14

To Alex,
From New Labour
to Conservatism ?
to Marxism to...?

Best wishes

Philip

LEGIONS OF PEACE

PHILIP CUNLIFFE

Legions of Peace

*UN Peacekeepers from the
Global South*

HURST & COMPANY, LONDON

First published in the United Kingdom in paperback in 2013 by
C. Hurst & Co. (Publishers) Ltd.,
41 Great Russell Street, London, WC1B 3PL
© Philip Cunliffe 2013
All rights reserved.
Printed in India

Distributed in the United States, Canada and Latin America by
Oxford University Press, 198 Madison Avenue, New York, NY 10016,
United States of America.

A Cataloguing-in-Publication data record for this book is
available from the British Library.

ISBN: 9781849042901

www.hurstpublishers.com

This book is printed on paper from registered sustainable
and managed sources.

In loving memory
Kate E. Cunliffe
1915–2010

CONTENTS

LIST OF FIGURES AND TABLES

List of Figures

List of Tables

PREFACE AND ACKNOWLEDGEMENTS

I came across the question of who contributes peacekeepers to the United Nations (UN) more or less accidentally. During my Master's studies in International Politics at Aberystwyth in 2003, my curiosity was sparked by seeing the successor states of the former Yugoslavia eagerly jostling to embed their armed forces in international peacekeeping operations and to function as adjuncts to the US-led operations in Iraq and Afghanistan.

It seemed ironic to me that the very countries that either had been or still were subjected to varying degrees of occupation by international forces stemming from the Balkan wars of the 1990s now wanted to deploy their own security forces abroad in the same manner. How did the projection of military force abroad become an acceptable token of international rehabilitation and respectability for countries seeking to establish themselves as good international citizens? How was it that certain types of armed force could be seen as peaceable and legitimate rather than as military aggression or unjustified meddling in the internal affairs of other states? These were the kinds of questions that initially motivated me.

Until that point I had assumed that at least since the end of the Cold War, international peacekeeping was essentially the monopoly of powerful, mainly Western states, whose military strength and wealth enabled them to exploit international law and organisation to justify their military excursions around the globe. Yet even the most superficial perusal of the data showed that the patterns of international military deployments were more complex. Foreign military adventures were by no means restricted to Western states or even to the more powerful states of the developing world. As early as the mid-1990s, poor and developing countries had become major participants in UN peacekeeping operations, and the end of the Cold War saw scores of states begin to participate in peacekeeping missions for the first time.[1]

Evidently the dynamics of international military deployments were more complex than I had initially assumed. Developing countries' participation in UN peacekeeping has remained entrenched even as UN peacekeeping has dramatically expanded since the turn of the century. I realised that the questions I had wanted to analyse through the defence policies of a few newly independent Balkan states potentially had a much wider resonance around the globe. Given the scale of UN peacekeeping, I also reasoned that exploring the question of troop contribution might enable us to probe more deeply into the underlying dynamics of post-Cold War international order.

A decade ago the study of contribution to UN peacekeeping was practically a blank slate. Although the character and motivations of troop-contributing nations had formed an important component of the study of Cold War peacekeeping, in the post-Cold War era, 'contributor studies' was all but overwhelmed by the study of how peacekeeping operates in the field.[2] Much of this vast and ever-expanding body of work was dry, highly specialised, under-theorised and made little effort to relate questions of peacekeeping to broader debates within the discipline of International Relations. The works examining the UN peacekeepers themselves, why they were there and where they came from, could almost be counted on the fingers of a single hand. Here again it was good fortune that I was put in touch with Darryl Li, who had written an unpublished critical synthesis of this literature, and that I came across a conference paper by Arturo C. Sotomayor, which explored peacekeeping contribution through the prism of civil-military relations in Latin America. Although brief, the richness of insight offered in Li's essay helped orient and inspire me throughout this research project, while Sotomayor's work helped me to contextualise peacekeeping in a vision of politics that went beyond international institutions and diplomacy. Such was the genesis of my doctoral research, conducted in the Department of War Studies at King's College London from 2004 to 2008.

Since I began my doctoral research the volume of material written about peacekeeping has not only continued to grow but has also improved in quality, as can be seen from the discussion in the first chapter. The availability and quality of the data on peacekeeping has also improved dramatically: when I began this project, an academic study of peacekeeping could gain credibility simply through the effort of accumulating data that was hard to find and compile. Now, the United Nations not only publishes detailed statistics on peacekeeping and peacekeeping contributions but the Internet has also made all this data more readily and widely available. This data is in turn more effectively mined and processed as a result of greater reflection on peacekeeping activities. Despite these advances in scholarship I maintain and argue in this book that not only are some vital answers still lacking in the academic literature, but even the right questions are still not being asked. Although we can say with greater confidence that we know much more about peacekeeping, our efforts to properly understand it still lag behind our factual awareness.

Since it has taken me an unconscionably long time to complete this book, I have incurred plenty of debts both during my doctoral research and since that I would like to take the opportunity to acknowledge. I was awarded a fully funded studentship by the UK's Economic and Social Research Council to pursue my research at King's College London for the first three years of my doctorate, for which I am grateful. A final round of interviews conducted in spring 2010 was supported by a Small Grant Award, given to me by the Faculty of Social Sciences at the University of Kent, for which I am also grateful.

I owe a debt of gratitude to my supervisors, Professor Mats Berdal and Professor Mervyn Frost. My initial views about the academic study of the United Nations were best expressed by Perry Anderson's unkind but all-too-accurate description of the world body as an 'intellectual sinkhole, down which swirl the drearily self-serving memoirs of its onetime functionaries and mind-numbing pieties from assorted well-wishers in the universities'.[3] Not only did Mats provide me with the means to frame my research, he also pointed me in the direction of some of the most creative work on the United Nations that had escaped the 'intellectual sinkhole'. Mats' own work on the UN Security Council and peacebuilding supplied essential insight and offered a model of how to write about UN peacekeeping in a way that kept international political realities firmly in mind. By putting me in touch with his many contacts in the United Nations and beyond, Mats greatly facilitated the interviews that I conducted for this book. I am glad I took his advice, as I realised the most insightful interviews were the ones that went off script.

Mervyn was always unfailingly generous with his time, and consistently encouraged me to dwell upon and return to the questions of international legitimacy, sovereignty and intervention that originally inspired the project in the first place. Both of my supervisors struck a balance between offering guidance and giving me sufficient space to allow my ideas to form independently. My doctoral examiners, Mark Hoffman and Professor Michael Pugh, provided sage advice about how to improve the argument and undertook a searching investigation of my assumptions and conclusions. I am grateful to them all, and I hope that this book that elaborates those earlier arguments does not disappoint.

Many of the arguments and ideas in here were variously tested and adapted in the course of numerous seminars, conference panels and informal discussions involving people unfortunately too numerous to mention, but they all have my thanks. However, it would be churlish not to make special mention of my colleague at the Defence Studies Department of King's College London, Professor Ashley Jackson, for providing guidance to the sources on the history of colonial armies and imperial defence. I also benefitted from discussions with Dr. Vincenzo Bove and Richard Gowan.

I must extend a special thanks to all those who took the time to read the draft manuscript in whole or in part and whose comments helped me to improve and clarify my argument: three anonymous reviewers, James Heartfield, David Maher, Frances O'Leary, Emily Paddon and particularly David Cunliffe. I am grateful to Suda Perera for help with the sections of the manuscript concerning the Democratic Republic of Congo. I would also like to thank Rahul Rao and Kudrat Virk for their guidance as regards India's policies on peacekeeping, Paula Drumond, Alex Hochuli, Danilo Marcondes and Kai Michael Kenkel for their help on Brazil's peacekeeping policies, and Richard Sakwa on Russian peacekeeping (see further chapter five). A colleague who would prefer to remain anonymous reviewed my coverage of Bangladeshi contribution to UN peacekeeping. Needless to say, I alone am responsible for all errors of fact and judgement in the text. I have established a blog where I build on some of the arguments in this book, and would welcome thoughts and contributions on questions of peacekeeping and contribution to peacekeeping: www.legionsofpeace.tumblr.com

I would also like to extend my thanks to Gill Woods and Helen Fisher for their patience with and support for me while I was a doctoral student in the Department of War Studies. Since completing my doctoral research at King's and after a temporary teaching position in the Defence Studies Department of the same institution, I joined the School of Politics and International Relations at the University of Kent in September 2009, where I finally had the opportunity to rework my thesis. From Kent, I would like to thank Gemma Chapman, Anne Haddaway, Nicola Huxtable, Frances Pritchard and Suzie Robinson for their support to me in my new post. My academic colleagues in the School have also provided an exceptionally friendly intellectual environment. Also, a special thanks to my publisher Michael Dwyer and his team at Hurst, for their tremendous patience throughout the process of publishing this book.

While studying for my doctorate, I lived at Goodenough College, which provides, I have no doubt, the best possible accommodation for postgraduate students in London: a welcoming and friendly community in the middle of Bloomsbury. I am grateful to all the staff of the College, but would particularly like to thank Annie Thomas, who was the highly supportive warden of William Goodenough House while I lived at the College. On repeat trips to New York across the years to conduct interviews with UN staff as well as various countries' representatives to the world organisation, I always benefitted from the hospitality and friendship of Nick, Danya, Alex, Tal and Forrest. Diolch yn arbennig i Ted Bach Llundain am awgrymu'r teitl i'r llyfr.

I conducted thirty-eight elite interviews with diplomatic representatives and UN officials in New York, who kindly offered me time out of busy schedules to answer my questions in 2005 and in 2010. Although these interviews were too few in number to be anything but exploratory, they nonetheless generated plenty of insights and new lines of enquiry. After completing this book I am more convinced than ever that the United Nations constitutes one of the most important limits on our political imagination, and that a more just and progressive global order requires overthrowing the vision of international politics enshrined and institutionalised in the United Nations and its Charter. Yet I could not help but be struck and impressed by the intelligence and dedication of many of the UN officials that I interviewed, whose commitment to a cause that goes beyond serving a single state is still rare in modern politics despite the pieties of globalisation—indeed one of my interviewees even lost their life in that cause. I am grateful for the insight that they all provided.

All such interviews were conducted under the condition of anonymity. When referencing interviews in the text, I have numbered them in the order they took place thus: UN1, UN2, etc., for interviews with UN officials and TCC1, TCC2 and so on for interviews with diplomatic representatives of troop- or police-contributing states. The date on which the interview occurred is also provided. If the same person was interviewed twice, it is referenced as UN1a, UN1b, and so on. Unless specified otherwise, all interviews can be assumed to have taken place in New York.

Two brief points about the text itself. First, I have occasionally taken the liberty of compressing and abbreviating some of the more sprawling academic debates with which I engage in the text, on the grounds that they are too large and complex to merit detailed recapitulation here. If readers wish to follow up my representations of particular debates, they can do so by consulting the sources in the bibliography. For UN reports cited in the text, where appropriate all references given are to numbered paragraphs rather than page numbers in printed editions, and I do not provide specific web addresses as they are all widely available online at a variety of sites. As the study of international institutions and peacekeeping is awash with acronyms, in order to avoid littering the text with capitalised ciphers, abbreviations that can be pronounced are spelled out in upper and lower case (so Unprofor, Unifil, Unicef) except in those cases where the fully capitalised abbreviation is more familiar (NATO).

Finally, above all I would like to thank my parents and sister, who always supported me throughout a protracted education and who have all always shown me more love and forbearance than I ever would have shown myself. The book is dedicated to the memory of my late grandmother Kate Enid Cunliffe, née Cole, who always reminded me of the value of education.

Philip Cunliffe   April 2013
@thephilippics
www.legionsofpeace.tumblr.com

LIST OF ABBREVIATIONS

AU	African Union
Ecomog	ECOWAS Monitoring Group
Ecowas	Economic Community of West African States
EU	European Union
FDLR	Forces Démocratiques de Liberation du Rwanda (Democratic Forces for the Liberation of Rwanda)
Minugua	United Nations Verification Mission in Guatemala
Minurca	United Nations Mission in the Central African Republic
Minurcat	United Nations Mission in the Central African Republic and Chad
Minurso	United Nations Mission for the Referendum in Western Sahara
Minustah	United Nations Stabilization Mission in Haiti
Monuc	United Nations Organization Stabilization Mission in the Democratic Republic of the Congo
Monusco	United Nations Organization Stabilization Mission in the Democratic Republic of the Congo
NATO	North Atlantic Treaty Organisation
Onuc	United Nations Operation in the Congo
Onuca	United Nations Observer Group in Central America
Onusal	United Nations Observer Mission in El Salvador
Plan	People's Liberation Army of Namibia
PT	Partido dos Trabalhadores (Workers' Party)
Recamp	Renforcement des Capacités Africaines de Maintien de

	la Paix (Reinforcement of African Peacekeeping Capacities)
Renamo	Resistência Nacional Moçambicana (Mozambican National Resistance)
SADC	Southern African Development Community
Shirbrig	Standby High-Readiness Brigade
Swapo	South West African People's Organisation
Unama	United Nations Assistance Mission in Afghanistan
Unamic	United Nations Advance Mission in Cambodia
Unamid	African Union/United Nations Hybrid Operation in Darfur
Unamir	United Nations Assistance Mission for Rwanda
Unamsil	United Nations Mission in Sierra Leone
Unavem I	United Nations Angola Verification Mission I
Unavem II	United Nations Angola Verification Mission II
Unavem III	United Nations Angola Verification Mission III
Unctad	United Nations Conference on Trade and Development
Undof	United Nations Disengagement Observer Force
Unef I	First United Nations Emergency Force
Unef II	Second United Nations Emergency Force
Unficyp	United Nations Peacekeeping Force in Cyprus
Ungomap	United Nations Good Offices Mission in Afghanistan and Pakistan
Uniimog	United Nations Iran-Iraq Military Observer Group
Unifil	United Nations Interim Force in Lebanon
Unikom	United Nations Iraq—Kuwait Observation Mission
Unita	União Nacional para a Independência Total de Angola (National Union for the Total Independence of Angola)
Unmee	United Nations Mission in Ethiopia and Eritrea
Unmibh	United Nations Mission in Bosnia and Herzegovina
Unmih	United Nations Mission in Haiti
Unmik	United Nations Interim Administration Mission in Kosovo
Unmil	United Nations Mission in Liberia
Unmis	United Nations Mission in the Sudan
Unmiset	United Nations Mission of Support in East Timor
Unmogip	United Nations Military Observer Group in India and Pakistan
Unoci	United Nations Operation in Côte d'Ivoire

Unomig	United Nations Observer Mission in Georgia
Unomil	United Nations Observer Mission in Liberia
Unomsil	United Nations Observer Mission in Sierra Leone
Unosom I	United Nations Operation in Somalia I
Unosom II	United Nations Operation in Somalia II
Unpredep	United Nations Preventive Deployment Force
Unprofor	United Nations Protection Force
Unscob	United Nations Special Committee on the Balkans
UNSF	United Nations Security Force in West New Guinea
Untac	United Nations Transitional Authority in Cambodia
Untaes	United Nations transitional Administration for Eastern Slavonia, Baranja and Western Sirmium
Untaet	United Nations Transitional Administration in East Timor
Untag	United Nations Transition Assistance Group
Untea	Untea United Nations Temporary Executive Authority
UNTSO	United Nations Truce Supervision Organization
Unyom	United Nations Yemen Observation Mission

1

INTRODUCTION

The might and reach of the United States (US) legions deployed around the world are often seen as integral to US global hegemony. But if this is so, how then should we understand the historically unprecedented deployments of United Nations (UN) peacekeepers, second only to the US in numbers deployed around the globe?

With bases and installations now in over one hundred countries, since the turn of the century US military deployments have expanded to reach levels not seen since the 1950s.[1] In that same period the number of UN peacekeepers deployed around the world doubled to just over 100,000. While these legions of peace are infinitely less powerful than the might of US arms, it is nonetheless UN peacekeepers that have been more consistently and directly engaged in sweeping schemes of political and social transformation in dozens of countries. UN peace-keeping is the most widely spread application of military power in international affairs today. UN propaganda boasts of the fact that 'Only the United States deploys more military personnel to the field than the United Nations.'[2] By the second decade of the twenty-first century, the UN peacekeeping operation in the Democratic Republic of Congo constituted the second-largest military expeditionary force in the world, after that of the Atlantic alliance fighting in Afghanistan.[3]

To be sure, the UN's legions of peace still fall far short of the military plans envisioned for the United Nations in its early years, when the US urged the permanent members of the UN Security Council collectively to form a combined force of twenty ground divisions (200,000 men), 1,250 bombers, 2,250 fighters, six aircraft carriers, ninety submarines, eighty-four destroyers, fifteen cruisers and three battleships.[4] Whatever the difference between the original conception for the UN use of force and its actual use of force, the fact remains that this world organisation so often derided today for its bureaucratic sclerosis, effete powerlessness and ultimate inconsequence in international affairs fields more military forces than the overseas deployments of any of today's major military powers and former colonial powers—barring one.

What is more, it is the member states of the UN General Assembly rather than the Security Council whose forces collectively comprise the overwhelming majority of these multinational legions of 'blue helmets'. While the Atlantic alliance draws its armies predominantly from the wealthy and powerful states of the North Atlantic rim, it is the poorer and weaker countries of the global South who fill the ranks of UN peacekeepers. These facts alone are sufficient to upend conventional assumptions about the constitution of military power in world politics, the relationship between wealth and military power and the use of force in international relations.

Understanding why developing countries have become so heavily involved in UN peacekeeping and exploring the implications of that involvement is the purpose of this book. The central argument of this book is that UN peacekeeping enables wealthy and powerful states to suppress and contain conflict across the unruly periphery of the international order without the encumbrance of open-ended political and military commitments. The institutions of UN peacekeeping allow states in the global North to displace the political risks and military commitments of international security onto poorer and weaker countries in the global South. In so doing, wealthy and powerful states reduce the global costs of hegemony.

As such, UN peacekeeping can be assimilated to a long history of imperial security in which metropolitan centres of power have sought to reduce the costs of policing empire by devolving these responsibilities to the periphery itself. The crucial historical difference is that today these functions are achieved through a system of imperial multilateralism rather than within a single, unitary empire. How did this latter-day system of imperial security emerge and how have the nations of the global periphery been integrated into it? What are the differences between empire and imperial multilateralism? These questions are for the book as a whole to answer. Before considering them, let us briefly review the terms that will set the parameters of the investigation, the themes that these terms will lead us to explore, and the structure of the investigation itself.

Remarks on method

The method of this book is critical, in the narrow sense that the argument develops from examining the internal contradictions and inadequacies of existing explanations of (poor) states' contributions to peacekeeping, and how well these sit with the evidence and data. The argument therefore cannot be so easily extricated from the method itself. In one of the most recent studies of contribution to peacekeeping, Alex J. Bellamy and Paul D. Williams argue that 'the quest for a general causal explanation [of contribution to UN peacekeeping] is illusory'.[5] While I share their scepticism regarding the possibility of identifying any overriding causal explanation of peacekeeping contribution, I do not think this eliminates the possibility of a general explanation, albeit not one focused on causal relationships between separate variables.

Instead I offer a general explanation by way of focusing on the conditions of possibility underlying contribution to UN peacekeeping. Therefore the type of explanation offered here is constitutive rather than causal, inasmuch as I seek to 'account for the properties of things by reference to the structures in virtue of which they exist'.[6] In other words, to explain poor countries' contributions to UN peacekeeping by reference to the nature of the international order of which they are a part. Thus the investigation does not proceed by way of case studies as I feel this would detract from the holistic perspective sought after by capturing the role of developing countries in UN peacekeeping as a whole. Nor does it necessitate the development of new data sets or the elaboration of existing ones, but rather a better developed framework with which to enable more consistent and profound interpretation of the existing data. Let us move to consider the parameters of the investigation.

What is peacekeeping?

Larry L. Fabian notes that 'peacekeeping' is one of those characteristically diplomatic terms debased by overuse and rhetorical manipulation, leaving it 'notoriously distended and imprecise' and 'used with a literalism that defies clarity: any policy or behaviour intended to keep someone's version of peace is labelled "peacekeeping"'.[7] The nebulousness of 'peacekeeping' reflects in turn the peculiar status of the word 'peace' in the modern political lexicon. Long before the United Nations deployed a single blue helmet, the slogan of 'peace' was already well established as political chloroform favoured for deadening public judgement. As Lenin observed in the midst of the First World War, the most bloodthirsty generals, politicians and monarchs declaimed their peaceful intent while abetting the slaughter: 'peace in general [is] a slogan ... entirely devoid of meaning and content. Most people are definitely in favour of peace in general...'[8] The real questions are, as ever, whose peace, what kind of peace and to what end? As an intergovernmental organisation of planetary scope, the United Nations has the advantage that it can be seen to extend a vision of peace distinct from the war aims or political interests of any particular government or state. For this reason, states in turn have sought to claim this mantle of cosmopolitan legitimacy by invoking 'peacekeeping' to describe their military actions, regardless of their scale or belligerence.

In the Cold War, peacekeeping was used to describe not only UN missions but also European states' interventions into their former colonies, the Soviet invasions of Hungary in 1956 and Czechoslovakia in 1968, the 1965 US invasion of the Dominican Republic and subsequent 1983 invasion of Grenada, the African Front Line States' attempts to contain the expansionism of apartheid South Africa, and Syria's 1976 intervention in Lebanon under the auspices of the Arab League—a peacekeeping mission that lasted until 2005.[9] With Western victory in the Cold War and the triumphant expansion of the 'Free World' into the 'international community', the invocation of peacekeeping has become even more promiscuous, being applied to virtually every military expedition of the last twenty years.

If we were to turn away from those peacekeeping missions debased by the self-interest of states to focus solely on UN military expeditions commanded from New York, we would still struggle to find a 'pure' peacekeeping that would form a stable basis for conceptualisation. Public discussion of UN peacekeeping rarely observes the distinctions which the United Nations purports to set such great store by—for example, 'peacekeeping', 'peacebuilding', 'peace enforcement', 'peacemaking', 'preventive diplomacy' and most recently the deployment of 'peace monitors' to the Syrian civil war—to name some of the allegedly distinct phases or types of UN response to conflict. The United Nations itself concedes that it is difficult clearly to distinguish these different types of mission, noting that 'Peace operations are rarely limited to one type of activity' and that the 'boundaries between conflict prevention, peacemaking, peacekeeping, peacebuilding and peace enforcement have become increasingly blurred ...'[10] To confuse matters still further, the UN Department of Political Affairs mounts its own field missions, which are also classified as 'peace operations' and carry out many tasks that are often assigned to peacekeepers. It is difficult to resist the conclusion that the vocabulary of modern peace operations constitutes little more than an arcane lexicon of 'blue-speak', as Jarat Chopra terms it, language whose function serves to mystify rather than clarify.[11]

Thierry Tardy's exasperation with attempts to define peacekeeping describes the frustrating variety of activities that have been lumped together as legitimate examples of 'peacekeeping':

If peace operations encompass the deployment of a military force to supervise a ceasefire line but also the establishment of a judiciary system in a post-conflict environment; if they can be legally consent-based or coercive, or both (within the same operation); if they can take place before, during or after a conflict with, in each case, different military and civilian implications; if they simultaneously refer to the activities of the UN in East Timor and of the Commonwealth of Independent States (CIS) in Georgia; if they can be peace-enforcement or humanitarian assistance; if all these activities belong to peace operations, then needless to say that this generic term is too large to be precisely defined and therefore conceptually coherent.[12]

Indeed, it has become something of a truism in peacekeeping studies to note the conceptual inconsistencies that are thrown up by attempts to define or classify peacekeeping, and then blithely go ahead and do it anyway.[13]

Distinctions are often drawn around the greater complexity of the so-called 'multidimensional' peacekeeping operations seen in the post-Cold War period. This complexity is cast as an evolutionary upgrade of peacekeeping operations in response to a new international environment whose conflicts were themselves more complex, with murderous civil wars fought between multiple factions with few clear battle lines around which peacekeepers could intercede. Yet this stylisation of post-Cold War peacekeeping obscures the crucial point that the aims and purpose of peacekeeping have, in the words of one study, been 'dictated by the interveners, not the targets'.[14]

The first generation of post-Cold War peacekeeping missions—in Central America, southern Africa and South East Asia—were all launched before the ill-fated expeditions despatched to quell wars in the Balkans, central Africa and the Horn of Africa—wars that would later come to be seen as defining UN peacekeeping. Thus change in the practice of peacekeeping is less reactive than commonly presumed, reflecting 'changes in the … dominant perspectives on the role of peacekeeping in global politics' more than it does any putative change in the nature of conflict.[15]

Thus our effort to understand peacekeeping must begin from the 'dominant perspectives' rather than working backwards from the operations in the field that are the end products of these perspectives. From this starting point, we are forced to consider what the plasticity of peacekeeping tells us about the changing needs of power rather than the changing character of conflict. It is reasonable to infer that the plasticity of purpose and function in peacekeeping constitutes part of its political utility to interveners.[16] This utility resides not just in camouflaging the use of military power in UN blue or redistributing the costs of imperial security across coalitions of states, but also in that multidimensional peacekeeping gives more flexibility to the exercise of power when intervening in conflict.

By virtue of its multiple dimensions, multidimensional peacekeeping evades proscribed limits—limits such as definitive statements of goals and purpose, settled standards or norms of assessment by which operational success would be measured, or clear strategic constraints against which success could be defined.[17] By reducing the costs of hegemony through its reliance on armies from the global South, UN peacekeeping gives even more political discretion and flexibility to interveners, as we shall see in greater detail in chapters two and six. Lured into limitlessness by the mirage of a globalised world without sovereign borders, the reflex expansion of peacekeeping to incorporate ever more aspects of life in post-war states shows that the political value of peacekeeping has come at the expense of its strategic and doctrinal coherence.

Hence attempts to cast peacekeeping in frozen definitions derived either from chronology (different generations of peacekeeping) or function (different types of operation) are ultimately self-defeating, as this strips away a real dimension of peacekeeping—its plasticity. Instead of seeking to define this plasticity away through intricate classification schemes or convoluted genealogies, it needs to be incorporated into the analysis from the outset. Following Philip Windsor's advice to 'establish what one is talking about by doing the talking first', I shall not be offering any one-sided definitions of peacekeeping here.[18] The historical development and institutional concatenations of peacekeeping will be discussed across the course of the book as a whole. I shall not be insulating discussion of different types of peacekeeping in scare quotes, nor offering standards by which to authenticate the genuine, pure variety serving the needs of the international community from the allegedly ersatz, corrupted peacekeeping serving the needs of selfish states. As peacekeeping scholar Alan James counselled, 'just as it is the scholar's job to describe the world as it is, and not as they would like it to be, so also they must use the terminology which is prevalent among states.'[19] Thus however frustrating and incoherent, 'blue-speak' is unavoidable if we are to study peacekeeping.

Here we can begin the process of demystifying the redundant categories of blue-speak by noting that I will take peacekeeping to act as a generic description of a variety of related activities and, unless specified otherwise, henceforward references to peacekeeping and peacekeepers in the text can be assumed to refer to UN peacekeepers (defined by the United Nations as military observers, soldiers or police). The varieties of peacekeeping that academics have expended so much energy refining into separate classes I shall assume to be essentially the same, with any distinctions meriting separate definitions to be 'worked towards' across the course of the discussion rather than 'stated at the outset' as Windsor puts it.[20] As I am interested here in the paradoxes stemming from attempts to use forces that are established and maintained by nation-states but deployed on behalf of an international organisation whose political claims refer to humanity as a collective, I will not be considering the growing numbers of civilian personnel, UN volunteers and other staff serving with peacekeeping missions in the field. This so-called 'civilianisation' of peacekeeping in recent years is in any case a function of the preceding militarisation of peacekeeping since the end of the Cold War, and reflects the growth in the scope and strength of peacekeeping operations around the world.

Who are the peacekeepers?

If peacekeeping is so difficult conceptually to isolate, what light is shed on our understanding of peacekeeping if we examine the peacekeepers themselves?

There are still very few studies of the dynamics of peacekeeping contribution within peacekeeping scholarship as a whole. Most peacekeeping scholarship is fixed around understanding the dynamics and outcomes of the peacekeeping missions once already deployed to the field. In his study of Cold War peacekeeping *Soldiers without Enemies*, Fabian states that his aim is 'not to resift once again the performance records of successive peacekeeping missions or the lessons to be learned from them. Theorists and practitioners have by now written authoritatively on these topics.'[21] What was true in 1971 is even truer today.

However, despite the recent best efforts of some academics to dislodge what Roland Paris branded the 'cult of policy relevance',[22] most peacekeeping studies continue to 'resift' the performance of past operations, typically ending with *bien pensant* conclusions culled from analysis of 'the diplomatic politics and techniques of peacekeeping, lessons-learned from operations and prescriptive agendas for improving performance'.[23] This focus reflects the extent to which peacekeeping scholarship remains more a form of policy lore than a field of theoretical inquiry, steeped in technocracy and bristling with detailed prescriptions, marching in step to the prevailing prejudices in world capitals.

Sandra Whitworth identified some of the problems of a scholarship fixated with these concerns some time ago—most glaringly a lack of attention to the 'most basic and important questions' of politics: who benefits, who is excluded, and whether countries should be involved in peacekeeping at all.[24] Whitworth elaborates, 'By asking only technical questions, a whole series of political questions remain unasked [for example:] whether particular interests are served within the United Nations, within particular member nations, or within particular national militaries, through the promotion of peacekeeping.'[25] A focus on countries participating in peacekeeping missions and their motivations for doing so provides a partial corrective to the problem identified by Whitworth, as such an analysis by its very nature forces us to reckon with the array of 'particular interests' that may be served through participating in UN peacekeeping.[26]

Yet even in this corner of the field of study, there is a strong policy-oriented focus, the overriding concern being how to squeeze more peacekeepers and materiel out of the current contributing nations, and how to expand the pool of contributing states.[27] Technical debates are characteristic of fields where all the key questions are taken to be settled or uncontroversial, a complacency that typically conforms to the settled prejudices and political outlook of an established elite.[28] In thinking only how to wring more peacekeepers out of states, the presumption has to be that peacekeeping is a legitimate and effective tool of world order.

To shatter this equanimity Whitworth enjoins ruthlessness in the study of peacekeeping: '[we must] expand our analyses from strictly policy-relevant questions of interest to the governments and militaries of advanced industrial societies to more critical analyses, even of the assumption that peacekeeping is a "good"'.[29] In other words, the deficiency in the literature on peacekeeping reflects a continuing failure to offer a sufficiently systematic and comprehensive critique of the institution of peacekeeping itself. Whitworth's demand for greater objectivity through a more reflexive and politically-focussed analysis will be the guiding framework for this book. To expand our analyses we must consider not only the national motivations behind peacekeeping but the role that peacekeeping plays in international order.

Table 1.1: Top Ten Contributions to UN Peacekeeping Operations, 1991–2000 (as percentage of total deployment)

1991–95	1996–2000
France, 9.9	India, 6.5
Pakistan, 7.0	Bangladesh, 5.9
United Kingdom, 6.0	Poland, 4.9
India, 4.6	Ghana, 4.7
Canada, 4.5	Jordan, 4.0
Bangladesh, 4.0	Pakistan, 3.8
Nepal, 3.2	Austria, 3.7
Jordan, 3.1	Finland, 3.6
Ghana, 2.9	United States, 3.5
Poland, 2.8	Ireland, 3.4

Source: Heldt (2008).

In the Cold War, sending UN peacekeepers abroad was seen as a characteristic attribute of middle powers—those intermediate states that were insufficiently strong to transform the status quo in their favour. As such, they could act as credible intermediaries in a conflict while simultaneously buttressing their own position by consolidating international institutions and networks of conflict restraint.[30] Examining the data on personnel contribution to peacekeeping across the last

Table 1.2 Top Ten (T10) Peacekeepers, Mean Monthly Deployment, 2001–11

	2001–05			2006–11		
	Country	*World Bank Ranking*	*Peacekeepers*	*Country*	*World Bank Ranking*	*Peacekeepers*
	Bangladesh	Low income	6,912	Pakistan[1]	Lower middle income	10,636
	Pakistan	Lower income	6,894	Bangladesh	Low income	10,177
	India	Lower income	3,975	India[2]	Lower middle income	8,889
	Nigeria	Lower income	3,182	Nigeria[1]	Lower middle income	4,744
	Jordan	Lower middle income	2,626	Nepal	Low income	4,044
	Ghana	Lower income	2,558	Jordan	Lower middle income	3,652
	Nepal	Low income	2,374	Egypt	Lower middle income	3,419
	Kenya	Low income	1,875	Ghana	Lower income	3,314
	Uruguay	Upper middle income	1,669	Rwanda	Low income	2,607
	South Africa	Lower middle income[3]	1,201	Uruguay	Upper middle income	2,526
T10 contributions as % of UN global deployment			60			58
Mean monthly deployment of UN peacekeepers per Western state*			388			385
Western contributions as % of UN global deployment			6			6

* West = Australia, Canada, Denmark, France, Germany, Japan, Netherlands, UK, US (defined as states that can rapidly deploy at least 5 per cent of their ground forces at short notice; O'Hanlon & Singer, 2004).

[1] Pakistan and Nigeria both transitioned to *lower middle income* in 2008.

[2] India transitioned *to lower middle income* from 2007.
[3] South Africa transitioned to *upper middle income* in 2004.
Low income: $1,005 GNI p.c.; Lower middle income: $1,006 to $3,975 GNI p.c.; Upper middle income: $3,976 to $12,275 GNI p.c.
Source: UN Department of Peacekeeping Operations. Figures on deployment and percentages rounded to nearest whole number.

two decades shows that the pattern of post-Cold War peacekeeping has been more fluid than the middle power associations of peacekeeping would lead us to assume.

The first decade of the post-Cold War period shows the traditional middle power peacekeepers such as Canada, Austria, Finland and Ireland being squeezed by the great powers (France, the UK and US) on the one hand, and new developing country contributors such as Bangladesh, Nepal and Jordan on the other. Other developing country contributors such as India and Ghana retain their pre-eminent positions across the Cold War through to the post-Cold War period, as table 1.2 shows. But as we can see in table 1.2, by the turn of the new century the great powers retreat from UN peacekeeping, taking middle, small power and formerly neutral Western states with them (Austria, Sweden, Ireland), thereby leaving UN peacekeeping as the preserve of poor and developing countries.

In his study of these changing patterns Birger Heldt is keen to mitigate the significance of this shift from rich to poor countries:

The conclusion is that the decreased contributions from wealthy countries have been replaced by contributions from a handful of less wealthy countries rather than from less wealthy countries in general. UN peacekeeping today is thus to an important extent the business of a few large and less wealthy countries ... rather than this category of states as a whole.[31]

Heldt's objections notwithstanding, there is no other obvious way readily to group countries coming from South Asia, West, Central and East Africa, as well as Latin America and the Middle East at the global level except to note that they are all developing and/or poor countries; as we see in tables 1.2 or 1.3 most were or are low income and lower middle income countries. Even the top boundary of upper middle income countries at $12,275 GNI per capita is still far beneath the average GNI per capita of high-income members of the Organisation of Economic Cooperation and Development—those states that we conventionally think of as the 'West'.[32]

Thus although the rankings have shuffled across the last decade with the rise of Egypt, Rwanda and Sri Lanka as peacekeeping powers, peacekeeping remains the preserve of poor, emerging countries. Their aggregate contributions far exceed those of Western states, and developing countries have contributed disproportionately to the larger UN operations. They have also met the UN demand for peacekeepers dur-

Table 1.3 The Next Ten (N10) Peacekeepers, Mean Monthly Deployment, 2001–11

	2001–05			2006–11	
Country	World Bank Ranking	No. of Peacekeepers	Country	World Bank Ranking	No. of Peacekeepers
Ethiopia	Low income	1,582	Ethiopia	Low income	2,316
Ukraine[1]	Lower middle income	1,211	Senegal[2]	Lower middle income	2,105
Morocco	Lower middle income	1,061	China[3]	Lower middle income	1,990
Senegal	Lower income	1,029	Brazil	Upper middle income	1,622
Argentina	Lower middle income	755	Indonesia	Lower middle income	1,448
Zambia	Lower middle income	645	Benin	Low income	1,275
Brazil[4]	Lower middle income	581	Sri Lanka	Lower middle income	1,086
China	Lower middle income	536	Kenya	Low income	998
Tunisia	Lower middle income	417	Argentina	Lower middle income	905
Sri Lanka	Lower middle income	379	Malaysia	Upper middle income	851
N10 contributions as % of UN global deployment:		24.6			24.3

[1] Ukraine was classified as lower middle income since 2002.
[2] Senegal transitioned to lower middle income from 2009.
[3] China transitioned to upper middle income from 2010.
[4] Brazil was upper middle income 2001–02 and lower middle income 2002–06.
Low income: $1,005 GNI p.c.; Lower middle income: $1,006 to $3,975 GNI p.c.; Upper middle income: $3,976 to $12,275 GNI p.c.
Source: UN Department of Peacekeeping Operations. Figures on deployment rounded to nearest whole number.

ing the same period as the number of peacekeepers deployed has doubled in size.[33]

If we were to sharpen the focus, we might also note the predominance of ex-colonial countries, and particularly former British colonies and protectorates among the top peacekeeping nations—namely, India, Pakistan, Bangladesh, Nepal, Ghana, South Africa, Nigeria, Kenya, Jordan and Egypt.[34] Jonah Victor innocently speculates that this might be attributable to the importance of English as the lingua franca of the United Nations and its field missions.[35] In his history of the United Nations Paul Kennedy more imaginatively attributes these states' propensity for global peacekeeping to their imperial history, having been part of a global empire: 'having campaigned as part of a larger coalition in the two world wars, they found it structurally and mentally easy to adapt to international peacekeeping.'[36]

As we shall see in chapter four, the British imperial armies involved in these war efforts were not equal partners in a joint enterprise as Kennedy's coy and anachronistic use of the term 'coalition' suggests, but rather imperial subjects whose numerous tasks extended far beyond the world wars to maintaining the imperial peace around the globe.[37] Indian Major General Dipankar Banerjee suggests that the tradition of imperial campaigning by the British Indian army has 'inculcated a tradition of overseas service that … remains alive to this day' in the peacekeeping operations of the Indian army and its South Asian cousins.[38] As the data show, the imperial tradition of overseas service is not restricted to the descendants of the British Indian army; but that is to get ahead of the argument.

If we take a larger purview of contributors to include the next ten ('N10') largest contributors (excluding Western states) as in table 1.3, we see that the mean contribution of each of these states across the last decade has been at the small end of a battalion-sized contingent (roughly 500 troops)—the building block of peacekeeping deployments—and often twice as large as that. By contrast the mean deployment of peacekeepers by individual Western states has fallen well beneath the level of a battalion to a company-sized contingent (roughly 200 troops) in the same period. The N10 group has contributed just under a quarter of total UN peacekeeping deployments across the last decade, in contrast to Western deployments, which have stayed well beneath 10 per cent of the total.[39] Within this expanded range of N10 contributors, we see that the imperial pre-history of peacekeeping encompasses more Anglophone ex-colonies (Zambia, Sri Lanka and Malaysia) as well as including countries that once constituted important sources of French imperial manpower such as Senegal, Morocco and Tunisia.

How the peacekeeping of today is shaped by the imperial history of proto-peacekeeping, including the differences between former British and French colonies in peacekeeping, is examined in greater detail in chapters four and five. Suffice to say here that across the last decade at least, there is no avoiding the fact that the United Nations has become dependent on developing, mostly formerly colonised countries to meet its prodigious and growing appetite for military and police manpower. Taking the T10 and N10 together, over three quarters of UN peacekeepers have come from nearly every region of the developing world across the last decade. Given the remarkable diversity of countries that comprise the T10 and N10 groups of peacekeeping powers, is it reasonable to speak of these countries as constituting a single group, and to invoke those other synonyms for developing states—the global South and the Third World?

Peacekeepers from the Global South

Long a by-word for corruption and poverty, the term 'Third World' was originally intended as a political designation, to characterise a grouping of states that championed national independence, were united by their global hostility to colonialism and whose ranks were persistently swelled by a continuing influx of newly independent states. Today, some analysts have argued that the image of a political clash between opposed North and South camps is simply a caricature in a post-ideological international order.[40] Although more newly independent states emerged in the aftermath of the Cold War, they came from the disintegration of the Eastern bloc rather than the global decline of European colonialism, and today there is no longer a politically coherent grouping of states organised around anti-colonialism and collaborating around projects of systemic international reform.[41]

Despite these changes, the disintegrating structures of Third World solidarity are buttressed by the quasi-parliamentary functions and institutions of the United Nations, which enables 'intergovernmental caucus groups' to 'articulate the views of the "global South" within UN forums and conference settings'.[42] The Non-Aligned Movement still comprises 118 of the 192 member states of the United Nations, and is still invoked in UN debates on peacekeeping. The persistence of common interests and shared disquiet among poor countries has in turn been sharpened by the growing assertiveness of (re)emergent powers such as Brazil, Russia, India and China, as well as the widespread international suspicion aroused by the Western proclivity for military adventures without UN sanction (the bombing of Yugoslavia by the Atlantic alliance in 1999 and the US-led invasion of Iraq in 2003). Indeed, the very fact that China, India and Brazil rely on UN peacekeeping to signal their enhanced global stature and to mount far-flung military expeditions which they would otherwise be unable to undertake is testimony to their rank as parvenu powers at best.

A North-South rift is certainly evident in UN peacekeeping, with persistent calls by developing countries for greater involvement in the political decision-making to deploy peacekeepers, accompanied by pleas to wealthier states to contribute more to peacekeeping by way of men and materiel. Reflecting on these inequalities, Richard Gowan characterises UN peacekeepers as proletarians hired by a bourgeoisie of rich countries to police the global lumpenproletariat of failed states. Colum Lynch describes this division as the 'blue helmet caste system': 'Rich countries pay most of the financial cost of keeping the peace. Poorer countries provide the peacekeepers. These days, they also die in far higher numbers than their wealthier counterparts.'[43] Simon Chesterman even goes as far as to speak of 'apartheid' in relation to the divisions on peacekeeping operations between Western and Third World forces.[44]

This institutional asymmetry in the global structures of peacekeeping is examined in greater detail in chapters three and six. Here we need only note that this inequality constitutes at once an index of growing detachment from traditional Third World concerns (notably the principle of non-intervention) as well as testifying to the continued political weakness and poverty of the majority of the world's states. This simple reality of lasting inequality—'defined in terms of economic, technological and military capabilities' as well as importantly the subjective awareness of such weakness, often underpinned by memories of historic humiliation before Western imperialism—imparts continuing validity to the use of the term 'global South'.[45] The fact that the 'global South' is a category hazy at the edges does not nullify its analytic value, as Mohammed Ayoob makes clear:

As with many other valid concepts in the social sciences that lack meticulously delineated parameters, the concept of the Third World has flexible frontiers rather than rigid boundaries. This flexibility helps the analyst use the term to encompass marginal and recent cases without losing sight of the contested nature of the concept's application.[46]

The study of Southern participation in UN peacekeeping missions allows us to study a large and diverse group of states in transition, as well as the emergence of the much-vaunted multipolar world with its putative new balance of power as Brazil, Russia, India and China breach the ranks of the great powers.

Why do they do it?

If we accept that the overwhelming majority of peacekeepers come from the global South, this immediately raises a very simple question: why do they do it?

Whatever their protestations to the contrary, it is not difficult to see that military interventions and conflict management activities by wealthy and powerful countries have a self-interested character, as these are the states with the greatest interest in preserving the international order on whose apex they perch. These are the states that are most likely to have the furthest-flung interests, along with the wealth and power to defend them. Poorer countries by contrast have fewer global interests to defend and in any case fewer resources with which to defend them. Their security concerns are more likely to be locked up in their own regions rather than in distant conflicts, and they are more likely to need their security forces to maintain stability at home. Developing countries have typically demonstrated deep suspicions over outsiders meddling in the internal affairs of other states, seeing this as a practice that is more likely to be applied to themselves rather than to stronger states.[47] Yet as we have seen Southern states have come to predominate in peacekeeping across the last decade, and a good number of developing countries were already important contributors to peacekeeping in the Cold War and early post-Cold War periods.

Of the few studies that there are of national motivations behind participation in UN peacekeeping, they are notable for their lack of attention to Southern states—despite the predominance of Southern armies in UN peacekeeping operations.[48] As we shall see in chapter five, there are plenty of reasons as to why developing countries might involve themselves in peacekeeping. Yet the very diversity of this wide range of countries suggests that an explanation that breaks down into the varied self-interest of different states is insufficient as an explanation of peacekeeping as a whole. There are at least two good reasons to treat such a reductive, state-centric explanation as insufficient.

First, the disjuncture between the range of states and interests at one end of the equation and a single, uniform collective policy—peacekeeping—at the other, suggests that it is possible analytically to unify the behaviour of these states by providing an explanation at a more general level. As Andrew Blum observes, 'Interest-based explanations have difficulty accounting for why the interests of so many different types of states have repeatedly converged in a sufficient manner to create these large and diverse coalitions of participants.'[49] These large and diverse coalitions have after all been sufficient to make the United Nations the world's second-largest military power in terms of numbers—and perhaps its most powerful, if measured in terms of the political effects proportionate to numbers deployed.

For the purposes of this book, I group systemic explanations of peacekeeping contribution into two schools of thought. The first I have labelled as democratic peace theories of contribution—theories which see the expansion of peacekeeping and the concomitant growth in peacekeeping contributing nations as a function of the spread of democracy in the international order. According to the terms of the theory, peacekeeping contribution can be explained by reference to the internal political structure of the contributing nations. The second type of theory explains peacekeeping contribution in terms of public goods analysis, whereby self-interested states overcome collective action problems to cooperatively produce the 'public good' of international security. Criticisms of these theories are elaborated in chapters five and six respectively. One of the problems common to both sets of theories is that they are insufficiently sensitive to the specific characteristics of the type of state in question—that is, states from the global South.

The fact that we are dealing with a particular kind of state—the weaker, poorer kind, the small or middling power—gives us further reason to be suspicious of reductive explanations rooted in the self-interest of such states. As the theorist of middle powers Carsten Holbraad noted, analysing the behaviour of smaller states has the advantage of helping us avoid the 'Olympian view of international politics' whereby world affairs are surveyed solely from the vantage point of the great powers. Yet at the same time studying weaker powers requires us to recognise that such states 'tend to be objects rather than subjects, in the sense that their international behaviour is highly conditioned by the politics and relations of stronger powers'.[50] It is safe to assume that these are precisely the countries whose motivations and behaviour count for the least in international relations. A framework whose explanatory content rested primarily on claims about the agency of those states with the least power and capacity to act would be logically suspect. Thus the motivations of Southern states must be treated as a necessary but insufficient component of an explanation of their peacekeeping participation. For a more complete account it is necessary to examine the larger framework within which these states operate—to identify the conditions of possibility that enable Southern states to take the lead in peacekeeping.

Theories of International Relations whose categories were moulded to fit the evolution of modern European states and to model the behaviour of a handful of great powers are not immediately suited to tackling the behaviour of large groups of weak and poor states, where the influence of powerful states is mediated and indirect although none the less real for it. Bearing in mind the limited agency of Third World states, analysis of peacekeeping thus requires us to adapt some of these categories so that our analysis can extend to include the place of the Third World in international order and how its political systems express the influence of wealthier and more powerful states. Martha Finnemore observes in her study of military intervention that 'There is an overwhelming tendency in analyses of [international] intervention (and of politics generally) to treat motivations or interests as obvious and to take for granted the context that gives rise to them.'[51]

Mindful of this warning, in this book neither is treated as obvious: the first part of the book examines the international context in which Southern states have come to predominate in peacekeeping. The explanation shifts across the course of the discussion to incorporate the motivations of the participating states, which are examined in the second part of the book. The direction of the argument is shaped by the fact that of all military assemblages, the formation of UN peacekeeping forces is the most institutionally decentralised, permeable and politically malleable, originating as it does not in the centralised structures of a single nation-state but within the fragmented structures of the international system at large.[52] This leads us to briefly review the third and final theme of this book, what I have called the system of imperial multilateralism.

Peacekeeping: from Empire to Imperial Multilateralism

The stark asymmetries between the North and South in peacekeeping inevitably pose the question of imperialism, not least in relation to the purposes and practices of peacekeeping itself. Questions of empire are never far from the debate, at least in scholarly discussion of peacekeeping. Kimberly Marten argues that the scenarios confronted by peacekeepers today would be familiar to the imperial expeditionary forces of the nineteenth century, embroiled as they often were in conflicts at the far edge of powerful states' spheres of influence, often forgotten or overlooked by remote metropolitan centres of power: 'tasks performed by imperial soldiers in many ways match what is being asked of today's peacekeepers, and we should therefore not pretend that peacekeeping tasks are unprecedented.'[53]

Marten is only one of a significant number of peacekeeping boosters who are disarmingly blunt about its imperial character. According to Roland Paris the values and institutions disseminated through today's enhanced peacekeeping operations amount to nothing less than a new *mission civilisatrice*: the diffusion of a new 'standard of civilisation' outwards from the metropole that peripheral states 'must accept in order to gain full rights and recognition of the international community'.[54]

Yet while discussion of imperialism is relatively frank and open in peacekeeping studies, discussion of UN peacekeeping is comparatively mooted in wider discussions of empire and imperialism or even International Relations more broadly. This is despite the fact that many of the metrics that are used to describe US empire could easily be applied to UN peacekeeping. Indeed, given the geographic scope, magnitude of political effect and transformational intent of UN peacekeeping efforts, US world power is the only comparator against which UN efforts could be reasonably evaluated.

Take for example the global scale of military deployments. Critics of US foreign policy have made much of the so-called 'empire of bases'—the colossal network of US military installations and troop deployments girdling the planet. Yet while there is an incipient public awareness of the vast scale of UN peacekeeping deployments, so far little effort has been expended to understand or contextualise these deployments in relation to wider theories and schemes of international order, let alone the kinds of theories that we might apply to US military deployments.[55]

At the time of the US invasion of Iraq in 2003, when discussion and fears of US imperialism were peaking, it was little observed that UN peacekeeping operations were growing rapidly in this same period, swelling the ranks of Southern troops deployed overseas through UN missions.[56] In October 2003, when the UN Security Council gave its imprimatur to the US occupation of Iraq, it also launched three major new UN operations in Africa (Liberia, Côte d'Ivoire, and Burundi) and one in the Caribbean (Haiti), and the Sudan and Congo missions already deployed were expanded. In the debate on 'new imperialism' US interventions have always been seen to be more intrinsically dangerous than even the largest and most invasive of UN missions. Yet the scale of UN peacekeeping operations in Namibia, Haiti, Sierra Leone and Côte d'Ivoire all constitute 'regime change' by any reasonable measure, while Kosovo and East Timor were directly ruled by UN viceroys.[57] According to Roland Paris, 'without exception, peacebuilding missions in the post-Cold War period have attempted to transplant the values and institutions of the liberal democratic core into the affairs of peripheral host states'. In a word, they have been engaged in nation-building, the same activity of which the US has stood accused in its imperial interventions.[58]

Another metric used to gauge US empire is the constant preparedness of the US military to intervene anywhere and at any point should they be required to do so.[59] But as Michael Hardt and Antonio Negri point out in their book *Empire*—one of the few theoretical treatises on empire to give prominence to the role of the United Nations—'The United States is the peace police, but only in the final instance ...'[60] It is UN peacekeepers who are more likely to intervene in the first instance rather than US troops. While the Obama administration has sought to rationalise and scale back US military commitments overseas, former US ambassador to the United Nations Susan Rice defended UN global peacekeeping commitments (see the discussion in chapter six). After US combat operations in Iraq were formally wrapped up in 2010, the United Nations launched two new peacekeeping missions in 2011: with a combined maximum strength of over 10,000 troops, both missions aim to provide a blue cordon sanitaire for the newly-independent Republic of South Sudan. UN Secretary-

General Ban Ki-moon also requested a 12,000 strong peacekeeping force for Mali to stabilise the country following the 2013 French intervention.

British ambassador to the United Nations Mark Lyall Grant reportedly questioned the scale of one of these missions to South Sudan in a closed session of the Security Council, as the United Nations sought to deploy 4,500 Ethiopian peacekeepers to the disputed border territory of Abyei between North and South Sudan. After all, according to Lyall Grant, it only took 10,000 British colonial soldiers to administer the whole of British India—why the need for half as many to monitor a much smaller sliver of Africa? The Indian envoy on the Council responded that Britain had not been engaged in a state building effort when it ruled over his country.[61] He might also have added that most of Britain's army in that era was in any case comprised of troops recruited from Britain's empire.

Indeed, it was in India that the British and French pioneered the imperial system of using indigenously-recruited soldiers to fight for them, which 'from then on', according to Victor G. Kiernan, became 'an indispensable part of Europe's ability to go on conquering. Afro-Asia was taught to conquer itself for foreign pay, most of it taken out of Afro-Asian pockets.' 'Shortage of numbers, need to economize costs, climate and disease were all arguments for use of native troops' in building the European empires, according to Kiernan.[62] If the various counter-insurgency, peace support, peacekeeping and stabilisation campaigns fought by Western armies since the end of the Cold War can be seen as lying on a continuum with the 'savage wars of peace' of the colonial era, so too it should be recalled that these 'savage wars' were fought not only against indigenous challenges to imperial rule but also with indigenous troops under imperial authority.

Outside of closed sessions of the Council at least, we are not accustomed to thinking of empire and peacekeeping in the same terms, despite the obvious similarities of scale and scope. The reasons for this are to do with the legitimacy that most peoples and states accord to the United Nations—a legitimacy that they do not to other types of political institution or individual states, no matter how powerful. According to Michael W. Doyle and Nicholas Sambanis, the 'mere presence [of the United Nations] guarantees that partial national interests are not in control', while UN values of impartiality, international equality and universal human rights 'make the quasi-colonial presence that a multidimensional peace operation entails not only tolerable but effective.'[63] Paris suggests that international peacebuilding missions have been 'considerably more charitable and consensual than the behaviour of many colonial powers'.[64] In other words, the United Nations is seen to compensate for the imperial instincts of states. The multilateral character of what Michael Ignatieff celebrates as the 'new humanitarian empire' is widely recognised: 'power is exercised as a condominium, with Washington in the lead, and London, Paris, Berlin and Tokyo following reluctantly behind.'[65]

The fact that this 'hegemony without colonies', as Ignatieff describes it, is dependent on the extensive support of weak states is less frequently acknowledged.[66] If it is acknowledged at all, the involvement of formerly colonised countries in peacekeeping is seen to redeem the practice, purging the sins of the imperial past. According to Andrea K. Talentino: 'Another argument against imperialism derives from the fact that states of all types promote intervention, not simply the most powerful. Indeed, if intervention relied primarily on Western or American participation it would rarely happen at all.'[67] Observing the political stress on rapid withdrawal in Western military planning, Ignatieff observes that 'No imperialists have ever been so impatient for quick results.'[68] But the impatience of latter-day imperialists reflects the fact that they can rely upon the United Nations to supply Bangladeshi, Ghanaian, Senegalese, Uruguayan and Jordanian blue helmets for longer-term and more labour-intensive military commitments.

In contrast to such insouciant views, I do not believe that the 'mere presence' of the United Nations or the involvement of Southern countries is sufficient to redeem imperial practices, however 'quasi', 'lite', 'virtual' or otherwise synthetic. There are as ever patterns of continuity and change in the history of imperial security, but the basic point is that in seeking to build up independent states in lands shattered by war, UN peacekeepers are not agents of a new colonialism but rather of an imperial multilateralism. This is a political order first envisaged by imperial reformers, imperial internationalists and liberal critics of empire, who dreamed among other things of empire without sin— without selfish national interests, conquest, exploitation and subjugation—or at least with these ugly aspects restrained to the greatest degree possible by controls and restraints embedded at the international level. The point of such reforms was not to abolish empire but to redeem it—to preserve it by elevating it onto a higher plane of cosmopolitan morality and multilateral cooperation. By its very nature, the effort to preserve empire by transferring certain functions from colonial empires to international institutions means that these functions are still imperial.

The transition from empire to imperial multilateralism has been a protracted process over the course of the last century, most obvious in the development of the League of Nations' mandates system and the United Nations' trust territories. In relation to security and peacekeeping, the evolution and dynamics of imperial multilateralism are discussed principally in chapters three and six. But as I have sought to craft the theme of 'peacekeeping and empire' as a 'moving prism' throughout the book the better to catch 'light from as many angles as possible',[69] we can begin here with a few preliminary remarks.

As far as the involvement of Southern states in UN peacekeeping is concerned, it would be a mistake to see their role simply as shabby auxiliaries deployed when needed to bolster flagging imperial efforts. For a start, changing patterns of troop contribution to UN peacekeeping are undergirded by specific configurations of interlocking and even fraught political agreements between different groups of states. Some of these agreements have an institutional form and expression—as with the remarkably resilient concert system that has developed within the UN Security Council since the end of the Cold War. Others are more tacit, such as the de facto bargain whereby Western states offer political and financial support for UN peacekeeping and Southern states the military and police forces. The international order that forms the backdrop to current patterns of UN peacekeeping contribution is sketched out in the next chapter, while its institutional and organisational dynamics are discussed in chapter six. The broader point is that the system of peacekeeping contribution could not function effectively if it were one that relied primarily on direct coercion: UN peacekeeping is ultimately dependent on the willing participation of the poorer and weaker member states of the world organisation.

More importantly, it would be wrong to see UN peacekeeping merely as a crutch for the imperial designs or expansionist efforts of individual states. On the contrary: the United Nations actively enables a greater range of political action than would otherwise be possible through say, direct occupation, conquest or even less blunt forms of outside intervention whether by single states or coalitions. UN competency in this regard can be measured by the greater depth with which the world organisation can often legitimately reach into societies to affect political change, as well as the geographic scope of its influence throughout the world.

One striking instance of this was when the US turned back to the United Nations in the aftermath of its botched 2003 invasion of Iraq despite the contempt that the Bush administration had earlier displayed for the world body (though even here the record is more ambiguous than commonly presumed; see chapter six). According to Mats Berdal 'through its envoys ... the UN did what the US never managed to do: consult and engage the informal power structures of Iraqi society in a dialogue on which the ultimate success of the political transition would depend.'[70] The UN Security Council can impart legitimacy to the collective actions of states in a way that no other agency can. This distinctive capacity stems in no small part from what the late Peter Gowan characterised as the 'unique ... popular aura ... of planetary inclusiveness' enjoyed by the world body.[71]

Simply to see UN peacekeeping as a covert extension of empire runs the risk of casting peacekeeping as an inadvertent subversion of the cosmopolitan ethos of the United Nations. This would be to gravely misconstrue the purpose and rationale of the organisation. The world body was explicitly founded with the purpose of unifying a globe fragmented among European colonial empires and spheres of influence under a 'trusteeship of the powerful' in the words of US President Franklin D. Roosevelt—that is, a great power directorate comprised of the permanent members of the UN Security Council which was in turn crowned by unrivalled US power.[72] The United Nations was intended to provide an institutional framework in which to encase the former vassal peoples of the European empires as they emerged from colonial bondage: an imperial multilateralism.[73]

In brief, there is an unexplored hinterland to contemporary debates on empire and imperialism—a hinterland ignored precisely because it is assumed to be the domain of the United Nations rather than the overt power of imperial states. Yet it is precisely in such realms governed by unchallenged assumptions that power can be exercised in a more insidious and unobserved fashion. Investigating this hinterland is one of the aims of this book. This is not to say that peacekeeping exhausts questions of empire in contemporary international politics. Peacekeeping is an important piece of this overall puzzle in that it is tied to questions of international security, and in that it involves the use of military force and, increasingly, police force. Moreover, the operations of other UN and non-governmental agencies will often be nested around a UN peacekeeping mission. Therefore, exploring the continuum between peacekeeping and empire today should hopefully push us to think through questions of power and imperialism more comprehensively and creatively than we otherwise might do.

Before briefly reviewing the argument of the following chapters, it only remains to be noted that I will not be offering any systematic analysis of non-UN forms of peacekeeping in this volume. This is not to say that the study of UN peacekeeping has no bearing on or implications for the study of alternative peacekeeping arrangements. Not only is UN peacekeeping larger in its collective effort and aggregate effect than any other types of peacekeeping, but all other forms of peacekeeping take place in the penumbra of historical precedent and international legitimacy bestowed by the United Nations. Oftentimes, peacekeeping missions mounted by regional or continental organisations are appended to and supported by distinct UN operations. Thus the international primacy of UN peacekeeping, as well the need for brevity, justifies the focus on UN peacekeeping alone in this book.

Argument in brief

The argument is presented so as to directly reflect the method of inquiry. Part I of the book is devoted to examining the role of peacekeeping in international order. Before examining developing countries' contribution to peacekeeping (and their motivations for doing so), we must establish what this peacekeeping is that they contribute to—that is the purpose of the first section.

In chapter two, 'Victor's Peace: Peacekeeping in the Post-Cold War Era', I seek to unfold the contradictions and pathologies of UN peacekeeping at the level of ideology and institutional practice since the end of the Cold War. The distinctive characteristics of peacekeeping in this era—notably that peacekeeping has become a globalised project of liberal post-war reconstruction—is best understood against the backdrop of Western victory over the Eastern bloc in the Cold War. Once this is grasped, then it becomes possible to understand the scale of post-war transformation that can be effected through peacekeeping without requiring the spread of empire through the occupation of subject nations. While much (though hopefully not all) the material presented in chapter two will be familiar to students and scholars of peacekeeping, the conclusions and analysis that I offer take a different view from most studies in the field. Laying the foundation for subsequent chapters, the discussion in chapter two is designed as a survey of peacekeeping as a whole rather than a detailed investigation of specific operations.

The discussion becomes wider in chapter three. Given the coercive and transformative character of peacekeeping missions and their role in reinforcing international hierarchy, the third chapter moves to contextualise the discussion of peacekeeping by portraying it as the highest stage of a long tradition of liberal imperialism. As we have already seen, empire is a familiar trope in peacekeeping scholarship: the sheer scale of contemporary peacekeeping inevitably raises comparison with empires of the past. In this chapter I tack closely to the work of other scholars in exploring the comparisons between peacekeeping and empire. Most scholars of peacekeeping who have catalogued the similarities between peacekeeping and empire recoil in the last moment from the symmetry of their own comparisons, finding sufficient analytic irregularities to convince themselves that peacekeeping missions can be distinguished from empire. It is this moment of recoil that I question, asking whether the reasons given to distinguish peacekeeping from empire are convincing, and by extension, whether the attempt to salvage peacekeeping is legitimate.

Thus to make the case that peacekeeping is the highest form of liberal imperialism does not require any radical re-interpretation of existing scholarship or invocation of hitherto unseen evidence. It only requires, I argue, a more systematic application of the standards that other scholars have used themselves in asking the same question. On this basis, I argue that we have good reason to see peacekeeping as belonging to a historic tradition of imperial security rather than representing its transcendence. As we shall see, this reframing leads us to a conclusion that it at odds with most peacekeeping scholarship.

Framing peacekeeping as a 'highest stage' of imperialism runs the risk of redundancy, multiplying a potentially infinite series of ever more rarefied and elevated 'stages' of imperialism. 'The Highest Stage of Capitalism' was the sub-title of Lenin's 1916 book *Imperialism: The Highest Stage of Capitalism: A Popular Outline*.[74] Subsequently, Ghanaian independence leader Kwame Nkrumah penned *Neo-Colonialism: The Last Stage of Imperialism* when he sought to account for the mechanisms by which imperial powers continued to exercise influence over their former vassals despite the dissolution of the colonial empires. There are variations on this theme by various lesser figures. While peacekeeping in some respects resembles a multilateralised form of Nkrumah's neo-colonialism, when I characterise UN peacekeeping as the highest form of liberal imperialism, I mean it in a more narrow and modest sense than that of either Lenin or Nkrumah, without implying any judgement on the long-term fortunes of global capitalism.

Peacekeeping is the 'highest' form of liberal imperialism in that it has developed out of earlier forms of liberal empire and in that it is the best adapted to fulfilling imperial functions in today's international system. I also argue that peacekeeping represents the most advanced rationale for imperial order based on the political ethics of liberalism. Today, spreading the benefits of liberal modernity entails restricting the political options of post-conflict societies to conformity with a model of 'good governance', as well as enmeshing states in regulatory frameworks of international oversight. It differs from earlier forms of empire in that, by virtue of being institutionalised in a system of imperial multilateralism, peacekeeping has been able to dispense with the need for long-term occupation or direct rule, and no longer operates to the monopolistic advantage of a single imperial metropole.

'Highest' implies transition, and the third chapter also considers how the 'liberal peace' constructed by peacekeepers is adapting in the face of imperial over-stretch, the withering war effort in Afghanistan and economic crisis, all accompanied by growing doubt and criticism of the validity of liberalism as a viable peace project. But criticism and doubt by itself is not sufficient to negate empire. Observing how imperial indirect rule developed out of the contradictions of liberal expansionism in an earlier period, I suggest that current criticisms of liberal peace—particularly those bundled together under the rubric of 'hybrid peace'—are likely tending in the same direction: towards reform and strengthening of the imperial framework rather than its overthrow. The theorists of 'hybrid peace' will provide the script for a new era of 'austerity intervention', which in turn will give greater weight to developing countries' suspicion of the liberal peace framework (see further chapter six).

For the sake of brevity I have excluded consideration of the political economy of contemporary imperialism. Vital as such analysis is, these debates are covered extensively elsewhere, and part of the premise of this book is that the political forms and institutions of contemporary imperial rule have been ignored in favour of the focus on US empire and globalisation.[75] Part of the purpose of this book is to correct this deficiency by widening the focus of the debate. Having outlined the place of peacekeeping in international order, we can then move to consider the role played by the legions of peace. Part II of the book shifts the focus from the place of peacekeeping in the international order to the peacekeepers themselves, and the countries that send them. These chapters also consider the political reverberations of peacekeeping in the contributing countries themselves. As such Part II is the engine room of the book.

Part II begins with chapter four entitled 'Constructing Imperial Security: From Colonial Armies to Capacity-building'. The chapter considers the patterns of peacekeeping contribution in the aggregate since the end of the Cold War. Scores of new states joined peacekeeping missions at the end of the Cold War—a development that looks on the face of it to be an impressively cosmopolitan commitment to global security. But this is I argue partly an error of perspective resulting from using the optics of liberal internationalism, which project peacekeeping deployments forward into a future system of global governance. If we consider peacekeeping contributions in the context of an international history that includes empires as well as nation-states, then these multiracial, multinational military formations deployed around the world under the command of a single centre of power appear less novel. Cognisant of Holbraad's theoretical warning about the limited agency of weaker powers, the chapter considers how these patterns of peacekeeping deployments are the indirect expression of underlying structures of imperial security.

How can we identify these structures of imperial security? As chapter four shows, peacekeeping in the present still bears the imprint of the colonial armies of the European imperial past. But these structures of imperial security are not merely the historical overhangs of old empires but are reproduced as part of an imperial security system in the present. History shows us that a consistent theme of imperial security is the indirect exercise of military power through the use of surrogates, either for reasons of economy and/or political expediency. These surrogates have varied historically, from the colonial armies levied by the European empires to the proxy militias and insurgents constructed and cultivated by US arms and money in the Cold War. We shall see in this chapter how UN peacekeeping by Southern states blends into this historic pattern of surrogate imperial intervention by providing specific political and strategic benefits to imperial power today.

As UN peacekeepers are state security forces, for our purposes it is colonial armies—the ancestors of today's peacekeepers—that are our prime focus, and the subsequent efforts to integrate the armies of newly independent states into the global military systems of imperial states—principally the US, Britain and France. Since the end of the colonial empires, imperial security has had to be effected through a multiplicity of structures: military alliances, bilateral treaties, arms trading, political linkages and of particular importance for the analysis in this book, peacekeeping training or 'capacity-building'. These latter are efforts led by Western states to bulk up the institutional and military capacity of states in the developing world so that they are able independently to mount their own peacekeeping expeditions. But at the same time as wealthy Western states seek to shed the burdens of imperial security, they do not wish to relinquish imperial influence—peacekeeping has to be on their terms. Thus the contradiction of capacity-building: on the one hand, the drive to devolve security to the periphery and, on the other, the need for control and influence that consistently undercuts the effectiveness of the policy.

As peacekeepers are the agents of imperial security, they are the 'Askaris and Sepoys of the New World Order' as the title of chapter five puts it. All the European empires levied military forces in their colonies—often heavily—both to garrison those territories and also to fight wars defending their empires throughout the world, with the combined ranks of colonial forces extending into the millions during the world wars. While 'sepoys' was the term used for Indian forces recruited predominantly by the Raj, 'askaris' became the term for African colonial forces recruited by European states, and later a generic term for military formations recruited from subjugated peoples (see the discussion in chapter five). Unlike the askaris and sepoys of the colonial era, today's forces are not a directly recruited imperial soldiery but the armed forces of independent states. Understanding the various rationales for national participation in peacekeeping is the purpose of this chapter. The patronising myth of 'mercenarism'—the idea that Southern states are simply seeking to extract hard currency reimbursement from the United Nations for their peacekeepers—is called into question in this chapter.

As discussed in chapter five, there are almost as many reasons for contributing to UN peacekeeping as there are contributing countries, with a spectrum of motivations ranging from pragmatic pursuit of advantage through to the less tangible goals of burnishing one's international reputation. As the global South is a fluid category in transition, this chapter also considers the peacekeeping roles of the aspiring giants of the global South, Brazil, Russia, India and China. All of these states have taken a variety of significant roles in peacekeeping at one point or another. These roles merit more detailed examination, as they are military actions of states that are often taken as the nodes of an emerging multipolar world order. According to the terms of International Relations theory, aspirant great powers are typically expected to brazenly flout international law and challenge practices of collective security, as these are seen to be the bulwark of entrenched interests whose demolition is required to accommodate the interests of new powers. The commitment to the United Nations demonstrated by the extensive involvement of today's rising powers in peacekeeping gives us the opportunity to rethink some of these views.

Given the variety of particular, country-specific interests in peacekeeping contribution, this poses the possibility of providing explanations at a higher level of theoretical generality. Chapter five engages with one such theory, providing a critique of the democratic peace theory of contribution by exposing its limited explanatory power. This theory is an 'inside-out' type of explanation, in that a foreign policy of peacekeeping is seen to be the outward expression of internal, democratic political structures. But what happens if we reverse the flow of explanation, and go from the 'outside-in' to consider the impact of peacekeeping on civil-military relations in contributing states? In so doing, we can expose the contradictory nature of a 'democratic' theory that elevates military power to such a degree. It is argued that little good for democracy can come from entangling the life and growth of democratic institutions and values with those of the military. If the outward face of this democratic Janus is democratic militarism, then the experience of some peacekeeper states shows that its inward face may well turn out to be that of the praetorian, as the sentinels of global democracy usurp the democrats.

Part III of the book pulls together the analysis offered in the previous two sections. The sixth and penultimate chapter examines the institutions of imperial multilateralism—how a world body composed of independent nation-states is, as the title of the chapter puts it, 'the last refuge of empire'. In Richard Kareem Al-Qaq's words the 'political grammar' of UN peacekeeping has been that of 'supreme umpire'—whether mediating between elites within post-war states or easing out imperial powers from a former colony.[76] Yet to accept this notion of the United Nations as an exogenous agent in peacekeeping rather than as an institution already endogenous to the conflicted political orders in question would be to allow the terms of analysis to collapse into the self-justification offered by the United Nations itself.[77]

Examining the peacekeeping institutions of the United Nations gives us an opportunity to examine the other forms of contribution to peacekeeping—specifically, the financial and political backing provided in the main by Western states. Hence we see how entrenched inequalities of power are refracted through UN institutions and how the great powers—particularly those on the Security Council—have sought to control the direction and magnitude of peacekeeping since the end of the Cold War. The chapter examines the allocation of roles and responsibilities in the construction of UN peacekeeping. The case is made that decision-making in UN peacekeeping is not only fragmented between various states and institutional actors, but also critically lopsided, with the majority of political, military and strategic risks falling upon Southern states.

The states that hold most of the decision-making power are not the states that have to implement those decisions. In the words of the longest serving Under-Secretary-General for Peacekeeping Jean-Marie Guéhenno, there is 'much less willingness among troop contributors to take risks if the risks that they are expected to take are not shared by those who make the decisions'.[78] In contrast to other studies of the United Nations, I argue that such institutional asymmetries are best understood not in terms of organisational dysfunction or misaligned incentives but as an expression of the political values and interests to which they conform and as such, one of the contradictions of imperial security in a multilateral age.

Examining the UN institutions that undergird peacekeeping shows that UN peacekeeping is expressly not the fledgling security arm of an incipient world state nor the police force of a post-national, cosmopolitan global polity. But nor is it reducible to interstate cooperation stimulated into hypertrophied growth in the uniquely benevolent environment of a unipolar international order. Rather, these institutions embody multilateral structures of imperial security. Once, imperial states would send gunboats in order to extract debt repayments from weaker countries or dependent regimes. As was seen in the global financial crisis after 2008, there has come to exist a sophisticated machinery of international economic institutions that intervene in balance of payments and debt problems both within and between core and peripheral economies. Just as these financial transactions have been transferred from bilateral relations between states to international organisations, so other functions of imperial ordering—such as the suppression of destabilising conflicts and the satisfaction of crusading humanitarianism—that would once have been undertaken by imperial expeditionary forces, are now carried out by UN peacekeepers.

I hope the discussion in this book will help to provoke fresh thinking on the larger questions of power, conflict and empire in the early twenty-first century as well as the United Nations. Michael Pugh has argued that a critical study of peacekeeping potentially has a 'totemic importance in exposing limitations in the foundational paradigms of international relations'.[79] Paris goes further, arguing that peacekeeping is relevant not only to international relations 'but also to the study of civil and ethnic violence, conflict resolution, democratic theory, transitions to democracy and capitalism, international ethics and law, postconflict justice, economic development, humanitarian assistance, psychological effects of conflict, and physical reconstruction of war-damaged infrastructure'.[80]

But this is just as if not more true of the United Nations as well. 'Select at random any standard litany of proposals aimed at the goal of "a strong, more effective United Nations"', writes Fabian, 'and almost without exception it will somewhere proclaim a need to bolster the organization's peacekeeping capabilities.'[81] Peacekeeping has expanded immeasurably by comparison with the peacekeeping of the 1970s, when Fabian wrote those words. Yet this expansion does not seem to have satisfied the demands of liberal internationalists, who exhort ever-greater strides to a cosmopolitan future that recedes into the distance the closer we collectively approach it. While I do not expect all or even most readers to agree with the arguments offered in this book, I hope by not limiting my conclusions to calls for peacekeeping reform and expanding the pool of peacekeeping contributors, that my contribution will be welcomed as a necessary departure from the existing debate.

PART I

PEACEKEEPING IN INTERNATIONAL ORDER

2

PEACE OF THE VICTORS

PEACEKEEPING IN THE POST-COLD WAR ERA

The blue helmets and white armoured vehicles of UN peacekeepers are a sight as familiar as to be innocuous in conflict zones around the world. This ubiquity testifies to the global legitimacy that peacekeepers enjoy, representing the most readily tolerated use of military power in international politics today. Typically, peacekeeping is distinguished from other uses of military force in three key respects: that peacekeepers use limited force beyond that used in self-defence, that they deploy only with the consent of the state on whose territory they are based, and that they remain impartial between warring parties. These three features—limited use of force, consent and impartiality—comprise the so-called 'holy trinity' of peacekeeping, a doctrine whose purpose is to transubstantiate profane military power into internationally consecrated peacekeeping. It is around these three distinct but interdependent aspects of peacekeeping that the discussion in this chapter is organised. We shall see how the three facets of this holy trinity transform into their opposite: how limited use of force transforms into militarism, how consent becomes a tool of coercion and how impartiality transforms from the disinterested stance of a diplomatic interlocutor into the indifferent detachment of the police, seeking to maintain stability across the turbulent periphery of the international order.

The contradictions of peacekeeping emerge within a specific context, and it is in this context that these contradictions must be understood. This context is shaped by the end of the Cold War and the changes that flowed from it. Of all field missions deployed by the United Nations since 1948, four-fifths have been launched since the end of the Cold War. That peacekeeping could only expand once the Cold War rivalries that had hitherto paralysed the United Nations had been overcome is self-evident. But the fact that peacekeeping is so ubiquitous speaks not just to the empowerment of a specific organisation, but also to the vindication of a distinctive set of ideas about the causes of conflict, the need for international involvement and the nature of post-war reconstruction and recovery. Underpinning this vision for peace, order and post-war revival are the pillars of market society and liberal political institutions.[1] Corresponding with the triumph of Western liberalism in the Cold War, this liberal vision of peace was also decidedly the victors' vision of peace. If peacekeepers are as ubiquitous as to be innocuous in international conflict today, this reflects the extent to which the victors' peace has come to be accepted as the preeminent form of post-war recovery for all humanity.

The fact that the expansion of peacekeeping is rooted in a victory settlement that ended a global geopolitical contest should remind us that for all its cosmopolitanism, the practice of peacekeeping is underpinned by power—and the inevitable concomitant of power is hierarchy. Against this backdrop of international hierarchy, we can see how the holy trinity of peacekeeping decomposes into the rationale for a multilateral imperialism in which peacekeepers are tasked with consolidating the victors' peace by implanting liberalism in a wide range of peoples and societies. We begin the investigation by turning to the use of force in peacekeeping, and examining how it relates to the dialectic of violence that entwines liberalism and war.

As we shall see, the liberal contradictions of peacekeeping are not restricted to the paradoxes stemming from peacekeepers' use of violence. They are also evident in the political and security institutions that peacekeepers are expected to help create and upkeep within states.[2] Here, peacekeeping goes beyond merely using deterrence or explicit force to contain or repress violence, and extends to nothing less than a far-reaching transformation of state structures and political processes, justified by the need to drain the very wellsprings of violence.

Peacekeepers and the use of force

In its most elemental form, peacekeeping is a response to conflict. As such, peacekeeping belongs to the venerable tradition of liberal internationalism, the highest goal of which is to suppress and eventually eliminate the 'scourge of war' from international politics in favour of a predictable, pacific and law-governed global order. Although peacekeeping relies on the agents and paraphernalia of state violence—trained soldiers and gendarmes, guns and armour—they are used towards different purposes. Instead of targeting an enemy for elimination, peacekeepers intercede between belligerents. If war embodies a clash of opposing political wills, peacekeepers embody the ultimate will of the warring parties towards peace. In this respect peacekeepers' promotion of peace and order is a universal aspiration in that it is addressed to humanity at large regardless of colour or creed. For peacekeepers, the dignity and rights of individuals are no less significant than the dignity and rights of nations: peacekeepers today are asked to protect refugees, defend convoys supplying humanitarian relief and guard aid workers, as well as offering military protection to civilians caught up in conflict.

Yet peacekeepers do not impose peace through force of arms. Unlike offensive armies, peacekeepers do not fight their way into a war zone in order to occupy land or seek out decisive battlefield encounters—they deploy only after ceasefires or peace settlements have been agreed. UN peacekeepers are too few in number and too lightly armed to conquer or hold territory for long periods: their helmets are famously painted blue and their armoured vehicles white so that they are clearly visible rather than disguising their movements from enemy forces with camouflage. Instead of eradicating enemy forces in battle, peacekeepers aid in repatriating prisoners of war. Instead of taking prisoners of war, peacekeepers help to demobilise combatants by cantoning their soldiers and irregulars, destroying their weaponry and aiding them in their reintegration into civil society. In so far as peacekeepers can deter armies from using force against each other, this capacity rests less on strength of arms than peacekeepers' moral authority: if launching an offensive or renewing a war requires overrunning peacekeepers' lines, the belligerent risks international opprobrium and condemnation as an aggressor.

But there is a paradox at the core of the liberal internationalist response to organised violence; a paradox exposed when the founding father of the League of Nations, US president Woodrow Wilson, declared the First World War a crusade to end all wars. The more that violence persists in international affairs, the more that liberal violence is justified in order to end the reign of violence. The more that violence evades the efforts to suppress it, the greater the violence needed to expunge violence from international order. UN peacekeeping has not escaped this paradox. 'Peacekeepers in armoured personnel carriers, facing enemy sniper attacks as they lumber through rugged dirt paths … are returning fire. Attack helicopters swoop down over the trees in search of tribal fighters.'[3] The war zone described is not Afghanistan but the Democratic Republic of Congo. 'It may look like war, but it's peacekeeping', according to the UN Force Commander at the time, Senegalese Lieutenant-General Babacar Gaye. Ostensibly seeking to clarify the situation, another senior UN official in the Department of Peacekeeping Operations said that the United Nations was 'not engaged in war. We are engaged in trying to create a peace.'[4]

According to the local UN commander in eastern Congo in 2007, Dutch marine Major-General Patrick Cammaert, forces under his command could 'match any peacekeeping operations of NATO or the EU'.[5] However exaggerated Cammaert's boast, it is noteworthy that this officer thought that a NATO military expedition was an appropriate point of comparison for the UN Mission in the Democratic Republic of Congo, known by its French acronym Monuc and since summer 2010 retooled as the UN Stabilisation Mission in Congo (Monusco). Indeed, at the time of writing, the Monuc-Monusco mission is the largest multinational military expedition in the world outside of Afghanistan. In mid-2011 Monusco was nearly 19,000 strong, equipped with 551 combat vehicles, thirty-seven naval vessels and forty helicopters (reduced, as we shall see in chapter four, as part of a political tussle over peacekeeping contribution between India and the UN in 2009).[6]

Attacks on Monuc forces are reported to have resulted in 'ferocious' retribution, with punitive raids by peacekeepers on rebel bases resulting in 'pitched battles' involving artillery, heavy weapons and close air support provided by Mi-35 gunships loaned to the mission by the Indian Air Force, and resulting in scores of insurgent casualties.[7] In 2006, Guatemalan special forces assigned to the UN mission sought to hunt down units of the Lord's Resistance Army that were operating in Congo's Garamba National Park. Following the fall of Goma to rebel forces in late 2012, the Security Council responded by militarising the mission further, authorising the establishment of a special 3,000-strong 'intervention brigade' in March 2013 comprising three infantry battalions, one artillery, one special forces and a reconnaissance company. The specific task of this brigade was to 'neutralise and disarm' rebel groups and launch 'targeted offensive operations'.[8]

If UN military operations in the jungles of central Africa are less widely known than those of the Atlantic alliance in the mountains of the Hindu Kush, doubtless this is in part because Monusco soldiers come from India, Pakistan, Bangladesh, Uruguay, South Africa, Nepal, Egypt, Morocco, Ghana and Benin, rather than from the US, UK, or France. The Monuc-Monusco mission is by no means the only mission where peacekeepers have used force; in some respects, it offers a distant mirror to the fate of an earlier UN venture in Cold War-era Congo. As we shall see in chapter four, the United Nations Operation in Congo that ran from 1960 to 1964, likewise known by its French acronym Onuc, was also a heavily militarised operation. More recently, Indian peacekeepers stationed with the Unamsil mission in Sierra Leone (1999–2005) used force to help push rebel forces back from the capital Freetown in 2000 and to rescue hundreds of UN peacekeepers held hostage by the rebels, while Untac peacekeepers stationed in Cambodia (1992–93) repulsed attacks by the Khmer Rouge on their peacekeeping posts. In 2011 several Ukrainian helicopter gunships stationed with the Unmil peacekeeping force in Liberia were re-deployed to UN forces in neighbouring Côte d'Ivoire, in order to be used as part of a French-led offensive to overthrow the incumbent government of Laurent Gbagbo—an episode we shall examine in more detail below.[9]

More well known to the Western public than any of these UN operations is the militarised peacekeeping seen during the UN missions to the former Yugoslavia and Somalia in the first half of the 1990s. In the Unprofor mission in particular, the UN could call upon far more air power than the handful of gunships later loaned to UN forces in Africa. As part of the UN-authorised no-fly zone imposed during the civil war in Bosnia-Herzegovina, UN officials on the ground could call upon the Atlantic alliance to launch punitive air strikes against recalcitrant belligerents. Extended into a full-scale bombing campaign that lasted over two weeks in late summer 1995, Operation 'Deliberate Force' involved 3,515 sorties and the dropping of 1,026 bombs on 338 individual targets, as well as the use of Tomahawk missiles and 10,000 rounds of depleted uranium, the latter suspected of causing heightened rates of cancer among civilians who formerly inhabited an ex-Serbian suburb of Sarajevo, which was subjected to heavy aerial bombardment during the campaign.[10] The militarisation of peacekeeping in the region was not restricted to the skies over the Balkans. According to the commander of the UN Protection Force in 1994, British Lieutenant-General Sir Michael Rose, it was Danish peacekeepers of Unprofor's Nordic battalion that 'changed the way to solve wider peacekeeping tasks forever' when two platoons of Leopard battle tanks inflicted the 'most significant military defeat' on Bosnian Serb forces prior to Operation Deliberate Force in a battle in central Bosnia in April 1994.[11]

UN operations in Somalia are best known to the Western public as a result of the deaths in combat of eighteen US soldiers following an operation by US special forces to rescue the crew of two US Blackhawk attack helicopters that were downed during a raid to capture senior leaders of the Somali National Alliance in south Mogadishu on 3 October 1993. The number of Somali dead in the battle—including many civilians—is estimated at 1,000.[12] In the event, the elite US rescue force had in turn to be rescued by Malaysian and Pakistani peacekeepers stationed with the Unosom II mission in Somalia.[13] Other peacekeepers of the UN force used military force repeatedly subsequent to the Security Council authorising its forces in Somalia on 6 June 1993 to take 'all necessary measures' to pacify Mogadishu.

The order was issued after a battle the prior day in which twenty-four Pakistani peacekeepers had been killed, along with 'at least as many Somalis'.[14] In retaliation the Security Council staked the credibility of the UN operation on military power, and its resolution was a declaration of war against the Somali National Alliance, the most militarily powerful of the various factions in Somalia's civil war. The UN offensive resulted in repeated raids by UN peacekeepers—frequently relying on close air support provided by US Cobra gunships—to capture or destroy various Alliance communication and military installations, and to kill or capture Alliance leaders. It was this cycle of raids that eventually culminated in the battle of south Mogadishu involving the US special forces and helicopter crew.

Behind the front lines

As the militarisation of peacekeeping has proceeded apace in the field, so it has necessitated the development of a more sophisticated military infrastructure behind the front lines, that is to say in New York, as well as new permanent bases at strategic locations in Mediterranean Europe. Since its establishment in 1992, the UN Department of Peacekeeping Operations has slowly but surely been shifted on to a permanent campaign footing, with the establishment of a 24-hour situation centre in New York, the creation of the post of Military Advisor, a dramatic increase in the secondment of military officers to the department, the formation of a 'lessons learned unit' (now the 'best practices unit'), attempts to recycle equipment from one mission to another, and attempts to establish a global rapid deployment capacity, aiming to get a 'simple' mission to the field thirty days after the passage of a Security Council resolution and ninety days after for a complex mission.[15]

The early 1990s also saw the formation of an office of planning and support and a special section for procurement for field missions.[16] Despite confronting political restrictions, bureaucratic rigidities and the wider resource constraints of the UN system, the Department of Peacekeeping Operations and subsequently its off-shoot, the Department of Field Support, have constructed a remarkably resilient and global system of strategic lift—that is airlift and sea transport to move UN troops and their equipment around the world—on the basis of commercial contracts and the support of UN member states (for which they are reimbursed by the United Nations). Impressively, this system was already capable of functioning independently of US support, at least in non-emergency situations, as early as the late 1990s.[17] At the turn of the century a logistics base in Brindisi, Italy was funded to develop strategic deployment stocks for the United Nations; it was expanded in 2009.[18] In 2007, in response to the surge in UN peacekeeping since the turn of the century and under the leadership of the newly appointed Secretary-General Ban Ki-moon, a new Department of Field Support was established to rationalise and strengthen the infrastructure undergirding global field deployments. Another support base was established in Valencia, Spain in 2007, to complement the one at Brindisi by acting as a global communications hub for peacekeeping operations.

Another key marker of the militarisation of peacekeeping is the growth in demand for 'field intelligence' and 'other capabilities' to face down 'violent challengers'.[19] The development of intelligence operations is a particularly striking indication of militarisation on the part of UN peacekeeping. Since the turn of the century, intelligence cells have been incorporated into peacekeeping operations in Burundi, Haiti, Sierra Leone, Liberia and the Democratic Republic of Congo.[20] In Congo the intelligence arm of the peacekeeping operation there was comparatively sophisticated, comprising 'basic signals and imagery intelligence capacity and a special forces component'.[21] In January 2013 the Security Council enhanced the mission's intelligence arm still further, by authorising the use of drones to enable peacekeepers to monitor Congo's eastern borders. UN peacekeeping missions are now expected to incorporate a 'joint missions analysis centre' in their head-quarters in order to allow 'senior mission leaders' to 'monitor developments and to understand the operational environment on a continuous basis' and to 'identify, prevent and/or respond to threats or emerging threats', among other tasks.[22] The Secretariat has also sought to re-establish an intelligence-gathering bureau at the strategic level in New York after the last one was closed down by the General Assembly over developing countries' disquiet about Security Council domination of the bureau.[23]

Peace means war: the origins of militarised peacekeeping

As was suggested in the first chapter, the growing use of violence by peacekeepers in the immediate aftermath of the Cold War onwards is often perceived to be a reaction to the unique nature of conflict that confronted peacekeepers in the post-Cold War world. In particular, it was the perceived inadequacy of UN forces in responding to atrocities witnessed in the civil wars of Somalia, Bosnia-Herzegovina and Rwanda that tarred the United Nations with the image of military impotence and moral compromise, and prompted the search for more resolute and forceful alternatives. Yet while it is true that peacekeepers were increasingly being deployed to civil wars, these conflicts were not significantly more bloody or destructive than the conflicts of the Cold War.[24] What was specifically different was the role played by the new expectations heaped onto peacekeepers.[25]

The vision for a more muscle-bound peacekeeping for the post-Cold War era was expressed by UN Secretary-General Boutros Boutros-Ghali in his 1992 report to the Security Council, *An Agenda for Peace: Preventive diplomacy, peacemaking and peace-keeping*. Among other innovations in this report was Boutros-Ghali's proposal for 'peace-enforcement units' that would be 'more heavily armed than peacekeeping forces' and be deployed to bolster the latter.[26] It was only later that same year that the missions in Somalia and Bosnia-Herzegovina were authorised (the ill-fated Rwanda mission, Unamir, was launched the following year). In other words, well before the humiliations endured by peacekeepers in the Balkans and Africa, Boutros-Ghali already planned to yoke greater military force to the UN peace project of the 1990s.

Although the remit of peacekeeping had already expanded in the new generation of early post-Cold War peacekeeping operations, large-scale military force had not been seen as necessary to buttress the deployment of peacekeepers in these instances, not even in the case of the UN missions in Afghanistan or Angola.[27] The link between the United Nations and the use of force was rather established by the 1991 Gulf War. Although not a UN-led mission, the conflict was significant in that the US mustered an unprecedented degree of international support for its war effort, including the backing of the UN Security Council and that of the US's erstwhile Soviet foe. The US-led war against Iraq demonstrated that armies could safely march under the banner of the United Nations without upending the balance of power between East and West, or calling into question the neutrality of the world body (at least a propos the permanent members of the Security Council).

With the Cold War schism over, the UN-backed war against Iraq reenergised doctrines of liberal internationalism, boosting hopes that international collaboration would revive the practice of collective security so that military force could be used with the full authority of international law to repel aggression and maintain international peace and stability. Conflicts could be ended through internationally coordinated efforts mounted under the auspices of the United Nations. It was in this inauspicious shadow of a bloody and ostentatious display of US military might that militarised peacekeeping emerged. In his notorious 'new world order' speech exulting in the US victory over Iraq, President George H.W. Bush assigned a central place to the United Nations in his vision for the post-Cold War world. It was to be an order in which 'In the words of Winston Churchill … the principles of justice and fair play protect the weak against the strong […] a world where the United Nations—freed from Cold War stalemate—is poised to fulfil the historic vision of its founders …'[28] The first UN mission to Somalia was launched the following year.

The drive to militarise peacekeeping was not therefore a response to the peacekeeping disasters of the early to mid-1990s. Indeed, it was the revitalisation of liberal internationalism that propelled peacekeepers into those difficulties in the first place. The new hopes vested in liberal internationalism raised expectations of what could be achieved through peacekeeping, and the burden of these hopes was piled onto peacekeepers in the field, as ever more ambitious and far-reaching mandates issued from the Security Council.

The greater the hopes vested in peacekeeping, the more that peacekeepers were expected to restore peace when it was shattered, rather than merely to monitor the maintenance or disintegration of ceasefire arrangements.[29] Instead of merely patrolling demilitarised zones, peacekeepers were expected to meliorate violence by monitoring the observance of UN-mandated human rights standards. The Vienna Declaration of the 1993 World Conference on Human Rights recognised the importance of peacekeeping operations in promoting human rights, and championed this involvement.[30] The 1991–95 Onusal operation in El Salvador was the first to have a human rights section embedded in the peacekeepers' headquarters and hence was a de facto 'human rights operation … deployed throughout the territory of a country for a lengthy period [with] intrusive powers', as well as constituting a precedent for most subsequent UN operations.[31]

The defence of human rights was extended when peacekeepers were tasked with relieving human suffering: peacekeepers were expected to provide a military guard to ensure the secure supply of humanitarian relief, guard aid workers and defend civilians caught up in conflict—notably in the infamous 'safe havens' of Bosnia—all in the midst of bitterly contested war zones. The more that peacekeepers were expected to meliorate violence, the more they were expected to create peace—and the more they correspondingly became protagonists within conflicts, bolstering their opponents by turning them into anti-imperialists by default. The more that peacekeepers became entwined in conflict, the more they were treated as belligerents by the warring sides—a status that inevitably involves the possibility of death, defeat and disgrace. Sixty per cent of all peacekeeping casualties occurred in the post-Cold War era, with the most lethal conflicts for peacekeepers being those in the former Yugoslavia and Somalia in the early 1990s, and more recently Liberia (2003) and Congo (2008).[32] Following the disgrace of peacekeeping in Africa and the Balkans, an embittered Boutros-Ghali wrote a chastened supplement to *Agenda for Peace* in 1995, retreating from the hubris he had expressed in the early post-Cold War era. As

Andrea K. Talentino observes, 'After Somalia ... intervention seemed likely to fade as an international strategy. Strangely however, the reverse has happened.'[33]

One of the preconditions for this growth in peacekeeping and was the ability of the Western victors of the Cold War to shift the burden of imperial policing in the new world order onto other states, as we shall see in chapters four and five. This shift was made in tandem with a process of reform and restructuring of UN peacekeeping, which ensured that it was brought into line with a Western vision for the post-Cold War use of force. The primary expression of this was the Report of the Panel on United Nations Peace Operations published in 2000, known for the name of the panel's Algerian chairman, Lakhdar Brahimi (prior to becoming a peace envoy for the United Nations Brahimi had served as foreign minister for the junta that voided Algeria's national elections and instigated the military repression of 1990–92).[34]

The Brahimi report made a number of recommendations in relation to the use of force by peacekeepers. In the first place, Brahimi urged that peacekeepers should be entitled to use force to secure their presence in the field. This entailed a more expansive view of self-defence, whereby UN peacekeepers would be entitled to seize the initiative to strike rather than merely react to violence against them. The report also argued that peacekeepers 'who witness violence against civilians should be presumed to be authorized to stop it, within their means, in support of basic United Nations principles'.[35] In other words, the Brahimi report was advancing peacekeepers' promotion of humanitarianism from monitoring human rights or defending aid convoys to the active military defence of 'basic United Nations principles'. The military defence of human rights required, as Brahimi acknowledged, more peacekeepers, who had to be more speedily deployed in greater numbers, with better provisions and weapons in order to combat 'obvious evil'.[36] These were to be 'robust peacekeeping forces'.[37] Peacekeeping was to be redeemed through force.

The Brahimi vision for peacekeepers whose moral virtue is to be measured by their military strength has been reaffirmed in subsequent UN documents, including in the first official statement of UN peacekeeping doctrine published by the Department of Peacekeeping Operations in 2008 as 'Principles and Guidelines' for peacekeeping, known as the 'Capstone Doctrine'. Robust peacekeeping was further expanded in two documents issued the following year—a non-paper published as part of the 'New Horizons' project for peacekeeping and a 'Concept Note on Robust Peacekeeping' produced by the Office of Military Affairs within the Departments of Peacekeeping and Field Support. Among other requirements, the 2009 'New Horizon' non-paper stressed the requirements of robust peacekeeping as having a 'high degree of mobility'; 'the willingness and capacity to operate at a high tempo for sustained periods, night and day'; 'effective mission command and control structures and units that can work together in larger formations'; 'regular joint training and exercises'; 'enhanced situational awareness and risk analysis'; 'scenario-based planning and reliable contingency arrangements'; 'modern technology' and 'responsive logistics support'.[38]

Peacekeepers in the field will inevitably fall short of the ambitious schemes for robust peacekeeping drafted by the planners in New York. Peacekeepers are still more likely to be criticised for insufficient and indecisive rather than excessive use of force.[39] But such criticisms should not deflect from the increasing militarisation of peacekeeping. 'Robust peacekeeping operations' are often taken as a post-Brahimi development; but as we have seen, the militarisation of peacekeeping stretches right back to the beginning of the 1990s. Indeed, in some respects peacekeeping has become more militarised than even Boutros-Ghali envisaged in his 1992 *Agenda for Peace*. Not only are many peacekeeping operations today spearheaded by 'peace enforcement units' as proposed by Boutros-Ghali (a development discussed further in chapter four), but peacekeepers themselves tend to be more heavily armed, deployed in larger numbers and with greater rights to use force. Boutros-Ghali envisaged his peace-enforcement units essentially as shock troops to restore and maintain fragile ceasefires.[40]

Today, ordinary peacekeepers can use force to defend peace agreements that are incorporated into the mandate of the mission, 'particularly', according to the Capstone Doctrine, 'in [those] situations where the State is unable to provide security and maintain public order'.[41] This too began to take shape before the publication of the Brahimi report: the UN mission to Sierra Leone launched in 1999 explicitly embedded 'protection' aspects into the mandate of the mission under Chapter VII of the Charter, which entitles peacekeepers to use 'all necessary means to protect civilians when under imminent threat of physical violence.' When Boutros-Ghali urged the reactivation of those articles of Chapter VII of the UN Charter concerning the use of force, he envisaged this to be separate to peacekeeping. Yet since the turn of the century most peacekeeping mandates issued by the Security Council have followed the pattern established by the 1999 Unamsil mission in Sierra Leone, with similar authorisation extended to operations in Burundi, Côte d'Ivoire, the Democratic Republic of Congo, Haiti, Liberia and Sudan.

Peace crimes

The Capstone Doctrine claims that 'although the line between "robust" peacekeeping and peace enforcement may appear blurred at times, there are important differences between the two.'[42] But for all the doctrinal attempts to articulate fine gradations in the use of force and to carefully delineate the different phases of peacekeeping operations, when peacekeepers wage war for human rights, initiate battles in pre-emptive self-defence, fight to enforce peace agreements and launch punitive raids against recalcitrant factions, there is little left but Orwellian absurdity: peace means war. Worse, peacekeepers' greater use of violence has inevitably led to their own record of excesses and atrocity, distinguished in the grim catalogue of contemporary conflict by the impeccably cosmopolitan cast of perpetrators, and the sanctification with which peacekeeping operations are endowed by the international community.[43]

On some missions, atrocities have resulted from the support that peacekeepers have extended to military actions launched by regimes that enjoy UN backing or in support of UN-sponsored peace settlements. The most notorious recent example is the support offered by UN forces to the Congolese armed forces in so-called 'collaborative combat operations' against a number of armed groups based in the eastern marches of the Democratic Republic of Congo.[44] In particular, Monuc provided intelligence, logistical and planning support as well as fire support and rations for a campaign known as 'Kimia II' that lasted for most of 2009 and was aimed at eliminating the Forces Démocratiques de Libération du Rwanda (FDLR)—a rebel group based in eastern Congo that included elements of the old Hutu regime responsible for the massacres that the United Nations failed to halt in Rwanda in 1994. UN support was traded for greater influence in the inner councils of the internationally-backed Congolese government (the United Nations had been excluded from government planning of previous campaigns). The price of this influence was a terrible one, to be paid by the peoples of eastern Congo.

Seeking to justify the support the United Nations gave to the offensive of 2009, one UN official is reported as saying, 'We believed that being on the inside would give us a better chance to protect civilians.'[45] In the event, the campaign was marked by great brutality against civilians: both by government forces seeking to forcefully consolidate the writ of the state over FDLR territory, as well groups within the government army using the military campaign as a cover to pursue ethnic vendettas, seize land and generally prey on the local population.[46] As the Kimia II campaign drew to a close, the Congo Coalition Advocacy group estimated that 900,000 people had been displaced, fled or expelled from their homes.[47]

The campaign left UN forces haemorrhaging whatever local support they had previously enjoyed, while also predictably prompting retribution by the FDLR, seeking to bolster its control over civilians unfortunate enough to inhabit the contested territory.[48] That a UN peacekeeping mission succeeded in augmenting the violence of what was already one of the most blood-soaked conflict zones in the world was a consequence of peacekeeping practice, and not a derogation from its principles.[49] That peacekeepers can so quickly become embroiled as protagonists within wars, with such seeming naïvety about the consequences of their actions, is a result of the near-angelic legitimacy granted to peacekeeping by the international community.[50] Styled as the international *deus ex machina* of human rights and peace, peacekeeping is launched into action without thought for the role peacekeepers will inevitably assume as political actors in a drama that they are part of and not outside of.

The establishment of the 'intervention brigade' in 2013 shows how the UN mission only ever gets sucked more deeply into local politics. To be comprised mainly of African troops from Malawi, Mozambique, South Africa and Tanzania, the 'intervention brigade' is specifically designed to deter neighbouring Rwanda from supporting Congolese rebel movements. The logic behind this selection is that African peacekeepers from the region will raise the political costs to Rwanda of clashes between its proxies and peacekeepers more than clashes with peacekeepers from Latin America or South Asia would.[51] Local UN commanders have simply become the best-armed warlords in eastern Congo, with the greatest level of international support.

The Monuc actions of the last decade are not the first time peace-keepers have extended support to dubious regimes or campaigns in defence of internationally sponsored peace settlements. During the 1989–90 Untag mission in Namibia, peacekeepers relied on the army of apartheid South Africa to act as the military arm of the mission, even though South Africa was still subject to a UN embargo at the time. The leadership of Untag consented to South African forces eliminating units of the People's Liberation Army of Namibia (Plan) in the interests of upholding the recently negotiated UN peace accords. This was despite the fact that the political leadership of Plan had not been fully party to the peace negotiations, and was therefore unaware of the full terms of the agreement when Plan military units crossed over from bases in Angola into occupied Namibia.[52] Describing this incident Thomas Weiss and Meryl A. Kessler observed that the 'first few days of the UN-supervised independence process ironically witnessed the highest casualties in twenty-three years of guerrilla struggle'.[53]

At other times, it is peacekeepers themselves who have been the perpetrators of atrocities. The most infamous actions of this kind must surely belong to the cycle of UN operations in Somalia across the 1992–95 period, which saw hundreds of murders and arbitrary killings of civilians as well as widely-publicised incidents of torture of both adults and children committed by elite Belgian forces, Canadian paratroopers and Italian troops. French, Malaysian, Nigerian, Pakistani and Tunisian peacekeepers also stood variously accused of numerous incidents of arbitrary arrest, casual brutality, banditry and looting, rape and excessive and indiscriminate use of force in dispersing crowds.[54] The local UN base came to be known as the 'camp of murderers' by residents of Mogadishu.[55] No less murderous was the indiscriminate use of devastating firepower, particularly that of US helicopter gunships, in densely populated residential districts of the capital.[56]

Less well-known than UN crimes in Somalia are more recent episodes on the other side of the world, with the excesses of the Minustah mission in its efforts to establish control of Haiti's capital Port-au-Prince since the mission was launched in 2004. Scores of civilian deaths have resulted from the de facto imposition of what one analyst called 'draconian martial law' on Port-au-Prince.[57] Brazilian General Augusto Heleno Ribeiro Peirera, a former Minustah commander, testified before the Brazilian national congress in December 2004 that he had been under 'extreme pressure' from 'the international community to use violence' in Haiti.[58]

The most notorious single incident is Operation 'Iron Fist' on 6 July 2005—when UN peacekeepers including 700 Brazilian troops armed with automatic weapons 'flooded' Cité-Soleil, a poor and densely populated district of Port-au-Prince. The tactics used mirrored those used by Brazilian security forces in their militarised incursions into the *favelas* of Rio de Janeiro and São Paulo—operations frequently accompanied by allegations of human rights abuses.[59] Redacted diplomatic cables released by the US embassy in Haiti speak of 'numerous civilian deaths' resulting from the raid. Only some deaths were admitted by UN officials though they conceded that 22,000 rounds of ammunition had been expended in the operation.[60] As one observer noted, in giving justifications for the civilian deaths resulting from the raids, peacekeeping officials began speaking in terms of 'collateral damage' sounding 'more like US generals than UN officials'.[61] Justified as crackdowns on criminal gangs, the districts targeted in the Minustah raids are also known for being popular strongholds of Haiti's former leader, Jean-Bertrand Aristide, ousted in a Franco-American intervention in 2003 prior to the UN mission. Subsequent protests by Cité-Soleil residents against the UN raids and the UN-backed government were dispersed with tear gas and rubber bullets.[62]

In other regions, peacekeepers use force not in support of UN-backed governments but directly as the security services of the ruling authorities themselves. On 10 February 2007 UN police in Kosovo shot dead two people and injured eighty others when they fired rubber bullets at the heads of Lëvizja Vetëvendosje! supporters ('Movement for Self-determination!') demonstrating against UN rule over Kosovo.[63] In East Timor, Untaet peacekeepers stationed in that country undertook sweeps against local pro-Indonesian militia, reportedly inflicting significant casualties in the process.[64]

War means peace: the liberal re-articulation of violence

It is worth pausing at this point briefly to consider how peacekeepers' use of force has pernicious consequences for our understanding of the nature and role of political violence in contemporary international politics, and perhaps more worryingly, how it debases the nature of peace.

As we have seen, in its efforts to suppress violence, peacekeeping recreates the basis for violence legitimated in a different form, in this case on the basis of liberal internationalism. The relegitimation of violence through peacekeeping marks the failure of liberal internationalism to transcend war. But this justification for force is not some atavistic remnant of an insufficiently purified liberal internationalism, nor a tragic recapitulation of a perennial theme. Rather, it is a distinctive re-articulation of political violence. What is distinctive about the use of force by peacekeepers is that it is a type of coercion endowed with the most exalted political and moral justification available to the armies of the world today. UN peacekeepers are mandated to use force by the Security Council, the only legal and political authority greater than the state that enjoys universal jurisdiction in matters of war and peace, and acts as custodian of the supreme ethical values of human rights embodied in the UN Charter.

That peacekeepers' use of force has the highest possible political, legal and moral sanction has the effect of polarising the nature of justification for the use of force. Relying on such glorified justification for their own use of coercion and violence, the violence with which peacekeepers are confronted is thereby rendered illegitimate by default. Hence the criminalisation and pathologisation of the violence of the poor and the weak, typically characterised in the categories of banditry, insurgency, war crimes, genocide, crimes against humanity and terrorism—all describing various types of depravity but all united by the fact of being intrinsically illegitimate expressions of violence.[65] Nothing exemplifies this perhaps as much as the notion of 'spoilers'— the generic term for all opponents of internationally brokered peace settlements and against whom peacekeepers are entitled to 'use all necessary means' according to the Capstone Doctrine.[66]

That this quintessentially technocratic term is used not only by peacekeeping planners, strategists, diplomats and policy makers but also as a near-universally accepted term of art in political science demonstrates the extent to which ideology has permeated both the study and practice of peacekeeping.[67] The result is not only that certain political aspects of conflict may be expunged by underlying assumptions about the defective morality and rationality of 'spoilers', but the legitimacy of any oppositional force on the part of the poor and the weak is called into question by default, no matter how imperfect a peace settlement, legitimate a grievance, rational an opposition or popular the support on which 'spoilers' can rely.

At the same time, force justified in the name of peace has serious consequences for how peace is understood and practised, the most serious of which is to insinuate violence into peace and consequently blur the boundaries between war and peace. This is most visible in the multiplication of conveniently amorphous transitional categories to describe the shift from peace to war and the role of peacekeepers within these various phases: 'peacebuilding', 'post-conflict environments', 'gray area operations', 'peace maintenance', 'peace restoration', 'peace enforcement', 'peace support', 'post-conflict reconstruction', among others, nearly of all which are predicated on the possibility of a relapse into conflict.

The persistence of generalised violence in 'post-conflict environments' ranging from small-scale to catastrophic proportions is an oft-observed feature of 'post-conflict' societies that have seen international peacemaking interventions.[68] But the proliferation of these categories between war and peace is not a more precise calibration of the conceptual space on the spectrum between war and peace, but rather marks the conflation of the two poles. The result is that the peace practised by peacekeepers and resulting from internationally brokered peace settlements no longer represents the classical liberal vision for the transcendence of conflict and violence. Rather, 'post-conflict' society is a twilight world where peace and violence are not mutually exclusive; violence is thereby normalised and does not call into question the basis of the new, post-war order, the governing regime or indeed the role of the United Nations in war-torn countries. Perhaps nowhere exemplifies the terrible costs of the ideology of 'post-conflict transition' more than its application to eastern Congo in 2004–08, a period which saw 'regular fighting among organized armed groups, torture and killing of civilians by soldiers and a frequent use of sexual violence ...'.[69]

Séverine Autesserre attributes this complacent ideology of 'post-conflict' transition to a specific 'peacebuilding culture' that ties together the many thousands of 'internationals' deployed across the globe in an self-enclosed world governed by its own procedures and bureaucratic fetishes, and replete with deep contempt for the Congolese (a contempt that Autesserre nonetheless refuses to label as racist).[70] But what the cultural explanation overlooks is the political functions that the ideology of 'post-conflict transition' serves and the political convenience of the blurring of the boundaries between war and peace.

Conceptualisation of conflict that does not draw sharp distinctions between states of war and violence and states of peace notably facilitates *refoulement*—the coercive repatriation of refugees. Thus states can shed their obligations to refugees on their territory by pushing them back into war zones deemed as 'post-conflict' by the international community.[71] Peacekeepers also smooth the path for *refoulement* by virtue of being obliged to provide protection to endangered civilians—protection which, as the recurrent atrocities in eastern Congo show, is inevitably inadequate.[72]

Mark Duffield has argued that changes in the provision of aid and attitudes towards refugees have driven changes in peacekeeping policy and doctrine, noting that it was the creation of humanitarian aid corridors and UN safe havens that was instrumental in the militarisation of peacekeeping. Whereas the Cold War international refugee regime was focused on the obligations of receiving states and the rights of asylum seekers, today international aid is targeted at cushioning states from the impact of refugee flows—either by discouraging refugees from fleeing war zones or through *refoulement* (forcible repatriation). The new peacekeeping order and the new refugee regime serve to contain the worst effects of conflict, while encouraging war-affected populations to remain relatively immobile, lingering in war zones in the hope of international assistance and relief.[73]

The flexibility of the categories of 'post-conflict' also blurs the standards by which external and internal agencies—be they the United Nations, leading powers, neighbouring states, donor agencies and nations, internationally supported post-war regimes—might be held to account for the specific consequences of their policies. As a result, persistent generalised violence, the breakdown of a ceasefire, an upsurge of fighting and a brutal Kimia II-style campaign to eradicate 'spoilers' do not need to be taken as indicators of the dysfunction of a peace settlement, oppressiveness of a state or political illegitimacy of a government, but rather subjected to strategies of management and containment on a spectrum where the difference between war and peace has been all but eclipsed.

Consent and coercion

One of the core precepts of 'robust' twenty-first century peacekeeping is the notion of civilian protection, as registered in the Capstone Doctrine: 'most multi-dimensional United Nations peacekeeping operations are now mandated by the Security Council to protect civilians under imminent threat of physical violence.'[74] The appeal of the idea lies in its commitment to defend the innocent and vulnerable *in extremis*: It solidifies peace into a moral project backed up with military power, rather than leaving it to the scraps of paper signed by haughty elites in distant capitals. Yet at the same time this claim encroaches on one of the key liberal justifications for state power—that states provide security for their citizens. The very core of liberal political theory is the claim that political authority rests on the capacity to provide effective security. In making such a claim, particularly in the conditions of civil disorder that peacekeepers frequently confront, the principle of civilian protection cannot but foster a non-representative and paternalistic vision of security.

As observed by Tara McCormack, this doctrine of so-called human security is predicated on a different type of security relationship than that between state and citizen:

The relationship between the intervening agents and those on whose behalf action is being taken is not a political relationship in which there is a formal relationship of representation and control. In this instance, there is a divorce between the exercise of power and the control or accountability of that power. Any agent that intervenes to empower and emancipate the individual tends to be one that has no reciprocal relationship of obligation and control.[75]

Perversely, the attempt to bring effective security closer to ordinary people widens the gap between people and the exercise of and control over power. For the people whom peacekeeping is supposed to protect have no formal institutionalised means by which to hold international agencies or peacekeepers to account—except by adopting the role of supplicant petitioners, 'spoilers', or by relying on the state to defend their interests against international organisations (that is, the same state whose role and capability is called into question by the international intervention in the first place). The consequence is that even in those cases where security is successfully provided by peacekeepers, the people in question are effectively reduced to passive receptacles of international forces and international humanitarian law. Under such conditions, where the United Nations can claim authority through its provision of security, the use of force for civilian protection can become a license for a much wider exercise of power, as most dramatically seen in the regime change mounted by UN peacekeepers in Côte d'Ivoire in 2011, with the overthrow of Ivorian president Laurent Gbagbo.

Regime change

If the UN has grown more accustomed to using military force in defence of mandate objectives and civilian protection, it has also begun to use it explicitly to achieve governmental change. While NATO jets were pounding Libya in April 2011, UN air power in Côte d'Ivoire was being used to attack a range of targets in cooperation with military strikes by French peacekeepers. In their air assaults mounted across the first weeks of April 2011, UN helicopter gunships (transferred from a UN mission in Liberia the previous year) targeted the presidential palace in the commercial capital Abidjan, where Laurent Gbagbo was residing, as well as a naval base and several military installations around Abidjan, destroying the president's heavy weapons and weapons stockpiles in the process.[76] At the same time Alassane Ouattará, Gbagbo's opponent, was being protected by UN peacekeepers at his base in Abidjan.

The elimination of Gbagbo's arsenal by UN forces operating in tandem with the French military decisively shifted the advantage in favour of Ouattará's army, the Republican Forces of Côte d'Ivoire.[77] The UN attack on Gbagbo's forces came over two weeks after heavy weaponry had been used against civilians in the capital, though only three days after Republican Forces marched into Abidjan, the culmination of a general offensive they had launched a month earlier. By the end of the year, Gbagbo was arraigned before the International Criminal Court in The Hague on charges of crimes against humanity.

One of the legal controversies over the NATO air campaign in North Africa was how it escalated from a no-fly zone justified by the need to defend Libya's civilians into an air offensive coordinated with a rebel uprising aimed at destroying Colonel Gaddafi's regime.[78] Yet in some key respects the UN intervention in Côte d'Ivoire went further than the NATO air campaign in Libya. While NATO airpower in Libya was deployed in support of a popular uprising against an entrenched dictatorship, in Côte d'Ivoire the United Nations intervened militarily in a closely fought democratic election between two long-standing opponents, in a country that was politically and geographically divided as a result of a prior civil war across 2002–03, and where neither side could legitimately be singled out as being overwhelmingly responsible for brutalising its opponents.[79]

The result of the November 2010 presidential run-off was decided in favour of Alassane Ouattará by the UN Secretary-General's Special

Representative Choi Young-Jin. Choi's decision included overruling the Ivorian Constitutional Court—the only national body constitutionally empowered to determine the results of presidential elections—even while he conceded the legitimacy of their concerns over the fairness of elections in the north of the country, dominated by partisans of Ouattará, and in the face of two conflicting election results.[80] Gbagbo's proposal to resolve the dispute—the establishment of an international commission to verify the election results on the precondition that both he and Ouattará recognise its authority—was turned down, 'despite the fact' as pointed out by former South African president Thabo Mbeki (a mediator in the crisis) that this 'would have resolved the electoral dispute without resort to war'.[81]

Once the UN Security Council affirmed the decision of the Special Representative in December 2011, the issue of civilian protection was redundant, as the United Nations had turned Ouattará into the internationally recognised Ivorian president. With UN credibility staked on Ouattará, coercion would inevitably be used to enforce the UN decision. The United Nations no longer needed the assent of the Ivorian government to keep its peacekeepers in the country, who in turn provided personal security for Ouattará. Even before the UN unleashed air strikes across Abidjan, the international recognition of Ouattará enabled sanctions to be passed against Gbagbo that cut off his government's access to banking services, thereby depriving him of his ability to pay state and army officials.[82]

While the use of force by peacekeepers to oust an incumbent head of state was novel, it was expanding already deep UN involvement in the country. With the national political system of Côte d'Ivoire tightly enmeshed into an externally-crafted peace process, it is not unreasonable to say that Côte d'Ivoire had effectively been placed into 'neotrusteeship' before Gbagbo's violent overthrow. Defined by two of its leading theorists as a 'postmodern imperialism' that comprises 'complicated mixes of international and domestic governance' involving 'a remarkable degree of control over domestic political authority and basic economic functions by foreign countries', neotrusteeship in Côte d'Ivoire could be dated to as early as 2005, the point at which the externally-driven peace process endowed the Special Representative of the Secretary-General with the power to certify future presidential elections.[83]

That UN peacekeepers overthrew an African government was also consistent with a long practice of sweeping political reconstruction carried out by UN peacekeeping operations for at least two decades prior to the Unoci operation in Côte d'Ivoire. At least three instances could reasonably be classified as episodes of regime change: in Namibia, Haiti and Sierra Leone. Instances of neotrusteeship are much greater still. Consent, the second aspect of the 'holy trinity' in peacekeeping, is what is supposed to distinguish peacekeeping from military occupation, dictatorial interference in the internal affairs of other states and imperialism. How then can consent be compatible with neotrusteeship, a political arrangement described even by its advocates as a form of 'postmodern imperialism'?

Liberal peacebuilding

The range of activities undertaken by today's UN peacekeepers extends 'to almost every sphere of human activity' in the words of former UN Secretary-General Boutros Boutros-Ghali. Reflecting on the early generation of post-Cold War peacekeeping operations, Boutros-Ghali noted that in 'Cambodia, Somalia and the former Yugoslavia, the United Nations' new duties were vast, encompassing food, water, land mines, disease, refugees, democratization, human rights, social and economic development and governance at every level'.[84] Or, as abbreviated by the British foreign secretary of the time Douglas Hurd, 'painting a country blue'.[85] It was this generation of so-called 'multidimensional' UN missions that set the pattern for subsequent peacekeeping operations. The enormous range of activities carried out by peacekeepers is at once predicated on the consensual character of UN peacekeeping and calls it into question. On the one hand, such sweeping programmes of social reform and post-war reconstruction could not be carried out without the assent of the state on whose territory peacekeepers deploy; they could only be otherwise carried out through sustained programmes of force. On the other hand, how can independent nationhood, the only basis on which meaningful consent can be offered, be compatible with such deep penetration of domestic political life by outside actors?

The justification for this vision of post-war recovery is given by the need to ensconce a lasting peace. The political expression of this vision was articulated by UN Secretary-General Boutros-Ghali in his *Agenda for Peace* as the difference between 'strategic' or 'political peace' and 'social peace'. Cribbing the idea of 'peace-building' from radical peace theorists of the 1960s, Boutros-Ghali envisaged rolling peacekeeping over into peacebuilding operations that would involve 'action to identify and support structures which will tend to strengthen and solidify peace to avoid a relapse into conflict,' as well as 'strengthening' public institutions, the 'transformation of deficient national structures and capabilities'.[86] This was an explicitly liberal vision of state power, in that the nature of the state was presumed to lie in its capacity to provide security for individuals, as well as giving prominence to specific attributes of liberal government, notably 'the rule of law and transparency in decision-making'.[87]

The scale of Boutros-Ghali's vision of peacebuilding was almost unseemly in its ambition, and the speed with which it expected to achieve its goals. This scheme for global peacebuilding effectively aimed to telescope political development and institutional accretion that took decades, if not centuries, in established democracies into a scant few months or years of a peacekeeping mission.[88] It was, in short, nation-building. There are several points that are noteworthy about the sheer ambition of this vision.

First, the speed with which peacekeepers were expected to achieve these transformations in numerous states betrayed the ambivalent if not disingenuous character of the political commitment to the purported goals of liberal peace. If liberalism and democracy were to be the fruits of the West's Cold War victory, why not cultivate them properly? Second, the fact that nation-building was taken as synonymous with peacebuilding reflects the strength of the ideological consensus that coalesced after the Cold War. This consensus took the liberal vision of political order as the natural form of government and successful nationhood for all humanity. The fact that the UN could, with no cognisance of contradiction, legitimate such forceful political and social transformation as a corollary of restoring peace—that is, *returning* to an antebellum period—indicates just how naturalised ideals of 'liberal peace' had become.[89]

That this vision of post-war recovery required the compression of self-determination in the conflicted countries was openly admitted. Nothing exemplified the imperial swagger of this new vision as much as Boutros-Ghali's casual depreciation of state sovereignty: 'The time of absolute and exclusive sovereignty ... has passed; its theory was never matched by reality.'[90] Boutros-Ghali further implied that consent might not be a requirement for future peacekeeping when he defined peacekeeping 'as the deployment of a United Nations presence in the field, *hitherto* with the consent of all parties concerned ...'.[91]

The suppression of sovereignty through UN peacebuilding initiatives reached its apogee in the Unmik (1999–2008) and Untaet (1999–2002) missions in Kosovo and East Timor, respectively.[92] The shabby authoritarianism and maladministration of what was euphemistically called 'transitional administration' by the United Nations in Kosovo and East Timor is widely known and well documented.[93] A large academic cottage industry has sprouted up dedicated to poring over these two cases alongside that of the 'European Raj' in Bosnia-Herzegovina.[94] That it is specifically these cases that have so focused the minds of academics is a reflection of several factors: the fact that the Balkans is on the periphery of the European Union; the fact that it was in these countries that the revocation of self-determination has been the most explicit; and the fact that Kosovo and East Timor were handed over to UN rule after widely acclaimed military interventions by Western armies.

Less well known are the other instances in which UN missions were endowed with enormous formal powers, often involving periods of de facto rule by UN functionaries, namely: Namibia (Untag, 1989–90); Cambodia (Untac, 1992–93); the 1996–98 Untaes operation in eastern Croatia and the post-Unprofor mission in Bosnia-Herzegovina; Unmibh (1995–2002). Aside from Bosnia, none of these other states were subject to the use of Western military force, and often relied on a range of non-Western peacekeepers for the maintenance of security. The breadth and intensity of liberal peacebuilding means that even in those countries where the United Nations did not rule explicitly, the organisation wielded extensive influence by virtue of being able to lead its programmes of restoring peace via political change. Keeping this wider context in mind, the periods of concentrated UN rule in Kosovo and East Timor should be seen as distilled forms of these wider trends. Surveying these developments as a whole, Roland Paris describes peacebuilding as a process of externally-driven social and political transformation operating through a system of 'proxy governance' founded on technocratic authority,[95] which places 'relatively narrow limits on the type of polity and economy that will be allowed to emerge' through peacekeepers' efforts.[96]

What facilitated this system of 'proxy governance' was the transformation in the meaning of consent in peacekeeping. Instead of being taken as substantive and necessary, its meaning was stripped back to a ritualistic formality. This is described by Eşref Aksu:

In several cases, as in Central America and Mozambique, comprehensive peace plans and agreements ... extracted parties' consent not only for the initial UN deployment, but also for subsequent UN activities in the field. By carefully placing the peacekeeping mandate on peace accords, international actors increasingly downplayed the requirement of seeking consent at every stage of the operation.[97]

If consent cannot be withdrawn at any stage of a process, it is legitimate to ask how meaningful such a notion of consent is. In practical terms, the slashing away of consent was testified to in the sheer size of peacekeeping missions, and as we have seen, increasingly permissive rules of engagement that allow peacekeepers to pursue offensive tactics beyond self-defence. Indeed, the distinction in the Capstone Doctrine between strategic consent—consent at the level of the national government—and 'tactical consent', the consent or lack thereof of belligerents in the field, is another means by which peacekeepers have debased the meaning of consent.

The texts of the comprehensive peace settlements that have often preceded the deployment of peacekeepers assigned a 'referee role' to the United Nations. This 'referee role' has enabled the world body to make judgements in relation to the domestic affairs of states. This was the case in El Salvador, Liberia, Mozambique, Rwanda and Somalia. UN officials helped draft the new Namibian constitution, while in El Salvador, Nicaragua, Guatemala and Cambodia international agencies have taught police forces, drafted electoral laws, overseen elections and even given classes on how to cast a ballot. In Mozambique, UN peacekeepers established commissions to oversee disarmament, organise elections and humanitarian activities.[98] In Angola, Rwanda, Mozambique, El Salvador, Nicaragua, Guatemala, Liberia and Sierra Leone, the UN was involved in nothing less than constructing liberal political systems and organising multiparty elections.[99] These political changes took place alongside the promotion of market-oriented economic reforms, including privatisation and the scrapping of wage and price controls in Rwanda, El Salvador, Nicaragua, Guatemala, Croatia and Mozambique.[100]

If the UN must continue to pay diplomatic lip-service to the idea of consensual peacekeeping, the theorists of peacekeeping have been more open though no less cynical about the need to subvert consent as much as possible, if not indeed dispense with it altogether. Michael Lipson describes this state of affairs as 'organized hypocrisy': the symbolic commitment to consent in UN peacekeeping is maintained in spite of the reality of growing coercion on the ground.[101] Michael Doyle and Nicholas Sambanis deny that consent should be treated as a 'bright line' dividing sanction from coercion, urging instead that that the 'key' to the new peacekeeping 'is usually finding a way to combine consent with coercion'.[102] Reflecting this intermingling of consent and coercion, Doyle and Sambanis also suggest that political authority be envisaged as a 'sovereignty spectrum', the implication being that international influence can penetrate more deeply into domestic political systems if it is not possible to sharply differentiate national political decision-making from the influence of outside actors.[103] James D. Fearon and David D. Laitin argue that the end goal of 'full sovereignty' be replaced with para-sovereign entities 'embedded in and monitored by international institutions'.[104] Reflective of this para-sovereign status, UN peacekeepers have even taken to providing personal security for national leaders who enjoy UN patronage: Liberian president Ellen Johnson Sirleaf is protected by Indian policewomen who patrol 'the gate to the president's office, while motorised Nigerian troops form part of the security detail'.[105]

Victors' peace

That consent and self-determination could be so restricted reflected the extent to which liberal peace was a victors' peace. This was important in a number of respects. In the first place the end of the Cold War balance of power denied developing countries the possibility of perching on the fulcrum of that balance and thereby preserving some freedom of movement. They could no longer hope to play off one side against the other in the contested world order, or seek Soviet aid to withstand US and Western pressure. It also meant a restriction of political choice insofar as the ideological spectrum was compressed by the dissolution of the USSR.

In the battlefields of the Cold War, peacebuilding was how the victory settlement of the Cold War was globalised. Thus UN peacekeeping helped to bring the Cold War to an end in those places where the war had been 'hot' and bloody: Afghanistan, Central America, South East Asia and southern Africa. It was the retraction of Soviet support for its allied regimes in Ethiopia, Angola, Nicaragua, Vietnam and for Cuban intervention in Africa that helped facilitate the 'flurry' of UN peace initiatives in this period.[106] Thus it was UN peacekeepers that monitored the withdrawal of Soviet troops across the Oxus River from Afghanistan back into Soviet Central Asia, and who watched as Cuban forces boarded the ships and planes that would take them back from Africa to the Caribbean. Peacekeeping missions thus provided a diplomatic rearguard and internationalist gloss for a Soviet Union in headlong flight from its imperial burdens.[107]

The new peacekeeping also reflected the changed nature of peace. With the Cold War over, peace was no longer the option between two visions of social and political order. The value of ending conflict was no longer the defence of an existing order (capitalism) or overthrowing it (socialism). Peace, no longer the choice between options, became synonymous with one vision—the liberal peace. National liberation and revolutionary movements that had once aspired to build socialism in their own countries adopted the principles of market democracy—free markets and procedural democracy—with alacrity.[108]

As part of the 1991 Bicesse Peace Accords, the People's Movement for the Liberation of Angola accepted market democratic principles over their previous Soviet-inspired vision of a command economy, with nationalised industries and collective farms.[109] In El Salvador, the Farabundo Martí National Liberation Front accepted the sweeping programme of economic liberalisation enacted by their conservative political opponents after the peace process and entry into multiparty elections.[110] In Namibia, the South West African People's Organisation abandoned the rhetoric of national liberation, state socialism and public ownership in favour of an explicit commitment to a free market 'enabling environment' that would protect foreign investment and allow for repatriation of profits and investments.[111] The Liberation Front of Mozambique came under pressure from Western governments and international donors to accept principles of market democracy as part of the peace process in that country.[112]

These moves facilitated international acceptance and unlocked large development loans and aid for the countries concerned. At the same time, movements that had been little more than counter-revolutionary war machines to grind away at popular movements in these countries were transformed into legitimate political actors as part of the peace processes: the Contras in Nicaragua, the National Union for the Total Independence of Angola (Unita), and the Mozambican National Resistance (Renamo). If the peace adopted in these societies was not under explicit duress, it certainly happened in restrictive international circumstances that necessarily limited the political choices available and determined the outcome of the transitions.

That democracy was seen as appropriate for developing countries wracked by civil war reflected a shift in US strategy in the closing decade of the Cold War. The shift away from supporting authoritarian regimes reflected a preference for governments that could elicit sufficient popular support in order to provide the stability that repressive dictatorships had thus far proved unable to provide (as testified by the Nicaraguan and Iranian revolutions at the end of the 1970s). Democracy was adopted then as part of a global struggle, a strategic instrument and expedient in a battle for political influence and ideological renewal. As part of the last US offensive of the Cold War, and democratisation was adopted as regional policy in those areas where authoritarianism seemed less viable as a political structure.[113]

Hence the designation of Barry Gills and Joel Rocamora—'low intensity democracy'—deliberately chosen to illustrate that democratisation lay on a strategic continuum with the low intensity warfare that preceded it, and that it was to be a controlled process that would defuse popular energies.[114] With the USSR in dissolution, such a process limited the range of political choices open to societies undergoing democratisation, including the fact that it immeasurably strengthened the appeal of Western models, not only for political systems but also economic ones—open trading economies with strong defences for private property. At the same time, the dissolution of the USSR helped to domesticate democracy in the developing world, ensuring that it could be tolerated by Western states as there was now less chance of democratic uprisings or change rolling over into support for state socialist policies such as nationalisation or restrictions on capital movement.

Democratisation involving post-conflict elections could not but have a plebiscitary character. In the context of peacebuilding, war-weary populations are asked to endorse externally crafted peace settlements, knowing that international support, both economic and political, depends on their positive assent to peace agreements that are strictly bounded by the decisions of external actors. Michael W. Doyle and Nicholas Sambanis see these efforts as part of a sensible process of political engineering: 'Like a good constitutionalist, the UN has helped embed external controls, such as democracy and the rule of law, and internal controls, such as power sharing and judicial reform, into effective peace settlements.'[115] But good constitutionalists have also understood that constitutions are only legitimate instruments of rule when they are created by those who are to be subject to them: this is what allows constitutions to act as a legal articulation of freedom rather than an arbitrarily-imposed order.

Since the 1990s there has been a concerted shift from rapid peace-building strategies of the early post-Cold War period to a longer-term vision embodied in the idea of state-building. The shift from peace-building to state-building can be characterised as a turn from the rapid liberalisation strategies of the early 1990s missions to a focus on cooperating with indigenous allies and building public authority rather than temporarily colonising certain state functions with UN cadre. The shift reflected the new understanding among policymakers that post-conflict societies were incapable of carrying the burden of democracy and market economies, requiring both a longer timeframe as well as stronger buttresses of state power to undergird the liberal peace.[116] The new focus on state-building looked to strengthen state institutions of public order as a means of 'locking in' peace settlements and their corollary political and economic reforms, along with a new stress on 'local ownership' of the peace process.[117] In this way, it was hoped that the failures of the early generation of post-Cold War peacekeeping operations could be avoided.

Part of this new approach was the adoption of the so-called 'light footprint' with the UN mission in Afghanistan. Explicitly crafted to rely more on informal influence than large numbers of peacekeepers, the United Nations took on this strategy out of concern that the US would expect nation-building to be carried out in the far more populous, underdeveloped and remote territory of Afghanistan along the lines established in East Timor and Kosovo a few years previously. The Secretariat explicitly warned the Council against saddling the United Nations with such a role. The Unama mission in Afghanistan was designed in contradistinction to the over-extended satrapies seen in Kosovo and East Timor.

Despite its comparatively modest size and budget, the Unama mission's importance to the US and NATO intervention in Afghanistan should not be underestimated, not only as regards its role in coordinating relief and humanitarian efforts but also in political reconstruction—that is, regime change. It was the efforts of Lakhdar Brahimi and the United Nations that were instrumental in the formation of the national conclave (the *loya jirga*) that laid the foundations of the pro-US, post-Taliban Karzai government. The United Nations also wielded extensive informal influence in order to secure the Bonn Accords that set out the vision for post-Taliban Afghanistan.[118] Thus operational size need not correlate directly with political influence, and nor should the 'light footprint' in Afghanistan detract from the continued UN extension of neo-trusteeship, particularly in Africa. Only one year after the establishment of Unama in 2002, the extent of the UN peacebuilding mission in Congo—a country more than twice as populous and three and a half times the size of Afghanistan—was likened to that of a 'protectorate'.[119]

There are several significant aspects of the shift to state-building from peacebuilding that must be stressed. The shift to state-building and 'local ownership' strategies speaks to a less direct exercise of international influence over post-conflict societies and their institutions, and an attempt to avoid the overt displays of power and social engineering carried out by UN functionaries in previous missions. 'Local ownership' is a strategy of making indigenous elites responsible for international policy—with the added bonus that the failures of policy will not rebound at the expense of international agencies. At the same time, this shift speaks to a downplaying of the values of democracy and the political benefits of liberalism such as multiparty competition or human rights, in favour of a 'satisficing' approach that prioritises order and stability more than transformation oriented towards progressive goals. Much like indirect rule sought to extend the sway of imperial influence, so too state-building strategies aim more firmly to fix international regulation of post-conflict societies by ensuring that solid structures are in place that cannot be easily eroded by subsequent political changes.

As peacekeeping has debased peace, so too has peacebuilding. The ideas of peacebuilding have helped to sever the link between peace and autonomy, with peacebuilding taking place under conditions of diminished, if not meaningless, consent and coercive democratisation. If we return to the original vision of liberal peace, for Immanuel Kant peace was not valuable in itself: he noted that peace could be the peace of the grave or an imperial and despotic peace where peace was predicated on snuffing out individual initiative and national autonomy.[120] Peace was valuable insofar as it contributed to a project of freedom. The dismembering of Kant's vision of peace, democracy and self-determination is expressed in democratic peace theory.

Peacebuilding and democratic peace

In its multiple and varied efforts to establish peace around the world, it is logical to see UN peacekeeping as a vehicle for diffusing liberal peace. In so doing, UN peacekeeping helps expand the borders of the liberal zone of peace in world order: that is, the prosperous, secure and integrated core of advanced liberal capitalist states. This view reflects the enormously influential theory of liberal peace, which has shaped the diplomacy of Northern states for the last three decades, as well as a plethora of international agencies and institutions.[121]

At the core of the various expressions of the theory is the millenarian prospect that nothing less than eternal peace can be achieved in world politics if two basic conditions are met. First, that states enjoy liberal representative government internally, which by its nature has no intrinsic interest in perpetuating warfare. Second, that states have market economies, which will help spontaneously to intertwine states' interests through the creation of mutually interdependent trading networks. The more countries that meet these criteria, so the logic of the theory goes, the more that peace and prosperity will spread throughout the world, and the more that states will gradually become enmeshed in a matrix of international bodies that will help to peacefully regulate their affairs. If the Cold War can be seen as a worldwide contest over what type of political and social organisation was best suited for humanity, then post-Cold War UN peacekeeping can be seen as part of a global effort to consolidate the triumph of Western liberalism in that prior contest.

Indeed, while the theory of liberal peace holds that relations will be pacific between liberal democracies, it accepts and even ratifies predation by liberal states on the illiberal (or insufficiently liberal) periphery, as the theory predicts that liberal states will seek to remould other states in their own image. The theory is predicated on the separation of the two zones—so that the interventions of the superior, democratic zone into the subordinate zone will slowly absorb the latter into the former. This is without consideration of the extent to which the two zones might already be integrated and interdependent, or that the blessings secured in the zone of peace might be won at the expense and subordination of the zone of conflict.

Such conditions of coercive democratisation and peacebuilding, where peace is not seen to be exclusive of violence, corresponds more to a policing order than a Kantian vision, where peace is not predicated on the transcendence of violence and disorder but on constant coercive intervention to contain it. If UN peacekeeping is a means of consolidating Western victory in the Cold War, it is at the same time a system of 'poor relief and riot control' in the words of Michael Pugh, a globalised policing order aimed at subduing the restive periphery of disorder that encircles the prosperous liberal 'zone of peace' at the core of the international system.[122]

Neutrality: from diplomacy to policing

Neutrality is the third aspect of the 'holy trinity' and gives peacekeeping a distinctive rationale. In place of targeting a specific enemy for elimination in battle, peacekeepers act impartially between warring parties—neither as foreign mercenaries nor as allies of a particular belligerent, but as third parties with no political interests or stakes in the conflict. This lack of direct strategic or political interest in a conflict is supposedly what endows peacekeepers with whatever authority they may possess, and reflects the classical view of peacekeeping as an adjunct of diplomacy rather than coercive military intervention. But in tandem with changes in the use of force and the meaning of consent already discussed above, the meaning of neutrality too has changed. This is expressed by Michael W. Doyle and Nicholas N. Sambanis in the language of policing: 'Good cops act impartially but not neutrally when they stop one individual from victimizing another.'[123]

Doyle and Sambanis's invocation of policing is by no means idiosyncratic. As Richard Kareem Al-Qaq observes, the vocabulary routinely used to frame international peacekeeping in public discourse—'blue helmets', 'policing', 'fire fighting'—is distinctively civil rather than international.[124] Policing has been at the core, both of thinking about the United Nations as a security system and for peacekeeping specifically. One of the founding fathers of peacekeeping, Canadian statesman Lester Pearson, described the first UN peacekeeping mission deployed to Egypt in 1956 (discussed in greater detail in chapter six) as the 'first genuinely international police force of its kind.'[125] That such descriptions are perceived as legitimate and acceptable indicates that peacekeepers are to some extent seen to be the forces of a single, integrated political order, much like the forces used in the domestic realm.

Talk of policing also reflects real changes in the practice of peacekeeping. Today the proportion of UN peacekeepers recruited from gendarmerie or police forces rather than mobile light and medium infantry is greater than ever. The numbers of international 'policekeepers' leapt from 5,840 in 1995 to over 17,500 in 2010.[126] This is seen as a mark of institutional progress for the United Nations because it represents a more effective deployment of resources. Unlike infantry, whose primary purpose is to destroy enemy forces in battle, police are more likely to be trained to deal with the kinds of public disorder that confront peacekeepers in the aftermath of civil conflict. Police forces are seen as better able to establish the 'rule of law' after civil wars, a precondition for the restoration of public order, civil authority, state services and ultimately, peace.

But the conventional understanding of policing as the enforcement of domestic order by a state apparatus presupposes precisely what is missing from the international arena—an overarching sovereign authority. So what can the category of 'policing' mean when it is grafted from the domestic onto the international realm?

At a minimum, policing provides a contrast to the classic model of power politics based on rivalrous sovereigns jealously guarding their interests, who neither recognise nor claim any higher power in their relations with each other. That police forces—those security forces most associated with maintaining domestic order—can be so readily transferred from one sovereign jurisdiction to another under the authority of the United Nations clearly presupposes a greater degree of legal and political homogeneity across borders, and this can only mean that the space for the political and legal articulation of a wider range of outcomes has been limited.

In terms of peacekeeping missions in the field, the former eastern commander of Monuc forces Major-General Patrick Cammaert expounded the philosophy of neutrality as understood in relation to 'robust peacekeeping': 'Being neutral means that you stand there and you say "Well, I have nothing to do with it", while being impartial means that you stand there, you judge the situation as it is and you take charge.'[127] In practice of course, peacekeepers 'taking charge' will inevitably favour one side at the expense of another in a civil war, as we saw above in relation to Côte d'Ivoire. But what is significant here is the authority on which peacekeepers claim to act. That the authority of peacekeepers is now measured less by their behaviour in relation to the warring parties and more by how they enact their own political and legal authority (the UN Security Council). This has significant implications for the balance of power between peacekeepers, belligerents and the states hosting peacekeepers.

From acting neutrally between belligerents, the authority of the United Nations has decisively shifted into claiming authority over belligerents. Impartiality has not been repudiated insofar as the UN is still in itself formally indifferent to the programmes of particular political actors. But post-Brahimi impartiality gives the UN greater authority not only because it formally extracts consent 'on a one-time and comprehensive basis'[128] but also because the UN must now militarily oppose 'obvious evil'.[129] This tokens an important shift of power away from states hosting peacekeepers to the United Nations, and as a result belligerents and host states have had to accept the logic of UN mandates as interpreted by the United Nations itself.[130]

All of this reflects wider geopolitical changes. During the Cold War, UN neutrality was justified and necessitated by the hostility of the two antagonistic blocs, both contained within the UN system. As the United Nations could only act if seen to be independent of either side, UN neutrality was a species of diplomatic neutrality, in that UN peacekeepers were solicited and accepted on the basis that they had no direct strategic or political interest in the outcome of any particular conflict. This is still likely to be the case in many peacekeeping operations (though see further the discussion in chapter three). The difference is that whereas the neutrality of the Cold War era was defined negatively, today neutrality has a positive meaning, embodying international law and the liberal peace. That this can still be presented as 'neutral' reflects the lack of ideological or geopolitical schism in international affairs, and the fact that the values of international law and liberal peace are taken to be beyond legitimate political contestation.

Cosmopolitan law enforcement?

How have theorists sought to make sense of these developments in terms of international politics? It is political theorists of cosmopolitanism that have gone the furthest in this respect, arguing that peacekeepers represent the proto-police force of global governance—the network of multiple institutions and authorities that signifies an incipient globalised political system, bound together by a body of cosmopolitan law focused on upholding the rights and claims of individuals over those of states.[131] This is the vision of a cosmopolitan or 'post-Westphalian' global polity, where cross-cutting political and legal relations spill over the borders of increasingly vestigial state forms with the old, 'Westphalian' order receding into history.[132] The duty of upholding law both within and across states—human rights law, international criminal law and international humanitarian law, or 'cosmopolitan law-enforcement' in the words of Mary Kaldor—is a task closer to peacekeeping than traditional military operations and lies 'somewhere between soldiering and policing'.[133] Kaldor takes the performance of the British state in Northern Ireland as an appropriate model of how to combine 'military and policing tasks' for this new era.[134]

The development of UN peacekeeping has indeed followed this model since Kaldor issued her prescriptions back in 1999. Many of the UN 'policekeepers' despatched around the world are special police deployed not as individuals but as formed paramilitary units—that is, roughly company-sized (100 to 150 officers) constabulary detachments, equipped with heavy weaponry and armoured transport rather than just handcuffs and pistols. It is paramilitary police formations that are particularly prized in UN policing—for example, the Italian *carabinieri*, the Spanish *guardia civil*, French *gendarmarie*, Argentinean *national gendarmerie* and Chilean *carabineros*.[135] Like Kaldor, Fearon and Laitin note that the Royal Ulster Constabulary (RUC), a police formation known for its role in British counter-insurgency in Ireland, was regarded by UN officials as the most effective of the police units deployed to Kosovo in 1999. Noting RUC 'methods may not always have been fully in accord with human rights conventions', Fearon and Laitin nonetheless accept this policing model as appropriate for post-conflict countries.[136] Seeking to expand the provision of such globalised gendarmes in June 2004, the Group of Eight industrialised nations agreed to support a 'Center of Excellence for Stability Police Units' to be established in Vicenza, Italy to scale up the training of 'stability police'.

In practice then, many of the proscriptions of cosmopolitan peacekeeping have variously pre-empted, echoed and recapitulated the kinds of policy recommendations one would find across any number of peacekeeping reports issued by the United Nations and various international bodies since the Brahimi report of 2000. They all variously urge more decisive and forceful military action, better and more materiel to be provided for peacekeepers, more international cooperation, more focused and purposeful political decision-making, greater observance of international law, more battalions earmarked for rapid deployment, more and better multinational training, international military exercises, joint and integrated command structures, and so on. Indeed, for all their idealism and self-proclaimed utopianism, cosmopolitan peacekeeping theorists pay strikingly close attention to the specific details of Anglo-French military doctrine in formulating their own proposals for peacekeeping reform.[137]

Given the correspondence between cosmopolitan theories of peacekeeping and the permissive rules of engagement and emphasis on civilian protection embedded in peacekeeping policy today, it would not be too much of a stretch to describe the current posture of UN peacekeeping forces as 'cosmopolitan peacekeeping'. Yet while cosmopolitan theorists welcome norms of civilian protection, many would be unsatisfied with peacekeeping in its current state, and would persistently urge further and greater reforms to break beyond the limits of a politics still anchored in the narrow concerns of nation states. Mary Kaldor perhaps strives farthest in this direction: 'Above all', she argues, 'the motivations of these new forces will have to be incorporated into a wider concept of cosmopolitan right. Whereas the soldier ... had to be prepared to die for his or her country, the international soldier/police officer risks his or her life for humanity.'[138]

For cosmopolitan theorists, current peacekeeping is an emergent security system at best, requiring much more global reform, institutional innovation and political restructuring before it could be said to be complete. Yet this telos gives cosmopolitan theory a flexible and correspondingly evasive character. Rather than seeing all the dysfunction, compromises and limitations of current peacekeeping as effects of structural or systemic constraints or expressions of irreconcilable interests, all such problems can be displaced on to a remote but glittering future of global justice, where all political antagonisms have been arbitrated, institutional asymmetries corrected and excesses compensated for. This vision of cosmopolitan peacekeeping is not, however, a world-state that would require concentrating political power into a single centre, but a process of constant refinement—in other words, an adumbration of the 'actually existing global governance' that we have in today's concatenation of multiple authorities and centres of power. If the vision of a future cosmopolitan polity offers a perspective from which to unify and comprehend seemingly contradictory developments in international security today, it is has the added benefit of being a future that never arrives.

In the perpetual interregnum between the present and the cosmopolitan future, even cosmopolitan theorists concede that today's 'cosmopolitan patriots' are likely to appear as 'neo-imperialists',[139] and that the post-national armies of cosmopolitan peacekeepers will resemble the multinational imperial armies of the recent past. For cosmopolitan peacekeepers, 'actually existing global governance' is:

> analogous to the situation that prevailed in Britain's global empire during the nineteenth century. Soldiers are required to participate in combat but not always in wars with other states. They also perform constabulary tasks, and provide engineering, medical and transport capabilities [and] municipal government where none exists. Like Britain's imperial army, they can also expect to serve alongside troops drawn from the four corners of the globe.[140]

This 'situation' was not restricted to Britain's empire and imperial army, nor indeed confined to the nineteenth century—multinational and multiracial imperial armies were fighting 'savage wars of peace' on behalf of imperial states well into the second half of the last century, as we shall see in chapter four. The link between policing and imperialism is also a familiar historical trope. The use of the domestic analogy of policing to describe the behaviour of imperial states in their spheres of influence indicates that the sovereignty of the subordinate states is effectively constricted by the state doing the policing (indeed Martin Wight even embedded policing into his definition of 'sphere of influence' offered in his classic *Power Politics*).[141]

While UN peacekeepers are not usually deployed to preserve an imperial state's exclusive sphere of influence, this does not change the fact that they act as imperial constabulary formations. The fact that the defining function of state authority—its legal monopoly on the use of force—is now seen to be legitimately open to displacement by foreign security forces and extensive external restructuring speaks to the depth and intensity of international intervention reached in early twenty-first century peacekeeping. If the police are preferable to the army as an instrument of domestic order, it is worth recalling that the police also have a mandate to use coercion in a range of circumstances far beyond the battlefield.

An enormous range of activities is undertaken by these UN paramilitary gendarmes/civilian police ('Civpols')—from monitoring the activities of local police to mounting their own independent patrols to uphold law and order.[142] The fixation in peacekeeping with restoring the rule of law has resulted in a distinctive new 'legal imperialism', with justice systems and legal processes that 'appear to be dropped in from on high', in the words of Matteo Tondini. The post-conflict court systems established under international auspices have often seen the use of:

'mixed' internationally-nationally staffed tribunals. Some have also been characterized by the establishment of courts composed of international judges in charge of the administration of a novel justice system, along with the imposition of human rights-inspired legal models derived from the idealistic character of military interventions that originated the civil reconstruction missions in the first place.[143]

Different uses for the police

Referring to the peacekeeping order of the early twenty-first century in terms of policing, as many analysts are wont to do, is not intended to emphasise a continuity with imperialism, but rather the positive aspects of peacekeeping, such as its relative lack of militarism, its concern with questions of public interest, its rootedness in authority that is based on neutral observance of the law rather than the arbitrariness of military might.[144] But the discourse of policing in international affairs is also revealing in another sense, albeit an inadvertent one: it reflects the vision of a world where security forces—military and paramilitary— are deployed to protect enclaves of global prosperity by pushing back the threat of constant low-level warfare, population movements of diseased migrants and globalised criminality. To speak of policing in international affairs is to 'lapse', as Lawrence Freedman observes, into the 'stereotypical images that can mark the view of the inner city from the suburban garden': 'Once we suppose that we are coping with an underclass—whether domestic or international—there is a tendency to adopt the mantle of police, social workers or authority figures, dealing with delinquents, inadequates, beggars and the hapless victims of abuse.'[145]

In some places the two tasks have already merged. The Brazilian army, deployed as peacekeepers in Haiti from 2004, was tasked after late 2010 with 'peacekeeping' in its own cities: Brazilian soldiers were sent to patrol two poor districts of Rio de Janeiro, a use of military force explicitly legitimated by the experience of Brazil's peacekeeping expedition in Haiti.[146]

Unlike domestic policing, peacekeeping concerns the fate of nations. According to Freedman, there are several consequences of treating international politics as a function of policing. With the assumption that policing is dealing with 'criminal elements that must be punished if they cannot be coerced', strategies may be adopted that 'fail to address the rationality of opponents, and the possibility that their security concerns may be real and deeply felt. Their strategic sense may be underestimated, while their propensity for mindless violence exaggerated.' On the side of those intervening, the chariness of getting involved in these 'rough neighbourhoods' of the international order produces a corresponding fixation on 'exit strategies' and a 'search for ways to influence events from a safe distance, especially through air power.'[147] Equally we might add, through the use of peacekeepers from the global South.

Imperial peacekeeping

The right to police is a civilizing mission, embodying a new standard that the states of the periphery 'must accept in order to gain full rights and recognition of the international community'.[148] Rather than states being seen as legitimate by virtue of being representatives of their people, legitimacy resides in meeting this new 'standard of civilization' that is set and defined by the powerful states and international agencies, with conflict-ridden states only being allowed to enjoy the rights and privileges accorded to other nations once they meet this standard.

The content of this cosmopolitan *mission civilisatrice* is taken to be beyond challenge: reified 'laws' of economics, good governance based on technical expertise, and ethical values are all assumed to enjoy spontaneous and universal support that obviates the need for political justification. Decisions about order and organisation are assumed to be a given, rather than requiring the active consent and support of its subjects. The intercessions of peacekeepers are seen in the words of one critic 'as the application of natural laws of economics, state creation and the ethical protection of human rights'.[149] The discourse of peacekeeping itself is a depoliticised, technocratic vocabulary of bureaucratic processes and administrative acronyms: 'DDR' (disarmament, demobilisation, and reintegration); 'SSR' (security sector reform); and 'executive policing' to name three of the most prominent. Technocratic administration and supreme ethical values march in step to the degradation of self-determination.

However this new standard of civilisation may be justified, there is no avoiding the fact that it undermines the rights of people who are supposed to be its beneficiaries. For all the plethora of rights that peacekeepers are tasked to uphold—human rights, non-combatants' rights, the rights of children, gender rights, minority rights, the rights of demobilised war veterans, the rights of child soldiers—political rights are given much shorter shrift. The single right that is foundational to the concept of political representation and accountability—self-determination—is the one right that can be relegated, ignored and derided with comparative impunity.[150]

The justification given for this new *mission civilisatrice* is that it will elevate its recipients into the comity of liberal states. It will do this by repressing war, eliminating the oppression, backwardness and poverty that give rise to conflict, and fostering national independence. Yet insofar as peacekeeping presupposes hierarchy—a division between the civilised/peacekeepers and uncivilised/peacekept—then this new *mission civilisatrice* will serve to recreate the conditions that it is supposed to abolish. Once a group is excluded from a political community by its dominant members, and different standards are applied to the behaviour of that group, their political actions become defined by their membership of the inferior group. The difference can then be used to justify and explain the behaviour of the marginalised group, with the end result being that inequality and marginalisation becomes self-reinforcing. Imperial peacekeeping has helped to roll back the equality achieved by anti-colonial nationalism since 1945, cleaving the international order into liberal and illiberal zones, the latter inhabited by the 'peacekept'. The nations that compromise the illiberal zone of the peacekept are assumed to be incapable of acting responsibly without international oversight and guidance, while it is precisely international oversight and guidance that confiscates political responsibility by eroding the self-determination in question.[151]

Conclusion

UN peacekeeping and peacebuilding missions are often contrasted with NATO expeditionary operations. The comparison is conveniently flattering to both the United Nations and to NATO, with UN peacekeeping placed at the softer, more pacifistic, reconstructive side of intervention, and NATO at the sharper, more militaristic end. This distinction is, as we have seen, overblown. The militarisation of UN peacekeeping should be judged not by comparison to NATO operations, but by reference to how UN operations themselves have developed. UN peacekeeping operations have become more interventionist even when less militarised, and in any case they exist in a world order in which intervention has become increasingly normalised, and one in which the NATO powers exercise enormous influence over the United Nations itself, as we shall see in chapter six. Indeed, to even place UN peace-keeping on a spectrum with NATO expeditions—something that would have been laughed at during the Cold War—is to admit that both types of intervention are seen to be serving the same essential purpose.

UN peacekeeping has become a key part of the post-Cold War world, consolidating the triumph of liberalism in the periphery of the states system. The means for consolidating this victory—democratisation, military intervention, human rights, nation-building, marketisation—are all policies pursued by the Western states that won the Cold War, foremost among them of course, the US. For all that peacekeeping is a liberal enterprise, it is no less an imperial one. Indeed, it is the very sweep and ambition of the post-Cold War liberal vision of peace that propelled the surge into imperial peacekeeping.

In this process peacekeeping operations have been transformed both in terms of depth—penetrating deeper into states and their societies—and geographic scope, as peacekeepers are deployed around the globe. The 'holy trinity' at the core of peacekeeping has remained intact even as it has been transformed as part of this process: limited use of force has become a new rationale for war; consent a means of degrading self-determination, and impartiality a basis on which to legitimate power that is not grounded in structures of political representation but in the ether of cosmopolitan law.

As more and more wars have ended with the deployment of peace-keeping operations, so too global peace has been made dependent on an extensive and prolonged international military presence. The establishment of democracy and liberalism has been made dependent on the use of force. Peacekeeping has helped to innovate ways of legitimating and normalising the use of military power, extending its role across various spheres of social life in the countries hosting peacekeepers, and prolonging a military presence long after the fighting is over. Peace-keeping has contributed to the normalisation of the use of force in world affairs.

That the 'holy trinity' of peacekeeping has been transformed in this way is testimony to the contradictions of liberalism—the inability of liberalism to realise its purported goals without undermining its own precepts, even as these precepts are invoked to legitimate illiberal efforts. With peacekeepers waging war for peace, to defend human rights, enforce resolutions drafted in remote councils of power, imperial peacekeeping has contaminated the classical liberal vision of peace. In the imperial peace, the classical liberal vision of peace as the transcendence of conflict has been muddied by the nebulous categories and phases of 'post-conflict' transition, where violence persists after peace settlements have been agreed. Efforts to meliorate conflict—whether it be modulating violence, containing 'spoilers' or providing humanitarian charity for hapless victims—have substituted for the vision of transcending war. Peace no longer means the absence of war—let alone the transcendence of war—for the United Nations it can even justify fighting wars.

So far, the discussion has been restricted to the imperial aspects of missions in the field. To complete this picture we must contextualise peacekeeping both within the historical development of peacekeeping and imperialism in world order. We turn to this task in the next chapter.

3

THE HIGHEST FORM OF LIBERAL IMPERIALISM

Introduction

Any sober and historically-informed appraisal of UN peacekeeping missions around the world today would leave the observer in little doubt that the kinds of tasks once performed by colonial armies, missionaries, comprador classes, imperial viceroys and colonial administrators are today carried out by the Special Representatives of the UN Secretary-General, UN peacekeepers and their camp followers of UN civilian staff, multiple UN agencies as well as international aid and development charities and non-governmental organisations, state elites and paragovernmental bodies. In place of the old imperial slogans of commerce, Christianity and civilisation, human rights, free markets and liberal democracy are promoted with no less commitment and vigour.

Yet UN peacekeeping is clearly seen to be legitimate and acceptable in a way that colonialism and neo-colonialism are not. Indeed, not only is UN peacekeeping not seen as imperialist, it is often seen as positively preferable to assertions of US imperial might or Western military intervention.[1] In contradistinction to imperial power, peacekeeping is seen to be legitimate because of the cosmopolitan authority of the United Nations that underpins its missions, the fact that the constitutional independence of its target states is preserved rather than annulled, and the absence of any single state at an imperial core monopolising whatever benefits that peacekeeping yields. In this chapter I argue that far from making peacekeeping anti-imperial, it is precisely these aspects that make peacekeeping the highest form of liberal imperialism.

In the global system of UN peacekeeping missions, we have an imperial order corresponding to the vision of the reformers of empire: a globalised political framework that places the wretched of the earth under a benevolent regime of international paternalism. At the same time, this political order is free of the colonial sins that exercised liberal critics of the old European empires: namely, the sins of economic plunder, conquest and narrow self-interest. This imperial residuum is not however an 'empire lite'—the form of empire minus the toxic substance of imperialism—but the distilled essence of empire: a hierarchic and paternalistic regime for maintaining order across a diverse set of peoples, while recreating political dependency as part of a global civilising mission. While this new imperial framework does not extinguish the forms of national independence, in practice it represents a more toxic subversion of self-determination precisely because it extends the fiction that substantive autonomy is compatible with sustained and systematic intervention by external agencies and foreign armies and gendarmes.

That these strategies of maintaining imperial order are carried out under the auspices of an international institution rather than those of a colonial empire is novel but nonetheless historically consistent with the evolution of imperialism across the last century. The twentieth century saw the spread of decolonisation correspond with the growth of international institutions to discipline and regulate the behaviour of newly independent states in place of old imperial strictures. Indeed, the gradual transfer of these imperial ordering functions from colonial empires to international agencies was one of the long-term goals of liberal imperial reform—that is, an attempt not to abolish empire but to salvage it from its opponents and its own internal contradictions.

This imperial peace has not arisen without controversy. Yet the political legitimacy and theoretical foundations of the imperial peace remain essentially intact despite increasingly vociferous scepticism about the liberal content of peacebuilding efforts. For all those who believe that the *'mission civilisatrice'* of UN peacekeeping can be freely indulged without neo-colonial guilt, increasingly there are those who fear that UN peacekeeping has trampled on peoples in post-conflict societies: that UN peacebuilders have casually imposed liberal institutions on fragile post-conflict countries without consideration for the wishes of local people, without thought for context and in ignorance of local customs, practices and initiatives. These critics and reformers of the liberal peace urge greater sensitivity to local concerns, they stress that more attention be paid to the legitimacy of post-conflict arrangements and instead of the mechanical reproduction of institutional blueprints drawn up in metropolitan capitals, they urge greater diversity of political institutions.

Critics of peacebuilding have certainly given external expression to the crisis of confidence that has beset the practice of peacebuilding in recent years. But as we shall see, for all the criticism of the liberal peace, the imperial peace remains unscathed. Although I will not survey the entirety of the critical debate on peacebuilding below, what should hopefully become evident is that critical debates over the validity of the liberal peace strongly echo earlier imperial debates over the benefits of indirect rule as opposed to direct colonisation. Under the system of indirect rule, the devolution of power to local structures of authority was not designed to dilute imperial rule but to transform indigenous centres of power into bulwarks of empire. As peacebuilders evolve new strategies that defer liberalisation and democratisation in favour of stability and 'local' solutions, I suggest we are witnessing the emergence of a new post-modern politics of indirect rule over post-war societies, this time legitimated by the radical critics of liberalism.

Making peacekeeping safe for imperialism

Ten years ago, the US invasion of Iraq and claim of a pre-emptive right to wage war generated an academic debate on imperialism so vociferous that the discipline of International Relations seemed to be on the cusp of being submerged into 'American empire studies'.[2] While suspicion over US imperial intentions in the Middle East fostered mass public opposition around the world, the theoretical and scholarly debate on US empire ranged far and wide. US empire was compared with previous historical empires. The role the US played in the development of twentieth century global capitalism was scrutinised, and the comparative role of military might as opposed to economic supremacy was discussed. This debate in international politics spilled over into the realm of history, as old controversies over imperial historiography and the long-term role and effects of empire in the developing world were re-examined. The debate was by no means one-sided. In tandem with the swelling opposition to US empire, a new generation of neo-imperialists emerged, comprised of conservative historians, Western strategists and International Relations thinkers dragging with them a long tail of broadsheet columnists, editorialists and assorted scribblers who openly welcomed the restoration of empire as an organising principle of international order. For all those who criticised US imperialism, there were those who exhorted US power to greater efforts.

Yet for all its historical sweep and controversy in other respects, the debate on empire offered a truncated view of contemporary imperialism. For all the talk of global capitalism, the critics of empire (fixated on the question of energy resources) rarely looked further than the Greater Middle East, occasionally straying as far as the Balkans, seeing the hypocrisies of humanitarian intervention as offering convenient cover for the extension of Western power. In some respects it was the neo-imperialists who had a wider purview of empire, as they saw in it the solution to problems of international order that went further than merely laying claim to natural resources.

What was striking about this hue and cry over empire was that it occurred at the point at which US power strayed from UN legitimacy due to the lack of UN support for the invasion of Iraq. Earlier displays of US power that were legitimated with UN authorisation or use of force that took the form of UN peacekeeping never provoked counter-imperial reactions on the same scale or intensity. Where the United Nations has deployed its own forces without US arms, discussion of empire has been even more muted. The omission of UN peacekeeping from debates on empire is peculiar given how it readily meets all the benchmarks drawn up to measure the breadth and depth of US imperialism today.

We have already seen in the first chapter that the United Nations is the only organisation that can approximate the geographic reach, if not the sheer might of US military power, and we saw that if measured by the metrics of nation-building and regime change, the United Nations arguably exceeds the US in the scale of its imperial ambition and transformative effects. One could go further. The attempt by the Bush administration to abrogate to itself the right to wage pre-emptive war, which stoked such legal and political controversy, is itself pre-empted in principle by no less an authority than the UN Charter, the first article of which allows for 'collective measures for the prevention and removal of threats to peace'. Long before the US intervention in Iraq, the United Nations had pioneered preventive military deployments, though not on the same scale as the US, with a small but highly regarded and uncontroversial peacekeeping deployment to Macedonia during the Balkan wars of the 1990s.

Given all this, why has the United Nations been ignored in discussions of empire? That the United Nations itself does not and cannot claim credit for the imperial management of the poor and the weak peoples of the world is unsurprising. Insofar as it is a forum for parliamentary diplomacy, the United Nations is its member states. To the extent that the United Nations is a bureaucracy independent of states, it must routinely efface itself before the member states. Beyond the niceties of diplomacy, why has the imperial role of the United Nations been so discounted in political and intellectual debate? Neo-imperialists have been muted in their public appreciation of the United Nations, tending to see it at best as an expedient prosthesis of imperial power and at worst as an unwieldy encumbrance. Even Michael Ignatieff—arguably the most liberal of the neo-imperialists—mostly ignores the role of the United Nations in his pleading for empire, limiting the reach of his 'empire lite' to those instances where Western intervention was most explicit prior to the 2003 Iraq invasion—namely Afghanistan, Bosnia-Herzegovina and Kosovo. Perhaps this contempt betrays a disinclination to share imperial glory with an institution that has succeeded more effectively to build a liberal peace than the US has in either Afghanistan or Iraq, and has done so moreover with less ostentation and military fanfare.

That the critics of empire share the same broadly contemptuous attitude towards the organisation is perhaps more surprising. When the United Nations is considered by the critics of empire, it is seen at worst as an accessory to US imperial power or at best as a makeshift restraint on that power and in those circumstances defensible. Perry Anderson's cursory dismissal of the United Nations could stand for many critics of empire today when he describes the organisation as 'a serviceable auxiliary mechanism of the Pax Americana'. He sees the 'multiplication of UN peacekeeping missions in the '90s' as an exercise in 'offloading policing tasks of lesser strategic importance for the American imperium'.[3] Yet that these peacekeeping missions have multiplied to the extent they have suggests that it is something more than a mere 'auxiliary mechanism'.

The exception to this dismissive trend is the theory of *Empire* by Michael Hardt and Antonio Negri. They give at least rhetorical significance to the role of the United Nations in their attempt to understand contemporary imperialism as a new, *sui generis* type of global political formation rather than a politics of state expansionism: 'The history of imperialist, interimperialist and anti-imperialist wars is over. The end of that history has ushered in the reign of peace. Or really, we have entered the era of minor and internal conflicts. Every imperial war is a civil war, a police action …'[4] Beyond these few descriptively suggestive passages scattered throughout the text, they pay little attention to concrete episodes of intervention or peacekeeping, adopting in effect the same contemptuous attitude towards UN practice that is visible among other critics.

If theorists of imperialism have tended to ignore UN peacekeeping, scholars of peacekeeping have had little choice but to compare the two. Aside from the occupation and reconstruction undertaken by the Allies in Germany and Japan after the Second World War, there is simply no historical precedent for the sheer scale of international involvement in countries subject to peacekeeping operations, aside from the League of Nations' mandates system and colonialism. The spectre of imperialism thus inevitably haunts the study of peacekeeping and its various permutations such as peacebuilding, post-war reconstruction, state-building and nation-building. Correspondingly, it is the analysts of peacekeeping who have taken this imperial analogy the furthest and detailed the differences and similarities between empire and peacekeeping most systematically. In examining the consistency of their reasoning and use of evidence we can decide whether or not it is legitimate to distinguish peacekeeping from empire.

Principles of order: peacekeeping and Empire

Roland Paris is perhaps the most prominent scholar of peacebuilding to argue that it is a 'modern rendering of the *mission civilisatrice*—the colonial-era belief that the European imperial powers had a duty to "civilize" their overseas possessions'.[5] But lest we confuse the 'old and new versions of *mission civilisatrice*', Paris admonishes us that 'European colonialism was practiced primarily to benefit the imperial states themselves'. According to him the 'motivation behind recent peacebuilding operations is less mercenary'.[6] Thus even when the imperial character of peacekeeping operations is admitted, it is held that peacekeeping can be rescued from the taint of empire. If peacekeeping is not simply to be ignored or rolled up into American empire, what reasons can be adduced for distinguishing peacekeeping from empire?

The defenders of liberal peace claim that peacekeeping is different from imperialism insofar as it is characterised by the following factors: (1) the absence of narrowly selfish motivations or strategic interests; (2) that peacekeeping is based on consent rather than conquest—what Paris describes as 'post-settlement' as opposed to 'post-conquest peace-building'; (3) that peacekeeping does not involve systematic economic exploitation of the countries concerned; (4) that peacekeeping is carried out through multilateral agencies and institutions; (5) that peacekeeping is not underpinned by ideologies of racial supremacy; and last but not least (6) the fact that the efforts of the United Nations are weaker in their effects than the results of classical imperialism.

Perhaps regretting his earlier labours to place the imperial analogy at the core of the modern research agenda of peacekeeping, Paris has lately argued that 'observing that there are echoes of colonialism in peacebuilding is quite different from asserting their equivalence. Not only is the colonialism-peacebuilding analogy overstated, but it also serves to discredit and delegitimize peacebuilding ...'[7] If Paris is right then the opposite is equally true: asserting the fundamental distinction between peacebuilding and colonialism directly serves to legitimise peacebuilding. Let us go through these claims in turn, before we turn to examine their validity.

The absence of strategic interests

Examining peacekeeping operations mounted in the 1990s, Marina Ottoway and Bethany Lacina share Paris's judgement. They point out that unlike peacekeeping operations, imperial domination was prolonged and driven by self-interested motives.[8] In his 2008 study *The Thin Blue Line* aid worker Conor Foley echoes these views, albeit inconsistently. On the one hand, while he concedes that it would be 'no exaggeration' to say that UN peacekeeping has resulted in the 'recolonization' of swathes of West Africa and claims that this 'is resented by many people' there,[9] he nonetheless rejects the overall charge of imperialism:

None of the major powers had any obvious selfish or strategic reason to intervene in places such as Somalia, Bosnia-Herzegovina, Haiti or East Timor. Indeed, it is precisely because western powers usually have not had ulterior motives to intervene that so many of these missions have suffered from lack of resources, planning and political will.[10]

The absence of economic exploitation

Closely tracking these arguments about the absence of selfish interests is the fact that UN peacekeeping operations, unlike old fashioned imperialism, do not involve the plundering of strategic raw materials or systematic economic exploitation. Michael Gilligan and Stephen J. Steadman have made the argument most forcefully against the idea that peacekeepers are deployed for the purposes of ensuring international access to imperialists' preferred form of loot—natural resources. They argue that there is no clear correlation between peacekeeping deployments and strategic stocks of raw materials.[11] While Ottoway and Lacina concede that there clearly is a concerted effort to impose new forms of political rule on other societies through peacekeeping, the comparison with imperialism is bogus: far from plundering the subject nations, peacekeeping missions pump massive resources into them as part of post-war reconstruction efforts.[12]

Post-conquest versus post-settlement peacebuilding

Roland Paris sets great store by the fact that peacekeeping operations are based on consent and that however much this may involve 'foreign intrusion in domestic affairs', it is important to keep in mind the distinction between intrusion that is based on conquest and intrusion based on 'the request of local parties after the negotiation of peace settlements to civil wars'.[13] It is this distinction at birth, according to Paris, that distinguishes peacekeeping from occupation, and peacebuilding from imposition of neo-colonial governing arrangements.

Peacekeeping is multilateral

The multilateral character of UN peacekeeping is taken as testimony to the lack of strategic interest behind peacekeeping, and consequently a political form that helps detoxify peacekeeping, ensuring it is free of imperialist contamination. The logic behind this view is that states seeking their own selfish interests would avoid the risk of diluting their gains by having to face the costs of coordinating allies and having to share the spoils. Michael W. Doyle and Nicholas Sambanis argue that the UN's 'mere presence guarantees that partial national interests are not in control', thereby making its 'quasi-colonial presence' not only 'tolerable but effective'.[14] Here, multilateralism is taken to check the pursuit of narrow national self-interest. James D. Fearon and David D. Laitin note that as the great powers abjure 'monopolized control of their imperial domains' today, so too the structures of these 'new forms of rule' are composed of a 'complex hodgepodge of foreign powers, international and nongovernmental organisations (NGOs), and domestic institutions ...'.[15]

To assume that the 'mere presence' of the United Nations is sufficient to annul imperial influence would be to assume that powerful countries cannot secure their interests through the United Nations. It would be generous to describe such a view as naïve, as we shall see in the next chapter and chapter six. But the notion that multilateralism is an intrinsically anti-imperial form of international politics is no less eccentric. As we shall presently see, the history of imperialism gives no prima facie reason to accept the proposition that multilateralism—at least in its peacekeeping guise—is the antithesis of imperialism.

Absence of ideologies of racial supremacy

It is argued that there is no ideology of racial supremacy driving or legitimating UN peacekeeping. Doyle and Sambanis celebrate the fact that UN peacekeeping operations 'mobilize a diverse and complementary set of national talents and serve by their multinational character to announce that cross-ethnic and cross-ideological cooperation can work.'[16] While Ottoway and Lacina acknowledge the gulf on many peacekeeping missions between a class of highly paid 'internationals' and the impoverished local people, they maintain that however stark this inequality, it is nonetheless radically different from the racial caste systems seen in the old European colonies.[17]

Peacekeeping ineffectiveness

Ottoway and Lacina add a final element when they maintain that peacekeeping operations have significantly failed to reshape the societies into which they are inserted. According to them, peacekeepers lack the vigour shown by imperialists in destroying resistance to their rule or overriding indigenous power structures.[18] Citing the example of

Bosnia-Herzegovina—a country subjected to the most prolonged experiments in 'transitional administration'—they claim that continued intercommunal hostility and the electoral success of nationalist wartime parties demonstrates just how limited the power of the international community to effect real change is.[19] As regards the limits of peacekeepers' power, others have cited the examples of Sudanese resistance to a UN peacekeeping force in its western province of Darfur, Congolese efforts to elbow Monuc out of the country and the attempts by Chad to secure compensation for hosting peacekeepers across the border from Sudan.[20] This point is affirmed by Doyle and Sambanis when they argue that the 'very inefficiencies' of the UN 'make fears of empire-mongering seem far-fetched'.[21]

Imperialism redux

It is worth pausing at this point briefly to draw out the implications of the way in which the imperial analogy is used in the study of peacekeeping. The first thing to note about these claims is that the imperialism against which peacekeeping is compared is the past forms of historical colonialism—the old European empires. The tacit assumption here is that imperialism is a thing of the past. No theories of empire or imperialism are cited or invoked. At the same time, while imperialism is safely consigned to history, there is no effort to engage with the complex historiography of empire to yield insights or points of comparison.

Having proven to their own satisfaction that UN peacekeeping is not an exact replica of nineteenth century imperialism, it becomes possible to make demands for rationalising and enhancing peacekeeping with a clear conscience. Ironically enough, having expended the effort of denying the imperial character of peacekeeping many of the proscriptions offered by the peacekeeping boosters are explicitly to make peacekeeping more like imperialism. Writing in 2001, Michael Doyle outlines the features of imperial rule from which peacekeeping and international intervention should learn:

Over the longer run, indigenous forces such as the political zamindars and the King's Own African Rifles and other locally recruited military battalions (not metropolitan troops) were the forces that made imperial rule effective, that preserved a balance of local power in favour of metropolitan influence—and that kept it cheap ...[22]

Doyle is not alone. James Mayall laments the lack of a UN cadre to match the old colonial administrators and their intimate knowledge of local politics and customs. He further claims that 'if the UN cannot reasonably be expected to act like an empire, it must find itself handicapped whenever it becomes deeply embroiled in attempts to preside over the transformation or reconstruction of a political system.'[23]

The United Nations seems to have learned some of its imperial history. As we shall see in the next chapter, by 2001 the reliance on relatively cheap Third World armies was already established as common practice in UN peacekeeping operations, including the descendants of the King's African Rifles so admired by Doyle. Not only does UN peacekeeping deploy 'locally recruited military battalions' therefore, it also deploys these battalions from one region of the developing world to another—much like the metropolitan states used colonial armies as imperial 'fire brigades' to suppress conflict across their far-flung imperial territories. If the 'internationals' on UN missions today cannot compare to the colonial administrators of the last two centuries, at the very least the United Nations can claim to have developed a cadre of envoys and proconsuls—Lakhdar Brahimi, Kofi Annan, Sérgio Vieira de Mello to name but a few of the better known—whose diversity of global experience would be the envy of many an imperial viceroy of yesteryear.

Roland Paris blames a culture of Western post-colonial guilt and political correctness as responsible for the shock therapy-style democratisation of the early post-Cold War peacekeeping operations, which he criticises for their failure to stay the course and mount long-term institution building. Paris prefers instead that democracy be de-prioritised and deferred to a future period after a process of externally directed state-building has been completed.[24] This is what Paris calls the 'IBL' strategy—'institutionalisation before liberalisation'. The boosters also urge greater self-confidence and vigour: Kimberly Marten decries 'squeamishness' that would stop us from thinking through the similarities between peacekeeping and imperialism. She asks us to 'learn' from the 'imperial past': 'the imperial era makes clear that when properly directed, disciplined soldiers can do a good job of providing public order.'[25] Simon Chesterman attacks the political correctness over colonial sensibilities that get in the way of carrying out efficient post-conflict reconstruction.[26] Thus we see, as Paris intimated, the way in which the imperial analogy is used directly to legitimate the practice of peacekeeping.

Empires old and new

It is ironic that in the process of defending peacekeeping from charges of imperialism these liberal scholars should end up sounding more like vulgar Leninists in their doctrinaire insistence that there is only one type of imperialism and that anything that does not exactly correspond to their model is not imperialism.[27] Perhaps this crudity serves a purpose in so far as the lack of substance to the discussion makes the imperialist spectre the easier to dispel—for all this comparison really amounts to is saying that imperialism is 'nasty' while peacekeeping is 'nice'. By offering a negative defence of peacekeeping—it is legitimate by virtue of what it is not, namely old-fashioned imperialism—its benefits and successes can be safely assumed to outweigh its costs. But how accurate is this historical image of imperialism against which peacekeeping is so favourably compared? As we shall now see, all these supposedly anti-imperial facets of peacekeeping today are easily visible in the historical record of European imperial practice.

Imperial security

That there were narrowly 'selfish' strategic interests behind imperial ventures does not help distinguish imperialism from peacekeeping. Many of the overarching purposes of peacekeeping—buttressing regional and global stability, preventing the overspill or spread of conflict, reconstituting the credibility of state authorities ('aid to the civil power', as imperial counter-insurgency was termed)—often featured prominently among the purposes of various imperial ventures as well. As much as there were sustained campaigns of imperial conquest, imperial expansion also occurred in an ad hoc, fragmented and decentralised fashion through the decisions of local imperial authorities, remote from metropolitan power centres, with various local aims of consolidating borders, punishing indigenous resistance and securing lines of communication.

Managing Empire

We have seen in the previous chapter the various ways in which consent has been eviscerated in peacekeeping operations, thus begging the question of its authenticity. That Paris himself places 'peacebuilding post-conquest' and 'peacebuilding post-settlement' as poles on a spectrum, with the 1999 NATO bombing of Yugoslavia lying in the murky grey zone between the two extremes, indicates that the similarities between the two types of peacebuilding are difficult to ignore. Nor can the flagging up of formal state consent be removed from the context of a post-Cold War world in which developing countries' freedom of action is more constrained—not to speak of that of war-torn states.

Even in those two instances where US military power was deployed without UN authorisation—Kosovo 1999 and Iraq 2003—the post-hoc imprimatur of UN legitimacy has been crucial to stabilisation efforts in those countries. The United Nations ruled Kosovo for nearly a decade while it was occupied by NATO forces and home to a new US military encampment, while the Security Council retroactively recognised the US invasion of Iraq when it awarded the US occupation the status of the 'Multi-National Force in Iraq'—as cosmopolitan in its make-up as any UN peacekeeping mission. Nor should the importance of the United Nations to political reconstruction in Iraq be underestimated. According to Mats Berdal, the United Nations proved adept at engaging the informal power structures of post-Saddam Iraq in a way that eluded the US occupation authorities to the extent that by spring 2004 UN legate Lakhdar Brahimi had 'largely eclipsed [US proconsul] Paul Bremer in the management of US strategy ... for the restoration of Iraqi sovereignty'.[28]

Paris's desire to differentiate different types of peacebuilding is aimed at rescuing consensual peacebuilding from imperial peacebuilding. The comparison works in favour of UN peacebuilding not only by implicitly privileging it over the militarism of US interventions but also by contrast to their widely perceived flaws and failures. But if post-conquest peacebuilding cannot be so readily disentangled from post-settlement peacebuilding, it is also possible to argue that the latter embodies a more successful consummation of imperial power.

The factors that Paris identifies as making post-conquest peacebuilding more fragile than post-settlement peacebuilding—the illegitimacy of occupation forces and imposed regime change—echo what critics of empire have identified as responsible for the hollow character of US military intervention in a unipolar age. The overt use of military force in a world order organised around independent nation states experiences political contradictions and rapidly diminishing returns that undermine the efficacy and legitimacy of imperial power. In the words of Leo Panitch and Samuel Gindin, 'an American imperialism that is so blatantly imperialistic risks losing the very appearance of not being imperialistic—[the] appearance which historically made it plausible and attractive.'[29] From this point of view, UN peacebuilding strategies can be seen as more imperial precisely for being more successful.

The political economy of imperial peace

As far as economic exploitation goes, the notion that the presence of raw materials is necessary to 'prove' imperialism is exceptionally peculiar.[30] Taking the absence of deposits of precious raw materials as evidence for the absence of imperialism, as Gilligan and Stedman urge, is like a mirror image of the crudest war-for-oil theories—and no more convincing when reflected in reverse. The same is true of the notion that profitable extractive activities drove all imperial expansion in the past, with the implication being that the absence of obvious sources of profit means that peacebuilding cannot be imperialistic. Given the enormous extent of the European colonial empires around the world—including virtually the entire continent of Africa—they evidently comprised a plethora of territory that had zero economic value. Sometimes territory was seized with a speculative eye to future profits that required pre-empting and excluding potential rivals from a particular region. At the same time, gauging empire simply by measuring the quantity and direction of resource flows does not of itself generate any clear view of imperialism as a structural phenomenon. One of the long-standing controversies over empire was the role played by the export of capital to the colonies—that is, a flow of resources from core to periphery in order to subsequently realise and repatriate profits. To claim, as the defenders of peacebuilding do, that the economics of empire was purely about plunder would be to ignore the fact that when empires provide economic benefits to the core, they are not necessarily direct and obvious.[31]

Some of this lack of clarity stems from the fact that the debate on the political economy of peacebuilding and the extent to which it resembles that of empire confuses matters by mixing different levels of analysis. Paris challenges the critics of liberal peace by saying that 'those who claim that post-settlement peacebuilding serves the interests of "transnational capitalism" have yet to demonstrate that either the expectation or the desire for economic gain has driven the decision to launch any such operations.'[32] But it is not clear why an explanatory model rooted in political economy would need to demonstrate that the launch of interventions was immediately driven by the motivation for economic gain. There is no prima facie reason why explanations pointing to the effect of underlying structures could not be compatible with a wide range of proximate motives and causes of particular expeditions. Certainly this was the pattern of European colonialism centred on 'Christianity and commerce' that Paris himself accepts was driven by economic motives. What is not in doubt is that post-conflict societies subject to coercive reconstruction are being configured along lines that complement the economic agendas of the leading powers of the day.[33]

Imperial multilateralism

To accept that the multilateral character of peacekeeping distinguishes it from old-fashioned imperialism would be to ignore prominent examples of multilateral imperialism. One author cites the suppression of the so-called 'Boxer Uprising' in China by the Eight-Nation Alliance at the turn of the twentieth century as an example of 'multilateral counter-insurgency' of continuing relevance for the launching of multinational military expeditions today.[34] The suppression of the Boxer Uprising is perhaps the most well-known, but there are other examples of 'multinational imperialism' directed at the Ottoman empire in particular, which was dismembered in a piecemeal and collaborative fashion across many decades in order to contain explosive clashes of interest between the great powers looking to profit from Turkish decline.[35] Albania was established as an international protectorate in 1913 in order to help contain action by the Balkan states independent of any great power patrons.[36] Erwin Schmidl cites the establishment of the modern Albanian state after the Balkan Wars of 1912–13, and the multinational expedition that was scheduled to deploy there, as a model for enforcing order across the Balkans today.[37]

Nor were imperial interventions purely militaristic. International sanitary police forces were variously deployed in Alexandria, Constantinople and Tangier. International administrations in Tangier and Shanghai comprised a multinational gendarmerie, complete with white police officers and reserve military units to enforce their rule. Not unlike modern peacekeeping operations, these expeditions saw foreign-led administrative and judicial functions superimposed over local power structures.[38] Navigation police operated in Danzig and Memel, as well as international administrations in Cracow and Crete in the inter-war period—functions that were directly tied up with the League of Nations' field missions in those regions.[39]

The effort to describe the spectrum of international subordination and hierarchy today should not come at the expense of overstating the organisational coherence or political and legal integrity of the empires of the past. European colonialism was rarely monolithic: the spectrum of imperial suzerainty comprised a variety of political forms ranging from sovereign basing rights and trading concessions extracted by imperial power through fortresses, protectorates, international mandates, client states, dependent regimes, unequal alliances, treaties of military assistance, metropolitan control over key security functions in subordinated societies and systems of indirect rule, right through to direct rule, annexation and colonisation by European settlers. It is only from the perspective of the present with the benefit of having gone through a century of anti-colonial revolt that we see these 'imperial rainbow' patterns of rule of the past in the uniform colours of imperialism plain and simple. Lucidity about past imperialism should not allow us to mystify the reality of contemporary imperialism by overstating the contrast between the European empires and the 'post-modern imperialism' of the present.

In any case it is not clear that today's forms of 'post-modern imperialism' in post-conflict societies are any the better for being less centralised. Simon Chesterman notes that as the peoples of East Timor and Kosovo were ruled by representatives of the Secretary-General rather than under the formal trusteeship arrangements articulated in the UN Charter, the Timorese and Kosovars had even fewer structures of accountability with which to check their UN masters than those available to the peoples who lived in the League mandates, which themselves were little more than imperial annexations given legal sanction.[40] According to Paris, by virtue of being 'decentralized and lacking a single corporate identity' the structures of 'international governance' that we see in peacekeeping operations lack:

clear lines of accountability, meaning that even if we ... disapproved of the actions of the network of international agencies engaged in peacebuilding, there is no single mechanism through which we could demand a change of peacebuilding policy. Nor is there a single actor whom we could collectively hold responsible for the outcome of particular operations.[41]

When particular political outcomes can be clearly attributed to particular agents not only is there a formal basis for political accountability and critique, but social order is perceived as being the result of political decisions and the power vested by populations in specific individuals and groups. This offers at least a formal possibility of challenge and repudiation—the most basic elements of political contestation. This is what is denied in the networked structures of international peacebuilding.

Multicultural hierarchy for racial hierarchy

If outright racism has been expunged from the official language of international intervention, this should not let us underestimate the asymmetry between 'internationals' and 'locals' in these missions—a relationship that Michael Ignatieff characterises as 'inherently colonial'.[42] Ignatieff gives the example of Kabul as having 'the social attractions of a colonial outpost joined to the feverish excitement of a boom town'—one of the 'few places where a bright spark just out of college can end up in a job with a servant and a driver'.[43] Nor does the absence of doctrines of racial supremacy entail the absence of the arrogance and contempt that accompanied racism. Simon Chesterman—himself a defender of UN transitional administration—observes that the infantilising language routinely used by international policymakers to describe people in the Balkans would be seen as racist if applied to people of colour in East Timor.[44]

In her study of peacekeeping witnessed from below, UN officials interviewed by Beatrice Pouligny told her how they perceived the societies hosting them to be riven by anomie, their peoples 'debased with destitution', 'predisposed to submission', 'incapable of planning and without leaders'.[45] Evidently racism is not a necessary component of political subordination: economic inequality, technological backwardness, cultural difference and Western technical expertise all suffice to justify international hierarchies of power and privilege vis-à-vis the developing world. However virulent ideas of racial supremacy have been, no less important for imperialism, as we shall see, was the civilising mission that justified imperial tutelage and oversight as well as its inevitable corollary of contempt. In any case, the civilising mission preceded racial theories, and evidently it has outlived them.[46]

Incoherent empire?

To defend peacekeeping by saying it is more 'inefficient' or ramshackle than empire is a peculiar way to defend the reputation of an enterprise. If so inefficient, why bother with it at all? Even more peculiar to cite Bosnia-Herzegovina as proof of peacebuilders' powerlessness, given the vigour and ruthlessness with which international viceroys have sought to dismantle local power structures in that country and have overridden expressions of popular will, including that of democratically elected representatives.[47] The patterns of UN rule in Kosovo and East Timor were little different.[48] Michael Ignatieff, himself a firm advocate of imperialism as a solution to contemporary problems of world order, describes Bernard Kouchner's political persona when he ruled Kosovo as UN proconsul from 1999 to 2001:

He clearly loves the imperial governor side of the job: he bans newspapers …; he bars a politician from nearby Albania from crossing the border; and in perhaps his boldest stroke, he decides the [German] mark should become the official currency of the province. He affects not to remember whether he consulted UN headquarters on the currency decision, just so it will be clear that he and not New York, calls the shots.[49]

To claim that viceroys such as Choi Young-Jin, Bernard Kouchner and Sérgio Vieira de Mello were relatively 'powerless' cannot but appear perverse.[50] To condemn local suspicion of international peacebuilding initiatives speaks to an attitude of baffled incredulity that Southern peoples in post-war countries do not gratefully accept the benevolent paternalism directed at them. It does not seem inappropriate to describe this insouciant attitude as imperialistic.

Despite the vast asymmetry of power between 'internationals' and 'locals' in peacekeeping missions, strategists and theorists of peacebuilding and state-building still identify the central problem in these cases as one of granting too much power to the target states. Or more precisely, in the process of building functioning structures of independent government, outside agencies systematically undermine the basis of their own power and ability to shape the societies in question by giving local elites the political depth and legal space from which to push back against their putative allies, thereby consistently thwarting the goals of international policy.[51] The solution to this contradiction is to regulate, restrain and embed the institutions of political autonomy and legal independence in disciplinary regimes that constrain the reality of independence as much as possible. In the words of Robert Keohane, 'We ... have to reconceptualise the state as a political unit that can maintain internal order while being able to engage in international cooperation [but] without claiming exclusive rights [...] traditionally associated with sovereignty.'[52] Some of the theorists and planners advocating this process are cynical enough to openly counsel that the trappings of independence should be purposely exaggerated in these missions so as to placate the populace of the countries concerned, lest they refuse to accept the reality of international rule.[53]

It is for this reason that the disabling of self-determination is more far-reaching under UN peacekeeping and peacebuilding. The world organisation has the veneer of global legitimacy while at the same time not offering a single metropolitan capital or centre of power that could offer a target of opposition. Compared to previous forms of imperial multilateralism, it cannot but be a more insidious exercise of imperial power. As we have seen, peacebuilding and peacekeeping have been described as systems of 'neotrusteeship', thereby establishing a link between the present and the historical UN system of Trust territories, and before it the League of Nations' mandates system. But while international tutelage in today's peacekeeping is real enough, the terminology of 'trusteeship' also confuses matters in that it underplays the role of the United Nations in this framework.

For all the cynicism and hypocrisy that these earlier forms of imperial multilateralism embodied, by clearly demarcating dependence from independence the League mandates system and UN trusteeship held aloft national emancipation as a desirable and feasible goal for its wards. By contrast the practice of UN peacebuilding denies that the subordination of national decision-making to international policy is exclusive of national independence. Peacekeeping is predicated on the idea that independence is compatible with hosting large foreign military and security forces for protracted periods. Suppressing national independence through the explicit revocation of independence pays homage to the value of autonomy. Making independence meaningless achieves a more thorough subversion of self-determination than guns and bullets ever could. The political results of this scenario are described by Jean-Marie Guéhenno, who served as head of peacekeeping at the United Nations from 2000 to 2008:

There [is] not a statue ... to pull down from its pedestal, only the amorphous mass of a diffuse and imperceptible power. The new order makes policemen of us all, and there is no longer a police chief against whom we may direct our revolt. We are deprived not of liberty, but of the idea of liberty.[54]

The highest form of liberal imperialism

As we have seen then, there is a good deal of similarity between peace-keeping and imperialism. The way in which the imperial analogy is used in the study of peacekeeping betrays a historical sleight of hand whereby defenders of peacekeeping compare it to historical forms of imperialism, thereby implying that imperialism is historically redundant and peacekeeping cannot therefore be imperial. Yet all those features of peacekeeping that are cited as contributing to its anti-imperial character can be discerned in the historical record of imperialism. The fact that it is so easy to refute those specific points that are used to flatter peacekeeping by comparison to imperialism shows that the imperial analogy used in peacekeeping studies is simply not serious. How should we understand the proper place of peacebuilding in light of imperial history and the civilising mission of the past? In this section, I argue that peacekeeping represents the zenith of liberal imperialism.

On the face of it, doctrines of liberalism and doctrines of empire appear antithetical. Founded on assumptions of universal rights, equal capabilities of reason, representative government and individual autonomy, the values of liberalism would seem to exclude principles such as the stratification of humanity into hierarchy, the denial of people's equal capacity for self-rule, and the corresponding establishment of political systems based on authoritarianism and paternalism. Historically, empire has been the solution to the gap between liberal ideals and a non-liberal reality—imperialism being the means for realising liberal ideals where they do not exist. At the same time, liberals have been among the staunchest opponents of empire. If John Locke and John Stuart Mill saw no contradiction between defending liberty and defending empire, Denis Diderot, Immanuel Kant, Thomas Paine and J.G. Herder all variously criticised colonialism and imperial expansion.[55] Yet the liberal critics of empire have not been without their own contradictions, and it is the perennial liberal internationalist dream of international organisation that has been one solution proposed for these contradictions.[56]

Take the example of John Atkinson Hobson. Arguably the most renowned liberal critic of imperialism, he attacked the European and

US imperialism of the late nineteenth century for the exploitative commerce that powered it, the militaristic rivalries that resulted from it, and the barbarism needed to subjugate indigenous peoples extending even to the extermination of whole groups. Hobson deflated the self-satisfaction of European imperial civilisation at the height of its power and glory, famously puncturing the spurious justifications given for imperial expansion with his barbed phrase 'philanthropy and 5 per cent'.[57] Refined in Vladimir Lenin's later and even more influential theory of imperialism, many of Hobson's arguments would become intellectual ammunition for a wide range of anti-imperialist struggles across the twentieth century; the theory was sometimes even referred to as the 'Hobson-Lenin thesis'. Yet despite this anti-imperialist legacy, Roland Paris claims that UN peacebuilding most closely approximates Hobson's vision for international politics in the developing world.[58] Given the importance that Paris accords to this fierce critic of empire, it is worth briefly reviewing Hobson's arguments for and against imperialism, the better to clarify the links between peacebuilding and empire.

For all his criticisms of empire, Hobson did not himself believe that the peoples of the colonial world—whom he called the 'lower races' and 'backward peoples'—were capable of self-government in conditions of modernity. Hobson thus argued against the retraction of empire—that the 'white Western nations will abandon a quest on which they have already gone so far is a view', Hobson argued, 'which does not deserve consideration'.[59] Foreshadowing contemporary debates about globalisation, Hobson based this judgement on observing that new means of transportation and communication technology fostered international inter-dependence and opened up the possibility of exploiting hitherto inaccessible and untapped economic resources.[60] Nor did Hobson argue (as Lenin later would) for anti-colonial revolution as a precursor to self-rule. Rather, Hobson argued for the sublimation of rival empires into what he called 'international government', or a 'sane' imperialism that would among other objectives guide dependent peoples to political maturity.[61]

Hobson did not understand this proposed 'international government' as a world-state but something closer to what we would today call an international organisation or international regime, as it would incorporate an institutionalised set of mutually binding agreements and embody a system of reciprocal norms covering all states.[62] This 'government' would not dissolve imperial rule but rather would provide institutionalised international oversight of imperial rule. Hobson envisaged numerous functions for this 'international government'. He hoped that it would arbitrate between the claims of rival imperial states in their grabs for territory, and that this regime would monitor their performance in order to ensure that imperial policy was prejudicial neither to the subject peoples nor the interests of other imperial states or humanity as a whole. The international regime would be entrusted with supervising the development of the 'lower races' as well as embedding an international economic order of free trade, helping to collectively manage the exploitation of the natural resources to be found in the lands occupied by 'backward peoples'. For Hobson then the efficient functioning of the international economy was intertwined with governing the political and social development of the 'lower races', and he saw this global regime as a step towards an eventual grand federation of nations.

On the make-up and functioning of this 'international government', Hobson insisted that it be a 'genuine international council' that was 'genuinely representative of civilization', in contradistinction to the 1878 Congress of Berlin at which the European imperial powers agreed to the rules that would govern their conquest of Africa.[63] Hobson set three tests by which the 'political and economic control of lower races' should be judged: first, that 'interference with the government of a lower race' could only be justified if it secured collective interests rather than merely 'the special interest of the interfering nation'. Second, that such interference be 'attended by an improvement and elevation of the character of the people ... brought under this control'. Hobson's third stipulation was that the prior two conditions would be determined by 'some organised representation of civilized humanity', rather than proceeding from the 'arbitrary will or judgement of the interfering nation'.[64] As part of this 'trust of civilization', Hobson argued that 'force' be kept 'in the background as a last resort', counselling instead that 'we should endeavour to assume the position of advisers' and 'to make it our first aim to ... promote the healthy operations of all internal forces for progress [within subject societies] that we might discover.'[65]

In arguing for a 'responsible' imperialism, Hobson softened the liberal discourse of imperialism, hitherto exemplified in J.S. Mill's derision for 'barbarians'. Hobson self-consciously placed 'lower races' and 'backward peoples' in his own inverted commas to indicate that such descriptions could not be taken for granted. Indeed, again unlike Mill, Hobson manifested profound respect for India and China as bearers of great and ancient civilisations that made them more worthy of self-rule than those he termed the 'low-typed unprogressive races'.[66] In place of Mill's dichotomy between barbarism and civilisation, Hobson preferred the vision of a spectrum of moral progress and education that linked backward peoples with the superior civilised nations: 'The analogy furnished by the education of a child is prima facie a sound one,' argued Hobson, 'not invalidated by the dangerous abuses to which it is exposed.'[67] Steeped in ideas of pedagogic paternalism, global utilitarianism and economic 'efficiency', Hobson believed force and compulsion were not only justified but obligatory on all these grounds—*if* carried out through internationalised means that compelled moral progress and advancement towards eventual self-rule. Moreover, these means had to ensure the development of untapped economic resources, both human and natural, in the interests of humanity at large rather than the interests of a single state. In the interim, as the subjugated peoples were incapable of politically articulating their views, their interests would be represented by the 'combined voices of the imperial states'.[68]

While Hobson's excoriation of imperialism inspired Marxists, his ideas of 'international government' inspired the liberal reform of empire, including the Fabians and Britain's Labour party. Hobson has been credited as the theoretical progenitor of the League of Nations' mandates system (the Covenant of the League uses Hobson's terms of 'trust' and 'civilization' verbatim) and the later Trust territories of the United Nations.[69] Despite the extent of his intellectual influence in the early twentieth century, Hobson himself was deeply hostile to one of the forms his own proscriptions took, namely the League of Nations. As early as 1915 at the height of the First World War, Hobson prophesied that the victorious powers would use such a post-war international organisation to monopolise the claims of 'civilization' to the exclusion of non-European states and substitute a 'pax Europoea' for a genuine international government.[70] Although Hobson expected the great powers to play a leading role in his vision of 'international government',[71] he was nonetheless disturbed by the prospect of what he called 'inter-imperialism'—collusion between the imperial powers collectively to manage their own narrow interests rather than to transcend them, the better to enhance their exploitation of subject peoples rather than realising an authentic 'imperial trust'. It was on this basis that Hobson attacked the mandates system of the League.

Given that Hobson never ultimately untangled or reconciled the contradictions in his ideas on imperialism, his objections to the League notwithstanding, it is 'difficult to see', as David Long argues, 'how Hobson's internationalized "sane" imperialism could avoid producing exactly his dreaded inter-imperialism, the collusion of the Western nations in the exploitation of the rest of the world'.[72]

In contrast to the flawed mandates system, Roland Paris asserts that the peacebuilding of today does approximate to Hobson's vision of an ethical imperialism in that peacebuilding missions meet the first two criteria set by Hobson for a 'responsible imperialism'. First, peacebuilding is undertaken to 'secure the safety and progress of the world', rather than the national interest of the 'interfering nation', and second that peacebuilding aims at the 'improvement' and 'elevation' of the character of peoples 'brought under control'.[73]

It is not hard to see why Paris asserts that peacebuilding today is the realisation of Hobson's vision for an internationalised empire purged of the sins of imperialism. UN peacekeeping operations enable the political expansion of Western liberalism without conquest, social transformation without economic predation, the spread of market society and stabilisation of commerce without the formal abrogation of monopolistic privileges for a single state, thus avoiding the militarisation of great power rivalries in the developing world. At the same time, this empire promotes ethical goals of good governance and social transformation for the benefit of humanity at large—all achieved (for the most part) without even the need for suspending the constitutional independence of the target states. Therefore, it is consistent with this tradition of social liberal thought on empire to see peacekeeping as the highest stage of liberal imperialism.

If we follow Paris in his neo-Hobsonian reasoning then this must mean that the core values of empire have been preserved even as the form of empire has been abolished. That is, we have a stratified international order manifested in the establishment of a paternalistic regime for governing the political and social development of diverse peoples. Yet this sublimation of empire has not managed to dissolve the contradictions of liberal imperialism. Paris seems much less concerned than Hobson by the prospect of a new inter-imperialism. When Paris measures peacebuilding by Hobson's standards, he notably drops consideration of Hobson's third criterion for responsible imperialism—the need for an 'organised representation of civilised humanity'—perhaps to avoid the awkward fact that, as Paris himself concedes elsewhere, UN missions today 'still reflect the interests of the world's most powerful countries'.[74]

But the problem of 'inter-imperialism' is only one of the contradictions of imperial peacebuilding, as we shall see in greater detail across the next few chapters. We have already seen in the discussion in this chapter and the previous one that spreading the liberal peace involves the degradation of all the progressive aspects of liberalism in the efforts to realise it. Self-determination, international equality and representative and accountable government are all undermined through peacekeeping and peacebuilding. If, as we have seen, Hobson was dissatisfied with the way in which 'responsible imperialism' manifested itself in his own lifetime, then it is all the more incumbent on us to understand the systemic pathologies that subvert liberal attempts to spread the benefits of liberalism today.

Critical peacekeeping studies: one step forward, two steps back

As the fate of Hobson's ideas illustrates, the dialectic between criticism of empire and empire itself is complex. Criticism of empire, however well-intentioned, has just as often motivated reforms that enable imperial rule to function more legitimately and effectively as it has undermined empire as a political institution. To put the point even more forcefully, the rationale for empire has been built as much on the self-conscious critique of empire as it has on doctrines of liberal expansionism. In particular, theories of indirect rule developed in the latter part of the nineteenth and early twentieth centuries were explicitly formulated on the grounds of criticising the liberal approach to empire.[75] This historical pattern, by which critique of imperialism lays the ground for a restructuring of imperial rule, is visible in the most recent record of debates on peacebuilding and liberal intervention more broadly understood.

The debate on these topics is more febrile than ever, as an insular and staid body of scholarship was reenergised by a wave of critical scholarship. In 2005 Oliver P. Richmond wrote that the liberal peace was held in such unquestioning regard that it had 'effectively become a Leviathan which all must assume and accept unquestioningly as a counter to the Hobbesian state of nature'.[76] Only two years later Neil Cooper wrote that the 'liberal peace is in crisis', and four years after that Paris felt that this leviathan was sufficiently threatened to motivate his spirited defence of the project in an article entitled 'Saving liberal peacebuilding'.

The wave of critical peacekeeping scholarship can be usefully dated to a special issue of the journal *International Peacekeeping* published in 2004, when the co-editors of the special issue launched a call 'to think peace operations anew', explicitly echoing the meta-theoretical debates that had occurred some years previously regarding a 'next stage' in International Relations theorising. In making their call for a 'next stage' in the study of peacekeeping, Alex J. Bellamy and Paul D. Williams claimed that extant peacekeeping scholarship lamely accepted the international order as a given and thus failed to 'challenge or seriously reflect upon the global structures that contribute to human suffering'.[77]

This group of scholars was by no means the first to critically examine peacekeeping or to subject it to deeper theoretical reflection. Yet prior to this, such work had only emerged sporadically and critical insights remained dispersed.[78] Since then, the wave of self-consciously critical scholarship has grown into a flood directed against the 'liberal peace'. This vision of post-conflict order has been criticised for its militaristic underpinnings, for riding roughshod over the wishes of peoples in post-conflict societies and for the high-handed and dogmatic Western insistence on spreading a uniform set of economic policies and political institutions around the world.

This debate is far more wide-ranging than the reality of peacekeeping missions in the field, and this mismatch is partly, I suggest, a result of the fact that these critical debates reproduce certain assumptions about the liberal peace that intellectually recreate it rather than moving beyond it. Hence my purpose in the concluding sections of this chapter is not to synthesise the debate on liberal peace in its entirety but rather to issue a warning about the lack of reflexivity in the criticisms that are offered of the liberal peace.

For all that this new wave of scholarship—what we can call 'critical peacekeeping studies'—has invigorated debate in the field, the failure to shift from criticism of the liberal peace to a consistent critique of empire has entailed reproducing the pattern of earlier historical debates that begin from the vantage point of criticism and yet ineluctably mutate into rationales for empire. It is the lack of reflexivity underpinning these criticisms that results in the complementarity between the changing needs of power on the one hand, and the arguments provided by the critics of liberal peace on the other.

The way in which criticism mutates into an argument for expanding and rationalising peacebuilding is perhaps best exemplified by Sandra Whitworth, who we recall from the introduction encouraged us to excavate the bedrock assumptions of peacekeeping, including questioning whether it was a good thing in and of itself. Whitworth's criticism focused on the atrocities committed by elite Canadian units during the Unosom operations in Somalia.[79] Whitworth attributed the cases of torture and random murders by Canadian peacekeepers to the ideology of militarised and racialised masculinity on which armies are founded and perpetuated, arguing that this ideology was particularly virulent in the elite paratrooper units of the Canadian armed forces.[80] In response, Whitworth offered some 'wildly impractical but responsible' suggestions (apparently) without irony as the solution to peacekeeping militarism:

When the people of countries in conflict call for contributions ... [send] not platoons of warriors but contingents of doctors, feminists, linguists, and engineers; regiments of construction workers and carpenters; armies of mid-wives, cultural critics, anthropologists, and social workers; battalions of artists, musicians, poets, writers and social critics.[81]

The characteristic pattern of such criticism is exhibited here: the solution to the problem identified is to drastically expand the scale and scope of outside intervention into war-torn states. Whitworth's 'responsible' solutions sound like a much more systematic imperialist effort than the efforts of UN peacekeepers—not to mention the militarisation of civil activities that is implicitly advocated in her extension of martial vocabulary to a swathe of professional and social roles.

Whitworth's solutions are neither as impractical or remote a possibility as she implies—the US armed forces at least, if not the United Nations yet, seem to have taken her advice to heart with their deployment of squads of social scientists, including anthropologists, as part of the 'Human Terrain System' in Afghanistan.[82] Reconstruction projects, including civil engineering, medicine and logistics projects are an integral part of contemporary peacekeeping operations and, it should be noted, counter-insurgency theorising. At least one influential critic of UN peacebuilding, Séverine Autesserre, has already cited the 'Human Terrain' war effort as a model for re-energising the UN's 'bottom-up' conflict resolution techniques.[83] Whitworth embraces the language of international responsibilities as unproblematic in offering her suggestions, as well as being ambiguous about the role played by consent in episodes of intervention. But as we have seen, with the institutionalisation of non-representative models of law and security, what 'people of countries in conflict' might call for has been distorted. Here we have the very same theorist who demanded that we upturn the technocratic lore of peacekeeping, demanding in the same breath that peacekeeping be radically expanded in order to function more effectively and penetrate more deeply into its target states.

The same pattern, whereby the critique of militarism is seen to justify the redoubling and expansion of post-war reconstruction, is visible in other critical approaches to peacekeeping. Bellamy and Williams, who spearheaded the 'critical agenda' in the study of peacekeeping, argued that this agenda must be sensitive to the dangers of 'becoming a form of neo-imperialism' and should include advocacy 'for more money to be spent on medicines and alleviating malnutrition than on marines and mercenaries', in order to 'help reduce the number of occasions that peacekeepers are required to engage in political fire-fighting or global riot control'.[84] Principles of humanitarian relief and developmentalism as a means of making peacekeeping more effective are of course a routine part of peacebuilding policy. But the conceptual scaling-up involved in shifting the focus of analysis away from purely military questions has enabled a wider perspective on the role of peacekeeping in the international order.

One important insight from this strain of scholarship—and one that remains relatively underexplored in peacekeeping scholarship as a whole—is how peacekeeping is only one of multiple outside influences that might shape states on the periphery of the states system. The implication is that to be understood properly, peacekeeping interventions should be contextualised in the range of economic and political pressures emanating from other UN agencies, not least the international financial institutions. As Bellamy and Williams put it, the conventional treatment of military intervention including peacekeeping 'as a discrete act with a clear beginning and end' ignores 'wider relations of [international] interference in domestic societies'.[85]

This insight formed the basis of Williams' analysis of how the policies imposed by the international financial institutions helped precipitate the wars in Rwanda (1990–94) and Sierra Leone (1991–2002), both of which subsequently became the targets of controversial peacekeeping operations and French and British military interventions, respectively.[86] Here, the policing character of international peacekeeping was evident: force was used to contain the disruptive effects of the systemic functioning of international order.

But the use of critical theory in this instance cuts both ways. Bellamy and Williams suggest that if we are to properly grasp these 'wider relations of interference' we need a richer 'ontology' to comprehend more fully the nature of international order. Instead of seeing states as isolated entities clearly demarcated from each other, 'Critical theories ... recognise that interveners and recipients are bound together beyond the ostensible limits of the particular intervention in question.'[87] It is worth noting that the abstruse invocation of 'ontology', while characteristic of the 'critical turn' in International Relations theory, has a very specific effect in peacekeeping studies—namely, to normalise intervention. As military intervention is seen as only one aspect of these 'wider relations of interference', Bellamy and Williams's intent seems to be to make the use of armed force appear less exceptional or in need of justification. In this case the denser 'ontology' provides firmer ground for peacekeepers' boots: both authors jointly endorse 'strengthening the military might of the UN'.[88]

In linking their project to the critical theory strand of International Relations, Bellamy and Williams sought to fold peacekeeping operations into the wider project of cosmopolitan reconstruction of international order that would push beyond the restrictive confines of national political systems: 'as long as peace operations continue to be seen as acts of altruism rather than part of our responsibilities to fellow human beings, and as "rights" rather than "duties", real progress will be difficult.'[89] The language of ethical duties provides wider justification for military operations than the more contestable ground of political rights clashing between states and individuals.

Not all theorists of peacekeeping have deployed political economy to the purpose of demanding more and better-armed cosmopolitan legions. Some analysts, centred around the Peace and Conflict Studies department at the University of Bradford, have gone furthest in analysing the power of the international financial institutions and economic policy in post-conflict settings. Specifically, how these agencies restrict the menu of economic options available to post-conflict governments, and how they promote norms associated with these policies—hostility to public services, welfare, state spending and endorsement of mass petty entrepreneurialism as the best route to recovery. Doubtless such policies are of dubious validity for war-torn countries in fragile stages of recovery. Yet the focus on the content of economic policies can come at the expense of keeping in sight the strictly political questions of control and authority: 'our key point', argue several of these critics,

is that the overall framing of peace by external agencies reinforces neoliberal prescriptions, particularly in the realm of political economy, that neither take sufficient account of local needs and agency, nor reflect on the role of global capitalism and structural adjustment policies as drivers of conflict.[90]

Following these criticisms, it is not clear whether alternative policies would be preferable if they were driven by a different but no less imperious set of external agencies—such as the gelded UN Development Programme. Nor is it clear how distant such proposals are from those state-building prescriptions that aim to build market societies over the longer run, while consolidating structures of public power in the interim. A critique of the content of economic policy cannot substitute for a critique of imperial influence as such, regardless of the relative merits of one economic policy over another. At times, this critique of economic orthodoxy in post-war reconstruction hovers on a renunciation of the very goals of economic growth, modernisation and technological advance—a view that can all too easily rationalise the failures of these agencies to promote economic development.[91]

Hybrid peace: the post-modern politics of indirect rule

This broadly based scepticism over the liberal peace has led to the multiplication of alternative categories and models for post-war reconstruction—'eirenic peace', 'hybrid peace', 'post-liberal peace' and even 'republican peace', all of which for the most part remain on the academic drawing board, with often fuzzy distinctions between them. Nonetheless, most academic energy in this regard has been absorbed in questions of hybrid peace. The appeal of this category-cum-model is that it captures normative scepticism towards the liberal peace while also offering a template of empirical investigation to explore the admixture of institutions that emerge in post-conflict countries as a result of the confluence of international intervention and autochthonous social forces.

It is certainly true that post-conflict societies will look very different from the blueprints drawn up in metropolitan capitals and by external agencies involved in post-conflict recovery. In its claim to examine actual empirical processes of post-war recovery, the hybrid peace expresses something of the old radical tradition of conflict transformation that drew its energy from counter-posing the initiative of people in post-war situations—'bottom-up conflict transformation'—to the 'high politics' of post-war diplomacy, centred on peace treaties drawn up by haughty elites in remote capitals. With empirical investigation as its cutting edge, investigations of the 'hybrid peace' are a search for alternatives that are to be found in ordinary people's actual attempts to build peace and establish systems of post-war justice, infusing the ideas of radical conflict transformation with the language of post-colonialism.

There are a number of problems with ideas of hybrid peace, but here I will mention only a few germane to our discussion. In its attempt to overcome a binary opposition of 'international' and 'local', the category 'hybridity' strives to capture the fluid character of social institutions in conditions of globalisation.[92] This conceptual fuzziness, focused on the reciprocal influence of multiple societies upon each other, runs the risk of smudging out specifically political dynamics, including how power is exercised. The valourisation of alternative forms of peacebuilding in ideas of hybrid peace overlooks the extent to which international agencies have sought to buttress their initiatives through supporting or recreating nominally indigenous practices.

'Traditional' dispute resolution processes have been extensively supported by Western governments and the non-governmental organisations that they fund in Timor-Leste, Kenya, Burundi and Rwanda.[93] In practice, what is presented as a venerable tradition of customary dispute resolution will be reconstituted through external political support and hard cash. Perhaps the most notorious (and ominous) example of this is use of the Gacaca community courts in post-conflict Rwanda. In this instance, a 'traditional' justice system reserved for resolving land and grazing rights was used instead as an administrative procedure by a highly centralised, militarised and efficient authoritarian regime in its processing of many thousands of prisoners in post-war Rwanda.[94] As we saw above, anthropological science has been deployed as part of the US war effort in Afghanistan in order to achieve the same precision in social restructuring of 'tribal' society as that achieved in the much-vaunted precision technology of US air power. Analogous efforts were made to support US war-fighting in Iraq through cooperating with and co-opting Iraqi tribal and kinship structures. The efforts of the US army in this regard arguably make it the most advanced and sophisticated practitioner of hybrid peace, blending liberal war aims outwardly through reconstituting 'traditional' societies inwardly.[95]

For all the libratory impulse behind the urge to extend participation in peacebuilding beyond the corridors of power, the hybrid peace risks simply preserving the most conservative and patriarchal institutions and practices of developing societies. Here, criticism of liberal peace segues into what Chandler describes as a 'speculative and passive search for different, non-liberal, forms of knowledge'; a critique 'not essentially of power or of intervention but of the limited knowledge of liberal intervenors'.[96]

During the Cold War, opposition to imperial nation-building projects often complemented opposition to US support for authoritarian regimes—regimes that were often built on the most conservative and backward elements of the societies in question. Supporting anti-imperial visions of peace usually entailed support for movements that were believed to represent social progress, with the capacity to modernise and transform their societies through anti-imperial revolutions, with the implication that the process of conflict itself manifested an orientation towards progressive political and social change. But without identifying any agency capable of progressive transformation in these societies, today such anti-hegemonic aspirations can only end up reifying the societies in question, with no means of distinguishing progressive change from the reproduction of stasis in the flux of societies subjected to globalisation.

In the melange of claims made in opposition to liberal peace—scepticism of liberalism, demands for more empirical investigation, and the backhanded affirmation of indigenous institutions—the vision of hybrid peace echoes the earlier discourse on indirect rule pioneered by the British in India and gradually disseminated to the other European empires. Indirect rule was specifically predicated on the affirmation of 'native' cultures, and involved the political devolution of power to indigenous authorities. As Mahmood Mamdani points out in relation to the 'native authorities' in the African empires of Britain, France, Belgium and Portugal: 'Indirect rule was mediated rule. It meant that colonial rule was never experienced by the vast majority of the colonized as ruled directly by others. Rather, the colonial experience for most "natives" was one of rule mediated through one's own.'[97]

As Mamdani stresses, this was a scaling up of imperial power. Whereas the liberal *mission civilisatrice* achieved the absorption of a thin stratum of native society into the institutions and mores of metro-politan rule, indirect rule allowed for the extension of imperial power over a much greater swathe of colonised societies, precisely as this power was magnified by being refracted through indigenous institutions and authorities.

It is worth bearing in mind the context in which the hybrid peace has been theoretically elevated at the expense of the liberal peace. With the wilting of the Western war effort in Afghanistan and in the context of fierce budgetary pressures on UN peacekeeping (see the next chapter), there is a search for ways of driving down the overhead costs of peace-building while preserving imperial influence. Cheaper and smaller scale political peacebuilding missions are already being mooted as the alter-native to vast, militarised nation-building efforts.[98] Co-optation of tra-ditional sources of power and authority can substitute for expensive legions of peace. Indirect rule emerged from the crisis of direct rule: as the nineteenth century civilising mission exhausted itself and encoun-tered resistance, imperial rule was restructured to incorporate local allies and flatter and preserve native 'customs' as bulwarks of imperial rule, rather than sweeping them away through modernisation.[99] In this context, hybrid peace could provide the policy script of a new post-modern politics of indirect rule, with postcolonial theory finding its political consummation in the bureaucratic search for 'inclusive', 'par-ticipatory' peace and 'local ownership'.

A post-liberal peace?

David Chandler has gone furthest in identifying the symmetry between the boosters and the critics of peacebuilding. Chandler notes that the critics of peacebuilding often end up echoing the shallow commitment to liberal and democratic goals held by policy makers. For all the com-mitments to liberal goals, Chandler argues that that in practice policy makers have shown themselves all too willing to displace sweeping visions of social and normative transformation onto a distant future in favour of securing order and stability in the interim. More pointedly, Chandler argues that both the critical and orthodox perspectives tac-itly share the same premise—that of international hierarchy. For both boosters and critics assume an international order bifurcated between liberal and illiberal zones, the latter being truculent, resistant to reform, change and progress.

Critics of the liberal peace identify the differences of the non-liberal world as explanations for the failures of liberal peace. According to Chandler, at this point critique slides into apologetics, the critics of peacebuilding providing the script for policy makers to blame the non-liberal world for 'the lack of policy success, and, through this, suggest that democracy or development are somehow not "appropriate" aspirations or that expectations need to be substantially lowered or changed to account for difference' in the non-liberal world.[100] For reasons such as these, Chandler accuses the critics of peacebuilding of offering 'succour and consolation rather than critique', affirming that the failure lies in the backwardness of the non-liberal world rather than the failed liberal attempts at transformation.[101] But if the critics of peacebuilding are indeed paving the path of retreat for peacebuilding strategists, Chandler's effort results in the construction of a shrine at which the peacebuilders can cast forlorn sidelong glances in the course of their evacuation. If the critics of peacebuilding offer 'succour and consolation rather than critique', so too does Chandler, reminding peacebuilders of the nobility of their original goals.

Chandler achieves this by arguing that liberal peace is not authentically liberal but what he calls 'post-liberal' or 'institutionalist', a policy complex that 'reduces law to an administrative code, politics to technocratic decision-making, democratic and civil rights to those of the supplicant rather than the citizen, replaces the citizenry with civil society, and the promise of capitalist modernity with ... poverty reduction.'[102]

Chandler is ambiguous as to when this 'post-liberal peace' emerges, dating the fall from liberal grace to both the 1990s and the 1970s— apparently oblivious to the efforts at imperial nation-building in South East Asia in the first half of the Cold War that shares so many similarities to the pathological failures of liberal peacebuilding today.[103] If ambiguous about the emergence of 'post-liberal peace', Chandler is clearly sensitive to the incompatibility between liberal values and the means and results of peacebuilding. But what Chandler offers as an immanent critique of liberal peace based on the tension between means and ends is more a Platonic line of criticism, inasmuch as Chandler contrasts liberal peace with an ahistoric and idealised vision of liberalism.

The view of liberalism propounded by Chandler posits it as a perfectly formed and coherent body of thought existing in a timeless dimension free from internal contradiction and safely remote from grubby compromises and the complexities of post-Cold War politics.

But this leaves the origins of empire as obscure and mysterious. In fact, empire is the expression of contradictions that are *internal* to liberal thought and practice—contradictions that reach back to the very foundation of liberalism itself and which, as we have seen, even the fiercest liberal critics of empire could accommodate themselves to. The depoliticising features of modern day peacebuilding that Chandler decries are emphatically the results of attempts to apply liberal doctrine to war-torn societies. To borrow the rhetoric of the Cold War, the post-war societies emerging through peacebuilding are the 'really existing' societies of liberal peace, and it is by this standard that liberal peace must be judged.

Chandler attempts to evade this problem by redefining the terms of the debate through the multiplication of categories: liberal peace is not properly liberal but 'post-liberal' and 'institutionalist'. But this avoids the authentic dilemma that peacebuilding has posed for liberals: how to reconcile liberal ends with illiberal means? In the words of Simon Chesterman, one of the more clear-eyed exponents of peacebuilding: 'Is it possible to establish the conditions for legitimate and sustainable national governance through a period of benevolent foreign autocracy?'[104] In practice, liberals have been willing to accept the means of autocracy for the ends of democracy. In rescuing liberal peace from contamination by peacebuilding, Chandler ends up recreating it. In doing so, he renounces the possibility of immanent critique in favour of idealist denunciation. However morally satisfying such shrine-building exercises may be, it is difficult to see how Chandler does not also offer 'succour and consolation rather than critique'.

Conclusion

We have seen that all those features that supposedly distinguish global peacekeeping from past practices of imperialism are easily visible in the historical record of empire. The historical record of empire also includes criticism and reform of empire. However cutting criticism of empire has been, without the willingness to accept that the peoples in question are politically self-sufficient—that is completely and immediately capable of governing their own affairs—imperial prerogatives inevitably reproduce themselves, even if disguised in new forms—whether that be indirect rule or hybrid peace. Despite the multilateral history of empire, UN peacekeeping has escaped relatively unscathed from the debate on American empire that has raged in recent years, as exemplified by the comparative lack of controversy over even the most coercive UN peacekeeping operations. This despite the fact that the United Nations has been at the cutting-edge of political reconstruction in war-torn societies, and in so doing the most effective at disseminating the idea and institutions of liberal peace.

Part of the reason that UN intervention in war occasions less attention than one might expect is that since the failure of UN missions in Africa and Balkans, it was NATO that became the instrument of choice for the West's military expeditions. UN peacekeeping did not disappear however; rather it began to rely on forces from the global South. That this rendered UN peacekeeping largely invisible to the Western gaze is unsurprising. While the recent wars in Afghanistan and Iraq have drained blood and treasure from the states of the Atlantic alliance, so too disenchantment, war-weariness and public criticism have grown in those countries. As for UN peacekeeping by contrast, questions of policy, strategy and political aims rarely if ever filter down from foreign chancelleries and council chambers of the United Nations, even though it is Western countries that continue to dominate these international institutions.

That peacekeepers from the global South have made UN peacekeeping invisible to the critics of empire is one of the many ironies of imperial peacebuilding. For a key pillar of imperial systems of rule across the centuries has been the development of colonial armies—recruited from the periphery to supplement and spare metropolitan forces. That imperialism spurred militarism and stimulated the growth of armed forces provided J.A. Hobson with another point of criticism. Just as imperialism tended to substitute financial speculation for productive investment, so Hobson reasoned by way of analogy that the development of standing colonial armies would sap the will to fight in the metropolitan states, alluding darkly to the prospect of racial revolt and insurgency resulting from the reliance on 'cheap foreign mercenary armies'.

Hobson was puzzled by the enthusiastic abandon with which the 'imperial nations' mobilized and armed these enormous standing armies with such little thought for the unintended consequences of their actions, and was particularly worried by the decline in white racial solidarity seen in the deployment of colonial armies of colour against 'another white race' in the Boer wars. He saw in this process 'one of the most perilous devices of parasitism, by which a metropolitan population entrusts the defence of its lives and possessions to the precarious fidelity of "conquered races", commanded by ambitious pro-consuls.'[105] If imperial multilateralism has replaced imperialism, and UN peacekeeping and intervention the 'small wars' of empire, to what extent have UN peacekeepers substituted for the old colonial armies? We examine this question across the next two chapters.

PART II

PEACEKEEPERS FROM THE GLOBAL SOUTH

4

CONSTRUCTING IMPERIAL SECURITY

FROM COLONIAL ARMIES TO CAPACITY-BUILDING

Introduction

If UN peacekeeping is the highest form of liberal imperialism, what is the role of Southern peacekeepers in this enterprise, and how do we account for it? UN peacekeeping has provided international policing for the war-torn societies at the periphery of the states system, and in so doing has globalised a rejuvenated post-Cold War vision of the old *mission civilisatrice*. Southern peacekeepers are integral to this role insofar as their participation also provides a broad range of benefits for imperial interests. In so doing, I argue that the legions of peace from the global South represent a new generation of askaris and sepoys—the colonial forces once recruited by European powers to support imperial power around the world.

Much like the askaris of old, UN peacekeepers enhance imperial power by reducing the costs of imperialism: they provide vast pools of additional manpower at less cost than that of maintaining metropolitan armies. Deploying Southern peacekeepers in remote conflict zones in support of protracted and complex efforts at nation-building carries fewer strategic risks and political costs for metropolitan powers. Indeed, peacekeepers from the global South are arguably more effective instruments than the askaris of old. As the armed forces of independent countries, the tasks of recruiting and supporting them are effectively dispensed with, as they are carried out by the post-colonial states themselves, while the task of mobilising them for specific operations is left to the machinery of the United Nations. Insofar as Southern blue helmets represent independent states, the legitimacy their participation gives to UN peacekeeping makes possible a range of military interventions throughout the world that would otherwise be seen as foreign occupations or outright neo-colonialism.

There are two tasks to be carried out in this chapter then: first, to explore the role of Southern peacekeepers in UN peacekeeping, and second, to examine how their presence helps to secure imperial interests. In the first part of the discussion we examine how Southern peacekeepers serve to extend the dimensions of global intervention—how they enhance the legitimacy of military intervention including Western military operations, how they expand the resources available for global military intervention, and how they reduce the risks and costs of such activities in financial, political and strategic terms. These arrangements are historically consistent with imperialism: what appears as a cosmopolitan or post-national military formation in the post-Cold War period becomes less historically novel once we consider the role of former colonies in imperial defence, and make visible the continuity in Southern military deployments across the colonial and post-colonial periods. Far from representing a cosmopolitan break with previous patterns of military deployment, we shall see that Southern peacekeeping exhibits a strong evolutionary continuity with the imperial past. Indeed, the notion that a central site of imperial power could despatch many thousands of troops and gendarmes far from their homeland in one part of the developing world to another should not come as a surprise when considered against the backdrop of an international history capacious enough to encompass empires as well as nation states.

If we expand our range of political actors to include empires as well as states, equally we should ensure that we do not treat states in the international system as black boxes all alike. To understand the military behaviour of post-colonial/Southern states, I argue that we must provide accounts that are specific to the features of the Southern state itself. Hence the picture on Southern peacekeeping comes into sharper focus when we bring in patterns of 'dependent militarisation'. Just as much as poor and newly independent states tended to be economically and often even politically dependent on powerful states, so too we witness patterns of military dependency among states of the global South. That is, rather than Southern armed forces being formed straightforwardly as the military forces of stand-alone states, the armed forces of weaker states are shaped by the priorities and policies of the militarily powerful, whose vehicles of influence are the provision of arms, training, and control of international security structures and alliances including of course, the United Nations.

The discussion in this chapter necessarily presupposes a good deal about the United Nations—first, that the organisation provides the institutional machinery through which imperial interests can be secured through the proxy deployment of other countries' armed forces. Second, that the United Nations is able to legitimise both peacekeeping and peacekeeping contribution in global terms. In other words, the precondition of Southern participation in UN peacekeeping is that those states perceive the United Nations to be a bulwark *against* imperialism. The validity of these assumptions is examined in chapter six, when we shall see how the world organisation successfully sublimated the imperialism of the old colonial empires into a new, more legitimate imperial multilateralism. For the purposes of discussion in this chapter, these things must be assumed. We begin by considering the changing contribution patterns of international intervention, before moving on to consider the role of Southern peacekeepers in these military formations.

Trends in peacekeeping contribution

Multilateralism is integral to peacekeeping. Involving as it does foreign troops piercing the sovereignty of a state in order to deploy on its territory, a range of countries contributing their forces to a peacekeeping operation under the authority of the United Nations signals both wide international support and indicates a reduced chance of being dominated by the self-interest of a single state.[1] In the words of UN doctrine on peacekeeping: 'International legitimacy is one of the most important assets of a United Nations peacekeeping operation [...] The uniquely broad representation of Member States who contribute personnel and funding to United Nations operations further strengthens this international legitimacy.'[2]

UN peacekeeping is certainly cosmopolitan, even by the standards of the largest military alliances. By the end of the first decade of this century, the security forces of 118 countries had been deployed as peacekeepers, out of 192 member states of the United Nations. By comparison NATO—the world's most powerful military alliance—has only twenty-eight members. No other regional body with a military or peacekeeping arm, whether in Africa, Europe or post-Soviet territory, has as many members as there have been participants in UN peacekeeping.

As we saw in the previous chapter, multilateralism is taken as the political form that inoculates UN field missions against imperialism by endowing them with the requisite legitimacy. In keeping with this anti-imperial theme, it is not simply reliance on a diversity of participating states—peacekeeping is also seen to place a premium on the participation of explicitly weaker states. Forces from smaller powers are understood to strengthen the claim to legitimacy in contradistinction to the military interventions of more powerful states, whose aims and motives are rendered suspect by virtue of that power.[3] Martha Finnemore presents this view when she says that the participation of smaller and middling powers helps to ensure that peacekeeping action is not 'merely self-serving and particularistic but is joined in some way to community interests that other states share', while also helping to integrate these smaller states by giving them a direct stake in the constitution of international order.[4] Finnemore's views are echoed by other International Relations theorists. According to feminist Cynthia Enloe, 'United Nations peacekeeping forces, drawn from the militaries of its member states, are being looked upon by the governments of many industrialized and Third World countries as offering the best hope for a genuinely post-Cold War, nonimperialist military ...'[5]

According to Andrea K. Talentino the participation of Southern states is another 'argument against imperialism ... states of all types promote intervention, not simply the most powerful. Indeed, if intervention relied primarily on Western or American participation it would rarely happen at all.'[6] Canadian statesman and one of the founding fathers of UN peacekeeping, Lester Pearson, articulated the philosophy underpinning peacekeeping, itself a reflection of Canada's self-understanding on the world stage: 'We are big enough to discharge with effect the responsibilities that we undertake; we are not big enough for others to fear us.'[7] Being further down the hierarchy of international power, it has been generally accepted that allowing such states to act as the forces of international intervention reflects the fact that they do not themselves constitute any larger threat to international or regional order, and that they will not be able to significantly alter the local or wider balance of power in the country in which they intercede.

Yet this 'middle power philosophy' that sees peacekeeping as the preserve of smaller powers obscures the reality of UN peacekeeping today in the shroud of its founding myth. While much ink has been spilled examining the many functions of the expanded peacekeeping missions of the post-Cold War era, much less thought has been devoted to considering how changes in the practice of peacekeeping and in peacekeepers' roles and responsibilities map onto changes in the composition of peacekeeping forces and changing patterns of peacekeeping contribution. However cosmopolitan the legions of peace have been in the past and present, definite changes in the patterns of peacekeeping contribution are visible; multilateralism in peacekeeping is not a fixed or merely abstract quantum.

Let us quickly recapitulate the changing patterns of peacekeeping contribution discussed in the first chapter. These changes can be divided into three broad periods.

In the first, Cold War period, peacekeeping was dominated by neutralist and middle powers comprising Non-Aligned states (for example, India, Ghana), some Commonwealth and NATO states who could boast credible military forces but were not perceived as expansionist or aggressive (Australia, Canada, Denmark, Norway) and smaller European countries that fostered traditions of neutral diplomacy (Austria, Ireland, Finland).[8] In the second period running from the end of the Cold War to the close of the century, UN peacekeeping was led by the leading Northern military powers, principally France, the US and Britain, with Australia, Spain and Italy in tow. This was also the period in which the Cold War-era peacekeeping states Austria, Finland, Sweden and Ireland were absorbed into the Partnership for Peace scheme as part of NATO expansion, thereby relinquishing their traditional neutralism. Both periods included a significant proportion of developing world peacekeepers. But it is in the third period running from the turn of the century to the end of the last decade that we have seen other groups of peacekeeping powers eclipsed by developing countries. It is this last period that concerns us in this book and in this chapter. But to understand how these patterns of peacekeeping contribution developed, we must briefly review the prior period following the end of the Cold War.

Peacekeeping contribution in the post-Cold War era

There were two major developments in the pattern of peacekeeping contribution in this period that I want to stress. First, the great powers—and the three Western permanent members of the Security Council in particular—became involved in UN peacekeeping to a much greater degree, both in leading peacekeeping operations and in bending peacekeeping to their own purposes. In the early 1990s, Britain and France took the lead in the peacekeeping operations in the Balkans, while the US took the lead in Somalia and Haiti. The permanent three were also involved in peacekeeping operations in Cambodia and Latin America.

At the same time, the great powers sought and received UN blessing for their own political and military interventions in their spheres of influence in Latin American and Africa—interventions for which they would never have been either concerned or able to secure UN support for in the past, and would instead have comfortably relied on their relations with pliant allies and client regimes. Of the 1994 US-led intervention in Haiti, Danilo Zolo observes that here we saw 'the world's supreme international institution' giving 'legitimation to the *Realpolitik* tradition practiced by the United States ... known as the Monroe Doctrine'.[9] At the same time, beyond this 'spheres of influence peacekeeping', UN authority was invoked for operations that did not require it under the terms of international law. In the cases of military interventions in the Middle East and Balkans, for example, the respective internationally recognised governments gave their express consent to the military interventions and/or peacekeeping missions that took place. As the Council's decisions are binding, unlike treaties and bilateral agreements based on state consent, the legal redundancy of UN authorisation in these situations contributed 'to the inflation of the Security Council's extraordinary authority'—a theme we return to in chapter six.[10]

Thus the liberal internationalism of the post-Cold War era saw an enormous concentration of legal, military and political power into a single centre. For a brief period, the promiscuous extension of UN authority to a variety of military interventions—and particularly Western military expeditions—saw the coincidence of highest might with highest right. The swelling ranks of peacekeeping nations lining up behind Western leadership reflected a 'bandwagoning' effect resulting from Western victory in the Cold War: a wide variety of countries, including many developing nations, joined the victors in their attempts to consolidate the victory of international liberalism around the globe. The numbers of states involved in peacekeeping rose dramatically from the Cold War figure of twenty-six to over seventy by 1994, including forty-one that had never previously participated in such operations.[11]

Following the military setbacks to UN/US operations in Somalia and the Balkans and the collapse of the UN mission in Rwanda, there was a dramatic slump in peacekeeping operations. In 1993, over 70,000 UN peacekeepers were deployed globally; by 1996 it was only 20,000.[12] Subsequent to the disgrace and humiliation of the United Nations in these conflicts, peacekeeping was re-routed into regional organisations. That the problems that beset these missions were attributed to UN command and control structures was ironic, given that the latter had been purposefully malformed to accommodate US interests in Somalia, and those of NATO in the Balkans, where a rickety 'dual key' command system had been established for joint UN-NATO control over NATO airpower. But it was UN peacekeeping that suffered at the expense of NATO, as the creaking Atlantic alliance was given a new lease of life when Unprofor troops in Bosnia-Herzegovina were replaced with Ifor peacekeepers commanded from Brussels rather than New York. The shift from New York to regional peacekeeping missions was not restricted to NATO—the pattern was repeated around the world.[13]

But there were several important elements of continuity even as Western-led UN peacekeeping ebbed. In the first instance, the high water mark of Western involvement in peacekeeping left behind significant institutional and doctrinal innovations that became embedded in subsequent practice—particularly the militarisation seen subsequent to the Brahimi Report (on doctrine, see the discussion in previous chapters; the institutional re-ordering will be covered in the next chapter). Second, even while the overall numbers of peacekeepers fell and the rankings of contributing nations were re-shuffled, the overall diversity of UN peacekeeping contributors remained intact. The number of states contributing personnel to peacekeeping operations in April 1997, seventy-one, was still not less than the number of contributors as of 1993—from 1992 to 2001 the average number of participating countries was seventy-six.[14] Third, as the permanent three withdrew from direct involvement with UN peacekeeping, so too did the new NATO partner states and the traditional Western peacekeeping powers—Australia, Canada, Ireland, among others. Traditionally neutral Sweden, Finland and Ireland entered NATO partnership schemes in this period. If this was a measure of these countries' renunciation of neutrality, it also reflected the changing political authority and legitimacy of NATO as it became another arm of the all-encompassing 'international community', whose claims were taken to be so beyond challenge as to be effectively neutral (see the discussion in chapter two).[15]

While the permanent three extricated their forces from the command of New York and the Secretary-General, their retreat from direct involvement in UN interventionism was not just an absolute drawing down of numbers but also entailed restructuring their involvement with UN field missions, even as they continued to direct peacekeeping from their perch on the Security Council. Where Western forces were despatched on UN operations, they tended to be in the mould of 'spheres of influence' peacekeeping—with UK peacekeepers in Cyprus and the Balkans, France's in Lebanon, Haiti and Côte d'Ivoire, US and Canadian peacekeepers in Haiti and Kosovo, with Italy, Spain and Germany following in tow.[16] While the bulk of Western interventionary forces were directed through non-UN forms such as the NATO Operation Allied Force against Yugoslavia in 1999, or the Australian-led Regional Assistance Mission in the Solomon Islands in 2003, Western states also began to mount what Alex Bellamy and Paul Williams call 'hybrid' missions in conjunction with UN peacekeepers.

In these missions Western forces were coupled to UN peacekeeping operations manned by other countries' forces, in which Western states retained political and operational independence from New York. As a result, the majority of Western military expeditions undertaken since the end of the Cold War, whether unilateral or otherwise—in West, East and Central Africa, the Balkans, South East Asia, Afghanistan—have either been part of or coupled with a UN peacekeeping mission. At the time of writing, the hybrid model has been proposed for Mali following the drawing down of the French forces in that country, with UN Secretary-General Ban Ki-moon proposing a UN peacekeeping force over 12,000 strong. Already envisioned to incorporate seven mobile infantry battalions with 'robust rules of engagement', Ban Ki-moon nonetheless recommended the deployment of what he circumspectly called a 'parallel force' alongside the peacekeepers—presumably a French rapid reaction force.[17]

Western forces perform a variety of roles in these hybrid missions.[18] These may include acting as the military vanguard of a UN operation (for example, Interfret in East Timor in 1999, the 2003 Operation Artémis in Congo, known in UN-speak as the Interim Multinational Emergency Force; the 2003 Franco-US intervention in Haiti; the 2008– 09 EU peacekeeping force in Chad/Central African Republic), and long-term stabilisation and counter-insurgency efforts working in tandem with UN peacebuilding operations (for example, NATO forces in Kosovo and Afghanistan). Western forces may also act as military shock troops and deterrent forces in 'post-conflict' countries experiencing turmoil (for example, the British Operations Deliberate Force and Palliser in Sierra Leone in 2000; US amphibious and naval support for both regional and UN peacekeeping operations in Liberia in 2003 and EU 'reserve deployment' forces in support of Monuc in 2006). In western Sudan, the US and EU provided logistical and strategic lift support to the joint UN-African Union mission there. Even the upgrading of the Unifil mission in Lebanon following the 2006 war with Israel—the first UN peacekeeping operation to see a sizeable Western presence since the mid-1990s—followed a similar pattern in its early phase, exhibiting significant influence from Brussels.[19]

These operations vary in the degree to which they are 'coupled' with UN peacekeeping operations—some are more tightly bound, others less so—and as to whether they are led by a single state, led by a pivotal 'lead' state, or are submerged within larger military frameworks provided by NATO or the EU. For our purposes here, the distinctions between these 'hybrid' operations are less important than the fact that they all provide military support of UN peacekeeping efforts *outside* UN political and command structures; Western forces act as the military spearhead of UN peacekeeping operations, whether directly in theatre or in an 'over the horizon' role.

In their 2009 study of the West's new role in UN peacekeeping, Bellamy and Williams were troubled by these findings—notably the militaristic emphasis at the expense of broader peacebuilding initiatives, and the fact that operational timeframes are thereby dictated by the political restraints of Western military planners rather than the needs of the wider mission. Following Martin Shaw's analysis of contemporary militarism, they labelled these 'hybrid' operations a form of 'risk-transfer war', where the risks of military operations are distributed away from Western troops onto 'other elements of the hybrid operation'—that is, Southern UN peacekeepers and civilian staff.[20]

Yet even on its own terms designating peace operations in this manner is contradictory. By Bellamy and Williams's own reckoning, if Western forces constitute the shock troops of twenty-first century UN peacekeeping, then they are by definition more likely to be exposed to the risks and trials of combat, albeit for a short period. At least since 2003 the Western public, particularly the Anglo-American public, have shown themselves willing to tolerate higher casualty rates than previously suspected, as witnessed in the wars in Iraq and Afghanistan. Both are missions that public debate fails to differentiate from peacekeeping and which military planners, counter-insurgency theorists and strategists see as being highly similar in political and operational terms. Nor does the theory of risk-aversion explain the dynamics of initial Western participation and subsequent retraction from UN peacekeeping in the immediate aftermath of the Cold War. Applied to international politics, these theories borrowed from sociology have an indeterminate character in that they leave unspecified to what extent Western risk-aversion is a cultural disposition and to what extent a political decision assumed by state and political elites. The danger here is that international inequalities of power are reified, explained as variations in cultural predispositions towards war-fighting between North and South, the tacit implication being that Southern societies are more militarised and militaristic.

To correct for and avoid such distortions, whether tacit or otherwise, and to understand better the calculus of risk and reward in peacekeeping, peacekeeping missions and contribution patterns need to be contextualised in considerations of international power politics. If we think about peacekeeping contribution in relation to the global distribution of military power, then the most immediately striking point is that there is quite simply a shortage of power projection capacity outside of the US. The US remains the only country that can indefinitely sustain large military forces overseas in combat operations. Even then the operations in Afghanistan and Iraq have shown that the US enjoys ambiguous, if not sharply diminishing, strategic and political returns from the direct and particularly the unilateral use of military force in counter-insurgency and state-building operations. Within the Atlantic alliance, only Britain and France have some limited power projection capabilities; outside it, Russia retains some vestigial capacities, as we shall see in the next chapter.

While US military spending was and is colossal, its closest allies have slowly but surely reduced their military spending since the end of the

Cold War both in absolute but particularly in relative terms: Western Europe as a whole has seen the lowest growth in military budgets of any world region across the last decade.[21] Indeed, excluding US military spending, on average NATO defence budgets as a proportion of gross national product declined from 2.42 to 1.87 per cent from 1995 to 2004.[22] The year 2012 was the first year in which defence budgets in Asia exceeded those in Europe, with cuts to equipment programmes stemming from the financial crisis in the latter. This is partly a reflection of the changing military balance of power and growing strategic rivalries in Asia, but even discounting for this effect reduction in defence spending in at least sixteen European NATO member states occurred across 2008 through 2010, with cuts in real terms exceeding 10 per cent in many of these cases.[23] Troop levels have declined at even sharper rates, and the funds released in Western countries by having relatively lower personnel costs have not thus far been re-invested in systematically upgrading force projection capacities.[24]

As we can see in graph 4.1, of those US allies that can offer at least 5 per cent of their total ground forces for rapid deployment in military intervention, the overall pattern has been either of decline or stagnation—with a particularly sharp decline manifested by those two states with the largest overseas military presence and the greatest experience of expeditionary warfare—namely the UK and France.[25] Having to watch Europe's military sinews wither since the end of the Cold War—in spite of, it must be said, their frequent use—has been an abiding source of frustration to liberal internationalists. This atrophy is seen to limit the ability of European nations to militarily defend liberalism abroad, and has prompted a persistent search for new reserves of manpower, greater military efficiency, demand for more weapons procurement and development, blueprints for structures of international cooperation to concentrate military power dispersed across nations, and schemes to harness the power of those states with large armed forces who are not currently involved in peacekeeping.[26]

This context of shrinking armies and stagnant or declining military spending within the Atlantic alliance helps us to frame changing patterns of UN peacekeeping. Against this backdrop, we can see that the cross-border institutions of UN peacekeeping have granted Western states access to a much larger pool of manpower for expeditionary warfare and 'stabilisation' operations. Indeed, Southern participation in peacekeeping has grown in inverse proportion to the relative diminution of European military power.

Graph 4.1: Size of Western Ground Forces, 1990–2010

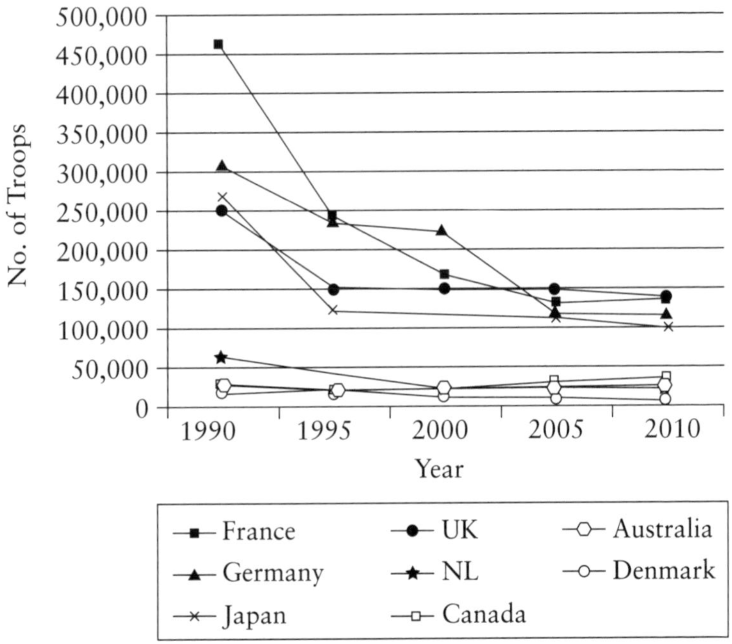

Source: International Institute for Strategic Studies.

Moreover, these forces can be tapped at much lower cost: according to Richard Gowan, a NATO soldier costs five times more to deploy than a UN peacekeeper.[27] This partly reflects the legitimacy accorded to UN peacekeepers, who do not need to fight their way into countries or hold territory—the types of operations that would require more manpower and larger outlays on armour, materiel and advanced air force and naval support. A study by the RAND corporation shows that the ratio of UN peacekeepers per thousand inhabitants of the host state—a standard measure used by armies in planning operational force sizes—has been consistently lower in UN-led than comparable US-led operations.[28] The same study also showed that per-capita financial assistance was lower in UN-led missions than US-led missions.[29] The relative cheapness of UN peacekeeping is not only a function of its legitimacy but also the fact that these monies can be spread across the relatively cheaper labour costs of Third World armies, as we shall see in the next chapter.

Much has been made of the non-strategic character of multilateral military interventions, as the institutions of multilateralism require the dilution of political and strategic control, divert energy into time-consuming and costly efforts at managing cooperation and coordination and require the sacrifice of power by leading states, all of which is said to compromise military effectiveness.[30] This leads Finnemore to the conclusion that 'Contemporary multilateralism is deeply political and normative not just strategic.'[31] But according to Susan Rice, the Obama administration's former Ambassador to the United Nations, the financial and functional benefits of multilateral UN peacekeeping are more obvious. For every dollar the US spends on unilateral stabilisation efforts the United Nations spends only 12 cents: 'That is a pretty good deal', she told US senators in her confirmation hearing.[32] The theme that consistently recurs in the liberal internationalist defence of UN peacekeeping is its cost-effectiveness, just as often demonstrated by pointing out how tiny the proportion of global military spending on peacekeeping is, and dramatising this contrast by showing that some peacekeeping operations even cost less than a single modern weapons system.[33]

The United Nations itself uses similar comparisons in defending its record, as demonstrated by the UN Under-Secretary-General for Peacekeeping Operations, Hervé Ladsous, in a statement delivered before a UN committee in October 2011:

the total expenditure on peacekeeping from 1948 to 2010 is estimated at USD 69 billion. By comparison ... some estimates indicate that the defense expenditure for 2010 of the fifteen top spenders alone amounted to approximately USD 1.6 trillion, or twenty-three times the cost of peacekeeping since its inception more the sixty years ago.[34]

Seeking a rapprochement between the United Nations and the Bush administration, a report on UN nation-building efforts by the RAND corporation noted a year after the invasion of Iraq that the cost of the US occupation in that country exceeded in one month the annual cost of seventeen UN operations running concurrently.[35] In a close study of the costs of the most recent UN mission in Haiti, which has run more or less concurrently with the US invasion of Iraq, a report by the US Government Accountability Office estimated that the UN mission cost half of what an equivalent US military expedition to the island nation would have cost.[36] Finally, on average, Western nations spend more on UN peacekeeping relative to the amount they budget for the military than do less developed countries.[37]

Such striking comparisons could be multiplied *ad absurdum*, and the various permutations of such contrasts need not detain us any further. Their implication is clear enough: for Western countries at least, UN peacekeeping is a bargain. Doubtless such arguments will only appear stronger in light of the ongoing global economic crisis and falling Western military budgets. UN peacekeeping already offers a tried and tested model of 'austerity intervention'. There are three conclusions that are worth drawing from these observations. First, the defence of UN peacekeeping in these terms in public, intra-governmental and inter-governmental debate clearly presupposes that UN peacekeeping is seen to be compatible with and advances Western interests in international order. The idea of 'cost-effectiveness' presupposes that Western concerns and interests are being secured at lower cost. Second, to calculate the relative benefits of UN peacekeeping in these terms is implicitly or explicitly to place UN peacekeepers on a spectrum that includes the deployment of Western or NATO forces, indicating that the former are to some extent at least seen as substitutes for Western troops. The comparison admits of the fact that peacekeepers, whether they be (Euro-American) NATO forces or (Southern) UN legionnaires are both seen as being available for essentially similar political and military tasks, the decision of which to use being a question of expediency rather than principle. Finally, that such a strong sense of Western proprietorship can be so casually expressed about UN peacekeeping as a whole—in the same breath as admitting its reliance on non-Western forces—speaks to a basic confidence that Western control over the organisation and its deployed forces can be maintained, whatever the national composition of those forces.

Yet if anything the liberal internationalists undersell the political benefits of peacekeeping in their attempt at a hardheaded, pragmatic defence of the institution in terms of dollars and cents. By grafting their military expeditions onto UN operations, Western armies have the opportunity to benefit from the legitimacy accruing to UN intervention without having to submit their soldiers to the limitations of a UN mandate, its diffuse command structures, problems of inter-operability across forces, and competing political pressures. With hybrid operations, Western states can mount military interventions independent of the United Nations while still advancing under cover of the legitimacy accorded to UN peacekeeping. They retain wider freedom of manoeuvre than that available to UN peacekeepers, while still being able to claim to be acting in support of the 'international community'—an international community that in any case they control, as we see in chapter six.

Freed from the direct constraints of UN institutional friction, diplomatic politicking and Secretariat bureaucrats, Western military planners can manipulate time-frames and military goals to suit national political purposes, notching military operations up as quick and clean successes even if the UN operation on which the Western operation is dependent continues long after the Western shock troops have departed. When it comes to UN command, other states must live by mandates drawn up by the permanent three member states, from which the permanent three's own forces are more than likely to be exempt, if they are deployed at all. Given the structure of hybrid operations, Western states can launch multiple military operations in support of the same UN mission, escalating or de-escalating their involvement at will without calling into question their policies or necessitating any clear expression of strategic intent and purpose. At the same time, should peace settlements disintegrate and war erupt, Western states can easily evade the political and strategic consequences of failure—UN peacekeepers are there to absorb these problems and take the blame.

Table 4.1 provides a partial snapshot of these hybrid operations— partial because it obviously excludes those UN peacekeeping operations that are not supported by Western military interventions, and partial in that some of these states are host to other Western military interventions and operations that are not directly in support of a UN mission but whose presence might nonetheless consolidate the nexus of international interventions in the country concerned (for example, Operation Barras in Sierra Leone in 2000, or the European Union police missions in the Democratic Republic of Congo). Nonetheless, we can see that on the whole UN missions last longer (an average of seven years and eight months) than the Western component of the operation (less than half as long), and are more likely to entail a larger military presence and sustain higher casualty levels commensurate with this larger size and longer timeframe. Even in those cases where the UN missions have been led by a Western state—Unprofor and Untaet—this should not lead us to ignore the large contingents provided by other states to the mission, which will invariably include developing countries.

That the United Nations is routinely derided for its incompetence and ineffectiveness in peacekeeping does not mean that these failures

Table 4.1: Hybrid Peacekeeping, 1999–2012

Missions & Country	Year(s)	No. of peacekeepers (max. deployment)	Duration	Largest contributor (at time of max. deployment)	Total Mission Casualties	Ratio of non-UN: UN peacekeepers
Unamid/Minurcat: *Sudan/Chad/ Central African Rep.*	2007–12 2007–10	23,447/3,814	5 yrs/3 yrs	Nigeria/Ghana & Nepal	114/8	1:5/1:1
Eufor Chad-RAC	2008–09	c. 4,300	1yr 6mns	France	1	
Minuci-Unoci: *Côte d'Ivoire*	2004–12	10,957	8 yrs	Bangladesh	90	1:2
Op. Licorne	2003–12	5,000	9 yrs	France	c.24	
Minustah: *Haiti*	2004–12	10,773	8 yrs	Brazil	170	1:3
Multinational Interim Force	2004	3,440	3 mns	US	1	
Unomil-Unmil: *Liberia*	2003–12	14,824	9 yrs	Bangladesh	165	–
Protection Force & warship	2003	–	N/A	US	N/A	
Monuc-Monusco: *DR Congo*	1999–2012	20,586	13yrs	India	199	1:9
Eufor RD Congo	2006	c. 2,275	8 mns	France	0	
Interim Multinational Emergency Force	2003	1,968	4 mns		0	1:10
Unomsil-Unamsil: *Sierra Leone*	1999–2005	17,368	6yrs	Pakistan	192	1:21
Op. Palliser	2000	c.800	1mn	UK	1	
Unmik: *Kosovo*	1999–2012	5,533	13 yrs	US	54	13:1
Kfor	1999–2012	42,500	13 yrs	US	43	
Untaet-Unmiset-Unmit-Unotil: *Timor-Leste*	1999–2012	4,776	13 yrs	Australia	52	
International Security Forces	2006–12	c. 930	6 yrs		0	1:5
Interfret	1999–2000	11,285	5 mns		1	40:1

Source: Bellamy and Williams (2009); Connaughton (2002); Guardian (29 May 2003); International Institute for Strategic Studies; Stockholm Institute for Peace Research. Ratios rounded to nearest whole number.

redound to the detriment of its leading member states. With brilliant counterintuitive reasoning, Inis L. Claude, Jr argued that UN failure could be politically functional for states—an insight applied to the post-Cold War actions of the United Nations by Mats Berdal. Berdal used Claude's paradoxical observation to suggest that the United Nations might be performing its function precisely when it seems to be failing.[38] Along similar lines Irish diplomat and ex-peacekeeping official Conor Cruise O'Brien argued that serving as a 'scapegoat for the vanities and follies of statesmen' was 'a large part of [the UN's] utility to national leaders'.[39] In a very real sense then, the 'UN's greatest successes are its failures'. O'Brien gives the example of the Unosom operations in Somalia, after which US President Bill Clinton baldly attempted to shed political responsibility for the debacle of the operation on to the United Nations:

in his address to the General Assembly [Clinton] coolly placed on the UN itself the blame for the US-fuelled over-expansion of UN peacekeeping activities. As the President put it 'If the American people are to say yes to UN peacekeeping, the United Nations must know when to say no.'[40]

The irony, as O'Brien points out, is that to 'resist the tendency about which the President was complaining, the UN would have had to say "No" to the United States, which has never been easy for the UN, and has been virtually impossible since 1990'. But 'taking the blame', O'Brien avers, is 'perhaps the greatest justification for [the UN's] continued existence'.[41]

Imperial peacekeeping: from Empire to the United Nations

Reflecting on his role in keeping the peace, one British officer observed:

None of the forces we served with were large enough or sufficiently well equipped to deal with foreign invasion or large-scale rebellion. We could, however, keep matters under some kind of control until help arrived [...] our role was to hold the fort until help arrived; while under normal conditions we acted in support of the local police forces. I like to think of us as Keepers of the Gates.[42]

This is not a description of hybrid peacekeeping operations today but rather the reminiscences of an anonymous, long since deceased British officer summing up how he saw 'scallywag soldiering'—that is, leading colonial armies drafted from native troops—in the many outposts of empire. Back then, the 'help' came 'sometimes from another Territory, but usually from the Navy or Army'.[43] Today that help, if it arrives, is at least as likely to come from New York, Brussels, Paris and Washington, D.C. as it is from London. Inasmuch as the help could involve the Royal Navy or US Army, it could also still include forces from 'another Territory' with the proviso that these forces will now be those of an independent state rather than a colonial army. But their role and duties will not be that dissimilar to those of their imperial forebears. Today's peacekeepers include the descendants of full-scale British imperial armies, as we shall presently see.

That there should be so many resonances between the experience of imperial policing by colonial armies and modern day peacekeeping is no mere coincidence, reflecting both historical continuity in the use of military power—the long shadow of the imperial past—and, more importantly, structural similarities in the security arrangements of empire and those of today—the imperial present. Indeed, once we are willing to think of peacekeeping as one type of military deployment among other possible configurations of military intervention, global military 'footprints' and force postures, we derive a wider context in which to map the changing geometry of military power. This gives us less reason to take the claims made for UN peacekeeping at face value—not least the belief that these peacekeeping deployments are harbingers of a cosmopolitan polity.

We have seen in the previous chapter the claim that multilateralism was styled the antithesis of imperialism, despite the history of multilateral imperialism. The 'pre-history' of modern peacekeeping too is intertwined with imperialism. In his history of the United Nations, Paul Kennedy observes that states of the former British Empire tend to be over-represented in UN peacekeeping from both the global North (Canada, Australia, New Zealand, Ireland) and South (India, Pakistan, Jamaica, Ghana, Nigeria, Bangladesh and Fiji).[44] The peacekeeping activism of Britain's ex-colonies in the South exceeds that of the white dominions of the British Empire many times over, as indeed during the Second World War the dependencies supplied more troops to the imperial cause than all of the dominions combined.[45] Kennedy's faux even-handedness notwithstanding, he attributes this peacekeeping activism to the history of these armed forces having been jointly deployed around the globe in a single coordinated effort: 'having campaigned as part of a larger coalition in the two world wars, they found it structurally and mentally easy to adapt to international peacekeeping.'[46]

One could trace these lines of continuity deeper: well before their peacekeeping duties for the United Nations as independent nations these armies were *already* fighting on behalf of the United Nations as British colonial armies. As Dan Plesch has shown, what we call the 'Allies' today styled themselves the 'United Nations' from 1942—a fact that is integral to understanding the war itself, insofar as US leadership of the anti-Axis campaign raised the banner of self-determination and international solidarity against fascist expansionism, rejuvenating with overwhelming military might the liberal internationalism that had been discredited by the military impotence of the League of Nations.[47] It was to the United Nations that Axis states formally surrendered; it was United Nations forces that were referred to in military orders written by US and British generals.[48] It was to the United Nations that the Jewish resistance fighters of the Warsaw Ghetto appealed for military aid in 1943 before they were exterminated by the SS, whose forces incorporated auxiliary units referred to as 'askaris' in German military reports—that is, colonial troops recruited from those the Nazis called the 'savage peoples' of the East, the subject nations of Germany's eastern European empire.[49]

That Britain's empire played a major role in the UN-cum-imperial victory is not in doubt, even if it has been forgotten in British public memory in favour of the more satisfying parochialism of 'Britain alone' after Dunkirk.[50] It was the troops of the King's African Rifles and the Royal West African Frontier Force that, along with the fourth and fifth division of the British Indian Army, helped destroy Mussolini's empire in East Africa (Britain's first victory on land during the war). 80,000 African troops contributed decisively to pushing Japanese imperial forces out of Burma, despite initial misgivings about the abilities of the African soldier to fight outside of his native continent against a foe as formidable as the Japanese Imperial Army.[51] Smaller numbers of African soldiers saw combat in the campaign in Italy and the Levant. Colonial armies contributed decisively to Britain's renowned victories in North Africa, not least in the form of a 100,000-strong African logistical support army upon which Montgomery's Eighth Army depended in its campaign against Rommel.[52] The largest imperial contribution however came from India, where a deep wartime famine and economic crisis directly resulting from the racial depredations of imperial rule prompted Indians to flock to their overlords' army in search of regular food and pay, producing the largest all-volunteer force in world history—2.5 million men.[53]

As the experience of Indian wartime volunteers attests, Britain's imperial armies were not equal partners in a joint enterprise but imperial subjects, deployed as the appendages of a single, global empire.[54] The active participation of the colonial armies in this global war effort reflected their imperial subordination. This subordination was manifest not only in the endemic racism confronted by these colonial soldiers and on which imperial armies were necessarily built, but also in that Indian nationalists and other colonial subjects who supported the British war effort hoped to trade their loyal military service to the empire for greater rights to self-rule—hopes ensconced in a larger global war effort legitimated by the Atlantic Charter of 1941 and its institutional expression, the wartime United Nations.[55] While still a satrapy of the British Empire aspiring to greater self-rule, India was one of the first nations in the world to sign the Declaration of the United Nations in 1942. The war thus had the paradoxical effect of solidifying the military might of the empire *and* spurring its dissolution as a result of the revitalised liberal internationalism that provided the ideological cast for the UN war effort:

The moral dimension of the war—a war of freedom versus tyranny, a war of peaceful nations against unsolicited aggression—heavily influenced the philosophy of post-war rule. Britain had to be seen ... not [to be] resisting the increasingly legitimate aspirations of colonial subjects.[56]

It was the experience of this globally coordinated UN war effort against the Axis alliance that spurred the formation of the institutions of military global governance. The UN Military Staff Committee was explicitly modelled on the Combined Chiefs of Staff that the US and UK operated during the war, while the experience of recruiting, deploying and joint combat of multinational, multiracial imperial armies deployed concurrently in varied regional theatres inspired confidence in the viability of a permanent, standing UN army that would be no less diverse in origin and global in scope.[57]

It was peacekeepers who would come to stand in for the absence of this standing UN army. Kennedy is right to observe that former British imperial subjects did indeed smoothly transition from military service in support of a global empire to service in support of an international organisation. The very same year that the Nigeria regiment of the Royal West African Frontier Force became the army of independent Nigeria, it was immediately re-deployed to the UN peacekeeping mission that had just been launched in the newly independent Congo (the

Onuc mission) in 1960. Here, the soldiers of Nigeria were joined by troops of their erstwhile comrades-in-arms of empire: the Gold Coast regiment of the West African Frontier Force, the Malay Regiment, the Ceylon Defence Force and the British Indian Army—all as the armies of independent Ghana, the Federation of Malaya, Ceylon/Sri Lanka, India and Pakistan, respectively. The history of the Gold Coast regiment moves from describing imperial-era campaigning to operations in Congo without skipping a beat.[58] Nor is this imperial history entirely forgotten by India's officers serving in peacekeeping today. A British journalist reporting from the war in eastern Congo in 2010 recounts receiving a commemorative mug from an Indian army colonel stationed there, bearing the emblems of the UN force in the region and the Jammu and Kashmir Rifles, embossed with the motto 'Reliving the history ... once again in the shadows of "Kilimanjaro" in east Africa 1918 to 1919 & 2009 to 2010'—referring to a previous imperial posting of the regiment.[59]

India's most famous peacekeeper, Major-General Indar Jit Rikhye, founder and long-time president of the International Peace Academy (now International Peace Institute) and one of the first theorists of peacekeeping, was born the son of a medical officer in the British Indian Army in 1920. Rikhye began service in a Punjabi Muslim squadron of the 6th Duke of Connaught's Own Lancers, better known as the Bengal Lancers, finishing the Second World War at the age of twenty-four in command of an armoured squadron that had seen combat in Italy and the Middle East. His UN peacekeeping duties as an officer in the army of independent India took him to Egypt, Congo, Yemen and Indonesia during the conflicts that followed decolonisation in those countries, and to Lebanon during the first Israeli invasion of 1982. Rikhye also acted as military adviser to two Secretaries-General, serving under U Thant during the Cuban Missile Crisis.[60] While serving with the Unef I force stationed between Egypt and Israel when the Six Day War broke out in 1967, Rikhye's peacekeeping headquarters was destroyed by Israeli shelling that killed several Indian peacekeepers. With their tyres shot out, 'bumping on the hubs' of their jeeps Rikhye and his remaining peacekeepers fled to the beach at Gaza where they radioed for rescue.[61]

Another renowned Indian peacekeeper, Lieutenant General Dewan Prem Chand, commanded the Indian division of UN peacekeepers whose offensive operations restored the breakaway province of

Katanga to the newly independent Congo, receiving one of India's most prestigious military decorations, the *Param Vishisht Seva* (Distinguished Service Medal) in the process (the campaign involving a fierce ten-day battle against Katangan separatists led by European mercenaries).[62] He subsequently served as UN Force Commander in Cyprus from 1970 to 1976, famously retaining UN control of the airport in Nicosia in the midst of the Turkish invasion of the island,[63] and as a UN observer when white Rhodesia seceded from Britain. At the age of seventy-two Prem Chand commanded one of the early post-Cold War UN missions—Untag, in Namibia. His military service began in 1937 initially in the Dorsetshire Regiment, before joining the 10th Baluch Regiment of the British Indian Army, in whose service he campaigned on the North West Frontier and with British counter-insurgency operations in Malaya. When Prem Chand met the Queen after having relinquished his UN command in Namibia, she reportedly greeted him by saying 'General, I understand that you have commanded more regiments of the British Army than most British generals.'[64]

If Paul Kennedy is coy about the character of the imperial war effort in the Second World War, he entirely ignores the more durable role of these colonial armies in providing internal security for empire, suppressing anti-colonial revolt and facilitating imperial expansion through conquest—all roles whose military functions approximate modern peacekeeping much more closely than the campaigns of the Second World War in North and East Africa, Italy or Burma. It was Indian troops who spearheaded a series of British military expeditions to China from the 1840s onwards to open the markets of the Celestial Empire to British trade and who, as we have already seen, contributed the majority of troops to the suppression of the Boxer Uprising. It was Indian troops who fought Britain's nineteenth century imperial wars in Afghanistan, and who shattered the Arab slave trade in East Africa in the late nineteenth century—all under white British officers.[65] Long before the Second World War the British Indian army fought in Abyssinia, Burma, Aden, Somaliland, Tibet and the Arabian Gulf. For these reasons the army of the Raj was seen as Britain's imperial 'fire brigade' (a metaphor used for UN peacekeeping today) which helped to buttress British imperialism from China to Africa via the Middle East and South East Asia.[66]

As the momentum towards Indian independence became irresistible in the aftermath of the Second World War, the empire turned increasingly to African colonial armies who, after the campaign in Burma, were seen as capable of fighting outside of Africa and for whom the prospect of independence was more distant. In 1952 three battalions of the King's African Rifles as well as the Northern Rhodesia Regiment were despatched to quell the communist Chinese revolt in Malaya.[67] This campaign, the 'last truly "Imperial Small War" to be fought under British command', was as polyglot, cosmopolitan and functionally segmented as any hybrid peacekeeping operation mounted by the United Nations today:

By the time the Communists had been defeated [in 1953] ... the British security forces had included Malays, Gurkhas, Africans, Australians, New Zealanders, Fijians, Indians and Chinese settled in Malaya, trackers from Borneo and of course the British themselves ... six cavalry regiments, six artillery regiments, twenty-nine infantry battalions ... five Gurkha battalions [plus British] Rhodesian and New Zealand SAS squadrons.[68]

By the time the third battalion of the King's African Rifles returned home in 1953, the Mau Mau revolt there had grown to such proportions that they were deployed once again in the service of suppressing anti-imperial revolt, this time of the Kikuyu people in their homeland.[69] The Kikuyu revolt would spur the process of Kenyan decolonisation, with the King's African Rifles becoming the army of an independent Kenya.

Kennedy also ignores the role of French former colonies in peacekeeping despite parallel continuities in French imperial military history. In the words of one historian, 'the North African *Tirailleur* was to the French Empire what the Punjabi Moslem rifleman was to that of Britain.'[70] Imperial France relied on her colonial armies even more widely and systematically than the British—in local and overseas campaigns of imperial conquest, occupation and counter-insurgency from Africa through the Levant to Indochina, and in defence of the French metropole itself. From the Crimean to the Franco-Prussian War of 1870, through Verdun to the campaigns of Vichy French forces in Africa and to Free French forces in Italy to the shattering defeat at Dien Bien Phu, Algerian, Tunisian, Moroccan and West African soldiers fought and died for the French empire.[71]

Nearly half a million North and West African troops served France on the Western Front in the First World War: French generals' eagerness to spare their hard-pressed white troops led to black French forces enduring casualty rates three times higher than white troops.[72] There

Table 4.2: Imperial Peacekeeping: T10 + N10 Peacekeeping States from Empire to United Nations

Empire/Metropole	State	Date of Independence	First UN mission: Start Date, Op., Region	Colonial Army	Regions of Imperial Campaigning/Colonial Policing
	South Africa	1902	1999: Monuc: C. Africa*	Union Defence Force	Home Region; N. Africa; E. Africa; Europe
	Egypt	1922	1960: Onuc: C. Africa	Egyptian army (British protectorate)	Home Region; C. Africa
	Nepal	1923	1958: Unogil: M. East	N/A	N/A
	Jordan	1946	1989: Unavem I: S.W. Africa	Trans-Jordan Frontier Force/Arab Legion	Home Region
	India Pakistan	1947	1956: Unef I: M. East	c.2/3 of British Indian Army c.1/3 of British Indian Army	Global
British Empire	Sri Lanka	1948		Ceylon Defence Force/Ceylon Planters Rifle Corps	
	Ghana	1957	1960: Onuc: C. Africa	Royal West African Frontier Force (Gold Coast regiment)	E. Africa; S.E. Asia
	Malaysia			Malay Regiment	Home Region
	Nigeria	1960		Royal West African Frontier Force (Nigeria regiments)	E. Africa; S.E. Asia
	Kenya	1963	1989: Untag: S. W. Africa	King's African Rifles (Kenya rifles)	Home Region; S.E. Asia
	Zambia	1964	1988: Uniimog: M. East	Northern Rhodesia Regiment	
Dutch Empire	Indonesia	1949	1956: Unef I: M. East	*Koninklijk Nederlands Indisch Leger* (Royal Dutch Indies Army)	Home Region

				Units	Home Region
	Morocco	1956		*Tirailleurs Marocains* + irregular *Goum* & *Spahi* units	Europe; Africa; M. East; S.E. Asia
French Empire	Tunisia			*Tirailleurs Tunisiens*	
	Senegal	1960	1960: Onuc: C. Africa	*Tirailleurs Sénégalais* & *Haoussas*	
	Benin		1998: Monuc: C. Africa		
West Pakistan	Bangladesh	1971	Unimog; 1988: M. East	some ex-officers of British Indian Army	Global/N/A

* South African participation in UN peacekeeping is usually dated to this operation, although South Africa had sent a handful of peacekeepers to earlier missions.

Note: Rwanda is excluded despite being in the T10 across the 2006–11 period: under the terms of the League of Nations mandate by which Belgium ruled Rwanda it could not be militarised and therefore had no indigenous colonial force.

Source: Banerjee (2008); BBC Country Profiles; Clayton (1998); Jackson (2010); Lunt (1981); Permanent Mission to the United Nations websites; United Nations Department of Peacekeeping Operations.

were so many black French soldiers involved in liberating France in 1944 that General Charles de Gaulle felt compelled to institute a policy of 'whitening' Free French forces to spare national honour at being liberated by its colonial subjects. In its war in Indochina, France deployed 18,000 West African, 30,000 North African and 200,000 locally recruited Indochinese, all to no avail.[73] Worse, some of the battle-hardened Algerian veterans defeated by the Viet Minh would form a steely core for the Armée de Libération Nationale, military wing of the Front du Libération Nationale, who would inflict on the French in North Africa what the Vietnamese had in Indochina.[74]

Table 4.2 summarises the development of peacekeeping from empire to the United Nations, showing that many newly independent states who inherited the colonial armies of their former masters quickly embroiled themselves in UN peacekeeping at its height in the Cold War—namely, the 1956–67 Suez mission and the 1960–64 Onuc mission in the former Belgian Congo—and that these early activists tended to be those states with experience of overseas campaigning in service of empire. The dramatic Congo operation put paid to ambitious peacekeeping operations until the end of the Cold War; had it not done so, perhaps we would have seen more continuous involvement by developing countries across the Cold War era through to the present. In any case, as table 4.2 shows, both the British and French imperial systems are well represented in the resurgence of peacekeeping seen since the turn of the century. Given how large peacekeeping operations have grown, in showing only the T10 and N10 contributors other ex-imperial states, which are smaller but nonetheless important peacekeepers, are excluded from the list—for example, Fiji, a small but stalwart contributor to UN peacekeeping whose soldiers campaigned for the British in Malaya, and Malawi, which had to fill quotas of men for the King's African Rifles as the Nyasaland Protectorate before independence in 1963.

Askaris and Sepoys, old and new

What then can we take from this imperial history of proto-peacekeeping, the better to understand UN peacekeeping today?

At the broadest level, the history of imperial armies exposes the historical naïvety of much International Relations scholarship, ignoring as it does the complex character of imperial forms in international history and the multiple ways in which empires built the consent of their subjects into transnational structures of coercion and oppression. As Tarak Barkawi and Mark Laffey point out, for the past 250 years of the modern era the dominant political form in international relations was empire.[75] From an historical viewpoint, multinational, multiracial armies organised around different global roles and functions that reflect international inequalities of power are no surprise, as these have been integral parts of imperial military and power structures.

As regards peacekeeping, we can go further than this: there is significant correlation between having a history of participation in imperial warfare and participation in peacekeeping, as the Nigerian, Ghanaian, Senegalese, Tunisian, Moroccan, Indian and Pakistani experiences all attest. While the descendants of the Royal West African Frontier Force, King's African Rifles, North Rhodesian Regiment, British Indian Army, Ceylon Planters' Rifle Corps and Malay regiment are still active around the world, the descendants of the Iraq Levies, Trucial Oman Scouts, the Sultan's Armed Forces, Aden Protectorate Levies, Hadhrami Beduin Legion, Somaliland Scouts, Somaliland Camel Corps, Sudan Defence Forces and Mauritius Regiment have not taken up modern peacekeeping duties—at least not yet. One of the differences is that the latter were never deployed in imperial expeditions outside their home region.

It seems therefore that experience of imperial warfare overseas—rather than merely acting as locally recruited 'keepers of the gates'—laid down a transnational military infrastructure of experience, doctrine, habit, organisation, training and manpower that was inherited by the United Nations via its newly independent member states and thereby re-directed to the purposes of post-colonial peacekeeping. Certain of these structures of imperial security have persisted well into the present. For example, former Belgian and French colonies—Senegal, Rwanda and Cameroon—are suppliers of highly prized gendarmerie units, especially well suited for the role of paramilitary policing now routine across many peacekeeping operations today. Their skills and interoperability with other Francophone countries' security structures is a transnational legacy of French and Belgian empire, further strengthened by patterns of bilateral, post-colonial security assistance that reproduced patterns of military dependence on the French metropole, a theme we shall shortly return to.[76]

Decolonisation—a managed, if fraught, process of imperial retreat—may also be an important factor here in contradistinction to the legacy of anti-colonial revolution. Although Algerians and Indochinese fought for the French empire as much and as hard as the Tunisians, Moroccans and West Africans, neither Algeria nor Vietnam have comparable experience of post-colonial peacekeeping, perhaps because their post-independence security structures (and political outlook) were not inherited wholesale from the French, but (re)constituted through the process of national liberation. Unlike the French, the British were on the whole more successful in managing their retreat from empire: none of the former British colonies now involved in peacekeeping underwent episodes of revolutionary upheaval comparable to those of Vietnam and Algeria.[77] The question, therefore, is the extent to which colonial armies are used as post-colonial instruments of nation-building, or whether they are substituted by new armies stemming from a war of national liberation.[78] Contrariwise, as table 4.2 shows, the army of independent Indonesia involved itself in UN peacekeeping early, despite the fact that the 1945–49 Indonesian revolution involved the overthrow of the Dutch system of imperial security in the archipelago (and, much like the *harkis* who fled independent Algeria for France, the independence of Indonesia saw the flight to the Netherlands of many of the native Ambonese recruits who had fought to the end to crush Indonesian independence on behalf of the Dutch crown).[79]

At the same time, there is a clear distinction in the contributions of peacekeeping powers of the former British Empire and those of the French. Darryl Li attributes the comparative underrepresentation of former French colonies in UN peacekeeping (despite the vast size of French colonial armies) to the security structures of the French empire. Under French rule colonial armies were directly administered by the War Ministry in Paris 'not in territorial formations [like the British colonial forces] but in elements of a centralised subdivision of the French Army'.[80] With the French empire as a whole more institutionally centralised than the British, its colonial armies were correspondingly more tied to the metropole, as described by Anthony Clayton:

The French Army in North Africa never possessed the same autonomy as the Indian Army, which from the latter part of the 19th century possessed its own Commander in Chief, General Staff, Staff College and permanent career officer corps with all that such continuity could provide in terms of relationships, training and administration.[81]

Li reckons that this resulted in post-colonial armies that were less self-sufficient and cohesive than their British counterparts, making them less well adapted to function as modular national armies in the aftermath of independence.[82]

Thus while the correlation is a strong one, having a history of colonial militarisation is neither a necessary nor sufficient explanation of peacekeeping participation today. Bangladesh's links to the imperial militarism of the past are more tenuous than those of Pakistan or India, yet Bangladesh is among the heaviest contributors to UN peacekeeping. The armed forces of Pakistan are as much descendants of the sepoys as the Indian army, and even though Pakistani peacekeepers were involved in Cold War-era peacekeeping it is only since the end of the Cold War that Pakistani peacekeeping has become comparable to that of India, which became consistently involved in peacekeeping less than a decade after independence. Morocco represents an analogous case to Pakistan for the French empire in that it has only recently entered peacekeeping in significant numbers (though interestingly, both Morocco and Pakistan did deploy their troops abroad repeatedly as part of various Cold War-era conflicts before they began deploying them as peacekeepers—see further below). Similarly, the descendants of the colonial army of Ceylon that saw action variously in the Boer Wars and the Second World War have only recently entered UN peacekeeping in a significant manner.[83]

Jordan is another exception. Although the Hashemite monarchy boasted a formidable colonial army in the form of the Arab Legion that conquered East Jerusalem and the West Bank in 1948, this force was not deployed on British imperial expeditions outside the Middle East. Despite this the Jordanians today constitute a significant military presence in UN peacekeeping. Equally, the Sierra Leonean descendants of the Royal West African Frontier Force, and the Ugandan, Malawian and Tanzanian descendants of the King's African Rifles have no significant peacekeeping duties as of yet. Nor indeed are Ivorian, Nigerien or Guinean soldiers as well represented as Senegalese peacekeepers in the United Nations, even though all are descendants of the *Tirailleurs* of French West Africa. The Latin peacekeeping states—Argentina, Uruguay, Brazil—as well as China, have no history of imperial warfare but are nonetheless involved in peacekeeping.[84] If participation in British and French imperial warfare is a factor that enhances the likelihood of participating in UN peacekeeping, clearly there is a range of other important factors. Participation in imperial warfare should certainly not be seen as a 'cause' of participation in UN peacekeeping. It is clearly a significant precondition in predicting propensity to participate in peacekeeping, but it is by no means decisive. The other factors, national and international, that motivate participation in peacekeeping will be examined in more detail in the next chapter.

Peacekeeping and imperial security

However much participation in imperial warfare and colonial policing may help explain predisposition to participate in peacekeeping, more important for our purposes here are the structural homologies between the security arrangements of empire and those of today.

Colonial armies constituted enormous reserves of manpower for imperial states, ranging from front-line, battle hardened combat troops through local security forces to vast support, logistics and porter units. The French, for example, reached deep into their subject populations in order to compensate for a birth rate that consistently lagged behind France's European rival, Imperial Germany.[85] For all imperial powers, askaris and sepoys were cheaper to recruit, cheaper to provision, cheaper to maintain and cheaper to deploy. At the turn of the century a *Tirailleur Sénégalais* in French West Africa cost less than half a white French marine infantryman.[86] Each soldier in the British Indian Army cost one-quarter of what it took to maintain a metropolitan British soldier. Demonstrating the imperative of imperial efficiency, Britain covered the costs of her Indian army entirely through Indian taxation alone—an arrangement that was less efficient from the Indian vantage point, with Indian government spending on defence reaching an astonishing average of 40 per cent during peacetime, devoted as Indian taxes were to maintaining a vast army whose global role and priorities were set outside of India itself.[87] The extent to which colonial armies made great powers great should not be underestimated. Mussolini dreamed of catapulting Italian military power to parity with the British and French empires by conscripting an army of 200,000 askari after his 1936 conquest of Abyssinia—a war in which Eritrean askari are believed to have borne the brunt of casualties on the Italian side.[88]

In the words of James Lunt, a former British senior imperial army officer: 'A great empire had to be kept at peace, defended, and if necessary, fought for. By far the most economical way to do this was with troops raised locally, trained and commanded by officers from the British Army.'[89] That this arrangement was 'economical' reflected not only the fact that the wage bill for 'native' troops would be less than that for metropolitan troops but also that these forces were often designed as inferior, auxiliary formations; the Indian army and the *tirailleurs* of French West Africa were the exception rather than the rule.[90] Colonial armies otherwise were comprised of scouts, levies, *goums*, *spahis*, guides, rangers, militia, military police, trackers, 'defence' and 'frontier' forces. They were intended as 'loose amalgams of local militia and constabulary forces' and 'guardians of a self-policing peripheral zone'.[91] Their training was correspondingly more limited and their equipment inferior, oriented toward manning garrisons, maintaining order and defeating technologically-inferior opponents in geographically contained revolts outside of wartime.

Material considerations aside, the lives of these troops of colour were also quite simply not as important as those of white soldiery. This enabled imperial capitals to avoid or delay the deployment of metropolitan forces in distant, protracted and potentially unpopular colonial campaigns. As imperial historian Ashley Jackson observes in relation to the British empire:

Colonial wars were ... considered 'small' in the minds of the British public because actual British losses were usually small ... Most importantly, they remained 'small' because the much greater loss of non-white lives barely registered in the public imagination because they were considered to be of far less value than white lives, and because the 'big' logistical effort involved in putting redcoats into battle—usually involving large numbers of indigenous labourers—was seldom acknowledged.[92]

Despite controlling the largest empire in world history, outside of wartime the British retained a modest, inexpensive professional army in contrast to the costly mass armies conscripted by Britain's continental rivals. As Barkawi observes, it was the Indian army that 'helped make the empire politically palatable in Britain by reducing the demand for British soldiers and taxes'.[93] The British were particularly effective at this, but imperialists in general 'sought to avoid expense': 'Keeping down the costs of Empire was important to both colonial and metropolitan treasuries. Ideally colonies were to pay their own way by balancing their budgets and [contributing] to the military needs of the metropole.'[94]

Proportionate to numbers deployed and resources expended, Europe's imperial security systems were remarkably efficient. In British Africa for instance, there were no British battalions south of Khartoum by 1930, while the sub-Saharan colonies were garrisoned by fewer than 12,000 locally recruited soldiers.[95] The most populous of Britain's sub-Saharan colonies was secured by the Nigeria regiment of the Royal West African Frontier Force, which was only 5,000-strong in peacetime. The King's African Rifles in East Africa were about 3,000 strong in 1930. The Belgian Congo—itself half the size of Western Europe—was controlled with a mere 20,000 men of the Force Publique in the 1920s. On the other side of the world, the Dutch empire controlled the entirety of the vast and dispersed Indonesian archipelago with the 'Army of the Netherlands East Indies' only 25,000 strong, two-thirds of which was non-European.[96] As David Killingray concludes, 'in the inter-war years, the gradualist policies of running Empire at minimal cost and with minimal force was a cause of self-congratulation by many colonial powers, who saw their systems of trusteeship as fulfilling the main criterion of good, if somewhat authoritarian, governance.'[97]

The effectiveness of this system relied on the entrenched prestige of empire and white supremacy and, from the early twentieth century onwards, improvements in weapons and transport technology that made it possible to rapidly deploy troops in support of local garrisons when required, overwhelming opposition with greater firepower and technological sophistication. Airpower in particular was seen too as a tool to enhance control over otherwise inaccessible areas without, in the words of Winston Churchill, 'eating up troops and money'.[98] Coastal and riverine areas had in any case long been open to bombardment with large naval cannon fire.[99]

The metropolitan contempt for Africans' fighting capacities expressed in this fetishism of military technology has persisted well into the present day according to Norrie MacQueen, with UN peacekeeping missions still clearly shaped by the assumption 'that armed groups in Africa, whatever their training, arms and motivation, will tend to disintegrate at the first encounter with disciplined military units'—an attitude that has cost peacekeepers their lives on a number of occasions.[100] The colonial-era security system also functioned because the use of colonial armies buttressed systems of indirect rule, whereby indigenous authorities were incorporated into the maintenance of law and order.[101] At the same time, colonial forces could be deployed from more remote territories—notably India—with less chance of imperial rule being undermined by fraternisation or links between local people and imperial security forces.

Historically, colonial armies were the means for reducing the security needs of the periphery through an imperial order in which security was devolved to regional imperial hubs, buttressed by metropolitan technology, firepower and superior forces hovering 'over the horizon'. Colonial armies therefore kept the costs of empire low: they reduced manpower costs, economic costs, and political costs. More than this, they made empire possible—the European empires simply could not have existed without colonial armies. The rationale for colonial armies—the advantages of lower cost balanced against their perceived lesser reliability—is strongly echoed in discussions of contemporary peacekeeping and its reliance on peacekeepers from the global South. Peacekeepers from the global South reduce the costs of imperial security in the post-Cold War era.

The financial advantages of UN peacekeeping we have already seen, as well as the comparatively lower force ratios per head of population in the host states. From the fantasy 'original position' adopted by liberal internationalists in surveying international security, peacekeeping is always seen as a malformed, inadequate affair, far short of what true ethical commitments to humanitarianism would entail in military terms. From an imperial perspective, these arrangements are not only resilient—having survived at least two decades since the end of the Cold War—but also remarkably efficient in sparing metropolitan soldiery the depredations of imperial occupation.

The post-Cold War era of Western military intervention and expeditionary warfare would simply not be possible without the support provided by peacekeepers from the global South. Much like colonial armies kept small wars small, so too peacekeeping allows for Western military interventions to be telescoped in terms of time, manpower and political costs. Hybrid peace operations replicate the old pattern of imperial policing, where locally or regionally deployed units are supplemented when necessary with metropolitan forces and firepower, which otherwise hover in an 'over-the-horizon' role. (On the extent to which the geography of peacekeeping contribution replicates the pattern of imperial policing, see further below).

UN peacekeepers spare metropolitan soldiers. The only state in the world materially capable of sustaining ground forces in expeditions overseas on the scale of contemporary UN peacekeeping is the US. We only need imagine the reaction both within the US and around the globe if every blue helmet in the world today turned overnight into a

US G.I. to know at once how politically unfeasible such a scenario is. Similarly, a British military presence on the scale of Unamsil in Sierra Leone is no more feasible than a French military operation in Côte d'Ivoire on the scale of Unoci. The converse is not true however, as Unamsil and Unoci make British and French military deployments in those countries not only possible but politically legitimate. Just as the use of colonial armies helped to blunt the edge of racial oppression that accompanied colonialism, so too peacekeepers from the global South help to mute fears of neo-colonialism that accompany the mass deployment of metropolitan soldiery today.

The imperial security system maintained by the United Nations differs from that of nation state empires in several key respects. For a start, its institutions are not integrated into a single, centralised state-empire but rather are built up through an externalised system of unequal inter-state cooperation mediated through UN institutions (on which, see chapter six). But that the imperial security structures of today can no longer rely on the mythos of white supremacy and the uncontested acceptance of empire does not necessarily make the imperial multilateralism of UN peacekeeping any weaker. UN legitimacy substitutes for the legitimacy once accorded to empire and to white supremacy.

The system of imperial security seen in peacekeeping is necessarily more politically consensual, relying as it does on the co-optation of willing governments rather than on directly recruiting or conscripting colonial soldiery. Today it is economic inequality, diplomatic pressure and institutional asymmetry that allow for the needs of imperial security to be met. But these processes still involve a degree of political bargaining whose outcome will not necessarily be set in advance and will perforce depend on a perception of mutually aligned interests. As the armed forces of independent states, the askari of today have a choice about involving themselves in peacekeeping in a way that colonial armies did not, however much that choice may be restricted and limited by the various political and economic pressures that cramp the foreign policy of developing countries. Nonetheless, as we have seen, this has not dented a basic sense of entitlement and ownership that Western states express over peacekeeping, demonstrating their insouciance about laying claim to the security forces of other countries for their own needs and purposes. The sustained continuity in Southern peacekeeping over at least a decade in the geopolitical conditions of US unipolarity and the continued Western stranglehold of international security institutions is evidence of the resilience and reality of this neo-imperial security system.

If the mechanisms of control in contemporary imperial security are reduced by virtue of being mediated through the interests of post-colonial states, so too the costs of imperial security are correspondingly reduced. As the armed forces of independent states mobilised and coordinated by UN machinery, the metropolitan powers can dispense with the transaction costs of recruitment, maintenance and deployment of colonial armies. If transaction costs are reduced, Western states have been happy to subsidise the financial costs of UN peacekeeping without compromising the political influence they retain, though how much of this subsidy developing states are actually able systematically to capture is ambiguous, as we shall see in the next chapter. Enhancing security self-sufficiency in the periphery also has the advantage that it can be promoted as part of a project of strengthening states rather than quashing their autonomy.

Dependent militarisation

That UN peacekeeping offers the same advantages for imperial power as colonial armies did for the old empires shows how international institutions are created and moulded by the underlying inequalities and power relations of the international order. The institutions are historically variable, reflecting changes in the underlying patterns of imperial power—notably the rise of the US—while imperial power itself has remained continuous.

One of the processes through which imperial security was recreated across the post-colonial era has been through relations of military dependence, whereby the security forces of independent nations have been reshaped by imperial concerns at various sub- and supra-state levels. At one level, this was effected through the provision of military assistance, advice and training. In the words of Victor Kiernan, too often post-colonial armies remained '"native troops", servants of a camouflaged Western ascendency in return for armaments and other means of maintaining their power'.[102] The colonial armies of imperial rule were often transferred intact to new states as nation state armies, which then frequently became the arbiters of national politics as the independence regimes slid into dictatorship, succumbing to neo-colonial pressures as they were sucked into the vortex of Cold War rivalry.

These structures of military dependence radiated outwards from this sub-state to the supra-state level, in which newly independent states were integrated into Western-led alliances, regional security systems, global networks of bases, overflight rights, electronic listening posts and port facilities, and enmeshed in one-sided rights of military intervention. Britain hoped to integrate independent India and Pakistan into a Commonwealth defence scheme and planned an anti-Soviet defence line in East Africa following the British retreat from its UN Trust territory in Palestine after the Second World War.[103] The French notoriously created an extensive system of unequal bilateral military alliances across Francophone Africa.[104] For the US, the separation of European dependencies from their imperial metropoles was a stepping stone to integrating the newly independent states into a new imperial security system, this time organised around anti-communism.

Typically the pattern of military dependence was shaped by structures of informal empire and the strategic need to contain Third World nationalist revolt and international communism on both the national and regional levels. The focus of this global military system was mainly inward—that is, the maintenance of national security through suppression of internal insurgencies and revolution.[105] To be sure, the US relied on a decentralised system of regional treaty systems modelled on the NATO pattern and anchored around regional gendarmes—for example, Pahlevi Iran, Saudi Arabia, apartheid South Africa—but in practice these regional groupings rarely deployed troops across borders, and certainly nothing like on the scale of contemporary peacekeeping.

The new era of post-Cold War peacekeeping has required some of these regional gendarmes to restructure their global force posture. Some of those who are peacekeepers today have a long post-colonial history of buttressing metropolitan security. Morocco deployed its forces to bolster Francophone Western allies in Africa, including deploying thousands of troops to Zaire ferried in French aircraft in the two 'Shaba' conflicts of 1977 and 1979, but also reportedly in Gabon and Equatorial Guinea.[106] Egypt had forces in Oman, Sudan, Iraq, Somalia and Zaire in the 1980s. South Africa had 14,000 troops stationed in occupied Namibia, which was in turn used as a base from which to raid Soviet ally Angola with forces up to 3,000 strong. Pakistan, a larger peacekeeping power than either Morocco or Egypt, had more troops deployed abroad during the last decade of the Cold War then it does today as peacekeepers. 10,000 Pakistani troops, including armoured units, were stationed in Riyadh as a praetorian guard for the Al-Saud dynasty until 1987, with a further 10,000 dispersed across Oman, the United Arab Emirates, Kuwait and Libya—as a deterrent against revolutionary Iran during that country's 1980–88 war with Iraq. Egypt, Morocco, and especially South Africa and Pakistan would all become significant contributors to peacekeeping operations in Africa and the Balkans in the following decade.

On the other side of the Cold War divide, Zimbabwe, Tanzania and Malawi—all small peacekeeping powers in the United Nations today—had a combined force of over 13,000 troops stationed in Mozambique in the 1980s to help that country's government crush the South African-backed Renamo insurgency. Vietnam and Cuba, who enacted their own understanding of 'good international citizenship' by overthrowing the Khmer Rouge and inflicting significant military defeats on apartheid South Africa respectively, have thus far not joined the ranks of global peacekeepers.[107] Indeed, it was UN peacekeeping missions that oversaw these countries' military disengagement from South East Asia and Africa. Shortly before the launch of the new generation of post-Cold War UN missions, a study in *The Washington Times* estimated that Cuba had up to 55,000 troops in Africa (37,000 alone in Angola), including perhaps as many as 10,000 more outside of Africa (most of them in Nicaragua supporting the government there against the US-backed Contra insurgency). Estimates put the Vietnamese military footprint in the late 1980s at 50,000 troops in Laos and 140,000 in Cambodia engaged in occupying the country and fighting the remnants of Pol Pot's ghoulish regime, the latter in turn supported by the US and its allies in the region.[108]

If nothing else, these figures remind us that peacekeeping deployments today are a reconfiguration of a preexisting global military dispensation and not a cosmopolitan military order that suddenly emerges after the end of the Cold War. Peacekeeping deployments by Southern states should be considered against the backdrop of those states' military deployments, and not simply within the self-referential terms of the waxing and waning of UN peacekeeping. Whatever rhetoric and political rationale is given to justify particular deployments, they remain first and foremost military affairs inevitably shaped by considerations of power, security and interests which are meshed into wider patterns, including those of imperial security.

The 'perennial themes' of imperial security are described by Karl Hack and Tobias Rettig as:

Policing the frontier, how to train local forces without losing control of them, who to choose as allies when one's friend's enemy will become your enemy too and how to turn "imperial" areas into security producers in partnership, rather than truculent security consumers: these are perennial themes.[109]

In terms of peacekeeping, these conflicting and contradictory dynamics of imperial security are most visibly expressed in relation to capacity-building programmes—those efforts by Western states to shed the burdens of imperial peacekeeping by strengthening peripheral states' capacity to mount their own military interventions—to turn them from 'security consumers' into 'security producers'.

The contradictions of capacity-building

Whereas anti-communism was the overarching purpose behind the military dependence created by the US during the Cold War, today peacekeeping and the war on terror are the major means by which Northern states have sought to mould the security forces of weaker countries to their own priorities. The countries that have taken the lead here are the US, Britain and France, stretching at least as far back as June 1997 when the permanent three jointly pledged to coordinate their peacekeeping training programmes.[110] In 2004, the Group of Eight (G8) industrialised nations set out an 'Action Plan' to enhance the global capacity to mount peacekeeping operations. This scheme was centred on Africa, whose lack of strategic importance more than its series of brutal wars explained Western desire to avoid military entanglements there—hence the need for 'frontier policing' to paraphrase Hack and Rettig. The Action Plan stressed developing peacekeeping in conformity with the militarised doctrine of the Brahimi report, with particular emphasis on the development of gendarmerie units, and a pledge to train 75,000 peacekeepers worldwide by 2010.[111]

The US has taken the lead in this regard, cycling through a series of peacekeeping training programmes in Africa reaching back to the first Clinton administration. Having effectively put Bosnia-Herzegovina under NATO occupation by the mid-1990s, the US wanted a policy that would spare it any further costly military interventions in Africa. With the almost uninterrupted series of wars launched by the US since the late 1990s, this has exacerbated the need to reduce the global burdens of imperial security. In his address to the UN General Assembly in September 2004, US President George W. Bush demanded that the world 'create permanent capabilities to respond to future crisis' and 'more effective means to stabilize regions in turmoil, and to halt religious violence and ethnic cleansing'.[112] The Clinton-era programmes, which had already trained 16,000 African peacekeepers by this point, were scaled up into a new 'Global Peace Operations Initiative' (GPOI) launched that year. The GPOI initiative adopted the G8 plan to train 75,000 peacekeepers around the world by 2010, as well as extend the provision of US logistical support to global peace operations.[113]

Africa has been subject to the most intensive capacity-building programmes but the initiative is wider. US South Command helps to sponsor and organise peacekeeping exercises in Latin America, including senior-level command post exercises, thereby enhancing the ability of US and Latin American staff officers to work together in military expeditions. The annual Cabañas field training exercises have focused on peacekeeping in recent years, with 'peacekeeping' in this context including offensive light infantry training as well as the policing-style tasks expected to arise in post-conflict scenarios and disaster relief operations.[114] US Pacific Command meanwhile has supported peacekeeping training in Bangladesh.[115] A US government report estimates that 54,245 troops and 3,350 trainers had been trained under the auspices of the GPOI programme by 2010. Of these, 46,115 peacekeepers from twenty-one different states have been deployed across eighteen different peacekeeping missions.[116]

The programme has also seen the establishment of twenty-two peacekeeping training centres around the world, and provided logistical and equipment support for peacekeeping to the tune of $64.8 million. The programme of training encompasses both UN and non-UN operations, with its students having deployed on ten UN missions, as well as the NATO operations in Afghanistan and Kosovo, and US combat operations in Iraq. Other students have participated in a regional peacekeeping force led by Australia to the Solomon Islands since 2003.[117] The GPOI funding has also been used to consolidate the US State Department's global counter-narcotics operations through extending peacekeeping training to include security scenarios related to drug trafficking.[118] Under the Obama administration, the programme was renewed until 2014 and further globalised—'beyond Africa'—with a range of partnership states established around the world, mostly concentrated in South Asia and the Pacific Islands.

Given the plasticity of peacekeeping discussed in chapter one, peacekeeping training has the useful purpose that it can serve as a means of disseminating counter-insurgency training—or in the words of a US government budget request, training for 'lethal peace enforcement'—safely bundled together with the more neutral blue package of peace-keeping.[119] Indeed, while certain Western programmes of military training, assistance and arms deals have come under intense scrutiny with regards to specific controversies or regimes (for example, US aid for Colombian and Mexican counter-insurgency efforts), peacekeeping training escapes notice, reflecting the broad international and post-ide-ological appeal of peacekeeping across the political spectrum. If any-thing, these peacekeeping training programmes are criticised for their lack of coordination, lack of resources and lack of long-term success in creating an indigenous, self-reliant transnational corps of global peacekeepers, rather than the fact that they are expanding the reach and legitimacy of military activity and global intervention.[120]

The British, French and European Union have followed with their own programmes of funding peacekeeping training along similar lines, the British under the 'conflict pool' programme; the French under the 1998 Reinforcement of African Peacekeeping Capabilities for Peace Maintenance (Recamp) programme, and the EU in its Peace Facility, which was established in 2003 and had disbursed €440 million by 2008 (funds redirected from EU development funds to peacekeep-ing).[121] All these programmes share similar features to US 'capacity building' initiatives—laying the organisational, doctrinal and human infrastructure of peacekeeping across African states and armed forces. Training under Recamp initiatives, for example, has ranged from reg-ular exercises in military manoeuvres through to crisis simulations, with emphasis on the inter-agency and cross-border cooperation needed to mount effective peacekeeping responses.[122] Gorm Rye Olsen's description of the European-backed 'African Peace Facility' could equally serve as an account of any of these capacity-building ini-tiatives, being primarily an instrument designed:

> to avoid deploying European troops on the [African] continent by offering financial contributions to African peace and conflict management operations. The other aim was to contribute to capacity building with the African partners which included a whole range of activities such as training of African troops to perform peace and security operations.[123]

In disseminating Western peacekeeping doctrine, military standards and approaches to peacekeeping, all of these capacity-building and training programmes share broadly similar emphases: to enhance the ability of African armies to substitute for and support Western military forces in their expeditionary operations. In other words, the concerns, priorities and practices of Western military intervention have been globalised across a wide range of national armed forces, solidifying the legitimacy and priorities of Western intervention even as it is diversified across borders. The aim of these programmes is to make other peacekeeping states indirect military interveners on behalf of Western states. Armies around the world are ready to cooperate with and deploy in support of Western military forces when called upon to do so, magnifying the reach of Western interests and power.

This leads us to the problems with these programmes. These problems are usually located in the lack of effective coordination between the US, UK and France at the international level, and the scepticism with which African leaders and officer corps hold these programmes. The solutions typically mooted are more resources and better coordination. But these problems are better understood less as maladministration and more as a symptom of an underlying contradiction—between the drive to devolve peacekeeping to the periphery on the one hand, and the attempt to extend the political and military influence of core states on the other. These two tendencies pull in opposite directions, the end result being the recreation of military dependency. With Western concerns uppermost, the programmes inevitably end by turning African armies into auxiliaries for Western militaries rather than autonomous actors in their own right. Of Recamp, a French officer said: 'We maintain control because there is no one to give it to, but we should nevertheless not confuse the current picture with the final objective.'[124] As the purpose of these initiatives is to consolidate Western interests over both the peacekeepers and the peacekept, they will inevitably reproduce the 'current picture' indefinitely.

African armies and states are interested in these programmes as potential transmission belts for finance and materiel. In practice, Western states have exercised tight control over the disbursement of resources, limiting the distribution of equipment and weapons and, in the case of the US, channelling funds through private security companies contracted to undertake the peacekeeping training—even the outsourcing is outsourced. In this way, the US retains tight control over the initiative and can regulate African states' engagement. African soldiers 'severely criticized' the quality of equipment provided under Recamp, with neither France nor anyone else willing to pay for the requisite resources and materiel that would be necessary to lay the ground of real military autonomy in African states.[125] Logistical support for peacekeeping operations is, of course, supplied on a discretionary basis, often for those operations adopted by particular governments for their own reasons, such as US support for the African Union/United Nations mission in Darfur or the mission in Liberia. Training rather than provision of materiel occupies the preeminent place in these programmes, despite the fact that many African states have plenty of peacekeeping experience themselves—sometimes reportedly more than their Western trainers.[126]

'Partnership' may have replaced the more sinister, Cold War-era vocabulary of 'military assistance', and 'peace support operations' the language of military intervention, while unilateral military intervention has been diversified through multilateral peacekeeping initiatives and training. Whatever the rhetoric, the parochial self-interest of metropolitan capitals reasserts itself: the lack of coordination among Western states reflects the competitive desires of Paris, London and Washington to ensure that they retain control over and capture whatever benefits, by-products, influence and prestige results from these programmes.[127] Thus Paris succeeded in capturing the EU Peace Facility (funded by the Commission in Brussels), turning it into a multilateral prop of French military policy in Africa. According to one analyst, African concerns occupy the 'least' important position in priorities for the Peace Facility.[128] Mark Malan similarly notes that there 'is little doubt that the United States' peacekeeping capacity-building programs are motivated to a large degree by self-interest'.[129]

We should also bear the wider international context in mind. Today US training of African peacekeeping forces must be related to renewed US strategic interest in the continent, with the Bush administration having established Africa Command (Africom) in 2007 as a full-fledged pillar of the nine pillars of US global combat command distributed around the world. In Africa, the new command is perceived as a means for the US to pursue its war on terror in the Sahel and the Greater Horn, to erect barriers to growing Chinese influence on the continent, and to protect Africa's energy supplies.[130] Indeed, programmes such as Recamp and the predecessors of the GPOI have also extended the reach of Western states in legitimising prepositioning—that is, the stockpiling of equipment at strategic points and bases in Africa.[131]

The patent self-interest behind these programmes unsurprisingly generates scepticism among their African recipients, which in turns spurs further attempts to devolve 'responsibilities'.[132] However many thousands of troops trained to Western 'standards' may be churned out through these capacity-building measures, they have not yielded independent structures for continental peacekeeping in Africa (the latter would raise the possibility of action independent of and potentially running against the interests of Western states). The result is the perpetuation of military dependence. The original goals of Recamp, for example, were to devolve the burden of French military intervention in Africa to French client states on the continent. Following Operation Licorne in Côte d'Ivoire in 2002—hitherto the largest French military operation in Africa since the end of the Cold War—Recamp was restructured as a multilateral, African prop to French arms rather than a substitute for them.[133] The fact that the United Nations has had to take over regional African-led operations in Burundi, Côte d'Ivoire and Liberia across the 2003–04 period is evidence enough that the 'ten years of Western capacity-building programs' prior to GPOI have failed to bear fruit.[134] More recently, although Africa consumed three quarters of global UN peacekeeping deployments in 2010, only a third of these came from African states, the other third coming from South Asia—a situation not dissimilar to that of the British empire when African colonial armies were buttressed by the 'imperial fire brigade' from the Raj.[135]

Conclusion

Congolese independence leader Patrice Lumumba, whose overthrow, kidnap and murder was aided and abetted by no less than UN Secretary-General Dag Hammarskjöld and his subordinates,[136] asked:

How can a beret coloured blue, erase ... the prejudices of conservative officers from Sweden, Canada or Britain? How does a blue armband vaccinate against the racism and paternalism of people whose only vision of Africa is lion hunting, slave markets and colonial conquest; people for whom the history of civilisation is built on the possession of colonies?[137]

If blue berets provide no defence against imperialism, nor does having the armies of formerly colonised countries operating as peacekeepers in other newly independent countries. Although Hammarskjöld feared that certain African and Asian peacekeepers among UN forces in 1960s Congo would sympathise with Lumumba—whom he feared and hated—he knew he could rely on Moroccans, Ethiopians and

Malays as a counterweight in the UN army, the loyalty of senior Indian officers such as Indar Jit Rikhye, as well as that caste of European 'conservative officers' identified by Lumumba.[138] Moroccan peacekeepers in particular are credited with a major role in helping to instigate and support the seizure of power by Colonel Joseph-Désiré Mobutu, who would subsequently rule Congo/Zaire for the next three decades as the archetypal anti-communist African strongman and US ally.[139]

Despite the Western-led power structures and networks in which the armed forces of the developing world are entangled, they are nonetheless more removed from metropolitan power than the directly recruited imperial soldiery of the past. The added political benefit of this is that Western states can not only, as we have seen, redistribute the costs of imperial security to those on the periphery, they also have the added benefit of declaiming political and strategic responsibility for the UN operations that they fund and direct. As UN legate Lakhdar Brahimi observed at the turn of the century, the 'vast majority of troops in the most dangerous UN-led operations are drawn from developing countries alone. To add insult to injury, the very nations which refuse to commit their own, will be the first to criticize the weakness of troops who actually risk their lives.'[140]

If this is an effective system of imperial security, it is not without its costs to global political development, notably in that it subverts the promise of liberal peace. One of the pillars of liberal peace theory is the notion that representative, accountable government will reduce the likelihood of war as it is the people themselves that will have to bear its costs; they will thus discipline their representatives to avoid war. With the new peacekeeping order, this key assumption of liberal peace theory is exploded and scattered across an imperial security system: in place of a self-governing, unitary liberal actor with an incentive to avoid war, we have a hub and spoke system of principals and agents, with the uppermost hierarchy of liberal states using their power and wealth to displace the costs of occupation, intervention, reconstruction, global deployment—the waging of the savage wars of the post-Cold War peace. That Western states are able to shift these costs onto weaker and poorer democratic states shows that the liberal democratic zone of peace, far from having transcended politics, is divided against itself—an internal division that is a redoubling of the wider inequalities between the liberal core and illiberal periphery of the international states system. By making military options less costly, perpetual peace is deferred and the basis for war recreated through liberal means.

What of the views among the peacekeepers? In the past, anti-imperialists lamented the system of colonial armies that supported imperialism: African-American writer W.E.B. Du Bois noted that 'the darker world is held in subjection to Europe by its own darker soldiers', while Motilal Nehru, father of Indian independence leader Jawaharlal Nehru, described the British Indian army as 'a mercenary army employed by foreigners to put down their own countrymen, and to keep them under foreign heels'.[141] UN peacekeeping is evidently seen to be legitimate in a way that imperialism is not. We can now turn to consider why the countries of the developing world help to construct this new system of imperial security.

5

ASKARIS AND SEPOYS OF
THE NEW WORLD ORDER

Introduction

The history of imperial armies and dependent militarism show that there is no *prima facie* reason to accept that multilateralism in international security scrubs out the possibility of imperialism. On the contrary, multilateral peacekeeping operations can be seen as a continuation of imperial practice, which enjoys all the more legitimacy today for relying so heavily on the armed forces of decolonised countries. Yet insofar as UN peacekeeping gives imperial power a greater global reach, it also means that metropolitan influence is that much more mediated and dependent on the willing cooperation of a diverse range of foreign states whose interests will not always align with that of metropolitan powers. If peacekeepers from the global South do indeed help to buttress a new imperialism, it is incumbent on us to explain why Southern states choose to do so. Unlike the askaris of old, peacekeepers from the global South are not directly recruited by the imperial powers in question. The participation of the askaris and sepoys of the new world order depends on the consent and active support of their own states and ruling elites. Explaining the rationale for this support is the purpose of this chapter.

One of the most common and least convincing accounts of this participation is the assumption of mercenarism: that developing countries are primarily motivated by monetary gain—an explanation as cynical as it is limited, understating the range of benefits that may accrue from peacekeeping. It is here that the discussion in this chapter begins. Criticising this explanatory model powers the discussion, shifting us from narrow financial interests to considering the wider range of benefits at both the state and sub-state level that arise from participation in peacekeeping. Given that the rising powers of Brazil, Russia, India and China all deploy their militaries abroad as peacekeepers, a brief survey of these countries' peacekeeping diplomacy is then offered. I argue that even if peacekeeping allows these states to fumble towards a greater imperial role for themselves, their political and strategic dependence on the United Nations clearly demonstrates the proximate limitations of their newfound power.

Given the variety of motivations involved in peacekeeping, what can be said of more general accounts of Southern countries' participation? The last third of this chapter deals with one such account: the democratic theory of peacekeeping contribution, which sees participation in peacekeeping as a function of democratic polities. As such, it can be thought of as a flanking theory of the wider democratic peace theory. Here peacekeeping is essentially seen as the means by which democratic states export their institutions and values and help to build a more peaceful international order. I argue that of the many gaps in this theory, the most troublesome is the explicit link it makes between democratic values and military adventurism abroad. In venerating peacekeepers as the crusaders of post-Cold War democracy, political scientists—not for the first time—betray a deep naïvety about the role of military institutions and martial values in spurring political modernisation and development. Sharing the teleological assumptions of democratic peace theory, democratic explanations of peacekeeping contribution are blind to the anti-democratic potential that results from according the military a central place in the life of the nation.

The myth of mercenarism

As we saw in the previous chapter, the participation of Southern states is seen as crucial to the legitimacy of international peacekeeping. Yet the motivations behind such states' participation are rarely considered. As Laura Neack observes in one of the first efforts to systematically study UN peacekeeping contribution, 'Expanded scope or not, the UN cannot function without the voluntary compliance and full and committed participation of its members.'[1]

When the motives of Southern states are considered, the patronising but typical assumption is that their motives are straightforwardly mercenary. Southern states continue to have large armies relative to the smaller, expensive and more technologically intensive armies of Northern states. As US-dollar remuneration is available at the flat monthly rate of $1,028 per individual peacekeeper for participating in UN peacekeeping (a rate established in 2002), and as developing countries have a comparative advantage in manpower, they can exploit this advantage by exporting peacekeepers.[2] The corollary of this assumption is that Southern peacekeepers can disrupt missions with their lack of commitment to mission objectives, thereby imperilling the promotion of liberal internationalism. In the words of one commentator, 'less wealthy countries are perhaps more prone to participate in peacekeeping operations as a way of subsidising the upkeep of their military forces (rather than for cosmopolitan objectives).'[3] *The Economist* concurs: 'Poor countries send by far the most men on UN missions. Asians predominate, with Bangladesh, Pakistan and India in the top three spots. They fund their armed forces by sending them abroad at the UN's expense.'[4] A senior Unprofor commander, French Brigadier-General Jean-Michel Loridon, in a thinly veiled attack on Southern peacekeepers sharply criticised those states contributing troops for financial gain, and these troops' participation in black market profiteering.[5] Stephen Kinloch-Pichat sums up this view of a particular type of peacekeeping:

The defects generally ascribed to ad hoc national contingents voluntarily contributed by Member States to the UN today are precisely those historically attributed to mercenary forces: foreign allegiance, corruption, and unwillingness to take the necessary risks when it comes to fighting.[6]

Southern peacekeepers bear the brunt of criticisms for failing to live up to the selfless ethics demanded by liberal internationalism. Underlying such criticisms is the assumption that elevation in the moral hierarchy of liberal internationalism corresponds with wealth: the rich countries are altruistic and the poor essentially venal, despite the poor demonstrating their commitment to liberal internationalism in supplying the legions of peace.

Certainly it is true that that there are plenty of opportunities for individual peacekeepers from Southern states to significantly boost their earning power through participation in such missions. A BBC report recounts the experience of South Asian peacekeepers:

'It's every Nepalese policeman or soldier's dream to serve with a UN peace-keeping mission'. he says. 'There's so much competition but also rampant favouritism and nepotism.' ... The salary of $85 a day helped him to build a house in Kathmandu and send his children to decent schools. '[Without having served with the UN mission in Haiti] I don't think my savings at home would have helped that much—whatever we make here is hardly enough to survive'. he adds. According to Fazle Elahi Akhbar peacekeeping is a 'much-desired assignment' in Bangladesh too ...[7]

The Economist estimates that half of Bangladesh's annual earnings of $300 million derived from UN peacekeeping go to its soldiers. The article gives the example of a military intelligence officer as a 'representative peacekeeper' from that country:

His one-year UN tour in Côte d'Ivoire netted him savings of 2m taka ($30,000), enough to buy two plots of land back home. He describes the tour as his pension fund, a reward for 15 years of service. 'Without a UN mission, majors like me, we're not that solvent' he says. To improve their chances of landing a UN gig, Bangladeshi recruits are most likely to opt for an infantry, sapper or signals unit. Or for the navy, which can offer a few places on a hydrography course in Bordeaux. The opportunity to learn French is precious, since this is the language of many UN missions.[8]

It is estimated that every Bangladeshi soldier gets a chance to serve on a UN operation once in his career and an officer perhaps twice.[9] Some reports suggested that the 2009 mutiny of the Bangladesh Rifles, a 67,000-strong paramilitary border security force, was partly due to the fact that the earning opportunities available to regular army units through participation in UN peacekeeping was closed to the border force.[10]

Yet if such accounts help consolidate the impression of mercenarism they do not take us very far by way of directly explaining national participation in peacekeeping. While peacekeeping may have extensive support among national officer corps and even rank and file troops within particular countries, the people that actually deploy on such missions are not necessarily the ones that make the decision to deploy. This requires a process of political decision-making at the state level. While military support for such missions may factor in and even sway this process of national decision-making, there is no reason to assume that it is the only factor that comes into play.

There are certainly opportunities to earn significant quantities of foreign exchange at the national level. Given the flat UN reimbursement rate there are clear opportunities for countries to tap the United Nations in order to subsidise military expenditure at the national level. National treasuries can also profit by pocketing the difference between receiving dollar reimbursements while paying their peacekeepers in national currency according to national pay scales. It is estimated that Uruguay has subsidised a large part of its military budget by deploying between a quarter and a third of its forces on peacekeeping operations at any one time.[11] The Uruguayan government estimated that it earned $129 million from peacekeeping from 1992 to 2003, with annual earnings in 2002 surpassing the value of the country's beef exports, making peacekeepers Uruguay's most profitable export industry.[12]

It is worth recalling however that the truly fat profits in peacekeeping lie not in supplying personnel but in provisioning logistics, providing peacekeeping training and in the post-conflict reconstruction market. According to the Indian Lieutenant-General Satish Nambiar, commander of Unprofor from 1992 to 1993, it is Western entrepreneurs and companies who have a stranglehold on contracts for provisions and services for peacekeeping, as they are the ones who are most familiar with UN procedures and have the necessary contacts in the Secretariat.[13] The roughly $500 million disbursed through the Global Peace Operations Initiative since 2004 for US-sponsored peacekeeping training around the world, for example, is captured by US private security contractors.[14]

The data on peacekeeping earnings is inevitably crude due both to the quality of the data and the fact that such data is often confidential or disguised. Despite difficulties such as these, the data in table 5.1 broadly correspond to the results of Ugurhan Berkok and Binyam Solomon's econometric modelling of peacekeeper earnings.[15] But while Berkok and Solomon estimate the quantity of dollars earned through contributing personnel to peacekeeping, they do not contextualise these earnings in relation to national rates of military expenditure. Thus when they estimate that India earned at least $35 million from peacekeeping in 2008, this is put into perspective in table 5.1. Against the backdrop of India's vast military expenditure, that such earnings would be sufficient to motivate India's participation in peacekeeping becomes dubious.

The data depicted in table 5.1 is likely to somewhat underestimate earnings from peacekeeping, but notwithstanding these limitations

Table 5.1: T10 estimated peacekeeping earnings as % of annual military expenditure 2002–11

	2002	2003	2004	2005		2006	2007	2008	2009	2010	2011
Bangladesh	11	11	10	10	Pakistan	2	2	2	2	2	2
Pakistan	2	2	2	2	Bangladesh	14	13	13	12	10	10
India	>1	>1	>1	>1	India	>1	>1	>1	>1	>1	>1
Nigeria	2	4	4	4	Nigeria	6	5	4	4	3	3
Jordan	5	4	4	4	Nepal	24	24	24	22	21	22
Ghana	53	43	43	43	Jordan	5	4	3	3	3	3
Nepal	19	17	14	13	Egypt	1	1	1	1	1	1
Kenya	5	5	5	5	Ghana	53	35	40	40	40	46
Uruguay	3	3	4	4	Rwanda	47	51	48	46	46	46
South Africa	>1	>1	>1	>1	Uruguay	5	5	5	4	4	4

Source: Stockholm Institute for Peace Research; United Nations Department of Peacekeeping Operations. Percentages rounded to nearest whole number. Figures on military expenditure calculated in constant 2010 USD.

they do give us some sense of the movement of national earnings from peacekeeping across time. They also allow us to compare how earnings from peacekeeping compare in relative terms across the T10 contributing nations over the last decade.[16] The waxing and waning of earnings from peacekeeping reflects both the growth in operational deployments across the last five years until their peak at the end of the last decade, and the growth or decline in the military expenditure of the country in question.

We see that the picture is highly varied, ranging from tiny proportions of reimbursement in the cases of India and South Africa to peacekeeping reimbursement constituting half a country's military spending in the cases of Ghana and Rwanda. Some of the largest peacekeeping contributor nations in the world thus 'earn' comparatively little from peacekeeping, undermining claims that participation in peacekeeping is simply a means of subsidising large armed forces. This alone is sufficient to call into question claims that reimbursement constitutes a single, uniform explanation of countries' participation in UN peacekeeping.[17] Even Bangladesh, often cited as an example of peacekeeping mercenarism, earns comparatively less from UN peacekeeping than smaller peacekeeping contributors such as Ghana and Nepal. Moreover, according to Rashed Uz Zaman and Niloy R. Biswas, Bangladeshi earnings through peacekeeping constitute a relatively small proportion of total remittances (only 8 per cent between 2009–11).[18]

Thus there are good reasons to be suspicious of mercenary style explanations at the national level too. For UN reimbursement to be 'profitable', we would have to ask whether the pecuniary benefit of peacekeeping exceeded the opportunity cost of deploying peacekeepers. This might involve not only financial considerations of military budgets, but also the potential political and strategic risks of running down a country's military defences and undermining its ability to respond rapidly to natural disasters or domestic unrest—both of which tend to be more prominent roles for the military in developing countries.[19]

It is worth recalling that due to standard rotation cycles in military planning the absolute number of a country's forces contributed to a peacekeeping mission at any particular point in time will understate the actual burden of that deployment. Military planners usually operate on the basis that any unit deployed for six months to a year will require one equivalent-sized unit preparing to replace the deployed unit, and another unit in post-deployment recuperation. In short, any deployment has to be multiplied at least by a factor of three to better approximate the burden carried by the contributing nation's armed forces.[20]

Participation in peacekeeping may also require expensive prior investments: Uruguay had to purchase second-hand tanks, frigates, minesweepers and river patrol vessels from NATO and former Warsaw Pact countries in order to meet UN eligibility criteria for deployment in operations since the turn of the century (their suppliers reportedly delivered some of the stock straight to Uruguayan peacekeepers in Congo without even shipping it to Uruguay first).[21] Some states explicitly structure their peacekeeping contributions so as to ensure that any potential mercenarism is contained. Pakistan, for example, aims to limit its soldiers to only one 'external assignment' in their career in order to maintain the national integrity and focus of the armed forces.[22]

When all is said and done, an explanation for peacekeeping participation that effectively takes the United Nations as a treasure chest for plundering by poor countries must be suspect. Not only is the world organisation notorious for its empty coffers—usually as a result of expenses incurred through UN peacekeeping—but even when the cash is available, reimbursement may be frequently and severely delayed for any number of bureaucratic reasons.[23] Richard Thornhaugh characterised participation in peacekeeping as a 'financial bungee jump, often undertaken in blind faith that timely appropriations will be forthcoming'.[24] Data collected by the Global Policy Forum show that the United Nations was owed between $1 billion and nearly $3 billion by its member states for peacekeeping expenditures incurred across 2001–5. In 2005, for example, while peacekeeping arrears had reached nearly $3 billion, expenditures had reached over $4.5 billion. It is safe to assume that it would be the large troop- and police-contributing countries that would be those to have suffered most from the effects of these arrears.[25] For reasons such as these, in global terms it makes more sense to regard UN reimbursement for peacekeeping participation as a 'palliative' that helps offset the costs of peacekeeping contribution and provides a basis on which other goals can be pursued through participation in peacekeeping, rather than a direct cause or straightforward explanation of participation.[26]

National interests in peacekeeping contribution

If money is the cynic's explanation for poor countries' peacekeeping efforts, it is hardly a rigorous explanation even by the cynic's standards. Simply focusing on the cash earned through peacekeeping contribution underestimates the range of other possible benefits that might accrue to armed forces in peacekeeping. Indeed, peacekeeping reimbursement could be better seen as a 'bridge' across which countries can cross to access these other benefits. These might be not only material benefits (such as retention of UN-provided equipment used on missions) but also intangible (such as on-the-job training, exposure to war zones, experience of international deployment, the opportunity to learn from interacting with other countries' armed forces, and the possibility of enhancing coordination and inter-operability with the armed forces of allied states). Participation in UN missions can serve as a spur to military modernisation, and factor into national efforts to reform, restructure and upgrade a country's armed forces to meet international standards.

Deborah Norden describes the range of non-financial perks of peacekeeping in relation to Argentinean peacekeepers deployed to the former Yugoslavia:

On the personal level, participants enjoy unique opportunities to travel, as well as important monetary incentives. The opportunity to 'see the world', a familiar refrain of US military recruiters, has historically not been available to young Argentines in the relatively smaller, and more locally focused military of … a … peripheral country […] Army officers and NCOs stationed in Croatia take advantage of these opportunities to travel through Europe, often taking wives along as well. … Perks such as these seem to dominate many military discussions of peacekeeping's benefits.[27]

If nothing else, perks such as these build up broad constituencies for liberal internationalist policies. Sotomayor estimates that 40 per cent of Argentina's officer corps were exposed to peacekeeping over the 1992–2000 period, while half of all Uruguayan officers and a third of that country's non-commissioned officers have experience of peacekeeping abroad.[28] As a result of force rotation cycles, a sustained period of peacekeeping contribution even at fairly modest levels to a few UN operations could expose a large proportion of a country's military forces to peacekeeping throughout the world.

One Indian officer deployed as a peacekeeper in Congo suggests that overseas posting through peacekeeping is also a matter of status within armies: 'It's such a big army [the Indian army], you always take pride in an overseas posting. The unit has to prove itself as one of the best to get sent here.'[29] Nor should ideological commitment to liberal internationalist goals be assumed to be beyond the ken of soldiers in developing countries. Indian Major-General Indar Jit Rikhye, whom we encountered in the last chapter, described his commitment to peacekeeping in the following words:

I am motivated by Gandhi's philosophy for nonviolent social change, Nehru's doctrine of *Pench Sheel* [non-alignment] and Hammarskjöld's advocacy of the role of international organizations in promoting peaceful settlement of disputes and strengthening international systems for the maintenance of peace and security.[30]

If UN peacekeeping during the Cold War was overshadowed by the high drama of arms races, superpower summitry and East-West stand-offs, then the UN rise to prominence after the end of the Cold War gave participation in UN peacekeeping correspondingly more prestige. This was particularly true for foreign ministries watching the rapid changes as the Cold War order crumbled, and for the diplomatic missions exposed to UN debates in New York.

Of the range of new and old Southern contributors to UN peace-keeping in the post-Cold War era, a range of motivations came into play. For some states, contribution to peacekeeping helps to boost their international reputation and legitimacy, with peacekeepers even serving a generic ambassadorial function as representatives of their nation abroad.[31] Of South Asian contributors to peacekeeping, *The Economist* observes:

Bangladeshis delight in donning the blue helmet [due to its] prestige. They want to be known for something other than bad politics and natural disasters. Pakistan's army is similarly keen to be known for more than its habit of starting wars and launching coups. India, on a grander scale, likes to see global policing as a sign of its emergence as a world power ...[32]

Bangladeshi Prime Minister Sheikh Hasina thanked Bangladeshi peacekeepers for boosting their country's national image in a speech on the International Day of UN Peacekeepers in 2011.[33] According to the first president of Fiji, Sir Penaia Ganilau, participation in peacekeeping 'greatly enhanced our national image internationally'.[34] Argentina hoped that participation in peacekeeping would help restore the country's international reputation after its occupation of the Malvinas/Falklands, and its subsequent defeat by Britain.[35]

Questions of prestige have been particularly important for new governing regimes, which have often deployed their forces on UN peace-keeping missions as a means of consolidating their reintegration into the international community. Eastern European states enhanced their involvement in UN peacekeeping at the same time as the European Union and NATO began their eastwards expansion after the Cold War. Croatia, Serbia, Argentina and South Africa are all examples of states that have participated in UN peacekeeping as a means of bolstering their international credentials following the demise of internationally ostracised or authoritarian regimes. For other states, peacekeeping represents a shift away from the Cold War-era diplomacy of power blocs and bilateral alliances to involvement in a more integrated international community: Pakistan is one such example of a state that restructured its military posture in the aftermath of the Cold War, as we saw in the last chapter.[36]

Prestige in turn can be harnessed to the strategic advancement of national interest. Peacekeeping can be used to boost a state's standing in seeking one of the elective, rotating seats on the Security Council. Guatemala, for example, contributed to the high-profile Unifil II mission in Lebanon in 2006 as a means of building support for its election to the Council.[37] Contribution to peacekeeping may be a collaborative means of contributing to regional, and thereby, national security. This is the pattern of much peacekeeping in Africa, but it is also visible in the contributions of East and South East Asian nations to the UN missions in Cambodia and East Timor.

Equally, dynamics of competition for regional leadership may spur contribution to peacekeeping as a means by which countries promote their international standing over that of regional rivals. Nigeria, for example, has sought to establish itself at the core of a 'Pax Nigeriana', while competitive patterns of peacekeeping contribution are visible in the struggles for regional leadership between Chile, Argentina and Brazil. Similarly, Indo-Pakistani rivalry led to large contributions by these countries to the UN missions to Somalia, and continues to propel Pakistani contributions to peacekeeping.[38] Peacekeeping can also be used to send economic as well as political signals: interviews with the representatives of African missions to the UN emphasised participation in UN peacekeeping as an attempt to signal Africa's emergence from conflict, with the hope of enhancing Africa's appeal to foreign investors.[39]

Trevor Findlay suggests that some states contribute to peacekeeping both as a form of repayment for being previous beneficiaries of peacekeeping and by way of setting up 'a beacon'[40] in the expectation that they might require such international protection in future. Examples given here include the Baltic states, Egypt, El Salvador, Jordan, Namibia, Nepal and Zimbabwe.[41] Participation in peacekeeping can also be used as a means of building up international credit towards settlements of long-standing conflicts. Morocco contributes significantly to UN peacekeeping while also being one of the protagonists in a long-standing conflict over the Western Sahara, which the United Nations has thus far failed to resolve, while Pakistan uses its peacekeeping credentials to project its concerns over the disputed territory of Kashmir at the UN Security Council.[42]

In virtually all interviews conducted by the author, representatives of Southern contributing states stressed their desire for greater involvement by Northern states in UN peacekeeping, stressing in particular the need for contribution of specialised units, technological and logistical support and equipment beyond the reach of poorer states. Perhaps this too helps to motivate Southern participation in UN peacekeeping, as such claims may offer the possibility of exerting moral pressure on Northern states. Participation in peacekeeping missions gives peacekeeper contributing states the possibility of engaging with the Security Council and the richer powers.[43] On a more basic level, contributing states gain the right to attend and participate in diplomatic meetings concerning the peacekeeping mission, to sit on various committees and commissions associated with peacekeeping, as well as gaining access to political and operational intelligence associated with the deployment. Nor should the benefits of informal 'corridor diplomacy' resulting from these scenarios be underestimated, for example, the opportunities to cultivate personal relations between senior officials and put across national concerns to countries that might otherwise be difficult to access.[44] Pakistan reportedly extracted a promise from the US that sanctions against Islamabad would be lifted if Pakistan committed their forces to the Unamsil mission in Sierra Leone in 2000.[45]

Sub-State motivations for participation in peacekeeping

Beyond the external benefits of contributing to peacekeeping, there may be putative internal benefits, too. One defence advisor stationed with the permanent mission to the United Nations of a significant African contributor to peacekeeping claimed that one boon of peacekeeping participation was its 'educational aspect': African troops deployed to crisis zones abroad had the opportunity to witness at first hand the dangers of national disintegration, intercommunal strife and taking up arms against the state.[46] Several representatives of contributing states mentioned the importance of their contribution to UN operations in Bosnia-Herzegovina, and how deployment to a European conflict gave them a new perspective on their role in world affairs.[47] A defence advisor from a South Asian mission claimed that his army's experience in counter-insurgency helped in peacekeeping operations, and the experience of peacekeeping operations helped in domestic counter-insurgency.[48] Another South Asian official posted in New York noted how the post-conflict reconstruction activities of peacekeepers complemented the domestic role of the military in fostering national cohesion, and that peacekeepers could function in lieu of diplomats in cultivating international relations with other states.[49]

The impact of participating in peacekeeping on contributing states, and particularly on a country's armed forces, has been worked up into an explanation of peacekeeping participation known as 'diversionary peace'. The theory was developed in relation to the peacekeeping activism of Latin American states after the end of the Cold War. The theory is based on the link between the growth in these states' peacekeeping participation and the fading away of the military dictatorships on the continent.[50]

In the case of Guatemala, for example, the Guatemalan government exploited the deployment of its forces to the Minustah mission in Haiti as a means of gaining greater control over the military decision making process as well as effecting a broader transformation of the military apparatus inherited by the civilian regime from decades of military rule and bloody civil war.[51] The theory has also been used in relation to Egypt during the early 1990's phase of political reform (according to Angela Kane) and Bangladesh during the same post-Cold War period.[52] According to C.R. Abrar, the international standing that the Bangladeshi army has achieved through peacekeeping should discourage any praetorian instincts: 'they would think twice or thrice before engaging in such adventurism. So in that respect I think it [peacekeeping] would have a deterring effect.'[53]

According to Kenkel, in the case of Brazil it is precisely the experience of that country's armed forces under military dictatorship that allows them to act effectively in the era of post-Brahimi peacekeeping:

… extensive experience in implementing infrastructure, development and health programmes, as well as internal missions to quell crime and political unrest. Disadvantageous though this may be for democratic control in the country, in the context of peace operations it presents an important comparative advantage over Northern troops [who have less of this experience].[54]

As suggested in the last chapter, patterns of military rule in developing countries reflect in turn the development of post-colonial informal empire and military dependence. With many newly independent countries inheriting a state apparatus with hypertrophied security functions but little else, one predictable result was the descent into military and one-party rule. As described by Victor Kiernan, 'when countries emerging from imperial rule resumed, or began for the first time, an independent existence, among their many predicaments might be a soldiery trained by the foreigner, dragon's teeth with a harvest of wars and army coups.'[55] How far peacekeeping has helped to recreate patterns of military dependence we shall examine below.

Diversionary peace

According to the theory of diversionary peace, for those states that have suffered military incursions into domestic politics in the past peacekeeping can become a way of neutralising such threats. The mechanisms of this process may be multiple. On the one hand, entangling peacekeepers abroad helps preserve civilian rule by deflecting the military from meddling in domestic politics. Another, perhaps complementary process is that peacekeeping deployments may help to 'socialise' military forces into the values of international liberalism, such as respect for international law and human rights, as well as articulating clearly differentiated civil-military relations and establishing an ethos of military professionalism. The theory thus effectively sees peacekeeping as a form of externalised nation-building, whereby military engagement abroad helps consolidate processes of domestic democratisation, political development and modernisation.

It would seem on the face of it to be a welcome development that armies that once waged wars on their own people are now deployed abroad monitoring elections, helping to stabilise conflict and assisting countries in their political transitions—a self-reinforcing cycle of political development across countries. Yet the pathways down which diversionary peace is supposed to work—pathways rarely disentangled in the literature—may have a special importance. As the example of Brazil suggests, participation in peacekeeping may simply extend rather than nullify or sublimate an army's traditional roles—roles that may involve domestic counter-insurgency and authoritarian practices. Thus, whatever the pathways down which diversionary peace is supposed to travel, it is not clear that peacekeeping abroad dissolves the role of the military as a caste with distinctive, praetorian functions in specific countries.

Whether the military is guarding the honour of the nation against domestic subversion and foreign conspiracy or helping to spread liberal internationalism abroad, in both cases the survival of specific political values is made critically dependent on the behaviour of the military. If diversionary peace is indeed an accurate account of peace-keeping participation for states undergoing democratic transition, it is also an explanation that has troubling implications for the character and vitality of the democracy being consolidated in the contributor state. For this explanation implies that democracy exists at the sufferance of the military.

No less implicit in the theory of diversionary peace is the claim that peacekeeping has served to launder the reputation of armed forces whose major role for the last few decades has been repressing their compatriots rather than defending their nation's borders. That peacekeeping helps to restore the prestige and credibility of the military in former military dictatorships raises the question as to whether peacekeeping may sow a new generation of dragon's teeth. Indeed, a harvest of praetorian peacekeepers may have already sprouted, as we shall see when we examine the democratic peace theory of contribution later in this chapter. Before that, we shall briefly review the motivations and peacekeeping behaviour of the four rising, so-called BRIC powers of Brazil, Russia, India and China.

The peacekeeping of the rising powers

It is a staple of classical thought in the discipline of International Relations that aspiring great powers are 'revisionist'. On the model of the Axis powers Italy, Germany and Japan in the inter-war period, it is assumed that rising powers will be compelled to reshape the international order to better fit their own needs and interests, as the international status quo will necessarily reflect the interests of the dominant powers of the day.[56] If that status quo is cemented by an international security organisation with universalistic claims, as with the League of Nations in the inter-war period, then the offensive mounted by revisionist powers will lead to the flouting of international law and the eventual evisceration of international organisation. The current international order is said to have four such powers (re)-emerging—the BRIC states. What does the behaviour of these countries in the field of peacekeeping tell us about the emergence of a new multipolar world? What follows is neither a comprehensive nor exhaustive account of these countries' changing fortunes in recent years; only a consideration necessarily brief in the context of this book, of the role that peacekeeping has played and may continue to play in these countries' rise.

That the term 'BRICs' was coined by Goldman Sachs chief economist Jim O'Neill presents the 'rare example of an investment bank's research paper provoking a geopolitical change'.[57] But it also draws attention to the artificiality of the category, at least in political terms.[58] While it is true enough that these countries' rapid economic growth in the years prior to the global crash of 2008 corresponded with a growth in international clout and political self-confidence, their respective geopolitical positions remain highly divergent.[59] For our purposes in this discussion, the most striking discrepancy among the BRIC powers is the unevenness of their integration into international security institutions. While Russia and China are already veto holders on the UN Security Council, India and Brazil are seeking this status through pushing for expansion of the Council.

Certainly all four powers have repeatedly voiced their suspicion of various Western military adventures across the post-Cold War period.[60] Yet viewed from the perspective of (UN) peacekeeping, not only are these powers not undermining international organisation, they are actively engaged in supporting it. Each has revised its peacekeeping policy in line with its re-emergence as great powers. Each has become a significant peacekeeping contributor: India and China on the global stage, while Brazil and Russia are both important regional peacekeepers. Let us examine them in turn.

Brazil

Of the four states, Brazil is the smallest peacekeeping power, and like Russia more of a regional peacekeeper than a global one. Of Brazil's participation in peacekeeping, its heavy involvement in the Minustah operation in Haiti since 2004 is the most important, although Brasília also took command of the naval component of Unifil II, with a Brazilian frigate patrolling the eastern Mediterranean since 2010. Brazil effectively assumed the leadership of the UN operation in Haiti following the ouster of the democratically elected President Jean-Bertrand Aristide by Franco-American forces in 2004. The year following the establishment of the UN force on the island, *The Economist* placed UN peacekeeping at the core of a transformed Brazilian foreign policy: 'This move marks a new departure. Brazil has long been a gentle and introverted giant, content to be a bystander on the world stage. Now that is changing.'[61] This was also the year that Brazil joined the 'Group of Four' alongside Germany, Japan and India in their campaign for permanent seats on the Security Council. Peacekeeping helped to consolidate Brazil's claim to a permanent seat on an expanded Council.

To the extent that Brazil was 'gentle' in its external relations from 1943 to 2004, its introversion was correspondingly brutal, seeing a military dictatorship across the 1964–85 period. Yet today it is not a military regime but the formerly repressed Partido dos Trabalhadores (Workers' Party, PT)—arguably the largest and most successful working class party in the world today[62]—that has spearheaded Brazil's newfound geopolitical assertiveness and neo-interventionist bent across three consecutive administrations from 2003. The year after PT leader Luiz Inácio 'Lula' da Silva assumed presidential power, Brazilian troops replaced Franco-US marines and led Argentinean, Chilean and Uruguayan peacekeepers in 'propping up a regime of ex-generals and former death-squad leaders in Port-au-Prince', in the words of Brazilian sociologist Emir Sader.[63]

As the UN operation got under way in Haiti, US Secretary of State Condoleezza Rice reportedly told UN Secretary-General Kofi Annan that 'If there were not 6,000 Brazilians in Haiti, there would be 6,000 American marines.'[64] There were never that many Brazilian troops in Haiti, but doubtless both Kofi and Lula got the point. In 2005, Brazil established a national centre for peacekeeping training, which trained 15,000 troops by 2010, over 2,000 of whom have served in Haiti.[65] This peacekeeping activism represents a departure in Brazilian diplomacy, Brasília having hitherto been opposed to the expansion of UN peacekeeping mandates as well as exhibiting scepticism towards intervention in the internal affairs of states.[66] Brazilian diplomats have thus engaged in all sorts of contortions in order to reconcile their country's enhanced interventionism with its supposed support for states' rights to non-interference by outside powers.[67]

Yet the supposedly introverted Brazilian giant has a longer history with both the United Nations and peacekeeping. Brazil was one of the first Latin American states to join the Second World War in 1943 following the Declaration of the United Nations the previous year, sending over 25,000 Brazilian troops and a fighter squadron to the UN campaign in Italy.[68] Brazil was also a not insignificant contributor to UN peacekeeping missions during the Cold War, although these being on a smaller scale, they did not consume great numbers of Brazilian forces. In total, Brazil has sent 27,000 peacekeepers to thirty-three missions since 1956.[69]

Brazil extended a patina of regional legitimacy for the US invasion of the Dominican Republic in 1965, providing both nominal leadership and 1,130 troops for the regional peacekeeping mission established by the Organization of American States on the island following the US incursion.[70] Brazil also played an important role in post-Cold War peacekeeping missions deployed to lusophone states, identifying Portugal's former colonies in Africa as ideal markets for Brazil's military industry. In Angola in particular Brazil used UN peacekeeping to deepen economic relations already established during the Cold War.[71] In addition to consolidating its foreign markets, peacekeeping allows Brazil to assert its regional leadership. In the words of Monica Herz, 'Brazil's elite thinks peacekeeping is part of the price you have to pay to be among the nations who make the rules.'[72]

The genuflection to the US seen in Haiti and the echoes of the Dominican invasion have stirred some misgivings over Brazil's foreign policy within the Workers' Party and the broader Latin American left. Resistance within the legislature has emanated from rural and *favela* parliamentarians who would prefer the government to solve problems closer to home. In April 2004, intellectuals, trade unionists and politicians from left-wing parties, including the PT, signed a letter protesting Brazil's military involvement in Haiti, while in 2007 the Brazilian Bar Association sent a mission to Haiti to investigate allegations of abuse by Brazilian forces. The Brazilian Landless Workers' Movement (Movimento dos Trabalhadores Sem Terra), in cooperation with the International Peasant Movement (Via Campesina), has a team of around ten members working in Haiti since January 2009, while various other civil society groups within South America have also organised solidarity missions to Haiti involving activists from Brazil and Argentina.[73]

A document released at a PT party congress in 2010 under the title of 'The Great Transformation' criticised the 'arrogant and predatory' attitude of Brazilian corporations abroad and voiced fears that Brazil's regional support would shrivel if neighbouring states came to fear the establishment of a 'Brazilian sub-imperialism'.[74] Such fears reflect a venerable tradition of critique of Brazil's international role by the Brazilian left, the term 'sub-imperialism' itself coined by Brazilian Marxist Ruy Mauro Marini, expressing a more critical variant of the idea of 'middle power' used in International Relations theorising.[75] Formulated in the 1960s based on observing the 'Prussianism' of the newly established dictatorship and its eagerness to support US military intervention in the Caribbean, Marini sought to root Brazil's 'dual role of surrogate and antagonist to US initiatives' in the country's intermediate position in the structure of the global economy.[76]

Applying the theory Daniel Zirker finds that sub-imperialist patterns of Brazilian foreign policy persisted across the democratic transition of the mid-1980s, with further evidence that they extend into the period of PT rule. On the one hand, municipal governments of the Workers' Party hosted the World Social Forum in 2001–2. This was at the same time that its government signed compacts with the international financial institutions and endorsed their economic orthodoxy.[77] While on the one hand Brazil played the loyal lieutenant's role in the 2004 invasion of Haiti, on the other it has championed calls for a multilateral order to restrain US unilateralism and sought to spearhead the developing nations of the G20 in their attempts to chisel away at Northern dominance of global markets and global economic governance. Brazil has also tangled with the US over nuclear policy, both in regards to its own state-run nuclear industry and over Iran's attempt to secure nuclear energy, as well as seeking to dissolve the rigidities of the global intellectual property regime in the interests of its public health system.[78]

Whether Brazil's economic transformation will be sufficient to enable it to break out of the subordinate sub-imperialist role outlined by Mauro into a fully-fledged imperial power (or developed state for that matter) is an open question; the aggressive expansion of Brazilian corporations abroad may confirm Mauro's theses on the internal structural weaknesses of the Brazilian economy more than they refute them.[79] As regards Brazil's new peacekeeping, two more immediate conclusions can be drawn. First, Brazil's compliance in Haiti has not helped it secure reform of the UN Security Council, let alone a permanent seat on an expanded council. To be sure, Brazil has secured two two-year stints (2004–5 and 2010–11) as an elected, non-permanent member of the Council across the tenure of the Haiti mission. But Brazil had a long record of successful election to the Council before leading Minustah.

Second, peacekeeping abroad has strengthened the position of the military in the Brazilian state, allowing the armed forces to stave off greater civilian control over 'defence' policy as well as extending the military's 'policy leverage over Brazil's international agenda'.[80] Running against claims that peacekeeping has helped to accommodate the military to democratic and civilian rule,[81] the Haitian operation has reinforced the traditional role of the Brazilian military as a counter-insurgent force, deployed to suppress revolts in remote regions of the Amazon and to mount militarised policing of the urban centres of Rio de Janeiro and São Paulo—expeditions frequently accompanied by reports of brutality, excessive force, exacerbating violence and extra-judicial killings (a pattern repeated as we saw in chapter two in Port-au-Prince).[82] We shall return to issues of praetorian peacekeeping presently.

Russia

While Brazil has burnished its reputation for pliant cooperation with the US in the field of peacekeeping, Russia by contrast has tended to arouse international suspicion for its peacekeeping endeavours in Europe and Central Asia—suspicions that reflect long-standing patterns of rivalry and suspicion between Moscow and Western states, and the fact that Russia has for the most part mounted these peacekeeping expeditions beyond the reach of Western influence. During the Cold War, Soviet Russia exempted itself from UN peacekeeping missions as a permanent member of the Security Council in order to maintain the neutrality of the institution, as did the other permanent members. Poland acted as the representative of the Eastern bloc on Cold War UN missions. Having lost most of its client states from the Cold War, Russian peacekeeping missions have often been taken as the paragon of cynical peacekeeping. Borrowing the authority of the international community in a bid to maintain its hegemony over the former Soviet imperium, Moscow made a mockery of peacekeeping with large, heavily militarised expeditions in neighbouring states overwhelmingly led by Russian troops.[83]

Yet it is not clear that the contrast between cynical, self-interested Russian peacekeeping and cosmopolitan, altruistic UN/NATO missions can be drawn so sharply. Given that Soviet Russia's global military footprint (once exceeded only by that of the US) disappeared virtually overnight with the end of the Cold War, Russian peacekeeping today should be seen less as a new round of expansionism and more as a rear guard attempt to maintain some lingering Russian influence abroad, particularly in areas where Russian influence is contested, such as Moldova and the southern Caucasus. Nor is Russia's peacekeeping activism exceptional among the great powers. As we saw in the previous chapter, the permanent members of the Security Council have taken to UN peacekeeping and routinely invoke UN authority for military escapades in their respective spheres of influence.

Unlike the cosmopolitan peacekeepers, Russia has not used peacekeeping to push into new spheres of influence as France, Britain and the US did with the UN/NATO missions in the former Yugoslavia. As Isabelle Facon observes, the militarisation and growth in size of UN peacekeeping operations after 2000 meant that UN peacekeeping came to more closely resemble the model of peacekeeping that Russia developed in its former Soviet 'backyard'.[84] From this point of view, the Russians have not derogated from the principles of UN peacekeeping so much as pioneered its twenty-first century model of 'best practice': more troops, more weapons, more permissive rules of engagement and large concentrations of militarily-robust 'lead nations'.

Given all this, it is not difficult to identify other reasons for the suspicions evoked by Russian peacekeeping. By contrast with the other three rising powers and indeed non-Western states in general, Russia stands out for having its own strategic lift capability and 'organic sustainability'—that is, capacity to maintain troops outside its borders for a protracted period. These capacities are otherwise a privilege only enjoyed by a handful of Western military powers (the US, Britain and France) in the former case, and only by the US in the latter.[85] Russia is also encircled by a belt of ex-Soviet states over whom it can continue to exercise political influence, again a privilege mostly enjoyed by former colonial states and the US. It has sought to translate this political influence into a militarily integrated regional grouping—the Collective Security Treaty Organisation—with its own rapid deployment and peacekeeping forces.[86] Contrast this with China and India whose proximate neighbours include proportionally more rivals and strategic competitors. Even in its 'near abroad', Moscow faces Western encroachment, with competition over Ukraine, NATO peacekeeping in Afghanistan and Western-backed attempts by neighbouring states to wrench themselves out of the Moscow orbit.[87] For reasons such as these, it would seem to be Russian audacity in sharing some of the privileges of Western power more than the operational doctrine and procedures of Russian peacekeeping that has so exercised Western observers since the end of the Cold War.[88]

India

Of the four emergent powers, India's peacekeeping commitments have been the most enduring, if arguably not the most consistent. Since the inception of UN peacekeeping, India has contributed over 160,000 troops to UN missions, sustaining 154 casualties and awarding over forty officers and soldiers commendations and decorations as a result of participation in UN missions.[89] Unlike Russia, India is a fully-fledged global peacekeeper, its soldiers having served in large numbers under the UN banner around the world.

In Indian elite circles there is a clear sense of peacekeeping being tied to India's international identity, with the country constitutionally mandated to foster and strengthen international peace and security. This is evinced in Indian peacekeeping practice.[90] Unlike the more common six month deployment pattern for Western troops, traditionally Indian peacekeepers serve with the United Nations for a year.[91] Since 1994, India has been committed to UN stand-by arrangements for rapid deployment of its peacekeepers, despite concerns that this would divert troops from domestic roles.[92] Yet despite this peacekeeping tradition, there are clear signs that India's policies on peacekeeping may have changed across these periods, and that it may be changing again to better fit with the Indian elite's new global ambitions. India's contribution to peacekeeping can be divided into three periods: the Cold War, a post-Cold War period running to the end of the first decade of the twenty-first century (1989–2009), and more recently an ambiguous interregnum, as we shall see below.

Corresponding with India's peacekeeping tradition is a middle power philosophy expressed by Major-General Rikhye as a fusion of 'Gandhi's philosophy for nonviolent social change, Nehru's doctrine of *Pench Sheel* (non-alignment) and Hammarskjöld's advocacy …'[93] Such sentiments are echoed by other elite figures. Discussing Indian participation in the UN mission in Sierra Leone at the turn of the century, the news magazine *India Today* argued that peacekeeping reflected the Indian army's role as a nation-building force as much as a military one: 'a "developmental army", not just an aggressive unit but a force equipped for larger community service ... This is what makes valiant ... India's ambassadors to the land they hope to calm'.[94] Major-General V.K. Shrivastava claimed that peacekeeping, 'besides being noble, signifies a nation's destiny and capacity to play its part in world affairs'.[95] Another former peacekeeper, Major-General Dipankar Banerjee opined that in contrast to her more cynical neighbours India's 'participation in UN peace operations is a particularly honourable activity'.[96] For the late Lieutenant-General Dewan Prem Chand, through participation in peacekeeping India contributes to the 'greatest organisation the world ever had, the world has ever known'.[97]

Reverence for peacekeeping is not restricted to senior officers. In self-professed 'Dworkin-esque' mode comparing Indian achievements to those of US liberal democracy, historian Ramachandra Guha rhapsodises that, among many other achievements (and in pointed if implicit contrast to US expansionism):

We [Indians] have demonstrated that nationalism can be made consistent with internationalism; without ever having waged war on another nation, we have contributed to peacekeeping efforts in other countries and continents, and lent moral and material support to such causes as the anti-apartheid movement in South Africa ...[98]

As with military officers and intellectuals, so too with the Indian bureaucracy. The strength of India's commitment to UN peacekeeping has been attributed to the strength of an urbane mandarinate that shapes foreign policy in line with its commitment to Third World non-alignment and classical anti-colonialism.[99] Modelled on the British White Hall system, bureaucratic control of foreign policy is institutionally dispersed and insulated from popular and political pressure.[100] Indian diplomats have been eloquent critics of the shift in the focus of UN activity from traditional Third World concerns with development to Western concerns with security. India's former ambassador to the United Nations, Nirupam Sen, described the 'Security Council's legislative decisions and those on the use of force ... as an arbitrary and alien power: this is an alienation not of the individual or class but of countries.'[101]

India was suspicious of the new generation of post-Cold War missions: India's circumspect involvement in Unprofor, for example, was seen as extending support to a Non-Aligned ally undergoing the trauma of partition that had also afflicted independent India.[102] Similarly, India supported the UN nation-building mission in Somalia with reservations, mollified in this case because there was no internationally recognised government in Mogadishu to either accept or reject UN intervention.

Concerns over meddling in the internal affairs of small states and militarised peacekeeping had receded by the turn of the century, as India began contributing heavily to muscular peacekeeping operations in Sierra Leone and of course Congo. This coincided with a newfound assertiveness in Indian foreign policy off the back not only of economic growth, technological advance and boosted defence spending, but also India's successful nuclear tests of May 1998, conducted in defiance of the US and subsequent sanctions.[103] The right-wing government of the National Democratic Alliance that assumed power in 1998 sought to strike a new path for Indian foreign policy by mounting an open bid for a strategic alliance with the US.

Since then, the Indian political class has shown itself eager to affect the Wilsonian chauvinism hitherto monopolised by Western states, increasingly asserting India's democratic tradition as a mark of her intrinsic superiority on the international stage, with an inevitable reference to the diversity of the Indian nation adding some local exoticism to the traditional Wilsonian recipe. In a speech in 2005, Indian Prime Minister (and former UN functionary) Manmohan Singh proclaimed 'Liberal democracy is the natural order of political organization in today's world' in the same breath as affirming the 'idea of India' as 'an inclusive, open, multi-cultural, multi-ethnic, multi-lingual society'.[104] Such posturing was warmly welcomed in Washington by the Bush administration, which was pursuing its own agenda of 'Wilsonianism on steroids' and was looking to cultivate India as a counterweight to growing Chinese power.[105]

Although India was opposed to the invasion of Iraq, that there was even a debate about supporting the occupation was striking enough.[106] New Delhi has been less ambivalent about the US war in the Hindu Kush, enthusiastically propping up the US-backed Hamid Karzai regime in Kabul as part of New Delhi's longstanding rivalry with Pakistan. New Delhi also actively collaborated with Washington in the international effort to manage Nepal's democratic revolution in 2006. The government of the National Democratic Alliance and a new generation of 'realists' steering Indian foreign policy retreated from India's traditional cultivation of the Non-Aligned Movement, focusing instead around securing a permanent seat on an expanded Security Council. The coincidence of a reduced interest in UN affairs as a whole, combined with the single-minded focus on Council expansion, likely lay behind the resurgence of Indian peacekeeping at the turn of the century.[107]

Although Congress won the two general elections since the end of the rightist government in 2004, that India's approach to peacekeeping is now more instrumental is evident in the shock decision by New Delhi to withdraw its Mi-35 gunships and some medium-lift helicopters from the UN mission in eastern Congo in summer 2011. This move ended 'years of Indian air superiority in the war-racked nation ... depriving the United Nations of its most vital military asset' in a region with few transport and communication links.[108] Although India had poor relations with the Kinshasa government, the withdrawal of the gunships was also seen as a fit of pique expressing New Delhi's frustration at being persistently lumped together with 'poor countries', in the words of Ramesh Thakur—states 'with bloated and antiquated defence forces desperate to earn foreign money'—a status unbecoming a rising great power.[109]

Indian officials claimed the helicopters were needed back in India to fight a powerful Maoist insurgency there. In announcing the move, India's deputy ambassador to the world organisation cited 'capacity restraints'—the Indian Air Force at the time being in possession of sixteen Mi-35 attack helicopters in addition to those deployed in Congo, as well as fifty multirole helicopters (that is, doubling up for both attack and transport functions) with another 150 on order, as well as 106 transport helicopters (the Indian army had another 200 multirole helicopters of its own).[110] India's willingness to jeopardise a mission so critically dependent on Indian airpower showed a newfound determination to extract greater benefits from UN peacekeeping.

International prestige notwithstanding, the geopolitical and institutional rewards of India's patient peacekeeping activism have thus far been slight. Although US President Barack Obama credited Indian peacekeeping when he extended US support for India's bid for a permanent seat on the Council in November 2010, the 2004–5 diplomatic offensive for Council expansion had long since withered. An attempt to revive the campaign from the General Assembly in early 2011 also failed,[111] though India had managed to secure two senior posts for her security officials in the Department of Peacekeeping Operations across the previous decade. Minor advances in the international bureaucracy had not prised open the Western grip on these institutions (on which, see the discussion in the next chapter).[112] When India demanded a 57 per cent increase in the UN monthly reimbursement rate per peace-keeper to off-set spiralling costs, the UN countered with a 7 per cent raise; India mooted the possibility of scaling back its peacekeeping con-tribution.[113] India failed to capture the post of Secretary-General when the rotation of the post reverted back to Asia in 2006, the highly regarded, longtime Indian UN functionary Shashi Tharoor losing out to the South Korean Ban Ki-moon.

India did secure election to one of the non-permanent Council seats across 2010–11 (only the second time since 1991–2, having been roundly beaten the last time they contested an elected seat in 1998).[114] India's performance at an open debate on peacekeeping held under the Indian presidency of the Council in August 2011 was regarded as underwhelming, the traditional stalwart of peacekeeping even being upstaged by a tiny newcomer to the field—Guatemala.[115] The debate itself was overshadowed by a terror attack on the UN headquarters in Abuja. Being the summer vacation month for diplomats, little could be expected to happen in New York in any case and the Indian presidency was further constrained by the need to steer between on the one hand the attempts of the permanent three to channel the mass uprisings in the Arab world against the regime in Syria, and on the other, Sino-Rus-sian attempts to shield their Ba'athist allies in Damascus.

Support for multilateralism has often been taken as a major axis of left-right division in Indian foreign policy.[116] On the one hand the right supports greater geopolitical assertiveness and strategic rapprochement with the US, and on the other the liberal-left supports India's tradi-tional Third Worldist and internationalist commitments routed through the parliamentary diplomacy of the United Nations. Two Indian thinkers, Parag Khanna and C. Raja Mohan, have enthusiasti-cally bid for a sub-imperial role for India, arguing for a 'neo-Curzo-nian foreign policy' modeled on the expansive role within the wider British Empire that Lord George Curzon, archetypal exponent of the 'Great Game' of imperial power play, carried out when he was the viceroy in Calcutta in the early twentieth century.[117] Raja Mohan in particular expressed hope that US President Obama would have the foresight to see in India 'a partner who is ready to work with the United States in constituting a post-colonial Raj that can bear the burdens of ordering the Eastern Hemisphere in the 21st century'. Raja Mohan vests his hope in Henry Kissinger's vision for India as sharing 'some of the security burdens now borne by the United States in the region between Aden and Malacca'.[118]

Pitched at the conservative wing of the US foreign policy establishment, it is not clear that these bold visions of future national glory as the regional sub-lieutenant for US empire would find the favour of the Indian public at large. Siddharth Varadarajan, editor of *The Hindu*, condemned the strategic alliance with the US as the outsourcing of hegemony.[119] But more to the point as regards peacekeeping is the fact that the contrast between the policies of multilateral non-alignment and a Delhi-Washington axis is over-drawn, a distortion in perspective that results from seeing through the prism of UN internationalism darkly. Even in its most impeccably multilateral moments, India has long been acting as a post-colonial Raj, its loyal *jawans* making up an obliging fire brigade ready to act virtually anywhere around the world, this time in the service of UN imperial multilateralism rather than the British Empire. As we have already seen in the last chapter, Indian peacekeepers have returned to many of the same theatres in which their forebears fought, and in not dissimilar roles.

When a young Indian republic sent its peacekeepers to Congo in 1960, it was conceived as a gesture of Third World solidarity in order to help the newly independent Congolese shake off separatism sponsored by Belgian mining interests and white supremacists in neighbouring Rhodesia. It was the Indian Brigade Group and light bombers of the Indian Air Force stationed with the UN army in Congo that played the decisive military role in cohering the fractious state. It was primarily Indian forces that destroyed a separatist army thousands strong bolstered by European mercenaries and led by Belgian officers.[120] In their contribution to the military defeat of Belgian neo-colonialism, Indian peacekeepers helped make Congo safe for US corporations and the rule of Mobutu Sese-Seko, the epitome of the Cold War-era anti-communist African dictator.[121] Under the command of Secretary-General Dag Hammarskjöld, Indian forces became pawns of the inter-imperialist rivalries of the Cold War, rather than defenders of Third World emancipation. More recently, much like Brazil obliged Washington in Haiti while the US was embroiled in the Middle East, so too New Delhi obliged in Africa, providing nearly 3,000 peacekeepers to support the expansion of peacekeeping under the US aegis in this period (on US support for UN peacekeeping in this period, see the next chapter).[122]

The commitment to self-determination of which India is seen to be such a staunch defender should be seen as expressing New Delhi's fears of international intervention in Kashmir and potential foreign sponsorship of domestic secessionist movements, at least as much as it is a principled stance. Indeed, India has not hesitated to launch military interventions as domineering as any other regional power in its sphere of interest: in East Pakistan/Bangladesh (1971), the Maldives (1988), as well as exercising coercive diplomacy in response to the Nepalese revolution of 2006 and in relation to the final phase of the civil war in Sri Lanka in 2009. New Delhi has shown itself to be as willing as any permanent member of the Security Council to justify its military escapades as 'peacekeeping'—notably when the 'Indian Peacekeeping Force' of over 50,000 troops intervened in Sri Lanka from 1987–89. If UN peacekeeping helps to burnish India's international reputation, it is not the only motivation: the former commander of Unprofor Lieutenant-Colonel Satish Nambiar elaborates a range of strategic and security rationales to help explain Indian participation in peacekeeping.[123]

For all the changes in Indian foreign policy over the last century, Indian commitment to peacekeeping evinces a strong strain of continuity. The mantle of Wilsonian chauvinism that the Indian elite is now trimming down for its use shares with classical Nehruvian foreign policy the same sense of Indian grandeur and exceptionalism, the same ambitions to great power status, and the same ruthlessness and hypocritical obliviousness when it comes to the use of force both within India and its near abroad. Peacekeeping is compatible with both visions, and given the British Indian army's history of imperial warfare, the fact that Indian peacekeeping has been so easily pressed into the service of the US imperium should not come as a surprise.

Thus instead of seeing Indian peacekeeping in the context of the pious conceits of India's foreign policy elite, Indian peacekeeping should be seen against the backdrop of India's rivalry with Pakistan, of India being the largest weapons importer in the world,[124] of India undergoing a vast and sweeping programme of military modernisation (expected to reach $80 billion of spending by 2015), of Indian attempts to militarily deter and contain Chinese power, and of schemes aimed at levering India higher on the world stage.[125] Inasmuch as Indian peacekeeping is not merely strategic but also ideational, India's tradition of UN peacekeeping can be seen as an integral part of what Perry Anderson calls the 'Indian Ideology', a remarkably self-satisfied creed asserting India's superiority through its cultural and political exceptionalism. Indeed, one would struggle to find another country where elite nationalism so readily blends pacifistic smugness with pride in martial prowess.[126]

Indian peacekeeping should also be seen against the backdrop established by Indian diplomats themselves when they withdrew their helicopter gunships from Congo—that is, of counter-insurgency back in India.[127] If the Indian army's external success in peacekeeping reflects its internal role in domestic nation-building, it should be remembered that this role has involved counter-insurgency campaigns that could match those of any Latin American state for brutality, even if India has never endured a military dictatorship at the national level. Overseeing the longest military occupation in modern history in Kashmir, Indian forces have also been repeatedly deployed to suppress internal dissent under the 1958 Armed Forces (Special Powers) Act. Described by Anderson as 'perhaps the most sanguinary single piece of repressive legislation in the annals of liberal democracy', the Act has enabled the military to repeatedly impose de facto mini-military dictatorships over swathes of Indian territory since being legislated.[128] Indian peacekeepers in the eastern Congo explicitly compare their efforts there to fighting back in India 'where we usually operate. The hills look a bit like this.' As one Indian peacekeeper told a visiting journalist, 'We've had a lot of experience with low-level insurgencies.'[129]

China

If the Russians were taken by Western analysts as the exemplar of cynical peacekeeping in the 1990s, Moscow nonetheless never had the temerity to encroach on a Western sphere of influence. This is the original sin of Chinese peacekeeping. One of the vectors of China's growing influence abroad are its UN peacekeepers, with China oscillating between being the largest and second-largest peacekeeper among the permanent five members of the Security Council. As it is in Africa where most peacekeeping missions deploy today, peacekeeping has become one of the means by which China has enhanced its political penetration of the continent.

Hitherto assumed to be the exclusive domain of Western charity since the end of the Cold War, the simple fact that China's economic growth has expanded the range of options available to African states is often taken by many Western commentators as an aggressive subversion of Western interests in the continent. Worse, by allowing African governments to extricate themselves from the many restraints painstakingly woven by Western governments, aid agencies, international institutions and civil society organisations, that African states enjoy more autonomy is seen to be damaging to African interests.

China's entry into UN peacekeeping displays the most dramatic change from the last century to the present period. Of the four emergent powers, China has the most complex history with the United Nations. Despite not being one of the 'enemy nations' referred to in the UN Charter, China is one of the few states that have fought UN forces in a conventional war lasting more than two years. China's intervention in the Korean War cost the lives of 900,000 of her soldiers, while UN forces by contrast endured 53,472 casualties of whom about 40,000 lost their lives.[130] China intervened in the Korean War in 1951 to repulse the armies of UN Command that were menacing the Chinese border, and then rolled back the UN conquest of northern Korea until they fought the United Nations to a standstill and eventual armistice along the 38th parallel in 1953. Mao Zedong's government branded the United Nations the 'imperialists' international police division' and the UN flag flies to this day on the armistice line that cleaves the Korean peninsula.[131] At the time, it was the rump nationalist Republic of China—restricted to the island of Formosa/Taiwan after the revolution of 1948—that enjoyed the Chinese veto on the Security Council (the People's Republic assumed China's seat only in 1971).

In 1965 the *People's Daily* denounced the Security Council for having 'degenerated into a dirty international political stock exchange in the grip of a few big powers; the sovereignty of other nations, particularly that of small ones, is often bought and sold there by them like shares'.[132] China has since had fewer qualms about engaging in such 'trading'. In 1999 China punished Macedonia for establishing diplomatic relations with Taiwan, when it vetoed the extension of the long-established Unpredep mission in the Balkan country.[133] In 2004, China deployed a battalion of peacekeepers to Liberia when that country switched diplomatic recognition from Taipei to Beijing.[134] China only permitted the Minugua operation in Guatemala to go ahead after the

Guatemalan government dropped its support for a General Assembly vote on allowing Taiwan entry to the world body.[135] In 1965, the *Peking Review* condemned the establishment of the Special Committee for Peacekeeping Operations as a means for 'converting the United Nations into a US-controlled headquarters of international gendarmes to suppress and stamp out the revolutionary struggles of the world's people'.[136] Today, Chinese gendarmes are helping, if not quite to stamp out revolutionary struggles, at least to disseminate 'best practice' policing: China sent police units to the Untaet mission in East Timor and riot police to Haiti.[137]

China's active participation in peacekeeping indicates just how far Chinese attitudes towards the world organisation have changed. In 1960 the Chinese state denounced the UN peacekeeping force in Congo: 'when the patriots in Congo defended their independence and fought bravely with the Belgium [sic] aggressors, the so-called "UN army" with "blue helmet" under flag of "maintaining the order", actually intervened and invaded Congo.'[138] Today, China has troops deployed with the Monusco operation in Congo. What is more, Chinese peacekeepers have been involved in a number of missions that have prioritised elections as part of their peacebuilding mandates—notably in Congo, Côte d'Ivoire, Liberia, Timor-Leste, Rwanda. China gave its political support on the Security Council to the Untac mission in Cambodia, which rescinded Cambodian self-rule in favour of UN governance for the duration of the operation, as well as contributing military observers and engineers to the mission.[139] It would seem that while the Chinese government still jealously defends its own sovereign integrity, the sovereignty of other nations, particularly small ones, is less important.

China's support for these expansive peacebuilding initiatives, extending even to support for post-conflict democratisation programmes, would seem to be at odds with China's reputation as a staunch defender of the prerogatives of the sovereign state as opposed to the claims of the international community. Along with Russia, in International Relations literature China is often portrayed as a bastion of the traditional rights of sovereignty (so-called 'Westphalian' sovereignty), her rulers' attachment to sovereign rights a mark of their authoritarian determination to monopolise concentrated state power. But to overplay the distinction between China's alleged Westphalian outlook and Beijing's support for post-Westphalian peacebuilding would be a mistake. It requires little reflection to realise that the doctrines of peacebuilding and state-building—with their emphases on intricately coordinated and tightly controlled processes of political and institutional reform designed to constrain and disperse popular energies—are eminently compatible with the philosophy of government that prevails in Beijing.

If peacekeeping today is not incompatible with Beijing's views on governance, this does not account for why China participates in peacekeeping. In the words of the Chinese Ambassador to the United Nations, Wang Guangya, 'We want to play our role.'[140] What accounts for this desire? A senior strategist of the People's Liberation Army, Major-General Peng Guangqian, claimed that 'Unlike some Western countries, China does not take advantage of peacekeeping to push national interests in other countries.'[141] But whatever the rhetoric, China's interests in Africa are expressed clearly enough in Chinese foreign policy statements describing the continent as a 'vast expanse of land' encompassing 'rich natural resources and huge potential for development'. China's Vice Commerce Minister Fu Ziying admitted that 'China's presence in Africa is ... more and more market-driven.'[142]

The pattern of Chinese African investments overlaps with Chinese peacekeeping. In Liberia, investment 'chased after peacekeeping deployments'. In 2007 China cancelled $10 billion of Liberian debt, waived import duties on Liberian goods and offered loans, and in 2009 a Chinese firm signed a $2.6 billion contract to restart iron ore mining in the war-ravaged country. In Sudan, the pattern was reversed—Chinese peacekeepers deployed there, helping to mollify a government deeply suspicious of Western states battering at their gates over the conflict in Darfur. The peacekeepers arrived long after strong trade relations that saw Sudan sell 60 per cent of its oil to China. Chinese peacekeeping and Chinese investments can also be presented as different prongs of international conflict resolution efforts: the Beijing government encourages its enterprises in post-conflict societies to employ former combatants.[143] With Chinese economic growth has come the expansion of the Chinese diaspora of traders and entrepreneurs, and peacekeeping is one means by which the Chinese government can claim to be protecting the interests of its citizens and ethnic compatriots everywhere, including Africa.[144] Nor is Chinese peacekeeping restricted to Africa: China's prime minister declared that the deployment of a Chinese battalion to the enlarged UN mission in Lebanon in 2006 was intended to raise China's profile in the Middle East and to build stronger ties with the European Union, whose core states were leading the mission there.[145]

These deployments help to extend the modernisation of a vast military machine undergoing rapid technological and professional advancement. In particular, peacekeeping allows for the accumulation of operational experience in conflict zones around the world, an opportunity that has otherwise been denied the People's Liberation Army since its invasion of Vietnam in 1979. Peacekeeping also provides a rationale for regional and bilateral military manoeuvres and training exercises with other nations. The 'Peace Mission 2005' exercises for instance, conducted with Russia and some Central Asian states, was one of the largest joint military exercises China has ever carried out on a multilateral basis.[146] Arguably most important of all, Chinese peacekeeping allows Beijing to manage its international image and to sooth international fears concerning China's precipitous ascent. Peacekeeping is an integral part of China's grand strategy of building a 'harmonious world' in which to ensconce its own 'peaceful development', in the rhetoric of China's public diplomacy.[147]

Yet while China has not been above using peacekeeping as a way of expanding its international reach, this policy has nonetheless been pursued in a way that is as compliant as to be timid in the face of Western leadership. In keeping with the inveterate caution and conservatism of China's ruling bureaucratic caste, Chinese peacekeeping deployments exhibit a muted militarism. Blue berets rather than blue helmets, China's peacekeepers are comprised of police units, medics, engineers and logistics experts whose focus is on development and reconstruction rather than fighting. China's peacekeepers have built up a reputation for their efficiency in drilling fresh water wells, upgrading transportation and communication infrastructure ravaged by war and dispensing medical services to local populations.[148] China's peacekeepers stand as a global rebuke to the paratroopers, marines and drone bombing raids associated with Western military interventions and peacekeeping.

While China has forcefully exercised the privileges of permanent membership of the Security Council over the question of Taiwan, and notwithstanding Chinese truculence over intervention in the Syrian civil war, at most other times Beijing has obligingly accommodated Western demands when it comes to questions of war and peace. China retroactively granted the imprimatur of UN legitimacy to the 1999 NATO war against Yugoslavia that saw the bombing of the Chinese embassy in Belgrade—this despite the fact that the Chinese government themselves maintain that the bombing of their embassy had been deliberate. China prevailed on Sudan to accept a UN/African Union peace-keeping force in the face of Western hostility to the government in Khartoum in 2006, and Beijing refused to veto the NATO bombing campaign against Libya in 2011.

Nor does the emphasis on developmentalism in China's peacekeeping operations mean that Chinese policy is any freer of imperial overtones. As Shogo Suzuki's study of Chinese modernisation theory suggests, China's views on such questions are no less hierarchical and ethnocentric in conception than classical Western modernisation theory. Except that in this case China is emplaced at the core of the theory as a paternal guide for developing countries, the latter reduced to a passive source of raw materials for Chinese industry and grateful recipients of Chinese wisdom on economic progress.[149] In any case the Chinese government hardly needs to mint its own imperial doctrines of international intervention. While China's Communist Party cannot credibly lay claim to the democratic chauvinism that is drawing India's political classes, the tenets of liberal internationalism provide more than sufficient ideological resources to serve Chinese interests. With the public discourse of international affairs thick with the language of responsibilities—global responsibilities, economic responsibilities, humanitarian responsibilities, environmental responsibilities, responsibilities to the poor—a Chinese ruling elite claiming to be leading a 'responsible state' will not struggle to find many ready-made ideas in the discourse of liberal internationalism amenable to their paternalistic vision of domestic and international governance.[150]

Peacekeeping of the rising powers: reformist revisionism?

According to Barry Buzan, there are three types of revisionist states: orthodox, reformist and revolutionary. Perhaps the middle label describes China best, in that such a state accepts 'some of the institutions of international society for a mixture of calculated and instrumental reasons. But it resists, and wants to reform, others, and possibly also wants to change its status.'[151] To the extent that UN peacekeeping has enabled the rising powers to deploy their forces internationally, it signals their global ambition in both military and political terms. Doubtless their military forces derive some benefit from participating in expeditionary field missions and exposure to a variety of operational theatres and conflicts, accumulating the kind of diverse experience abroad that would otherwise be restricted to the members of the Atlantic alliance.

But whatever benefits they gain also expose their military dependence. With the partial exception of Russia, the three remaining BRIC states are all dependent on the logistical infrastructure contracted by the United Nations to ferry their forces around the world. None have the strategic clout or political self-confidence to mount independent military operations outside their regional spheres of influence, let alone operations on the scale of the Atlantic alliance. Russia only deploys at a distance from its borders in tandem with NATO or UN forces. Even in the Balkans, historically a Russian sphere of influence, Russian forces deployed there are adjuncts of NATO armies. In Bosnia, the Russians even demurred to NATO command. Its nuclear arsenal notwithstanding, Russia's regional peacekeeping deployments in post-Soviet territory underscore the fact that it is a regional military power rather than a global one.

The BRIC powers possess no institutions with which to translate military power into hegemony, yoke the strength of smaller allies or alternatively to pool their power on the scale available to the Atlantic alliance.[152] If the United Nations provides the stage on which these rising powers can test out geopolitical expansion and perhaps fumble towards an imperial role through peacekeeping, their reliance on that stage shows the proximate limits of their nascent power.

If the BRIC states will struggle to disentangle themselves from the United Nations, could they perhaps change peacekeeping from within, usurping the Western domination over the purposes and practices of peacekeeping—a stranglehold that has remained intact at least since the Brahimi report of 2000? The evidence suggests otherwise. The more that the BRIC states have sought to oppose Western interventionism, the more energetically have they thrown themselves into UN peacekeeping as a multilateral alternative to Western militarism—even while control over peacekeeping remains firmly in the grasp of Western states. In so doing the BRIC states have thereby helped to push peacekeeping beyond barriers that were once seen as insurmountable for their foreign policies and as impenetrable with regards to the sovereign rights of the states being intervened in.

In stressing its 'peaceful rise', China has supported reconstructive peacebuilding operations—operations whose intrusiveness is however contingent on the normalisation of larger, Chapter VII operations. The Brazilian military, initially hostile to peacekeeping in Haiti, has since developed an appetite for intervention, seeing Port-au-Prince as a laboratory for militarised policing back in the Brazilian *favelas*, and developing a new role abroad since the demise of the Communist foe.[153] Brazilian diplomats, struggling to reconcile Brazil's interventionism with her classical anti-interventionist stance, have sought to cover the mailed fist of Brazilian peacekeeping in Haiti with the velvet glove of an expansive vision of social reconstruction—paradoxically extending the scope of intervention even as they try to downplay its repressive features.[154] For all its musty Third Worldism, India has compliantly fed the UN's growing appetite for manpower, finding its massive, well-equipped army in high demand for the new era of militarised peace-building operations. Russia, meanwhile, renounced any principled opposition to interventionism when Moscow established protectorates over Abkhazia and South Ossetia following its intervention in Georgia in 2008, belatedly replicating the logic of UN/NATO interventions in the Balkans.

On this historic pattern, we have no reason to expect the BRIC states will affect any changes to the modus operandi of peacekeeping—or if they do, it will be because such changes reflect a new agenda in Western capitals. As long as peacekeeping remains the most tolerated form of military intervention, it will be seen as a refuge from Western interventionism and therefore will remain intact. What this further reminds us is that none of these states is able to mount a political challenge on the scale of either the Axis alliance or the USSR to international liberalism, and none has the ideological resources to justify military interventions independent of UN sanction—whether that be spreading democracy, halting human rights abuses or waging a war on terror unlimited in time and space. The scoffing that greeted Russia's claims to justify its invasion and subsequent dismemberment of Georgia in 2008 in terms of the humanitarian responsibility to protect, make clear that hypocrisy is another monopoly to be exclusively enjoyed by the Atlantic alliance.[155]

Theories of peacekeeping contribution I: peacekeeping contribution and democratic peace

The preceding discussion of national motivations behind peacekeeping participation provides a survey that is both contingent and context specific, varying from state to state. Is it possible theoretically to unify explanations of peacekeeping contribution at a more general level? One influential contender for this role is the democratic peace theory of contribution—a theory that can be seen as a buttress to the larger theory of democratic peace.

In its most elemental form the theory of democratic peace holds that liberal democratic states will not go to war with each other, creating a zone of peace that can transcend the pressures toward conflict built into the anarchic structure of the international system. At the same time, the very factors that explain peace between democratic states—reciprocal normative affirmation between democracies—suggest that democratic states will seek to spread liberal democracy by using force against non-democratic states. The larger the zone of peace, the more that violence is eliminated from international order. When linked to theories of peacekeeping contribution, it is assumed that peacekeeping is an instrument for disseminating democratic peace: we expect the peacekeepers to be democrats, and the targets of peacekeeping to be despotic or, at the very least, unstable states whose disorder threatens liberal and democratic values.

In the words of Andreas Andersson, 'although essentially shaped by *idealpolitik*, the democratic community may use UN operations in an instrumental fashion in an attempt to improve long-term global peace and security by targeting non-democratic states.'[156] Or, in other words, spreading democratic peace. Andersson finds that the more consolidated the democracy, the more likely it is to participate in peacekeeping. Subsequent studies have built on Andersson's findings. Richard Perkins and Eric Neumayer go further, identifying 'a similar positive relationship between domestic respect for human rights and countries' involvement in multilateral' peacekeeping operations.[157] James H. Lebovic is keen to point out that it is 'important to recognize that *democracy* here is not synonymous with *NATO* ... or *Western Europe* [but also includes] the democracies of India, Argentina, Uruguay, Australia, Thailand, Brazil, the Philippines, Botswana, New Zealand, Japan, Chile, and Colombia ...'[158]

The strength of the theory is that it knits together a number of distinct trends in international politics since the end of the Cold War: the dramatic rise in peacekeeping, the equally dramatic diversification of contributors to peacekeeping, the spread of democratic governments to regions historically mired in authoritarianism, as well as linking internal political structures to external foreign policy behaviour, and to membership of international regimes and institutions. Democratic peace can also help explain the distinctive character of contemporary peacekeeping operations, insofar as they claim to go beyond purely strategic or narrowly self-interested military intervention.

Andersson for example points out that peacekeepers have been allowed to penetrate traditional great power spheres of influence, with UN missions to Cold War Afghanistan, the post-Soviet Caucasus and Central Asia, the US's 'backyard' in Central America, as well as to British and French former colonies in Africa.[159] Moreover, according to Andersson the emphasis on social transformation through peacekeeping is incompatible with military intervention understood to be purely self-interested.[160] Reasons such as these lead Andersson to suggest that narrowly self-interested explanations of peacekeeping participation do not work.

But when these insights are presented as the findings of large-scale quantitative studies associating democracy and peacekeeping contribution, it is difficult to ignore the sheer banality of the conclusion that many democracies are also peacekeeper states. For these studies all end up recapitulating what is already known, that the number of democracies and the numbers of peacekeeping contributors have both grown since the end of the Cold War. Little effort is made to disentangle the effect of internal political structures from that of bandwaggoning behaviour, as the new peacekeeping nations flocked to the banner of Western-led liberal internationalism after the fall of the USSR.

To be sure, some of these studies were conducted too soon after the end of the Cold War or else simply omit the first decade of the twenty-first century, which would enable them to capture the growth of Southern peacekeeping contribution in recent years.[161] But even disregarding questions of periodisation, by virtue of the fact that these studies tend to lump together democracies of all sorts, more subtle changes in the patterns of contribution do not have to be reckoned with (notably the evacuation of a small group of democracies—the Western states—from UN peacekeeping). Thus the distinctions *within* this group of states—inequalities of power and wealth *between* democracies—are blurred. Importantly, by more or less tacitly accepting a 'community of democracies' as the agent in the theory, the ways in which contribution patterns are articulated through international institutions is ignored. This failure to build institutions into the

explanatory models means that the range of possible interests accruing from peacekeeping participation—interests that are tied up with
specific institutions—are ignored. 'Interests' are restricted to those
associated with sending troops to a specific country, rather than being
associated with a specific type of intervention.

More broadly, the explanatory model shares the weaknesses of democratic peace theory. The shift to values-driven and transformative policies as a distinctive attribute of post-Cold War military intervention is
left unexplained in the terms of the theory. After all, the very size of the
non-liberal zone of world politics, and the many problems associated
with democratic transition, can in many instances be plausibly attributed to the prior behaviour of Western states in their support for
authoritarian regimes during the Cold War and earlier. Yet while all
these studies begin with the premise that the structure of international
order was transformed by the end of the Cold War, no effort is made
to account for this transformation in the terms of the theory itself. This
oversight cannot but undermine the claim that peacekeeping contribution is primarily a function of the internal constitution of states.

There are some putative exceptions to this trend of democratic
peacekeeping participation that are worth considering in some detail.
Specifically, there are instances where precisely the opposite effect has
been registered, with participation in peacekeeping leading towards
military incursions into domestic politics or outright dictatorship.
Strikingly, this includes some of the largest and longest serving peacekeeping contributors and is an effect that is also visible in regional
peacekeeping operations (though here I will focus on the former). I
argue in this section that these counter-examples are not isolated
exceptions, but rather expose the weakness of democratic peace as an
explanation for peacekeeping contribution.

Peacekeeping Praetorianism

Andrew Scobell argues that the Fijian military's experience of UN
peacekeeping directly led to the series of coups in that country in the
late 1980s, partly a result of the fact that it was peacekeeping which
established the military as a socially weighty and politically-significant
institution in Fijian society (the Fijian military expanded ten-fold
between independence in 1970 and the first putsch of 1987).[162] When
a Labour government came to power in an ethnically fractious Fiji in

1986, it was seen to threaten the national status of the military when newly elected prime minister Timoci Bavadra branded the army a 'band of mercenaries' and promised to forge a new neutralist foreign policy. These pronouncements stoked the fears of a military whose peacekeeping missions in Lebanon made them at once suspicious of Third Worldist ideology and fearful of a descent into violent intercommunal conflict.[163] Lebanon's war has since ended. Fiji's peacekeepers have in the meantime made a habit of praetorianism at home: *The Economist* suggested peacekeeping contributed to the coup d'état of December 2006.[164] Jean-Marie Guéhenno, UN Under-Secretary-General for Peacekeeping at the time, protested the *Economist* article in a letter to the newspaper, defending the reputation of the institution and arguing that 'Service with UN peacekeeping also provides other benefits, exposing militaries to key international norms and standards including human rights training, gender parity, support for elections and a doctrine of civilian control.'[165] But Fiji is not the only example of peacekeeping praetorianism.

Eboe Hutchful's 1997 study of civil-military relations in Ghana attributes to UN peacekeeping a role in that country's recurring bouts of military rule. Specifically, Hutchful suggests that it was the exposure gained to the command cultures of other armies through participation in peacekeeping operations that emboldened Jerry Rawlings and other junior officers to usurp the upper echelons of the military that sat on Ghana's Supreme Military Council, which was overthrown by Rawlings in 1979.[166] Hutchful also argues that the revenues earned through participation in UN peacekeeping allowed the military to weather a period of declining defence budgets, while also allowing the Rawlings regime to polish its international image.[167] More recently, it was reported that Major Salou Djibou, who fronted the 2012 coup in Niger, is also an ex-peacekeeper.[168]

Another national stalwart of peacekeeping on the other side of the world, Pakistan, has exported its peacekeepers across periods of both military and civilian government during the Cold War and post-Cold War eras. It was under the rule of General Pervez Musharraf across 1999–2008 that Pakistani peacekeeping reached its apogee: Pakistan has been ensconced among the top five largest peacekeeping contributors since the turn of the century. Indeed Musharraf is himself a former peacekeeper, having deployed with Pakistani forces in both Somalia and the Balkans. The general, whose torturers would become so important to the waging of the war on terror only a few years after he seized power in 1999, relates in his memoirs how deeply he was moved by the suffering of Bosnia's children during the Balkan wars:

There were some dozen or two dozen children [outside the camp], begging and crying for food. My eyes swelled with tears, both at their misery and at my helplessness to assist them. I gave them all the dollars I was carrying and turned back, full of pain and sorrow.[169]

It is in Bangladesh that the link between peacekeeping and praetorianism has assumed more chilling proportions. In this country, on whose troops the United Nations has relied so heavily to spread democracy to war-torn lands, the world organisation helped instigate a coup d'état in January 2007 using the institutional links it had forged with the Bangladeshi military from 1988 onwards, leading to the suspension of fifteen years of democratic rule in the country.[170]

The United Nations and the 2007 coup d'état

Although only a quarter as long as the rule of Lieutenant-General Hussein Mohammad Ershad (1982–1990), the most recent bout of dictatorship in Bangladesh succeeded in cramming the usual depredations of military rule into a brief two years. With a caretaker government headed by an aging ex-World Bank executive, the military established an elaborate system of censorship, banned criticism of the new regime, stripped back civil liberties, placed the judiciary under military supervision, brutally suppressed a campus uprising, launched a wave of mass arrests that would eventually net up to half a million people, many of whom were held without charge, presided over summary trials and torture, handed down lengthy prison sentences to hundreds of politicians, all at the same time as 'Bangladesh's dreaded intelligence agency became the foremost decision-maker'.[171] Economic policy followed in a similar groove, with bountiful spending on prestige projects, military agencies awarded lucrative economic privileges and international development banks availing themselves of the suspension of democracy aggressively to extend economic liberalisation, prevailing on the military regime to reduce government subsidies and sell off public enterprises. Together these policies helped boost inflation to a rate not seen for decades.[172]

Western states enthusiastically supported the putsch with an eye to preserving the integrity of the wider war against Islamism in south and central Asia. The British High Commissioner and European Union envoy to the country lavished praise on the new regime, while avoiding mention of the word 'coup'.[173] The World Bank and the Asian Development Bank propped it up by opening up generous new lines of credit to support 'anti-corruption' initiatives spearheaded by the military. In this regard the Bangladeshi putsch followed a long-established pattern that has seen the US and its allies support military dictatorship in preference to democracy incorporating Islamists: Algeria in 1991; Turkey in 1996, Palestine in 2006; Egypt in 2011–13. What differed in Bangladesh from these other countries is that one of the levers that helped to hoist the military regime into place was UN peacekeeping.

By threatening Bangladeshi access to UN peacekeeping and the money the military earned thereby, Bangladesh's Western donors and allies persuaded the Bangladeshi generals to intervene in an electoral stand-off between Bangladesh's two major parties on the eve of a general election. Although the precise role of UN officials in the sequence of events prior and subsequent to the coup is difficult precisely to establish so soon after the fact, what is clear is that the United Nations did play a major role. To begin with, the world organisation withdrew its support from the general election scheduled for early 2007 on the eve of the military seizure of power (Bangladeshi legislators have since charged the United Nations with supporting an unelected military government).[174] *The Economist* attributed a major role in instigating the coup to the UN representative in Dhaka, saying that the military 'intervention was strange on the face of it, because the UN is not known to go around inciting army takeovers'.[175] According to the report, the United Nations set the pace for the period of military rule by using the military's access to UN peacekeeping missions as a way of prompting the military to eventually hold the controversial elections after they had 'rebooted' national politics. According to a report in *The Nation*, it was the local UN representative who suggested the method of the so-called 'soft coup' to preserve Bangladesh's international image as a peacekeeper, by ensuring that instead of direct military rule there should be a civilian 'caretaker' administration.[176]

Moeen U. Ahmed, the Bangladeshi Chief of Army staff, claimed in his memoirs that the Under-Secretary-General of Peacekeeping at the time, Jean-Marie Guéhenno, supported this indirect military rule in preference to allowing the troublesome general elections scheduled for 2007 to go ahead.[177] The United Nations for its part neither denied nor confirmed the claims of the army chief. If the general's claims are true, it is safe to assume that Guéhenno did not act without the support and knowledge of UN Secretary-General Ban Ki-moon. Certainly, Army Chief Ahmed attributes great significance to the communiqué from Guéhenno in shaping his decisions, a decision based on the importance of peacekeeping to the morale, status and earnings of the military.[178] In the general's line of reasoning, the fate of Bangladeshi democracy was weighed against the need to preserve the military's access to peacekeeping assignments abroad.

Whatever the precise role of the United Nations in the military take-over, on the basis of what is already known we can extract some broader implications of the 2006 coup. Firstly, as suggested earlier, hopes vested in the 'diversionary peace' thesis (which were being applied to Bangladesh right up to the eve of the coup) are misplaced.[179] Not only does the idea of diversionary peace render new democracies hostage to the military, but it overlooks the fact that peacekeeping may exacerbate as much as restrain praetorian instincts. Hobson worried at the turn of the last century that the combination of imperial despotism and colonial armies would redound to threaten the liberty of the metropole by tying the 'fidelity' of the 'conquered races' to 'ambitious pro-consuls'.[180] Today, with the domestic political costs of imperial security buffered by the peacekeeping nations of the developing world, it is the political institutions of these countries that are threatened by 'ambitious pro-consuls'.

If Bangladeshi peacekeepers are not helping to expand the borders of a colonial empire, it is nonetheless not too great a leap from over-seeing the management of democracy abroad to overseeing it at home. Many of the justifications given for the coup by its apologists at home and abroad were impeccably technocratic, transposable to a Security Council script hammered out for any peacebuilding mission in Africa. The focus was on rooting out political and state corruption, enacting electoral reforms, insulating state institutions from political influence, hemming in party political competition, defusing heated electoral antagonism, and acting as the overseer of credible elections with the stamp of international legitimacy.[181] 'Diversionary peace' reverses the flow rather than the logic of praetorianism: from managing politics at home, peacekeeping allows a nation's soldiers to manage it abroad, but there is no reason the flow cannot be reversed again. Peacekeeping has served to globalise the role of the military as the praetorians of political order, the trustees of political reform, modernisation, democratisation and election oversight.

Dragon's teeth of the new world order

As regards the terms of the theory of democratic peacekeeping, these counter-examples could be cast as 'outliers'. Idiosyncratic exceptions to the general rule, peacekeeping praetorianism in Fiji, Pakistan, Bangladesh, Ghana and perhaps Nigeria, the Gambia and Niger are all worthy of investigation in and of themselves to explain their deviation from the overarching trend, but of insufficient importance to call the trend as a whole into question. Such a view would be a mistake, for these instances are not outliers but holes in the theory itself—holes through which we can see the fragility of its theoretical foundations, resting on a naïve conflation of democracy and peacekeeping in a chimerical liberal militarism.

This is to be sure a distinctive type of militarism. The classical liberal telos envisaged the institutions and ethics of the military withering away through rationalisation and the spread of commercial society. As a concept militarism is still associated with the illiberal societies of modernity: fascist states with their reverence of martial values, the ostentatious May Day parades of the Eastern bloc and the shabby Third World dictatorships of the Cold War era. Michael Mann's definition of militarism as 'a set of attitudes and social practices which regards war and the preparation for war as a normal and desirable social activity' cannot easily be stretched to accommodate peacekeeping, predicated as peacekeeping is on the suppression of war.[182]

If however by militarism we mean that military success becomes the yardstick for measuring national development and progress, or that the use of military force is accorded a central role in the foreign policy of a state, or that national purpose becomes entwined with the success of military initiative and enterprise, or that a large, strong military is needed to promote national interests abroad, then militarism is easily visible in peacekeeping. If by militarism we mean the cultivation of a romantic view of soldiers and soldiering, or the glorification of the ethos of a professional military caste, then it is hard to think of an ideology that would provide as sentimental a view of soldiering as that of peacekeeping. This militarism is more insidious than any outright glorification of war and martial valour precisely because the reverence of military power is camouflaged by the circumlocutions of liberal militarism that sees international policing, peace operations, cosmopolitan peacekeeping and cosmopolitan law enforcement in place of military intervention and combat. In the evolutionary telos of democratic peace, the achievement of liberal democracy is taken as a state of such social perfection that the only remaining outlet for systematic political change is the export of democracy. The notion that the systematic export of democracy might come with political costs resulting from the concomitant elevation of military power in national politics is simply ignored.

In the same breath as noting the positive relationship between democracy, domestic respect for human rights and countries' peacekeeping participation, Perkins and Neumayer innocently note that states' military capacities are also 'found to positively influence countries' propensity to provide troops for peacekeeping missions', not seeing any possible contradiction with their other findings regarding peacekeeping states' democratic political systems and putative respect for human rights.[183] We do not need evidence of military coups to see that peacekeeping has buttressed the weight and role of the military in many new and emerging democracies—we have already seen that for the Brazilian military, peacekeeping has strengthened its traditional domestic roles. In his study of civil-military relations in Uruguay for example, Sotomayor shows that peacekeeping has served to perpetuate the political power and social weight of the armed forces since the end of the Uruguayan dictatorship in 1985.

Through tight control of their peacekeeping operations, the armed forces of Urugay have succeeded in shielding military training and procurement from civilian oversight or legislative accountability, the overall effect of peacekeeping being to boost the 'policy leverage of the (mostly uniformed) Ministry of Defence' within wider government structures.[184] Although the armed forces are professional rather than conscripted, they still have only 6,000 fewer members in 2011 than they did in 1981—still one of the highest ratios of men under arms to civilian population on the South American continent.[185] At the same time, peacekeeping missions have allowed the Uruguayan military to perpetuate their 'traditional roles and values' by 'developing more policing techniques than strictly military skills', so that 'as during the dictatorial regime' the military is dedicated to providing 'law and order where chaos prevails'.[186]

What such examples show is that it is not merely a question of rulers that are draped in brocade and medals, but wider questions of democratic accountability, parliamentary oversight of defence, security and intelligence bureaucracies, legal restraints on the military, freedom of information, public understandings of state security, among many other aspects of democratic control over the instruments of state power.[187] As Robin Luckham observes, 'the dangers of authoritarian regression within a formally democratic shell may be as great as, and certainly are more insidious and difficult to detect than, those of direct military reintervention.'[188] While the impact of peacekeeping on state security bureaucracies and civil-military relations may differ across states, what is clear is that the greater the role given to peacekeeping by a state, the greater the role given to the military in the national self-image and political life of that state. It is not possible to elevate the security institutions of the state without feedback effects on the democratic polity.

Conclusion

Lamenting the lack of power projection capacity among the world's armies for the purposes of peacekeeping and humanitarian intervention, Michael O'Hanlon and P.W. Singer observe that 'most countries, even those with strong militaries are like caged tigers at best: fierce if fought on their home turf, but relatively harmless beyond.'[189] Judging by laments of this kind, one could be forgiven for wondering whether there would ever be enough men and materiel to satisfy the military demands of liberal internationalists. Since the founding of peacekeeping, over one million personnel from 130 states have participated in peacekeeping operations around the world.[190] By providing the political support and ideological, institutional and logistical infrastructure for peacekeeping, the United Nations has opened these cages, freeing the tigers to prowl.

Armies across the world have accumulated extensive overseas tours and operational experience of conflict zones. In dozens of countries, soldiers and gendarmes from around the world have been given powers to oversee and protect the social and political reconstruction of whole nations and societies, with tasks ranging from training newly formed armies through monitoring post-conflict elections to battling recalcitrant insurgents. Through ever more intrusive and far-reaching mandates issued by the Security Council, peacekeepers have become the praetorians of political development, order and modernisation around the world. Small wonder that the military may come to think of itself not as the servant of the state but as its highest guardian, endowed with authority higher than that of any elected representative and exhibiting an 'attitude of impunity and exceptionalism', to paraphrase Jean-Marie Guéhenno.[191] Evidently, traditional conservatism and fascism are not the only visions of society that justify military and authoritarian rule: spreading protectorates abroad and ensconcing praetorianism at home, so too international liberalism has helped to relegitimise dictatorship.

The theoretical justification for this blithe amalgamation of peacekeeping and democratisation in democratic peace explanations of peacekeeping reveals an apolitical and sanitised view of international order. Naïve about the character and practice of peacekeeping missions, theories of democratic peacekeeping contribution portray an international order without power, ideology, sources of systemic inequality and domination, or political structures and institutions with their own logics and interests. The most glaring oversight here is the lack of any attention to the structures of the United Nations, both institutional and ideological, in providing for peacekeeping. Unable to account for the predominance of specifically Southern states in UN peacekeeping, such theories cannot discount imperial multilateralism as the most consistent and powerful explanation of the role of Southern states in peacekeeping.

We saw in the previous chapter that patterns of contribution in peacekeeping have changed across the last two decades, with Western states restructuring their engagement so as to avoid long-term entanglements with its associated strategic and political risks. The role played by Third World peacekeepers is not simply that of auxiliaries however, as their very presence makes possible sweeping tasks of political transformation that in other circumstances would be seen as outright neo-colonialism. The involvement of Southern peacekeepers therefore is integral to the activity, their complicity in reproducing international structures of imperial security all the more glaring.

But whether the motives are those of egotistical self-interest or of a magnanimous democratic messianism, explanations based in national motivation will only take us so far in understanding the phenomenon of peacekeeping contribution by Southern states. For it is implausible to reduce peacekeeping contribution to the motivations of those countries whose motives generally count for so little in world affairs. Nor can research on the issue be exhausted simply by accumulating more intensive case studies of particular countries' policies; we must consider the institutional context that frames the decisions available to Southern states. The role of the United Nations, long seen as a citadel of Third World sovereign rights and anti-colonialism, is crucial. It is to understanding the immensely supple and creative role played by the world organisation that we now turn.

PART III

IMPERIAL MULTILATERALISM

6

THE UNITED NATIONS

LAST REFUGE OF EMPIRE

Introduction

In arguing that UN peacekeeping is the highest form of liberal imperialism and that blue helmets from the Global South are its askaris, I have presupposed that the United Nations provides the means whereby imperial control can be maintained over peacekeeping and imperial benefits thereby secured. We shall explore the institutions of this control in this chapter.

The United Nations provides not only the institutional infrastructure but also the legitimacy for this imperial security system by virtue of its claims to be an anti-colonial organisation. The importance of the United Nations to maintaining the anti-imperial reputation of peacekeeping should not be underestimated. In her study of peacekeeping Kimberly Marten avers that 'Multilateralism is the one thing that removes any hint of individual state gain from what might otherwise appear to be a colonial effort ....'[1] Paradoxically then, if it is clear from the preceding chapters that UN peacekeeping perpetuates liberal imperialism, this is because of—and not in spite of—its anti-imperial credentials. In other words, the highest form of liberal imperialism is not a perversion of the ethos of the United Nations, but is entirely in keeping with the founding vision and historical rationale for the organisation.[2]

We have examined the organisation of peacekeeping in the field in the first two chapters, and the patterns of peacekeeping contribution across the previous two chapters. These give us a partial image of peacekeeping. For if peacekeepers were the forces of a single nation or empire, their deployment would correspond to the will and designs of that state. Investigating their deployment would be that much more straightforward. Yet nor can we be satisfied with an explanation that simply aggregates the participating countries' individual motives, or distils a theory by extrapolating from the attributes common to this mass of states. For in the case of UN peacekeeping, the states that contribute forces to peacekeeping are not the same as those who control and finance peacekeeping. It is this political and institutional asymmetry that enables us to identify the power relations underlying UN peacekeeping. To complete the picture of peacekeeping and peacekeeping contribution, therefore, we need to examine the leadership structures and institutional machinery of peacekeeping.

It is here that the investigation in this chapter begins—by examining the means through which imperial influence over peacekeeping is secured, beginning at the apex of the organisation—the Security Council—and moving through the financing of peacekeeping to the Secretariat, focusing mostly on the Department of Peacekeeping Operations. In this process, we shall see the extent to which since the end of the Cold War the United Nations has been reorganised around the concerns of wealthy and powerful states at the expense of developing countries.

If these are the means by which imperial influence is secured through peacekeeping, these means are predicated on the claims of the United Nations to be an anti-imperial institution. The anti-imperial reputation of the United Nations stems from its tradition of parliamentary diplomacy during the Cold War. This period of anti-colonial revolt saw the newly born nations of the Third World organise themselves in the chambers of the organisation to repeatedly denounce and embarrass their former overlords.

But the reputation that the United Nations acquired as a bastion of weak and developing countries was a by-product of the Cold War rivalries that deadlocked the Security Council, thereby allowing the General Assembly to gain greater prominence.[3] I argue that the way in which the United Nations has functioned since the end of the Cold War is not a deviation from the ideals of the world organisation, but rather approximates much more closely the vision of the organisation's founding fathers: that of a concert system for legitimating great power rule and intervention. Even during the heyday of Third World nationalism, the notion that the United Nations helped to enfranchise developing countries needs to be tempered. Specifically, it should be recognised that channelling the ambitions of the ex-colonial states through UN diplomacy helped to buffer the challenge that they posed, and helped to absorb them into institutional structures designed to cohere US leadership of the post-war world. Once this containment of the Third World is recognised, to be conceptually accommodated it requires us to develop a broader account of international organisation.

International organisation is conventionally seen as a response to the problem of war.[4] But inasmuch as modern wars have been tied to inter-imperial rivalries and anti-imperial revolutions, so too international organisation has been a response to the problems posed by imperialism. Hence it should come as no surprise that efforts to contain and suppress conflict through international organisation have also seen these organisations—the League of Nations and the United Nations—being used to help to disestablish colonial empires. This process, spearheaded by the US in its rise to global supremacy, led to the displacement of European colonialism and neo-colonialism by a new type of imperial hegemony based on indirect modes of domination. Indirect domination necessarily had to be exercised through the institutions of formal independence, and for these the United Nations provided the props. The end of the Cold War has allowed the United Nations to establish a more coercive regime with which to discipline the behaviour of states and regulate their internal life—and it is a regime in keeping with the overall rationale for the United Nations, namely to institutionalise US hegemony.

Although the imperial character of UN peacekeeping has become most explicit in the aftermath of the Cold War, we shall see below that the imperial prerogatives of peacekeeping reach back to the very origins of the institution, in the deployments of the 1950s and '60s. My argument thus cuts across much of the contemporary scholarship, which usually proceeds by way of assuming fundamental qualitative differences between the character of peacekeeping in the Cold War and post-Cold War eras. By examining the Cold War history of peacekeeping, we see how the present peacekeeping order is rooted in the past. The sequence of the discussion reflects this analytical claim: the past history of peacekeeping (discussed towards the end of the chapter) is observed through the optic of the present (discussed in the first part of the chapter), rather than beginning our discussion in the past and then wading through to the present. Hence we avoid the dangers of implicit teleology by suggesting that the present order inevitably resulted from that of the past.

In brief, the imperial functions of peacekeeping are therefore a congenital component of the United Nations and not merely a by-product of the overstretch resulting from the multiplication of UN missions after the end of the Cold War. The history of international organisation is intertwined with attempts to regulate colonialism and curb interimperial rivalry, leading to the partial sublimation of national imperialism into an 'imperial multilateralism' embodied first in the League of Nations and, more successfully, in the United Nations.

Peacekeeping and the Security Council: a new condominium

The authority to deploy UN forces (including peacekeepers) has been battled over both openly and covertly, explicitly and informally, since the founding of the United Nations. In this time, political authority over UN use of force and field missions has passed from the Security Council to the General Assembly and back again. Peacekeeping initially emerged through the actions of the General Assembly led by the US in the creation of the 1956–67 Unef I operation. The Assembly also created Untea (1962) and UNSF (1962–63). It was following the controversy of the 1960–64 Onuc mission that the Council took decisive control over peacekeeping, and has retained it ever since.[5] These tussles over peacekeeping remind us that the United Nations is an institutional site of struggle rather than an inert monolith. They also help us to clarify the power relations underpinning peacekeeping. Wallensteen and Johansson make clear that since the end of the Cold War, the Council has beaten back the role of the General Assembly in the field of international peace and security.[6] For when Cold War rivalries on the Council came to an end, the stage was already set for a newly united Council to dramatically expand the remit of peacekeeping.

Although the end of the Cold War is often dated either to the fall of the Berlin Wall in 1989 or alternatively to the implosion of the USSR at the end of 1991, the beginning of the post-Cold War era in the United Nations can be backdated to 1988—the period of 'New Thinking' in Soviet foreign policy which instigated the new era of peacekeeping.

In articles published in 1987 Soviet premier Mikhail Gorbachev called for the permanent five to act as 'guarantors' of international security and to extend the use of military observers and peacekeepers to 'disengage' warring sides in conflicts as well as monitoring ceasefires and armistices.[7] It was in early 1988 that the USSR suggested a UN peacekeeping navy to protect the shipping routes in the Arabian Gulf threatened by the 'Tanker War' between Iran and Iraq, which saw repeat attacks on oil shipments.[8]

1988 also saw two new peacekeeping operations established after a decade-long hiatus: the UN Good Offices Mediation in Afghanistan and Pakistan (Ungomap, 1988–90) and the Iran-Iraq Military Observer Group (Uniimog, 1988–91). The missions in Iran/Iraq and the 1989–90 mission in occupied Namibia even saw Soviet airlift combined with US logistical support on behalf of the peacekeepers deployed there.[9] After that, the number of new UN operations continued to grow until the collapse of the USSR, with three new operations launched in 1989 and five new operations in 1991, respectively.

Greater geopolitical cooperation resulted in behavioural change on the part of the five permanent members of the Council, including changes in working procedures that helped to consolidate the dominance of the permanent five and in particular the US.[10] One trend is restraint and collaboration, in order to prevent the Council becoming a lightning rod for international rivalries: '[The Council] is more cooperative, it is making serious decisions, and it is more deeply involved in the issues on its agenda. This has enhanced the standing of the Security Council.'[11] As Susan C. Hulton points out in an informative study of Council working procedures: 'Disputes over procedural issues—one of the hallmarks of Council meetings during the Cold War era—have all but vanished, with most such issues now being resolved in consultations.'[12] Another dimension of this new condominium is the declining use of the veto, with the 1991–2000 period seeing only seven vetoes cast, the lowest for any decade in the history of the world organisation.[13] Put simply, fewer vetoes cast means fewer openings for smaller powers to exploit. Safe in the knowledge that the UN authorisation for the use of force would no longer be paralysed by rival use of vetoes, the permanent five began to exercise their power with abandon.

The growth of peacekeeping therefore needs to be contextualised against the backdrop of a Council that grew more confident in its use of power. The newly enlarged power of the Security Council, including the tighter control that it exercises over UN activity, indicates that the growth of peacekeeping can only have come about with the active support of the Council. This follows the pattern set during the Cold War. Although peacekeeping initially emerged as a product of a divided and paralysed Council (see further below), since at least 1963 peacekeeping has waxed and waned in direct proportion to the harmony of the Council itself. Periods of great power accord have allowed peacekeeping to flourish. The period of détente between the US and the USSR in the 1970s saw peacekeeping expand with the Unef II, Undof, Unyom and Unifil missions, all in the Middle East and all but one designed to defuse the Arab-Israeli confrontation from sparking superpower conflict.[14] Peacekeeping then diminished during the era of the 'second Cold War' during the 1980s until the Cold War itself ended. There were no new UN peacekeeping missions between 1978 and 1988, and then twenty new missions across the next ten years.

If peacekeeping correlates with periods of geopolitical cooperation, the end of the Cold War did provide its own distinctive, ideological element to the mix. The rhetoric of Soviet 'New Thinking' in foreign policy—'interconnectedness', 'interdependence' and 'comprehensive security', terms as commonplace as to be innocuous in international affairs today—ironically originated as nothing 'more than the other face of the ... collapse of [the Soviet] empire'.[15] The end of the Cold War established geopolitical cooperation on the Council laced with a post-ideological, post-Soviet discourse of common threat and shared interests as the basis for the new peacekeeping.

Small powers, peacekeeping and the Security Council

The changed context of harmonious relations on the Council forces other states to behave in different ways. Notably, it changes the pattern of political calculation, as noted by Thomas Weiss: 'Excluded countries wanted a part of the action, to defend their own viewpoints from the risk of being ignored by a new ... P-5 condominium ...'[16] Anthony Parsons welcomes the fact that the permanent five now cooperate 'rather than competing, the old parliamentary arithmetic of East versus West bidding for the non-aligned majority a thing of the past ...'.[17] This was particularly true due to the role of the US in controlling the Security Council agenda, at least since the signing of the Dayton Accords that ended the war in Bosnia in 1995.[18]

This is not to say that peacekeeper contributing states have not gained greater prominence corresponding to the growth of peacekeeping in the post-Cold War era. To be sure, the Council has gradually expanded its consultations with peacekeeper contributing countries over the last few years.[19] The Council also now accepts reports from peacekeeping force commanders in the field, and keeps a tight leash on the missions themselves, actively renewing them at intervals usually of either six months or a year. Yet questions of control over peacekeeping remains a perennial source of friction between the Council and Southern peacekeeping states, testimony to the latter's lack of control over the process.

The need for more consultation with contributing countries was put across as one of the major themes and concerns of the open debate on peacekeeping held under the Indian presidency of the Council in August 2011. The possibility for consultation thus represents one means by which troop- and police-contributing countries can secure access to the Council and curry favour with its members, constituting one advantage of being a contributor to peacekeeping. However, if this privileged access to the Council boosts the standing of peacekeeper contributing states, it also reflects the enhanced authority of the body conferring that privilege.

Since the end of the Cold War the Council's expanded consultation procedures reflect the extension of Council authority, which draws on a broad variety of 'constituents': the Ecosoc committee, the Secretariat, non-governmental organisations and the wider UN membership.[20] The shift in power to the Council away from the General Assembly has also seen the Secretariat put on a tighter leash.[21] Thus, poor contributing states have been coerced by a Council that has consolidated its control over UN procedure and institutional politics.[22]

One means by which smaller powers can articulate their interests is through the election of non-permanent members to the ten rotating seats on the Council. Non-permanent membership of the Council offers 'the ability to raise points of interest in discussions; to learn about the views of others and about the leanings of the Council on given issues; and to appear to be at the center of important things'.[23] In these elections the Charter requires the General Assembly to pay due regard to member states' contributions to international peace and security and to ensure equitable geographic representation.[24] But the power of these elected positions is severely limited. Most obviously, 'effective decision making [on the Council]... is monopolized by the Permanent Five'.[25] But there is a raft of means by which the power of non-permanent members is circumscribed. To minimise the disruption of this quasi-democratic incursion into the permanently-sitting upper house of the world organisation, the US ensures the loyalty of elected members by reportedly increasing its aid to these states during their two-year tenure on the Council—aid that falls away once their tenure expires.[26]

Table 6.1: Elected/Non-permanent members of the UN Security Council, 1999–2013

Jan 2011–Dec 2013: Colombia, Germany, **India**, Portugal, South Africa
Jan 2010–Dec 2012: Bosnia and Herzegovina, **Brazil**, Gabon, Lebanon, **Nigeria**
Jan 2009–Dec 2011: Austria, Japan, Mexico, Turkey, Uganda
Jan 2008–Dec 2009: Burkina Faso, Costa Rica, Croatia, Libya, Vietnam
Jan 2007–Dec 2008: Belgium, **Indonesia**, Italy, **South Africa**, Panama
Jan 2006–Dec 2007: Congo, **Ghana**, Peru, Qatar, Slovakia
Jan 2005–Dec 2006: **Argentina**, Denmark, Greece, Japan, Tanzania
Jan 2004–Dec 2005 Algeria, Benin, **Brazil**, Philippines, Romania
Jan 2003–Dec 2004: Angola, Chile, Germany, **Pakistan**, Spain
Jan 2002–Dec 2003: Bulgaria, Cameroon, Guinea, Mexico, Syria
Jan 2001–Dec 2002: Colombia, Ireland, Mauritius, Norway, Singapore
Jan 2000–Dec 2001: **Bangladesh**, Jamaica, Mali, **Tunisia**, Ukraine
Jan 1999–Dec 2000: Argentina, Canada, Malaysia, Namibia, Netherlands

Source: Global Policy Forum. Countries in bold if in T10 or N10 in that period.

It is not only the power of the five permanent members but also Charter stipulations on equitable geographic representation that curb the influence of Southern peacekeeping states. Given that Asia and Africa count as one geographic region for the purposes of Council elections, the number of Southern peacekeeping nations that can be elected to the Council is obviously limited as most peacekeeping powers hail from these two continents. The list of countries elected to the Council across the last decade only weakly correlates with patterns of Southern peacekeeping contribution. France and Britain used their activism in UN peacekeeping in the early 1990s to justify their permanent seats on the Security Council in the post-Cold War era. Such justifications do not apply to the poorer countries, regardless of how heavy their contributions.

As we can see from table 6.1, there is no particularly strong correlation between T10 and N10 contribution, and election to the Council, let alone peak deployment and presence on the Council.

If the end of the Cold War changed the relations between the permanent members of the Council, it also changed the nature of their geopolitical and strategic interests in the wider world. That UN peacekeeping operations were allowed to penetrate great power spheres of influence that were formerly sealed against international intervention is read by Peter Viggo Jakobsen and Norrie MacQueen as a measure of declining geopolitical interest in these formerly contested regions. This decline in geopolitical interest corresponded to a general decline in the strategic significance of the Third World in the post-Cold War era.[27] But if geopolitical interest in peripheral regions has declined, that does not mean that the great powers have ceased intervening in these regions. Rather, their intervention was scaled up into a UN condominium, and mediated by reliance on the askaris and sepoys of the new world order, whose use allowed the great powers to buffer the costs of imperial security.

New horizons for intervention?

Another avenue through which the global South has sought to mould the new peacekeeping to better fit its interests is through the various committee structures associated with the General Assembly and peacekeeping, notably the Special Committee on Peacekeeping Operations and the UN Peacebuilding Commission. Discussions through the Special Committee have, for instance, contrasted a vision of 'effective peacekeeping' to the Western understanding of 'robust peacekeeping'. The 'New Horizons' initiative launched by the former Under-Secretary-General for Peacekeeping, Alain Le Roy, was partly designed to placate the global South by better integrating developing countries' concerns through talk of 'partnership' with 'stakeholders'. Here, Southern concerns over militarised peacebuilding were used to rationalise resources by devolving some of the burden of peacekeeping onto regional organisations and generally rolling back from the imperial overstretch afflicting peacekeeping at the end of the first decade of the twenty-first century. The next Under-Secretary-General Hervé Ladsous sought to continue this placation, proposing in early 2013 the establishment of a new peacekeeping directorate 'to support Member States, by providing timely and accurate feedback to troop and police contributing countries on a broad range of issues, including missions' utilization of contributions against endorsed requirements, as well as on training, best practices, and safety and security issues'.[28]

Certainly debates within the Special Committee and the New Horizons project itself are testimony to the continued North-South asymmetry in peacekeeping structures. Whatever the scope of Southern disquiet over 'robust peacekeeping', they have nowhere to retreat to outside of UN conflict management processes. The more Southern states oppose 'robust peacekeeping', the more they reaffirm peacekeeping interventionism by having to justify alternative models—developmentalist models that, if less militarised, are no less sweeping in their visions of post-conflict reconstruction.

Great power disputes and peacekeeping in the post-Cold War era

Making a case for the enhanced power and authority of the Council means considering the diplomatic crisis over Iraq. This was widely seen as having shattered the consensus that had hitherto prevailed across much of the 1990s.[29] No period of great power 'concert' lasts indefinitely, eventually succumbing to the centrifugal pressures of self-interest, as happened in 1999 over Kosovo and in 2011–12 over Syria. In both instances, the Council was divided between the Western permanent three on the one hand, and Russia and China on the other.[30] What was significant about the 2003 Iraq invasion was that it was the Western bloc itself that fragmented, France joining with Russia and China.

Yet this clash failed to dent the Council's penchant for peacekeeping. Other clashes of interest have also been contained. While Chinese oil interests in Sudan are often cited as responsible for protecting the regime in Khartoum, over the last ten years Sudan has become one of the most heavily peace-kept countries in the world. Moreover, as Mats Berdal writes of the diplomatic crisis over Iraq:

Notwithstanding the deep divisions among member states that emerged over Iraq in 2003, and which many predicted would have a lasting and paralysing effect on the Security Council, new [peacekeeping] missions have been authorised and existing ones substantially expanded ... at an unprecedented rate.[31]

Indeed, it can be argued that the launch of new peacekeeping operations was used to affect reconciliation on the Council after the bitterness engendered by the dispute over Iraq (see further below). Judging by this historical pattern, we might expect that the permanent members of the Council will seek to mend their dispute over the Syrian civil war—already in its second year at the time of writing—through the expansion and extension of UN peacekeeping operations in the Levant once that war comes to an end.

In light of the preceding discussion, it is worth re-stressing at this point the absurdity of the charge of mercenarism levelled against Southern peacekeeping states. The idea that Southern countries are draining a compliant United Nations is seen to be ridiculous, given the reality is that Southern countries confront a united Council, more willing than ever to use punitive and coercive measures to enforce its will and extend its reach. Insofar as Southern states have expanded their involvement in UN peacekeeping, they have become further enmeshed in a United Nations dominated by the great powers as never before.

US: UN

Of course, there is one state in particular whose actions need to be reckoned with if we are to grasp the post-Cold War dynamics of UN peacekeeping. Here again however, the dynamics are different to what we might expect.

There is a widespread conventional view that the US is schizophrenic as regards its relations with the world organisation. Enhanced support for multilateralism and the United Nations is believed to correspond with Democratic ascendency in US domestic politics, with unilateral aloofness and suspicion of the world body corresponding with Republican ascendency. The latter in particular was believed to hold sway during the two administrations of President George W. Bush. Bush notoriously appointed the neoconservative UN-sceptic John Bolton as his ambassador to the organisation, and the president snubbed the world body when he ordered the invasion of Iraq without the unanimous backing of the Council.

Yet the Bush administration was heavily supportive of peacekeeping, as described by Lise Morjé Howard: 'At the beginning of Bush's first term, there were approximately 35,000 UN peacekeepers in the field but, by the end of his second term, the UN was fielding over 110,000 ... troops in seventeen different missions—more than ever before.' The UN peacekeeping budget tripled in the same period, while the administrative budget for the organisation doubled—unprecedented growth for both budgets.[32] This simply could not have occurred without the active support of the United Nations' most powerful member state. It was also the Bush administration that launched the Global Peace Operations Initiative in April 2004 (discussed in previous chapters), to rationalise and expand US support for peacekeeping around the world.

This turn to the United Nations by the Bush administration was partly dictated by necessity. As we have seen, UN peacekeepers took up the slack around the world for a US embroiled in two military campaigns in the greater Middle East. The Bush administration also needed the United Nations for the purposes of political reconstruction in Iraq, particularly given the administrative experience and political credibility that the world body could lend to the US-sponsored elections in the country. The United Nations also helped court Iraqi Shia leader Grand Ayatollah Sayyid Ali al-Sistani, who snubbed the US occupation authorities but proved amenable to the overtures of the UN's more urbane and cosmopolitan envoys.[33] John Bolton himself advocated the revival of the UN Military Staff Committee, approved the expansion of the Unifil mission in Lebanon in 2006 and voted to expand the management budget of the world organisation.[34]

But even before Bush's imperial adventures began to draw more heavily on multilateral support, the isolationism of the first Bush administration saw a boost in US support for the UN. It was in this period that a deal was brokered on US arrears to the organisation, and the cap on financial assessments for peacekeeping held to by the Clinton administration was also lifted. This early burst of support for the world body by the Bush administration can be explained by the fact that Bush's foreign policy team wished to ensure that it was the United Nations and not the US that shouldered the burden of Clintonite nation-building experiments inherited by Bush's presidency.[35] The elder President Bush—himself a former US ambassador to the world organisation—was even keener on the United Nations. In the flush of Cold War victory, President George H.W. Bush gave the United Nations a prominent place in his vision of a new world order, issued instructions that peacekeeping training for US forces was to be renewed, and argued for the establishment of a UN rapid reaction force.[36]

The Clinton administration initially continued these early policies of Bush senior, even countenancing the possibility of US forces serving under foreign UN command. Clinton was also content to see the definition of threats to international peace and security extended. After the losses incurred by the failed nation-building experiment in Somalia, the Clinton administration retreated from its early liberal internationalism into the neo-isolationism expressed in Presidential Directive 25 (PDD 25), which ruled out the possibility of US forces' involvement in peacekeeping. But this should be tempered by recognising the fact that PDD 25, in the very act of recoiling from peacekeeping also ensconced peacekeeping as an integral part of US foreign policy: PDD 25 reiterated that peacekeeping was a 'cost-effective tool' of advancing both 'American and collective' interests.[37] Andrea K. Talentino writes that in the wake of 'Somalia … intervention seemed likely to fade as an international strategy. Strangely however, the reverse has happened.'[38] Part of the reason for this is the cost-effectiveness of peacekeeping—cost-effectiveness resulting from the loyalty and cheapness of the sepoys and askaris provided by developing countries to the United Nations.

Thus the US presidency that exhibited the greatest hostility towards the United Nations in a generation was also the one that boosted the organisation financially and materially. Beneath the rhetorical froth that often occludes US-UN relations, it is clear that the US has persistently used the world body to consolidate US power. Even in those periods of headlong retreat from engagement with the world body, the US has sought to use the United Nations to maintain US interests around the world and reduce the costs of imperial power to the US in terms of blood, treasure and political credibility. Whether the policies of a particular administration are supportive or hostile, the United Nations remains a quintessentially 'American product' in the words of William E. Rappard, as much a manufacture of US power as 'the jeep or atomic bomb':

Conceived at Dumbarton Oaks near the American Capitol, inspired by American ideas, born under American chairmanship on the American West Coast, having decided on a permanent site in America, it is even endowed with an American surname. In fact as in word, there would be no United Nations were there not a United States.[39]

The politics of peacekeeping finance

In addition to its power on the Council, the other great lever of US power is money. While lamenting the absence of detailed figures on the UN budgetary process in 1961, one student of international organisation conceded, 'Not that the fate of the world rides on the United

Nations budget, or that matters of peace and war will be determined by the dollars and cents of the Secretary-General's estimates.'[40] Such a blasé attitude could not hold today. The scale of UN peacekeeping operations means that those dollars and cents count more towards reproducing the international order than at any other time in the organisation's history. Personnel are one component of a peacekeeping operation; the other is the financing—to pay for the troops, gendarmes, materiel, logistics and administration. Financing is the other great source of contribution to peacekeeping operations.

The structure and functioning of the UN budget system is notoriously Byzantine even by the standards of public procurement and accounting, and I have no intention of reconstructing all this complexity here. Rather, all I wish to demonstrate is that first, financing involves political decision making, and that this includes constant recalibration and reassessment in relation to other powers' decisions, as well as political struggle over payments and arrears.[41] Second, the pattern of peacekeeping financing shows the reverse mirror image of personnel contribution: the rich countries lead here. This allows us to draw out the implications of Western support for peacekeeping.

The United Nations remains chronically under-resourced. Formally, all member states of the United Nations share the costs of peacekeeping. This is an integral part of the burden-sharing that gives the world body its legitimacy as an organisation, and is mirrored in the burden-sharing of personnel contributions for multinational peacekeeping forces. Given the absence of any detailed guidance in the organisation's Charter concerning financing,[42] UN finances and particularly UN peacekeeping financing, has evolved in as haphazard a way as peacekeeping itself.[43]

For our purposes here, it is the results of this evolution that are the most important. By the early 1970s, a new form of peacekeeping assessment developed that extended the inequality at the core of the UN system to peacekeeping. Specifically, the new assessment pattern recognised the responsibility of the permanent members of the Council for establishing peacekeeping mandates by ensuring that the financial provisions for peacekeeping reflected the permanent members' privileged position.[44] The system of financing for peacekeeping developed from the methods of assessing contributions for the regular UN budget. It was based on percentage contributions assessed on individual members' capacity to pay (though according to the United Nations, many countries voluntarily make additional resources available, above and beyond their assessed share of costs, to support peacekeeping, for example, transportation, supplies, personnel and financial contributions).[45]

The two basic differences in the peacekeeping assessments system are first, the surcharge for the permanent members of the Security Council reflecting the constitutional privileges accorded them by the Charter, and second, the division of other member states into multiple groups classified alphabetically. So for example, the peacekeeping budget rates for member states in groups C and D was based on their regular budget rates, reduced by 80 and 90 per cent respectively, while group B paid the same rate for peacekeeping as they did for the regular budget.[46] This system of peacekeeping assessments remained in place from 1974 to 2001, after which point a modified system came into play that remains to this day. This modified system expanded the range of bands from four (A-D) to ten (A-J).[47] The new system was based on gross national income, adjusted for low income and debt in particular cases.

According to the analysis of the new financing system offered by William J. Durch, the modifications to the assessment system at the turn of the century have on balance reflected a net decrease in Western payments to UN peacekeeping, with the exception of the UK, Canada and South Korea. The greatest offset in costs has been in the share of the US budget paid.[48] According to Durch: 'Under the new system, the P5 states were relieved of approximately two percent of UN peacekeeping costs.'[49] At the same time, forty-nine countries spread across the group J and I categories received a 90 and 80 per cent discount, respectively.

What this means is that at the same time that Third World peacekeepers came to predominate in UN operations, Third World states were being further incentivised to contribute by the new financing system, because it had become less expensive for them to do so.[50] With the exception of Russia and China, who carry surcharges as members of the Security Council, since at least 2005 the top twenty assessed financial contributors to UN peacekeeping are all wealthy, Northern states, the top five being the US, Japan, Germany, the UK and France.[51] As we saw in the introductory chapter, in this period Western contributions of uniformed personnel to peacekeeping operations have shrivelled to a sub-battalion average.

More recently, in the wake of the global economic crisis Western states have sought to slash UN spending as part of cutting their own expenditures on foreign affairs (states' UN payments often come out of foreign ministries' budgets). The Obama administration rounded on the world organisation for failing to reduce its spending on administration with sufficient speed (the US representative for UN Management and Reform saying in a speech in 2011 that 'the United Nations cannot afford business as usual').[52] On peacekeeping however, it is the US that has held the line against European efforts to enforce an austerity budget—Paris and London targeting in particular those large, expensive missions that are close to US interests (in Liberia, Haiti and Sudan—with, at the time of writing, the greatest number of peacekeepers on these missions coming from Pakistan, Brazil and India, respectively). Developing countries have grumbled about the expenses spent on the special political missions in Iraq, Afghanistan and Libya, seen as UN props to US war efforts.

Former US Ambassador to the United Nations Susan Rice staunchly defended the peacekeeping budget, refusing to allow a drawdown of peacekeepers in Liberia and accusing the European states of seeking to redistribute the budget in favour of their own preferred missions in their spheres of influence—such as the French-dominated mission in Côte d'Ivoire. Rice said, 'We pay 27 percent of the bill while the Europeans pay a smaller percentage', and thus for the Europeans 'to be holier than thou is a bit rich, to say the least'.[53] With his government in London seeking to impose an austerity budget, Deputy British Ambassador to the United Nations Philip Parham discovered a concern for the sentiments of the peace-kept, expressing his worry that 'many ordinary Haitians' had come to see UN peacekeepers as an 'occupying force'. Susan Rice batted aside such concerns, saying in which case Britain should never have voted to authorise the mission 'in the first place, because the nature of it hasn't changed', and insisting that the 'Haitian people and the Haitian government are not asking for it to leave now'.[54]

We can draw several conclusions from this survey of peacekeeping financing. First, even since the modified financing system came into effect, peacekeeping continues to be financed by the wealthy states of the North.[55] If we examine the figures for financing contribution and the ranking in personnel contribution across the last five years, we see the image of personnel contribution inversed: the biggest financiers are also the lowest personnel contributors. Second, attempts to ensure international equitability notwithstanding, Ross Fetterly points out that the assessment rates effectively mean not only that a small group of rich countries support UN peacekeeping, but that this group of countries have an incentive 'in limiting the approval, size and duration of peacekeeping missions funded by UN peacekeeping assessments'.[56] But Fetterly mistakes incentives for techniques of discipline and control. The institutionalised system of arrears means that the payment to the United Nations is a political process rather than an automatic one—one that involves decision making: payments can be used to influence debates, operations, opinion.[57] Article 19 of the UN Charter allows for the suspension of membership after two years' of non-payment of dues. Since the days of the Reagan administration the US has skirted close to this on a number of occasions but always paid before suspension proceedings could get underway.[58] This practice of using financing to control UN process and reform is most directly associated with the US, but it holds true of all the major financing powers: arrears and payments are an intrinsically political process that allows the wealthy states to discipline the expansion of peacekeeping and regulate its rhythm.[59]

The United Nations is frequently lambasted both for its failure to resource peacekeeping properly, and to match its ambitions to its resources. In the words of Michael W. Doyle and Nicolas Sambanis: 'At its worst, the Security Council appears ... to be seeking rhetorical solutions to strategic problems and satisfying CNN and the domestic publics of the member countries, making those more important than providing well-designed missions with sufficient forces.'[60] But the fact that no single actor fully confronts the complete costs—political, financial, and military—of collective UN decisions on peacekeeping greatly expands the possibility for political evasion and its corollary, the tendency to inflate the rhetoric and scope of peacekeeping mandates.

Thus what is often described as organisational dysfunction is better understood as the satisfying of political interests. The lack of institutional integration between the Security Council and operations in the field is the very precondition of UN peacekeeping, inasmuch as its allows for the provision of international order by reducing the political, strategic and personnel costs of maintaining that order. That these asymmetries reflect separate political interests, and not merely organisational maladaptation, is evident in the clashes that they engender. One example is related by ex-peacekeeping boss Jean-Marie Guéhenno, which occurred at the turn of the century in Sierra Leone when two of the major troop-contributing countries to the Unamsil mission, India and Jordan:

announced their intention to withdraw their personnel from the mission, threatening its complete collapse. They argued, not without some merit, that they had not signed up to engage in an enforcement operation, and moreover, that it was untenable that they would have to pay in blood while members of the Security Council and western nations were only willing to pay in dollars at best, or through lip-service at worst.[61]

This was a classic case of UN overreach: the Council extended the mandate of the operation after it had already deployed, thereby inviting the fury of contributing nations (India in particular), as their troops were now expected to perform functions for which they were not originally deployed.[62] These antagonisms can be traced in more systematic detail by examining the Secretariat.

The Secretariat

The struggle for control of peacekeeping has been waged not just between the Council and the General Assembly, but also through the body of the Secretariat itself. It was the disputes over peacekeeping in the Balkans and the Horn of Africa that led the Clinton administration to remove the strong-willed and clever Boutros Boutros-Ghali from the post of UN Secretary-General against the wishes of every other member state of the world body, and replace him with the mediocre but pliant Kofi Annan, whose name now adorns a peacekeeping training centre in his native Ghana. An official on Clinton's National Security Council explained the rationale for the palace coup in Turtle Bay:

Very few secretaries-general had worked with the US military. Here we were in an era where the US military was going to be a big part of the equation. You needed a secretary-general who understands that the US military is not the enemy.[63]

Michael Pugh points out that the common portrayal of an arthritic United Nations choked up with bureaucracy belies the degree of institutional flux that the organisation has undergone, particularly in the Department of Peacekeeping Operations, itself only a young offshoot of the organisation. The department was established in January 1992, with its logistics division truncated into a standalone Department of Field Support in 2007. Since the mid-1990s, the Department of Peacekeeping

Operations has seen a situation centre established, a post of Military Advisor created, the number of seconded military officers increased, a Lessons Learned (now Best Practices) unit set up, as well as a database of national pledges to the UN's Standby system drawn up.[64]

The Department of Peacekeeping Operations

According to Jocelyn Coulon, during the 1990s peacekeeping was the battleground for 'a bitter struggle for control between the UN and certain countries'.[65] As Coulon observes, the stakes were high in this struggle: 'If France captured this key position at UN headquarters, it would be in a position to wield considerable power in the political management of an army of Blue Helmets that numbered close to 80,000 soldiers in September 1994.'[66] Jostling for control of key posts has continued unabated, with the latest wave of restructuring coming in the wake of Ban Ki-moon's appointment as the UN Secretary-General. The retirement of Jean-Marie Guéhenno, the longest-serving Under-Secretary-General of the department, allowed the US to make a bid for the position when Ban initiated changes to the department's structure. In the end, France retained leadership of the department, the US receiving in exchange the position of head of the Department of Political Affairs.[67] Thus since the formation of the peacekeeping department, the Quai d'Orsay has retained a monopoly on the premier peacekeeping post: Alain Le Roy, who replaced Guéhenno in 2008, was in turn replaced by Hervé Ladsous in 2011. All three were highly seasoned French diplomats prior to their UN appointments.

According to another senior French diplomat, the French claim to the post of peacekeeping chief is justified by the fact that 'We are the only developed country that puts actual peacekeepers on the ground'—referring to France's role in the expanded Unifil mission in Lebanon since 2006.[68] But France's peacekeepers are few compared to those from countries of the global South—as we saw in the first chapter, French peacekeeping numbers have drastically shrunk from the early 1990s. If France's 'actual' contributions justify Paris securing the top position in the peacekeeping department, it does not seem that the growth of Southern contribution to peacekeeping justifies greater Southern influence within the Secretariat. Indeed, quite the opposite.[69]

Given that there is no generally accepted system for measuring non-pecuniary contributions to the United Nations—notably peacekeeping forces—Kabilan Krishnasamy argues that this cannot but prejudice the chances of peacekeeping contributor states, as the composition of the Secretariat is determined primarily by monetary contribution to the United Nations.[70] Thus rhetorical appreciation for the role of Southern peacekeeping is not matched by growth of Southern influence in the Department of Peacekeeping Operations: 'The pattern of appointing candidates mainly from Europe has led to claims from Third World countries that the UN's DPK [Department of Peacekeeping] is dominated by NATO military planners at the higher levels of military planning and execution.'[71] This was addressed by the creation of the post of Deputy Military Advisor in 1994, yet it remains an open issue, particularly given the fact there is flux in terms of contributions.

Across the years for which data are available (2005 onwards), in aggregate rich Northern states have retained on average roughly 40 per cent of the posts available in peacekeeping headquarters in New York, with just under a quarter of all posts across the Departments of Field Support and Peacekeeping Operations being held by the US alone.[72] Developing countries that hold proportionately large numbers of peacekeeping posts in New York tend to be US allies, such as the Philippines with its extensive military and political links to the US. While some major peacekeeping contributors, notably India, can claim roughly 3 per cent of posts across this period, this figure is comparable to a number of other Western states, each of whom have held a similar proportion of posts—France, Britain, Canada and Germany—none of whom contribute significant numbers of peacekeepers, let alone numbers to match those of India. For other major peacekeeping states such as Ghana, Nepal or Pakistan, the number of posts they hold is smaller and matched by the number claimed by Western nations such as Australia.

Then again, perhaps the French monopoly on peacekeeping spares the blushes of Southern peacekeeping nations by providing a European buffer for overweening US power: 'The Yanks can't have peacekeeping', one developing world ambassador told a journalist, as this 'would turn peacekeeping into a minor branch of the US army'.[73] In any case, the Western grip over the departments of Political Affairs, Humanitarian Affairs and Peacekeeping remains intact.

Securitisation of the United Nations

The United Nations certainly gives a means for extending one's influence across the range of UN activities. This applies as much to those poor contributing states who hope to benefit from UN consultation procedures as well as to those powers on the Council who shape the UN's overall direction. However, it is those states that are already powerful that will be more easily able to enhance that power through the machinery of the United Nations. That participation in the United Nations is not a zero sum game does not mean that the rewards of participation are not drastically skewed in favour of the great powers and wealthy states.

The restructuring of peacekeeping at the world organisation should be contextualised within a broader reorganisation of the United Nations—what we can call its 'securitisation'. Through this process the organisation's Cold War-era institutions of political advocacy for global trade, such as the Centre on Transnational Corporations, were variously eclipsed or wound down. Unctad, the UN agency that had spearheaded the developing world's diplomatic and ideological assault on the international economic order during the Cold War, saw its brief restructured and resources slashed in the early 1990s, alongside the formation of new UN ventures in cooperation with private business.[74] This restructuring was justified by the need to avoid duplicating activities conducted by the international financial institutions. Richard Kareem Al-Qaq describes this as a 'double transformation' in the 'axis of UN activity': 'a shift towards peace activities and away from political-economy advocacy, and a general transformation of these roles from an exogenous to an endogenous [that is, internal] focus'.[75]

Boutros-Ghali collapsed all units and departments concerned with economic, social or developmental concerns into a single Department of Economic and Social Development, while creating three new departments focused around preventive diplomacy, peacemaking and peacekeeping: the Departments of Peacekeeping, Political Affairs and Humanitarian Affairs respectively.[76] At the same time, developmental concerns mooted by the United Nations have shifted from macro-scale questions of technology transfer and the terms of trade between North and South, to developmental concerns focused on defending property rights, extending markets and cultivating an ethos of petty entrepreneurialism in place of large-scale investment.[77] Peacekeeping meanwhile has been placed at the core of UN functions in the new century, with peacekeeping and peacebuilding being allocated the role of providing the peoples of the world with 'freedom from fear'—one of three freedoms that Secretary-General Kofi Annan tasked the United Nations with pursuing in the new century.[78] In this, the organisation reflects the priorities and concerns of Western states.

Theories of peacekeeping contribution II: peacekeeping as a 'Public Good'

Having covered one set of general explanations for peacekeeping contribution in the previous chapter (the democratic peace theory of contribution), and having surveyed the institutional structures of the United Nations and their relation to peacekeeping in this chapter, we are now at a point where we can consider a final set of theories of peacekeeping contribution—public goods theories of peacekeeping. These seek to understand contribution to peacekeeping on the basis of seeing peace as a public good, analogous to the large-scale public services often provided by governments within countries.

Given the special characteristics of public goods, there are two classic problems that go along with the application of public goods-style explanations to the international realm. The first is explaining how or why these goods are provided in the first place. The fact that the benefits of public goods cannot be restricted means that every actor has an incentive to free ride on the efforts of others, with the collective result that the good in question is not produced. In this case, the public good produced by peacekeeping is that of 'system stability' in the words of Mark Bobrow and Davis Boyer—the international stability desired by all states, with the result that no single state invests the necessary effort in providing peacekeeping to the degree necessary to achieve the desired effect.[79] As Bobrow and Boyer put it, 'Self-interest works against the interest of the collective. If UN PKOs [peacekeeping operations] are indeed a pure public good, then they will not be produced to the extent needed by the international system.'[80] The second classic issue is the expectation that, in the international realm at least, it will be weaker states that will free ride on the efforts of the stronger, the latter having more interests and incentive to effect system stability.[81]

In terms of the theory at least, the fact that countries do export peacekeepers and support peacekeeping financially suggests that there are plenty of exclusive benefits that can be captured though involvement in peacekeeping as well as 'public' benefits of international stability. The theory has the advantage therefore of cleaving tightly to the self-interest of states, and does not require us to assume the spontaneous harmonisation of foreign policies across countries, as follows from democratic peacekeeping theories. While democratic peacekeeping theories collapse self-interest and group interest into the collective effort to usher in the democratic millennium, with public goods theories we can keep 'self interest' and 'collective interest' analytically distinct but without having to assume that they are mutually exclusive motivating factors in explaining states' peacekeeping efforts either.[82] Confronted with the right combination of self- and collective interest, states will be motivated into exporting peacekeepers and/or paying for peacekeeping (the latter, as we have seen, a particularly important aspect of the global peacekeeping order, and one which tends to be ignored in democratic peacekeeping theories).

Peacekeeping thus yields 'joint products'—some 'purely public' (system stability), some 'impurely public' (for example, enhanced regional stability) and private/country-specific benefits for those participating in the operation (for example 'stability for unique national economic interests in a particular country or region ... national status ... and even the financial and training benefits from military participation').[83] Exponents of the theory claim that it suppresses any dewy-eyed assumptions about humanitarian benevolence or democratic goodwill spilling over international borders: 'Benevolent intentions are not a necessary condition for positive results' argue Bobrow and Boyer, and nor does the existence of selfish motivations nullify the public character of the good produced: 'the presence of such motives does not in and of itself make participation simply a private good consumed only by the provider of the contributions.'[84]

Despite having some advances over theories of democratic peacekeeping, the quantitative application of public goods explanations are effected at such a level of generality that they rarely supply much added value to our understanding—and that is when the theory does not simply produce eccentric conclusions. Let us examine these problems in greater depth.

On the whole, public goods theories recapitulate insights that do not require the application of economic theories and econometric techniques to divine—for example that UN peacekeepers deploy to those regions where there tend to be fewer great power strategic interests (hence NATO peacekeepers in Afghanistan and UN peacekeepers in Congo);[85] or that factors such as proximity to a conflict zone and the number of refugees displaced by conflict influences the decision to deploy peacekeepers; or that countries with larger militaries are more likely to send peacekeepers abroad. All of these facts are familiar and well-established to students and observers of peacekeeping.[86]

More important for the conceptual coherence of the theory is the validity of the central premise—as to whether the peace resulting from peacekeepers' efforts can legitimately be treated as an impure public good at all. The benefits of regional peacekeeping for those states neighbouring a conflict zone and not interested in pursuing war are evident (though it should be noted that on the basis of post-Cold War conflicts in Western, Central and Eastern Africa, neighbouring states cannot be safely assumed to prefer regional peace over war). It is far less evident however why states on the other side of a continent or indeed the other side of the world should have any generic interest in 'system stability' as a whole. While it is plausible that rich and powerful states should have an interest in system stability, as they will be the states with the most far-flung interests, it is not clear why an analogous interest in system stability should apply to poor and peripheral states. As Andrew Blum notes in his criticism of this line of reasoning, it is 'not at all obvious why conflict in a distant part of the world is commonly understood to be a sub-optimal outcome among rational utility-maximizers'.[87]

Yet if this assumption of states' aversion to conflict is taken away, the bottom falls out of the theory, for there is no longer any compelling reason to treat peacekeeping in terms of public goods theory. In Bobrow and Boyer's case, the argument is vitiated by circularity: we assume that countries desire systemic stability; the evidence for desire is the hortatory rhetoric of the United Nations and countries' contribution to peacekeeping operations.[88] That peacekeeping has become increasingly difficult to disentangle from counter-insurgency efforts and war fighting further erodes the assumption that peacekeeping has a claim to be a 'public good'. Indeed, one study in this vein simply incorporates post-invasion military operations in Afghanistan and Iraq as another type of public goods peacekeeping on the grounds that they are highly similar in operational terms to UN peacekeeping missions—'guarding bases, patrolling cities, training Iraqi security forces, and performing humanitarian and reconstruction tasks'.[89]

Even if we accept public goods accounts as persuasive explanations of peacekeeping contribution, how should such contributions be weighed against other actions by states that might undercut these public goods? What are public goods theorists to make of Laura Neack's observation that a good proportion of peacekeeping nations in the Cold War were also the world's largest arms exporters, and that many of these arms went to the very same region that their peacekeepers did—the Middle East?[90] Or Paul Williams's observation that those peacekeepers sent to police the after-effects of devastating international economic policies are funded and supported by the same states that enact those policies in the first place?[91] Neack and Williams can reconcile these contradictory types of behaviour in the terms of their own theories; it is not evident that public goods theorists can.

Self-interest conceived in terms of utility maximisation makes it very difficult to account for the sheer diversity of peacekeeping contributors without making certain normative assumptions about the constitutive character of multilateralism in shaping military intervention. Yet such considerations have been treated as extraneous to public goods theorising. We could also note that these theorists make no reference to claims regarding the success or outcomes of peacekeeping operations, which should surely be a factor in deciding whether or not it is legitimate to treat it as a 'public good'. Even if we allow for the success of peacekeeping (however that may be defined),[92] it is not clear that this would be sufficient to prop up the theory if the majority of conflicts in the world do not receive the attention of peacekeepers. Thus Bobrow and Boyer rather miss the point when they claim that the 'fact that a double standard has sometimes characterized the choice of cases and degree of effort in UN PKOs ... does not eliminate the provision of (impure) public goods for those cases chosen and efforts made'.[93]

The 'Great Outsourcing Exercise'

The utilitarian logic of public goods theories sometimes generates bizarre lines of thought. While public goods theorists have to their credit often extended their analysis to include the UN financial assessments system as an embedded part of the global peacekeeping order, they reason that due to the involuntary character of the UN assessments system it is effectively a tax on wealthy states. Poor countries, which are assumed to profit from UN reimbursements, proportionately benefit more from UN peacekeeping, to the point that the weak are effectively exploiting the strong.[94] Were this conclusion simply counterintuitive, it would not be so problematic. But there is no avoiding the fact that such a conclusion is at stark odds with the developing world's perspective. The representative of Guatemala made this clear in the open debate on UN peacekeeping in August 2011, when he likened peacekeeping to a 'great outsourcing exercise, in which developed countries [have] contracted lower-cost troops from developing countries to do the hard and dangerous work ...'.[95]

Aside from the problematic character of mercenary-style explanations already addressed in chapter four, this reasoning jars with the view of UN peacekeeping held in the global North whose elites have, as we have seen, tended to look upon UN peacekeeping as a fantastic 'bargain', whereby benefits are extracted with lesser costs. In the words of Doyle and Sambanis:

> Nor is the United States discriminated against in the assessment of UN costs ... The United States and other large [financial contributors] will have to ask whether UN peace operations are worth the cost ... both the UN's Cambodian and Salvadoran operations look remarkably cheap and genuinely successful when measured solely in terms of U.S. national interests.[96]

Assuming that the weakest and poorest countries in the world lumped together in band J, at the bottom of the UN peacekeeping assessments system, are 'exploiting' the rich and powerful states in the upper bands would be to ignore the range of power that accrues to those states in the higher reaches of the assessments system—not least their ability to financially discipline the UN organisation as a whole in accordance with their wishes.

Even if we do not go as far as assuming that the global South is exploiting the North through the peacekeeping assessments system, public goods theories tend to dissolve all institutional friction and political clashes of interest into the bland calculus of narrowly economic rationality that will function with ever greater effectiveness as long as incentives are properly aligned. According to Bobrow and Boyer, the fact that the global South provides manpower and the North the money for the production of 'system stability' is an expression of a refined division of labour—a 'specialization in ... contribution [that] can [reduce] the opportunity costs to the contributors and [result in] gains in efficiency of provision (and thus an aggregate increase in the supply of public goods provided).'[97] James T. Fearon and David D. Laitin describe this as a 'natural trade between the rich, major powers and many developing countries', the latter characterised by large armies and weak extractive capacities vis-à-vis their own societies.[98] One defence advisor interviewed by the author in the New York embassy of a developing country described this 'natural trade' less enthusiastically as the 'blood-money trade-off'.[99]

This Panglossian rationalisation of a 'natural trade' between the developed and developing worlds evinces a remarkable political naïvety. Such is the result of grafting microeconomic categories onto the domain of political investigation. The results of this are described by Duane Bratt: 'The connotations of Pakistani or Jordanian soldiers serving American or British officers in some failed state would resemble European armies in Asia and Africa prior to independence and would reek of neo-colonialism.'[100] Bobrow and Boyer discount neo-imperial theories of peacekeeping by suggesting that if considerations of imperial security predominated then we would expect other powers' peacekeeping operations to directly correlate with US military interventions—apparently forgetting the fact that the US is the predominant power on the Security Council and retains military encampments of various kinds in over one hundred countries.[101]

Ultimately it matters little whether the blood money trade-off is viewed as a 'natural trade', and efficient specialisation in function, or as an inefficient underproduction of the 'public good' of international stability. The point is that this view simply ignores the structures of imperial security that are embedded in the institutions of UN peace-keeping. This is not least due to the fact that the 'rich, major states' do not merely pay the protection money and then retire from the field, but also influence how the money is used and directly control how their hirelings go about their business.

Thus for all the effort to rigorously place rational self-interest at the core of the explanation, public goods theories carry a number of concomitant assumptions, some more explicit, others less so, that require us to be naïve about the claims made by power and the means used by power. The end results are the familiar bromides of liberal internationalism—more peacekeepers, in greater numbers, with better coordination, to spread the values of peace, order and justice. For all that public goods explanations do not require us to assume that the democratic millennium is upon us as is the case with democratic theories of peacekeeping, ultimately public goods theories nonetheless rest on homologous assumptions about the end of history—assumptions that the era of systemic confrontation and transformation is over, and all that remains is to stamp out the embers of conflict to efficiently distribute the benefits of universal peace and plenty.

This is not to say that the application of economic categories to questions of international order is entirely redundant, whatever the contortions of public goods theories. Theorists of empire have often spoken in similar terms apropos certain imperial states—Britain in the nineteenth century, the US in the twentieth—who were seen to be providing certain global 'services' in order to cultivate imperial dependence among allies and clients around the world. It was Marxists who pioneered the application of economic categories to international order when they began to reason in the early twentieth century that the contemporaneous economic restructuring that they were witnessing would be replicated in the political realm.

Like most commentators of the time, German Social Democrat Karl Kautsky believed that imperialism was intertwined with economic expansion of the core capitalist states. Kautsky reasoned that the cartelisation of the economic realm would express itself in the political realm by states coordinating their actions in the colonial world so as to mutually satisfy their interests without destroying each other in damaging conflicts. This theoretical possibility of ultra-imperialism calls into question the view of peacekeeping theorists that the multilateral character of UN peacekeeping necessarily expunges imperialism. According to Kimberly Marten, 'Since multilateralism is what legitimates these operations, it is politically unacceptable to suggest that a single, powerful entity (with the authority equivalent to an imperial state) ought to be in charge.'[102]

In Marxist debates on imperialism the conceptual linking of the economic to the political realm did not mean simply grafting categories from one domain to the other, but translating economic concepts into specifically political forms. The main question that resulted was whether this political restructuring of global order would be peaceful or antagonistic. These have been the two poles of a recurring debate in International Relations across the last century, symbolised by the names of their most famous proponents Karl Kautsky and Vladimir Lenin, respectively. While Kautsky looked forward to the likelihood of coordination and cooperation between imperial powers in an arrangement he dubbed 'ultra-imperialism', Lenin held that such cooperation could never transcend the anarchic logic of capitalist competition that was both economic and geopolitical.

Peacekeeping and theories of Imperialism

On the face of it, peacekeeping perhaps most closely resembles Karl Kautsky's vision of ultra-imperialism from the early twentieth century—the view that Lenin took to task in his rejoinder *Imperialism: The Highest Stage of Capitalism: A Popular Outline*. Consider, for example, UN peacekeeping during the controversy over the US-led invasion of Iraq in 2003. Arguably the most damaging political divide between Western states since the end of the Cold War, the invasion of Iraq did not paralyse the Council as regards peacekeeping. As we have seen, new missions were authorised and existing ones expanded 'at an unprecedented rate'.[103] At the height of Franco-US bitterness over the Iraq invasion, Peter Hallward describes the equanimity that accompanied the international intervention in Haiti:

No brusque pre-emptive strikes, domestic carping or splintering coalitions have marred the scene ... In overthrowing the constitutionally elected government of Jean Bertrand Aristide, Washington could hardly have provided a more exemplary show of multilateral courtesy. Allies were consulted, the UN Security Council's blessing sought and immediately received [...] The Quai d'Orsay's offer of diplomatic protection would guarantee not only safe entry but painless withdrawal, as the proposed UN Stabilization Force, took up the burden three months later.[104]

Indeed, as we have seen earlier in this chapter, the integrity of a great power concert has been a precondition of the expansion of peacekeeping since its foundation. As Norrie MacQueen has argued, during periods of great power conflict peacekeeping efforts have been diverted into regional operations, while at times when great power rivalries have been suppressed, UN peacekeeping has expanded.[105]

Yet if peacekeeping bears traces of ultra-imperialism, many observations could be made to differentiate the world of today from that of Kautsky. Among the most obvious differences is that the two most populous nations in the world—India and China, the subjugation of whose ancient civilisations confirmed European ascendency—are now emergent great powers once again. China even sits on the UN Security Council and, as we have seen, pursues its own global purposes through peacekeeping. Insofar as the Security Council is a cartel-like great power directorate as envisaged by Kautsky, it did not emerge as Kautsky thought, arising from coordination between entities of roughly equal strength. Instead it arose under conditions of unparalleled US primacy, which itself was the product of the most catastrophic cycle of great power conflict in human history and could only be maintained in the face of a nuclear-armed systemic rival in the form of the Soviet Union. In that process, the national ruling classes of the advanced economies forged many instruments and ideologies of international cooperation to overcome the divisiveness of previous conflicts.[106]

On a more fundamental level, both Lenin and Kautsky's views presupposed the necessity of geopolitical expansion and armed competition to capitalist growth in the metropolitan economies. Yet it is clear that peacekeeping is not the corollary of economic expansion. On the contrary, the existence of peacekeeping is often tied up with the lesser strategic significance of particular states and regions: the existence of a peacekeeping operation shows that no single power is sufficiently motivated by self-interest to mount a unilateral operation excluding the possibility of other powers' influence in a particular area. Doubtless peacekeeping, where successful, helps facilitate the reintegration of particular states into the global economy and ultimately smoothes the path of commerce. Yet this process of integration is not itself integral to the functioning of the global economy, or indeed, to peaceful relations between the great powers.

In other words, peacekeeping is a function of the prior pacification of great power rivalries rather than the pacification of great power rivalries being a function of peacekeeping. It shows therefore that although some of the institutional forms that Kautsky divined have indeed emerged, the practice of peacekeeping is not consistent with the terms of the theory of ultraimperialism as a whole. This in turn reflects economic restructuring across the last century—a more globally integrated world under US leadership, which no longer requires colonial expeditions to secure access to new supplies of raw materials and markets, and where economic expansion is not dependent on the exclusion of other powers from these spheres of influence. That all this suggests that the world has changed since the early twentieth century is obvious—and trivial. The broader and more important point is that the theorisation of contemporary imperialism needs to account for peacekeeping if it is to have any claim to accurately depict the reality of the use of force in international politics today.

If peacekeeping fits the wider historical pattern of imperialism, it is a very specific form of the exercise of imperial power. For whatever influence is wielded by peacekeepers, its precondition is the anti-colonial credentials of the United Nations. In this respect, the United Nations and its imperial functions have developed within the larger international order shaped by the US since 1945. That is, an indirect imperialism predicated on disciplining the behaviour of subordinate states, remoulding their political and social structures when required, but not obliterating their nominal independence.

This imperial framework reaches back to the first pulse of US overseas expansionism following the 1898 Spanish-American War. While the US annexation of Spain's colony in the Philippines provoked insurgency in those islands and fostered anti-imperialist sentiment in the US itself, relegating the Spanish colony of Cuba to the status of a de facto protectorate while preserving its formal independence not only met less domestic opposition in the US but also integrated Cuban nationalists into the US-sponsored independence regime.[107] It was US President Franklin D. Roosevelt who scaled up this vision of anti-colonial imperialism onto a truly global level, when he envisaged the United Nations as a 'trusteeship of the powerful' to oversee the states that would emerge from the dissolution of the colonial empires. Roosevelt was evidently happy to describe his vision in terms borrowed from the imperial internationalism of the League era. Imperial peacekeeping by the United Nations thus shares many features with the non-territorial forms of US imperialism post-1945: constitutional independence of the subordinate states is maintained alongside projects of nation-building and internal transformation to meld with the transnational institutions of metropolitan power. If the precondition of a US-led imperial order is a framework of independent states, then the United Nations as the bastion of Third World decolonisation can be seen as a bulwark of this post-war US order.

But there are also important differences. Exercises of neo-colonial power—whether deploying military 'advisers', backing putsch attempts or responding to requests for 'help' issued by dependent regimes—always risk exposure and denunciation as malevolent foreign meddling. The fact that Western/US power has had to consistently resort to covert or proxy means in order to effect imperial aims was the homage that vice had to pay to virtue during the Cold War. The gap between the ideal of self-determination and the reality of imperialism was the basis for political critique and opposition. Even in the post-Cold War era, when Western powers have been able to mount open military interventions justified by the most extravagant and grandiloquent claims of defending humanity itself, they have never fully been able to shake off suspicions of imperial intent, as attested by the widespread popularity of 'war for oil' theories, or the mass incredulity that met the justifications given for the US-led invasion of Iraq in 2003. UN peacekeeping does not carry this burden, not least because it does not usually involve the mass deployment of Western forces. Its political influence is less suspect.

Theorists of imperialism who have sought to integrate accounts of post-colonial independence with the reality of US empire have typically proceeded in a teleological vein, seeing the formation of many independent states as fulfilling the highest needs of capitalist development.[108] In so doing they reduce a protracted planetary revolt against empire to a distracting sideshow alongside capitalist globalisation. But the two perspectives on the end of the empire, while contradictory, are not mutually exclusive: the regulation of independent statehood through the United Nations was a means of containing the disruption caused by the disintegration of the European empires and involved the extension of US hegemony over a more integrated world system.

End of Empire, birth of Imperial multilateralism: UN peacekeeping during the Cold War

Thus far the discussion in this book has focused on peacekeeping in the post-Cold War era—that period when peacekeeping became a keystone in the architecture of international security. In this respect the discussion has followed in the footsteps of many other studies of peacekeeping, which have reasonably presented the end of the Cold War as the defining moment of modern peacekeeping. As important as the end of the Cold War is in explaining the resurgence of peacekeeping, it also introduces several degrees of distortion into our observation—distortions that we can now correct by briefly reviewing some elements of Cold War-era peacekeeping.

First, overemphasising the impact of the end of the Cold War also overemphasises the link between peacekeeping and collective security. The fact that peacekeeping emerged during the Cold War while the Security Council was deadlocked by superpower rivalry—and then rapidly expanded once that deadlock ended—has solidified the view that peacekeeping was essentially a second-class substitute for the collective security that failed to materialise as a result of Cold War rivalries. Second, the optics of 'Cold War' versus 'post-Cold War' in the study of peacekeeping have introduced a distinct strain of nostalgia in peacekeeping studies, with certain traditionalists looking back to a 'classical' or 'golden age' of peacekeeping, when peacekeepers were less morally compromised and their tasks simpler.

This distorted stylisation means that we miss strong elements of continuity across the Cold War and post-Cold War periods, particularly as regards the development of imperial peacekeeping. As we shall presently see, imperial peacekeeping is not simply hypertrophied cooperation produced in a uniquely benevolent international environment. The imperial character of peacekeeping is visible even in the much reduced peacekeeping operations of the Cold War era. In examining the Cold War history of peacekeeping, we see how peacekeeping served to protect imperial interests in the process of decolonisation, and how functions of imperial ordering once carried out by colonial empires were internationalised as UN peacekeeping tasks.

In the first instance, peacekeeping operations were often mounted in order to buttress the retreat of colonial empires: UN peacekeepers provided cover to the retreat of British imperialism from Cyprus, Palestine and Egypt (Unficyp, Unscob and Unef I, respectively),[109] Belgian rule in Congo (Onuc) and Dutch colonialism in Indonesia (Untea). Other peacekeepers were deployed in the conflicted aftermath of partition stemming from imperial practices of divide-and-rule (the missions in Kashmir, Gaza, Sinai and Lebanon).[110] Some of the post-Cold War missions have even been belated instances of decolonisation, such as Namibia (Untag). A former German colony, then a League mandate and subsequently a UN trust territory administered by South Africa, the apartheid regime continued to occupy the country until the end of the Cold War as part of its own project of racist expansionism. East Timor was a similar case, annexed as it was by Indonesia following the collapse of the Portuguese empire in the 1970s. The UN ruled the country following the end of the Indonesian occupation in 1999 right through to 2002. But it is not clear that the people of independent Timor-Leste have since fully emerged from international tutelage.[111] Powerfully appointed UN missions operated continuously in the country across the first decade of independence. In other instances, UN peacekeeping operations have facilitated military interventions by Western states in their former colonies: the 2000 British intervention in Sierra Leone and the 2003 French intervention in Haiti and Côte d'Ivoire are notable examples.

The fact that late imperialism was so often intertwined with the rise of international organisation means that some of the countries hosting UN peacekeepers are already familiar with intervention by international organisation—quite unlike the popular image of UN peacekeeping as an international *deus ex machina* that swoops in on conflict from the outside to dispense peace and aid.

Take Somalia and Rwanda, two countries whose post-Cold War suffering is often attributed to the insufficiency and inadequacy of UN peacekeeping. Yet both had prior experience as wards of international institutions, as both countries had been UN trust territories. Rwanda was a 'class B' League of Nations mandate and subsequently a UN trust territory after the Second World War, while Somaliland was an Italian-run UN trust territory from 1949 to the formation of modern Somalia in 1960.[112] Italian rule was reasserted over the Horn of Africa after the Second World War—and against the wishes of Somalis—in return for Italy renouncing claims to its former colony in Libya. Extensive UN oversight was embedded into the restored Italian colonial regime in Somaliland. One of the legacies attributed to this particular phase of UN-led nation-building was the exacerbation of clan rivalries at the expense of earlier forms of reconciliation for dealing with intercommunal conflict.[113] The notorious construction of polarised racial identities in Rwanda—which laid the basis for the horrors of the 1994 war—occurred for the most part under the Belgian mandate, when Rwanda was ruled as part of the 'sacred trust' of civilisation bestowed upon Brussels by the League.[114]

The 1960–64 Onuc mission in Congo, when UN peacekeepers intervened in a state disintegrating in the midst of civil war, is sometimes taken as the forerunner of today's operations aimed at stemming civil wars and state collapse. Nor was Onuc the only Cold War mission where peacekeepers used force: subsequent missions continued to expand peacekeepers' rights to use force beyond defensive measures, as seen in the deployments to Cyprus (Unficyp, 1964-present) and Egypt (Unef II, 1973–79)—even though both missions were much smaller and less well-armed than the Congo operation.[115] There is also the example of the 1962–63 Untea mission as a forerunner of the Kosovo and East Timor missions in which the United Nations directly administered the territory of West Irian (albeit the UN mission there prepared the territory for absorption into Indonesia rather than prefiguring new states, as in the cases of Kosovo and East Timor). But the imperial prerogatives of peacekeeping can be uncovered even in the smaller and less powerful peacekeeping missions as well.

Take Unef I, deployed on the Egyptian border from the end of the Suez War of 1956 until the peacekeepers' withdrawal with the outbreak of the Six Day War of 1967. Unef I is worth examining in some detail because the peacekeeping textbooks treat this operation as the first 'proper' UN peacekeeping operation as well as being the paragon of the 'classic peacekeeping' of the Cold War era.[116] On closer inspection, we shall see that the prerogatives of imperial multilateralism shaped the Unef mission as well.

Unef I and the 1956 Suez War

In British public memory the 1956 war is generally remembered—even lamented—as a strategic retreat resulting in the scaling back of imperial ambition and yet another humiliating accommodation to US leadership. From the liberal internationalist perspective, Unef is seen as an institutional innovation by brilliant entrepreneurial diplomats and UN officials. Although there had been several de facto peacekeeping missions authorised by the United Nations prior to Unef, these were all small-scale observer missions, not involving significant armed forces.[117] Due to its origins in the Cold War, peacekeeping has often been cast as an attempt by the United Nations to carve out a role for itself in response to the paralysis of the Council resulting from the US-Soviet confrontation.

Unef was created by Canadian diplomats and the then UN Secretary-General Dag Hammarskjöld to help end the 1956 Suez War that saw Britain, France and Israel collude to destroy the government of Colonel Nasser in retribution for Egypt's nationalisation of the Anglo-French Suez Canal Company. The Unef mission was a small, lightly armed contingent of UN peacekeepers that monitored the ceasefire line on the Egyptian border with Israel after the end of the war. From the retrospective viewpoint of the civil conflicts that have characterised the post-Cold War era, the Unef mission appears straightforward: strong international support in a thinly populated area with a clear distinction between the forces of the two belligerent states.[118] The Achilles's heel of this classical peacekeeping mission was seen to be its dependence on the consent of the host state, which could be withdrawn at any point. When Egypt did withdraw its consent on the eve of the 1967 Arab-

Israeli War, the UN and its peacekeepers were powerless to prevent the renewed outbreak of conflict.

But this commonplace view of the origins of peacekeeping is misguided on several counts. For a start, it was not Soviet-US rivalries that paralysed the United Nations in this instance but rivalries between Western states. Due to the Franco-British veto in the Security Council, the United Nations had to create Unef using the 'Uniting for Peace' procedure in the General Assembly, which the US had originally crafted as a means of outflanking the Soviets on the Council during the Korean War. According to MacQueen, from the US point of view Unef I 'was a means of closing over without long-term damage the division that had opened up in the western alliance. It was also a means of containing, if not resolving, a situation that appeared to be on the point of spinning out of control.'[119] As British and French paratroopers began their airborne invasion of Egypt in early November 1956, Soviet tanks were penetrating into Budapest to destroy the uprising in Hungary. But while the Soviet intervention in Hungary did not alter the overall balance of power in the world, the Suez Crisis did threaten the solidarity of the Atlantic alliance. In other words, the UN response was a way of managing relations among the great powers themselves more than it was a response to the actual conflicts occurring in the world. Here the United Nations performed the function of imperial multilateralism by sublimating inter-imperial rivalries.

The scandal of the covert collusion between the British, French and Israelis to invade Egypt is so familiar that it is often forgotten that the justification for the Anglo-French assault given at the time was the need to end a regional war in the interests of the international community (it had been previously agreed that the Israeli invasion would provide the pretext for the Anglo-French intervention). The entrepreneurship of the United Nations consisted therefore less in ejecting imperial influence from the Middle East as much as making international intervention in the Arab-Israeli conflict legitimate. According to Al-Qaq's study of the diplomacy of the time: 'Egypt ... capitulated to more or less every Western demand *before* the [1956] invasion and *as a result* of mediation by Dag Hammarskjöld, and that by the time the British and French aerial attacks began, Egypt was in absolutely no position to reject a proposed UN force'.[120]

Canadian foreign minister Lester Pearson initially believed that the crisis could be defused simply by asking the Anglo-French invasion force to run up the UN flag on Egyptian soil in place of the Union flag and *tricolore*.[121] When this suggestion failed, the Canadians blithely offered the Queen's Own Rifles of Canada as a substitute for Her Majesty's British forces.[122]

But this is not all: the deployment of Unef did not cast the British and French as imperialists who had violated Egyptian sovereignty with Israel as their proxy. The international agreements that underpinned Unef treated each state as an equivalent disputant party whose consent was required for the operation to go ahead, retrospectively normalising the Anglo-French presence in Egypt even as they agreed to withdraw from Egyptian soil. The basis for the withdrawal included a secret agreement not to militarise the Gaza Strip (then under Egyptian sovereignty)—thereby meeting a key Israeli security concern.[123] For these reasons it is perhaps better to see UN forces as effectively replacing Israeli, British and French forces.[124] The agreements under which Unef forces deployed tied Egypt into accepting the presence of foreign troops on her soil until the crisis had been settled to the satisfaction of the United Nations itself.[125]

Al-Qaq further argues that the regime of Canal governance laid out in Security Council Resolution 118 (1956), which formed the basis of the post-war settlement, went even further than the original Convention of Constantinople of 1888 in its formal restriction of Egyptian sovereignty over the canal. While the original treaty recognised the Canal as located on Egyptian territory, the UN settlement defined the Canal as an international resource in its insistence that the operation of the Canal be insulated from the 'politics of any country'.[126] UN troops were only deployed on the Egyptian side of the armistice line, and their presence in Sharm el-Sheikh ensured the free passage of Israeli shipping through the Straits of Tiran—thereby meeting another one of Israel's strategic priorities in the 1956 war. Small wonder that Nasser's rivals in the Middle East mocked him for 'hiding behind the skirts' of the UN.[127] Nasser's need to show his independence from the United Nations helped spur him on to the showdown with Israel that resulted in the 1967 Arab-Israeli War.

To be sure, UN peacekeepers did not restore the Canal to Anglo-French control, nor did they overthrow Nasser or throttle Arab nationalism—all original aims of the tripartite invasion. Indeed, the simple fact that Nasser survived enabled him to consolidate his rule and emerge as an influential Third World anti-imperialist. But the mission also established some important precedents as regards the rights of peacekeepers against the rights and interests of their host nations, as well as opening up a new domain for the legitimate use of military force in international affairs. The history of Unef makes clear that the United Nations was far less impotent, and Nasser's triumph correspondingly more ambiguous, than is commonly believed.

As much as peacekeepers sought to intercede between belligerents in the superpowers' proxy wars in the Third World, their deployments also mapped closely onto the ebb and flow of European empires. As a whole, peacekeeping missions need to be seen in the context of the larger and often overlooked UN role in the era of decolonisation: the integration of newly independent states into a US-designed international order under the UN Security Council. In this protracted and uneven process, many imperial functions and prerogatives once attached to empire were in effect transferred to the United Nations. Across its history, peacekeeping provides one of the most striking and visible illustrations of the imperial multilateralism for which the world body was itself crafted.

The intersection between late imperialism and international organisation should not therefore be restricted to the mandates system. If we can see the rise of peacebuilding as signalling the transfer of trusteeship functions to those of peacekeeping, we should also conceive of the specific functions of the United Nations as an interrelated whole.[128] Even if the world organisation was absent from key security crises in the Cold War, which thereby contributed to the image of its perennial impotence, it was nonetheless functioning effectively on the front of decolonisation.[129] This is described by Sir Adam Roberts:

the greatest achievements of the UN in its first fifty years were probably not in the field of international security narrowly conceived, but rather in providing a framework for the most fundamental change in international relations since 1945: European decolonisation [...] its most important contribution was in providing a framework for entry into international society of the numerous new and reconstituted states, many of which were intensely vulnerable. For them, the UN was not just the means of securing diplomatic recognition, but also a world stage ... and a source of symbolic protection.[130]

It is often held that the Third World organised itself successfully through the United Nations to defend its gains and independence, dissolve colonialism and imperialism and generally embarrass their former colonial overlords.[131] The highest international achievement of decolonisation is often presented in terms of gaining recognition at the level of the United Nations and winning the right to membership of the organisation.[132]

As Roberts indicates, this was part of the successful integration of these states into the international order and the containment of the challenge posed by Third World anti-imperialism, not its apotheosis. The notion that the United Nations was captured by small states to hold great powers to account was a product of the Cold War, but also testimony to the success of the world organisation in integrating, and thereby blunting, the anti-imperialist nationalism of the Third World in this period. The more the Third World struggled to achieve recognition of their rights and interests through the world organisation, the more they enmeshed themselves in an institutional order designed precisely for the purpose of enmeshing them. The paradox of anti-colonial nationalism is that it rescued a quintessential US institution from being submerged by Cold War rivalries.

In as much as the United Nations provided a buttress for national self-determination, this was contingent on the paralysis of the Security Council during the Cold War, which was unable to combine effectively to marshal the member states of the organisation behind it. The Cold War allowed the General Assembly to outflank the Security Council, and to give maximum scope for its rhetorical efforts. This disguised the embedded inequality between the two chambers, the restrictions imposed on states through the award of rights of membership in the organisation, and the enormous power vested in the Council, as described by Martin Wight: 'the Hobbesian sovereign of the [Security Council] was a schizophrenic paralytic incapable of action.'[133] Wight was attentive to the way in which the UN Charter conditioned the venerable rights accorded to states under international law as a result of the powers granted to the permanent members of the Security Council: 'By a striking innovation, the traditional rule that international bodies can decide only by unanimous vote (which is the legal principle that a power cannot be bound by a decision to which it has not itself consented) was modified …'[134] This led Wight to conclude that the United Nations was a:

more authoritarian organization for world security than the League had been. The League had been able to do nothing except by the free cooperation of its members. The United Nations had the qualities of a governmental organization, that could in some respects order and override its members and perhaps even alter their legal rights.[135]

The Charter of the UN empowered the Council rather than member states to decide whether a breach of the peace had occurred, and its decisions are binding. Whereas the League emphasised international law and just settlements in the arbitration of disputes between states, the United Nations substituted for this the political discretion of the Council. In the Charter, states also lost the right to summon the Council, the right to decide war had occurred in breach of international law, and lost the right not to act if the Council demanded that they do so.[136] F.H. Hinsley summarised the situation thus: 'In all the Articles of the Charter which deal with its functions the powers of the Security Council are permissive as well as complete.'[137] Danilo Zolo notes in particular the abrogation of the right to wage war concentrated in the UN Security Council:

The Charter allows … states only the faculty of temporary resistance to aggression pending intervention by the UN Security Council. The Security Council, which is endowed with independent power ranking above that of either or any of the belligerents, has the authority to restore order by resorting for its own part to the use of force, without being compelled to take into account the military manoeuvres initiated either by the attacking or the attacked state.[138]

All of which is to say, quite simply, that however indecorous the General Assembly might have become during the Cold War, however daring and impudent its denunciations and proclamations against imperialism, the fact remains that by subscribing to a Charter that explicitly suborns them to the Security Council and revokes their sovereign right to wage war, Third World states were integrating themselves into a US-inspired and US-led vision of international order.

The United Nations also performed the function of setting the horizon of what was possible to achieve through the dismantling of the European empires, and helped to set limits on the loftier visions of the anti-imperialist leaders, whose ambitions went beyond inheriting state borders drawn by colonial administrators and aimed at unifying peoples across borders. Pan-Africanism and Pan-Arabism are the two most famous examples of such movements. What is more the process of national liberation was not simply about formal independence, but entailed a broader vision of social emancipation through modernisation and development. From the viewpoint of the anti-imperialism of the early to mid-twentieth century, the struggle against colonialism in the developing world lay on a continuum with the struggle for revolution in metropolitan countries. The sacralisation of the nation state achieved through the United Nations helped establish the institutional and ideological parameters with which to contain and limit the revolutionary energies and social changes unleashed across the course of the twentieth century.

If the UN citadel appeared to have been stormed by the Third World during the 1960s and '70s, no such illusions should cloud our thinking about the world body today. Indeed, I would argue that in the post-Cold War world we have come much closer to how the United Nations was supposed to function originally than we ever did in the 1940s—that is, as a great power directorate where the national self-interest of the great powers is disentangled from collective interests, the better to manage them together. Relative harmony on the Council has allowed the five permanent members to ruthlessly exploit the coercive powers available to them under the terms of Charter. If the United Nations is not coordinating the joint armed forces of the permanent members of the Security Council under the command of the Military Staff Committee as permitted by its Charter and envisioned by its founders, this is in no small part because the Security Council stumbled across a more expedient, cost-effective and politically valuable arrangement: the blue helmets.

Conclusion

According to Inis L. Claude, Jr 'International organization is fundamentally ... though not exclusively, a reaction to the problem of war'.[139] Modern day peacekeeping is one of the key innovations pioneered by international organisation in its manifold responses to conflict. Yet at the same time, international organisation has been intertwined with questions of empire and political dependence, not least because many wars across the last century have been bound up with inter-imperial rivalries. If modern international organisation has been crafted collectively to manage the security concerns of the great powers, the expansion of global capitalism and European colonialism inevitably entailed global imperial rivalries becoming ever more intertwined with conflict. So too were the efforts to neutralise this antagonism through international organisation, notably by disinvesting the European empires through international organisation—a vision which saw political oversight transferred from the narrow interests of single states to the more impartial vehicles of international organisations.

The intersection between imperialism and international organisation should come as no surprise. The League of Nations' mandates system was explicitly crafted to neutralise colonial rivalries: class A mandates were equally distributed between Britain and France, class B mandates were run under 'open door' trading policies to avoid economic rivalry and it was forbidden to fortify or militarise the territories of class C mandates.[140] Strikingly, the United Nations explicitly sought to radically expand the principle of trusteeship, as Chapter XI of the Charter made all those ruling dependent territories commit themselves to the proposition that colonial possessions constituted a 'sacred trust' that had to meet certain international standards.

Rather than seeing the evolution of peacekeeping *ex nihilo* or in relation to the proto-peacekeeping efforts of the League, or before it the Congress of Vienna, peacekeeping operations should be seen in the context of UN organisation and purpose as a whole, as well as the wider intertwining of imperialism and international organisation.[141] The liberal vision of global post-natal social work implicit in the UN idea of trusteeship is shared with the UN vision of peacekeeping, as it has increasingly sought to reconstruct the political and social structure of conflict zones in line with its vision of liberal peace.[142] The United Nations represents the sublimation of imperial rivalries, the transfer of the management of political dependency from colonial states to international institutions.

We have now seen in some detail that the extension of Southern peacekeeping contribution has been reliant on certain conditions prevailing in other spheres of the United Nations—the harmonious relations on the Council and the willingness of the financing powers to support peacekeeping. In more general terms, the point of showing the influence of rich and powerful states over the United Nations is to show that Southern states cannot but participate in peacekeeping on the forbearance of states other than themselves.

7

EPILOGUE

CONCLUDING THOUGHTS ON UN PEACEKEEPING, CONTRIBUTION TO UN PEACEKEEPING, AND INTERNATIONAL ORDER

That the political functioning of the United Nations and the public responses to it have a distinctively religious character is a peculiar and under-analysed phenomenon of modern politics. Conor Cruise O'Brien described this as the 'sacred drama' of the United Nations, while Danilo Zolo sees it as a form of political idolatry—the worship of graven images of international order.[1] According to O'Brien:

the United Nations makes its impression on the imagination of mankind through a spectacle presented in an auditorium with confrontations of opposing personages, it may be said to belong to ... *drama*. Since the personages, individually or collectively, symbolise mighty forces, since the audience is mankind and the theme the destiny of man, the drama may rightly be called *sacred*.[2]

One can think of the ritualistic character of UN Security Council crisis diplomacy, the way in which states seek the endorsement of the Council for their uses of military power in much the same way that the princes of medieval Europe would seek the blessing of the Pope, or the fact that the vision of human rights enshrined in the UN Charter and its associated covenants occupies the place of a new secular natural law, no less ethereal and equally able to justify a latter-day era of just wars and democratic crusades.

No metaphor is perfect: if the UN Secretary-General is the secular pope of the age, he can command, as we have seen, more divisions than any Pope in history could ever muster. But the language of religion is nonetheless analytically appropriate. According to O'Brien, due to the relative powerlessness of the organisation compared to states, it is better to understand the institution as structuring certain human needs and fears that are often associated with supernatural power—'needs which create prayer, ritual and holy symbols'.[3] In the case of the United Nations however, the fears which it is supposed to assuage are not those of divine wrath but of humanity itself: 'In this modern drama, man's fear is of man ...'[4]

But rather than seeing these needs as deep and primordial human attributes that recur across the ages, it is better to understand these needs as the products of a contemporary world order shaped by profound structures of political alienation—structures of which the United Nations must be among the most alienated and remote, and given its universal claims and reach, correspondingly the one invested with the most heavenly attributes. How else but in religious terms can one describe the naïvety of the belief that the blessing of the victors of the Second World War transubstantiates the soldiers of nation states into global warrior angels of peace, empowered to defend law and wage war without sin? The superstitious nature of this principle was most evident in the global anti-war protests of February 2003, with the mass demand for UN benediction of the US invasion of Iraq—the second Security Council resolution that never materialised—which would purportedly have transformed a US imperial expedition into a just war.

More routine and uncontroversial but no less superstitious is the belief that the doctrinal 'holy trinity' of UN peacekeeping—limited use of force, consent and impartiality—performs the same miracle of transubstantiation, with troops placed under the command of the Secretary-General. The superstitious response to the consecration of military power reflects the lack of theoretical reflection and controversy over UN peacekeeping, the practice of which remains dominated by the assumptions of liberal internationalism. When criticism of peacekeeping is raised, it is almost always to extend peacekeeping and devote more resources to it.

In the period between the two world wars, the attempt to suppress conflict through the collaborative efforts embodied in the League of Nations stimulated theoretical and political controversy that was sufficient to found the academic discipline of International Relations itself—the 'first great debate', which established the two contending camps within the discipline of realists and idealists, whose intellectual descendants continue to fight along similar battle lines today. Yet today similar efforts to suppress war on a far greater and more successful scale have yielded comparatively little theoretical controversy or deep public interest.[5] Yet if peacekeeping is an inferior substitute for collective security, it ultimately requires views that are no less naïve than those of the interwar idealists, even if today's peacekeepers and their defenders are content to have abandoned the goals of transcending conflict in favour of managing and suppressing it. As the predominant form of the international use of military force, UN peacekeeping has normalised extensive and highly intrusive military intervention on an unprecedented scale. Peacekeeping has helped to re-enchant the use of military power, not only in extending the domains into which military power can be legitimately applied but also in making the spread of liberal and democratic values contingent on the use of force. The success of UN peacekeeping in conflating the instruments and practices of warfare with that of peace would be the envy of any totalitarian ideologue.

That peacekeeping is treated in this way reflects its post-ideological character in that it represents the application of standardised techniques and preformatted solutions to political and social conflict, offering models that are to be disseminated to the peace-kept, rather than allowing for the creative exercise of political autonomy and self-determination. Yet for all that peacekeeping is endowed with attributes that supposedly distinguish it from state-led uses of military force, it is still a use of force that expresses and reinforces preexisting power structures and international inequalities.

This book began by contrasting the deployment of UN peacekeepers with that of US military forces. Yet on another level, rather than counterposing UN peacekeepers to US forces, peacekeeping would be better conceived as an adumbration of US power, even if one mediated through international institutions. For the scale of UN peacekeeping today is contingent on a world that is unipolar in terms of its power distribution and post-ideological in terms of its politics. The policing of smaller powers effected through peacekeeping is contingent on peace among the big powers. As such, the vast peacekeeping system we see today will only remain credible as long as the underlying power relations of the contemporary international order remain intact. As these relations are bound to change, at that point the capacity to indefinitely sustain such large deployments of armed forces around the world on behalf of a wraithlike 'international community' will no longer be possible. In the meantime, however, it is incumbent on all those interested and concerned with international politics and the deployment of military force not to be lulled into complacency regarding the nature of military power and the political costs of its repeated and extensive use. It is for the reader to judge how far this book has contributed to that goal.

NOTES

PREFACE AND ACKNOWLEDGEMENTS

1. Trevor Findlay, 'The new peacekeepers and the new peacekeeping' in T. Findlay (ed.), *Challenges for the New Peacekeepers*, New York: Oxford University Press, 1996, p. 1.
2. See for example Larry Fabian, *Soldiers without Enemies: Preparing the United Nations for Peacekeeping*, Washington, D.C.: The Brookings Institution, 1971. Rosalyn Higgins devotes sustained attention to the role of and UN relations with contributor states in her four-volume study of UN peacekeeping during the Cold War. Rosalyn Higgins, *United Nations Peacekeeping: Documents and Commentary*, Oxford: Oxford University Press, four volumes.
3. Perry Anderson, 'Made in USA', *The Nation*, 2 April 2007.

1. INTRODUCTION

1. Vincenzo Bove and Ron Smith, 'The economics of peacekeeping' in D. L. Braddon and K. Hartley (eds) *Handbook on the Economics of Conflict*, Cheltenham and Northampton, MA: Edward Elgar, 2011, p. 244.
2. United Nations, 'Background Note: United Nations Peacekeeping', June 2012. Online. Available HTTP: www.un.org/en/peacekeeping/documents/background-note.pdf (accessed 29 March 2012)
3. Monusco comprises the most military and police forces. At the time of writing, the single largest peacekeeping mission overall is the Unamid mission in the Sudanese province of Darfur. See UN Peacekeeping website for further details.
4. Soviet Russia's counterproposal was more modest: twelve ground divisions, 600 bombers, 300 fighters, five to six cruisers, twenty-four destroyers and twelve submarines. See John G. Ruggie, 'The UN and the Collective Use of Force: Whither or Whether?', *International Peacekeeping* 3, no. 4, 1996, pp. 3–4.
5. Alex J. Bellamy and Paul D. Williams, 'Introduction', in Alex J. Bellamy and Paul D. Williams (eds), *Providing Peacekeepers: The Politics, Challenges, and*

Future of United Nations Peacekeeping Contributions, Oxford: Oxford University Press, 2013, p. 5. Original emphasis.

6. Alexander Wendt, 'On Constitution and Causation in International Relations', *Review of International Studies* 24, no. 5, 1998, p. 105.

7. Larry L. Fabian, *Soldiers without Enemies: Preparing the United Nations for Peacekeeping*, Washington, D.C.: The Brookings Institution, 1971, p. 15.

8. Vladimir I. Lenin, 'The Question of Peace' in Lenin, *On National Liberation and Social Emancipation*, Moscow: Progress Publishers, 1986, p. 133.

9. Fabian, *Soldiers without Enemies*, p. 15. On Lebanon, see Norrie MacQueen, *Peacekeeping in the International System*, London: Routledge, 2006, pp. 13, 131; see also Paul R. Pillar, 'The Greater Middle East: Problems of Priorities and Agendas' in D.C.F. Daniel, P. Taft and S. Wiharta (eds), *Peace Operations: Trends, Progress and Prospects*, Washington, D.C.: Georgetown University Press, 2008, pp. 208–9. On Grenada and peacekeeping, see J.N. Moore, 'Grenada and the International Double Standard', *American Journal of International Law* 78, no. 1, 1984, pp. 145–68.

10. United Nations, *United Nations Peace Operations: Principles and Guidelines*, New York: Peacekeeping Best Practices Section, 2008, p. 14.

11. Jarat Chopra, 'Introducing Peace-Maintenance' in J. Chopra (ed.), *The Politics of Peace-Maintenance*, Boulder, CO: Lynne Rienner, 1998, p. 7. As the title of Chopra's volume suggests, his contempt for 'blue-speak' has not deterred him from coining more terms in the same debased currency.

12. Thierry Tardy, 'Introduction' in T. Tardy (ed.), *Peace Operations After 11 September 2001*, London: Frank Cass, 2004, pp. 2–3. On the definitional and conceptual haze in peacekeeping studies see also Michael Bhatia, *War and Intervention: Issues for Contemporary Peace Operations*, Bloomfield, CT: Kumerian Press, 2003, p. 11; *The Economist*, 'Call the blue helmets', 6–12 January 2007; Eşref Aksu, *The United Nations, intra-state peacekeeping and normative change*, Manchester: Manchester University Press, 2003, pp. 22–8; Paul Diehl, *Peace Operations*, Cambridge: Polity Press, 2008, p. 3; Oldrich Bures, 'Wanted: A Mid-Range Theory of International Peacekeeping', *International Studies Review* 9, no. 3, 2007, pp. 409–12; John T. O'Neill and Nicholas Rees, *United Nations Peacekeeping in the Post-Cold War Era*, London: Routledge, 2005, p. 6; Michael Barnett, Hunjoon Kim, Madelene O'Donnell, Laura Sitea, 'Peacebuilding: what is in a name?', *Global Governance* 13, no. 1, 2007, pp. 35–58. Others simply draw the conclusion of definitional futility, for example, Diehl, *Peace Operations*, p. 8.

13. For an effective criticism of such efforts, see Alex J. Bellamy and Paul D. Williams with Stuart Griffin, *Understanding Peacekeeping*, 2ⁿᵈ ed., Cambridge: Polity Press, 2010, pp. 14–8. Nonetheless Bellamy and his collaborators go on to differentiate between seven different types of operation.

14. Alex J. Bellamy, 'The "Next Stage" in Peace Operations Theory?', *International Peacekeeping* 11, no. 1, 2004, p. 28

15. Ibid.

16. On this point, see Tardy, 'Introduction', p. 3; Kimberly Zisk Marten, *Enforc-*

ing the Peace: Learning from the Imperial Past, New York: Columbia University Press, 2004, p. 5; and Michael Pugh, 'Maintaining Peace and Security' in D. Held and A. McGrew (eds) *Governing Globalization: Power, Authority and Global Governance*, Cambridge: Polity Press, 2002, p. 217 and *passim*.

17. On this point, see further Jean-Marc Coicaud, *Beyond the National Interest: The Future of UN Peacekeeping and Multilateralism in an Era of US Primacy*, Washington, D.C.: United States Institute of Peace, 2007, p. 64.

18. Cited in Mats Berdal, *Building Peace After War*, Abingdon: Routledge, 2009, p. 17.

19. Alan James, *Peacekeeping in International Politics*, New York: St Martin's Press, 1990, p. 10.

20. Ibid. At the broad level of international order at which much of the discussion takes place, unless specified otherwise I will take 'peacebuilding' and 'peacekeeping' to be interchangeable. On distinctions between peacebuilding and peacekeeping, see the discussion in the next chapter.

21. Fabian, *Soldiers without Enemies*, p. 5. See also Inis L. Claude, Jr., *Swords into Plowshares: The Problems and Progress of International Organization*, 4th ed., New York: Random House, 1971, p. 317. For more recent authors echoing these views see Paul Diehl, 'Peacekeeping Operations and the Quest for Peace', *Political Science Quarterly* 103, no. 3, 1988, p. 488; and Mark J. Mullenbach, 'Deciding to Keep Peace: An Analysis of International Influences on the Establishment of Third-Party Peacekeeping Missions', *International Studies Quarterly* 49, no. 3, 2005, p. 533.

22. Roland Paris, 'Broadening the Study of Peace Operations', *International Studies Review* 2, no. 3, 2000, p. 44.

23. Michael Pugh, 'Peacekeeping and Critical Theory', *International Peacekeeping* 11, no. 1, 2004, p. 39. See also Virginia Page Fortna, *Does Peacekeeping Work? Shaping Belligerents' Choices After Civil War*, Princeton: Princeton University Press, 2008, p. 175.

24. Sandra Whitworth, 'Where is the politics in peacekeeping?', *International Journal* 50, no. 2, 1995, p. 428.

25. Ibid., p. 434. The point is echoed by David N. Gibbs, who noted that the debate is dominated by the liberal internationalist supporters of peacekeeping with the result that the most 'basic questions are often elided'. Gibbs, 'Is peacekeeping a new form of imperialism?', *International Peacekeeping* 4, no. 1, 1997, p. 122.

26. In support of this shift in the focus of peacekeeping studies, see further Mullenbach, 'Deciding to Keep Peace', pp. 531–2.

27. For example, Alex J. Bellamy and Paul D. Williams (eds), *Providing Peacekeepers: The Politics, Challenges, and Future of United Nations Peacekeeping Contributions*, Oxford: Oxford University Press, 2013. See further Michael O'Hanlon and Peter W. Singer, 'The Humanitarian Transformation: Expanding Global Intervention and Capacity', *Survival: Global Politics and Strategy* 46, no. 1, 2004, pp. 77–100 and Daniel *et al.* (eds), *Peace Operations*.

28. Whitworth, 'Where is the politics in peacekeeping?', p. 434. See also Paris's effective critique of the limitations of policy relevance in scholarship, Paris, 'Broadening the Study of Peace Operations'. p. 32.

29. Whitworth, 'Where is the politics in peacekeeping?', p. 435.

30. On middle powers and Cold War-era peacekeeping, see Laura Neack, 'UN Peace-keeping: In the Interest of Community or Self?', *Journal of Peace Research* 32, no. 2, 1995, pp. 181–96.

31. Birger Heldt, 'Trends from 1948 to 2005: How to View the Relation between the United Nations and non-UN Entities' in D.C.F. Daniel *et al.*, *Peace Operations*, pp. 24–5.

32. The calculations in tables 1.2 and 1.3 are my own. In ranking the contributions of the T10 and N10 I followed Donald C.F. Daniel *et al.* in looking at the month when overall peacekeeping deployments were highest overall for that year, and then going to each country's contributions for that particular month. See Donald C.F. Daniel, Katrin Heuel and Benjamin Margo, 'Distinguishing among Military Contributors' in D.C.F. Daniel *et al.* (eds), *Peace Operations*, p. 29.

33. James H. Lebovic, 'Uniting for Peace? Democracies and United Nations Peace Operations after the Cold War', *Journal of Conflict Resolution* 48, no. 6, 2004, p. 922.

34. Although Nepal was never formally absorbed into the British Empire, it is reasonable to say that it fell in the British sphere of influence in South Asia.

35. Jonah Victor, 'African peacekeeping in Africa: Warlord politics, defence economics, and state legitimacy', *Journal of Peace Research* 47, no. 2, 2010, p. 227. Note that Victor is referring to the African peacekeeping states only, but as the case of South Asia shows, his point applies more generally.

36. Paul Kennedy, *The Parliament of Man: The United Nations and the Quest for World Government*, London: Allen Lane, 2006, p. 83. Kennedy includes Fiji which, although a stalwart of peacekeeping, contributes such comparatively small numbers that it no longer falls into either the T10 or N10 as detailed above.

37. See Ashley Jackson, *The British Empire and the Second World War*, London: Hambledon Continuum, 2006.

38. Dipankar Banerjee, 'South Asia: Contributors of Global Significance' in D.C.F. Daniel *et al.*, *Peace Operations*, p. 189.

39. Here I have counted 'the West' as those NATO member states that can offer at least 5 per cent of their total ground forces for rapid reaction military interventions and peacekeeping duties, plus Australia and Japan. This excludes therefore, Belgium, Italy and Spain, among others. See further O'Hanlon and Singer, 'The Humanitarian Transformation', p. 84. More expansive definitions of 'the West' do not go higher than a quarter of annual UN peacekeeping deployments. See Alex J. Bellamy and Paul D. Williams, 'The West and Contemporary Peace Operations', *Journal of Peace Research* 46, no. 1, 2009, p. 45.

40. Thomas G. Weiss, 'The Humanitarian Impulse' in D.M. Malone (ed.), *The UN Security Council: From the Cold War to the 21st Century*, Boulder, CO: Lynne Rienner, 2004, p. 44.

41. This is the argument of Vijay Prashad in his *The Darker Nations: A People's History of the Third World*, New York: The New Press, 2006.

42. Berdal, *Building Peace After War*, p. 159.

43. Colum Lynch, 'The blue helmet caste system', *Foreign Policy*, 11 April 2013. Online. Available HTTP: turtlebay.foreignpolicy.com/blog/16159 (accessed 12 April 2013).

44. The remark was made by Gowan to me at a brown bag seminar at the Center on International Cooperation, New York University, 13 April 2010. For Chesterman's characterisation see Simon Chesterman, 'The Use of Force in UN Peace Operations', Peacekeeping Best Practices Unit (undated), p. 11. Online. Available HTTP: smallwarsjournal.com/documents/useofforceunpko.pdf (accessed 6 April 2012).

45. Mohammed Ayoob, *The Third World Security Predicament: State Making, Regional Conflict and the International System*, Boulder, CO: Lynne Rienner, 1995, p. 15. See Ayoob's discussion more generally pp. 1–17.

46. Ibid., p. 13.

47. Andrew Blum, 'Blue Helmets from the South: Accounting for the Participation of Weaker States in Peacekeeping Operations', *Journal of Conflict Studies* 20, no. 1, 2000, p. 2. See also Kgomotso Monnakgotla, 'The Naked Face of UN Peacekeeping: Noble Crusade or National Self-Interest?', *African Security Review* 5, no. 5, 1996, pp. 2–3. See also Blum, 'Blue Helmets from the South', p. 13.

48. See for example Rachel E. Utley (ed.), *Major Powers and Peacekeeping: Perspectives, Priorities and the Challenges of Military Intervention*, Aldershot: Ashgate, 2006; David S. Sorenson and Pia C. Wood (eds), *The Politics of Peacekeeping in the Post-Cold War Era*, London: Frank Cass, 2005. From the global South, Utley's collection covers Russia and China, while the Sorenson and Wood collection covers Argentina, India and Nigeria. Note that both collections were published well after Southern states became established as the predominant group of contributors to UN peacekeeping. The D.C.F. Daniel *et al.* collection *Peace Operations* gives equal weight to the major regions of the world, regardless of their relative weight in UN peacekeeping.

49. Blum, 'Blue Helmets from the South', p. 15.

50. Carsten Holbraad, *Middle Powers in International Politics*, Basingstoke: Macmillan, 1984, p. 3. This is the general conclusion of the literature on small states and middle powers in international affairs. According to Michael Handel for example: 'the most obvious fact about small powers is that their foreign policy is governed by the policy of others. It follows that the student of small power policy, even more than the student of great power policy, must concentrate on the environment.' Handel, *Weak States in the International System*, London: Frank Cass, 1981, p. 4. Jeanne A.K. Hey concludes in a collection of essays studying the foreign policy of small states: 'the domestic level of analysis rarely emerges the most important criterion in determining small state foreign policy. Yet … domestic-level factors are crucial conditioners of foreign policy content.' 'Refining Our Understanding of Small State Foreign Policy' in

J.A.K. Hey (ed.), *Small States in World Politics: Explaining Foreign Policy Behavior*, Boulder, CO: Lynne Rienner, 2003, p. 191. Needless to say, all of these authors identify those exceptions in which smaller powers may gain more room for manoeuvre.

51. Martha Finnemore, *The Purpose of Intervention: Changing Beliefs about the Use of Force*, Ithaca: Cornell University Press, 2004, p. 4.

52. On this point, see further Mullenbach, 'Deciding to Keep Peace', p. 536.

53. Marten, *Enforcing the Peace*, p. 17.

54. Roland Paris, 'International Peacebuilding and the "Mission Civilisatrice"', *Review of International Studies* 28, no. 4, 2002, p. 670.

55. See for example Tony Judt, 'Is the UN Doomed?', *The New York Review of Books* 54, no. 2, 15 February 2007; Bruce Jones, 'The Limits of Peacekeeping', *Los Angeles Times*, 1 March 2006. The BBC has run an informative series of reports and profiles of UN peacekeeping efforts around the world; see for example: Patrick Jackson, 'When the gloves of peace come off', BBC News, 18 April 2007. Online. Available HTTP: news.bbc.co.uk/1/hi/6542399.stm (accessed 10 April 2012).

56. Mats Berdal, 'The UN After Iraq', *Survival: Global Politics and Strategy* 46, no. 3, 2004, pp. 88–9.

57. Marina Ottoway and Bethany Lacina, 'International Interventions and Imperialism: Lessons from the 1990s', *SAIS Review* 23, no. 2, 2003, p. 86.

58. Roland Paris, cited in Alex J. Bellamy, 'The "Next Stage" in Peace Operations Theory?', p. 32. According to Oliver Richmond, 'Comprehensive peace agreements provide an increasingly detailed and deterministic framework for peace, and often have similar formats and wordings.' *The Transformation of Peace: Rethinking Peace and Conflict Studies*, Basingstoke: Palgrave Macmillan, 2005, p. 113.

59. See for example, the writings of Andrew Bacevich on this score: *Washington Rules: America's Path to Permanent War*, New York: Metropolitan Books, 2010, *passim*.

60. Michael Hardt and Antonio Negri, *Empire*, London, Cambridge: Harvard University Press, 2000, p. 181. Unfortunately, their account of the United Nations is underdeveloped. See the discussion in chapter three.

61. Colum Lynch, 'U.S. and Europe fight over cuts in peacekeeping' *Foreign Policy*, 10 October 2011. Online. Available HTTP: turtlebay.foreignpolicy.com/posts/2011/10/10/us_and_europe_fight_over_cuts_in_peacekeeping (accessed 11 April 2012).

62. Victor G. Kiernan, *Colonial Empires and Armies 1815–1960*, Stroud: Sutton Publishing, 1998, p. 16.

63. Michael W. Doyle and Nicholas Sambanis, *Making War and Building Peace: United Nations Peace Operations*, Princeton: Princeton University Press, 2006, p. 318. On this point see also Marten, *Enforcing the Peace*, p. 19; Chopra, 'Introducing Peace-Maintenance', p. 9.

64. Paris, '"Mission Civilisatrice"', p. 653.

65. Michael Ignatieff, *Empire Lite: Nation-Building in Bosnia, Kosovo and Afghanistan*, London: Vintage, 2003, p. 17.

66. Ibid., p. 2.

67. Andrea K. Talentino, *Military Intervention after the Cold War: The Evolution of Theory and Practice*, Athens: Ohio University Press, 2005, p. 89.

68. Ignatieff, *Empire Lite*, p. 115.

69. C. Wright Mills, *The Sociological Imagination*, New York: Oxford University Press, 1999, p. 214.

70. Berdal, 'UN after Iraq', p. 88.

71. Peter Gowan, 'US:UN', *New Left Review* 24, 2003, p. 14.

72. Cited in Brian Urquhart, 'Looking for the Sheriff', *New York Review of Books*, 16 July 1998.

73. Richard Kareem Al-Qaq, *Managing World Order: United Nations Peace Operations and the Security Agenda*, London: I.B. Tauris, 2009, p. 168.

74. According to Eric Hobsbawm the original subtitle of Lenin's book was 'the *latest* stage of capitalism'; it was Lenin's Soviet publishers who were more premature in their assessment of the future of global capitalism when they changed 'latest' to 'highest'. See *The Age of Empire: 1875–1914*, London: Abacus, 1987, p. 12.

75. See for example Alex Callinicos, *Imperialism and Global Political Economy*, London: Polity Press, 2009; James Heartfield, 'Zombie anti-imperialists vs. the "Empire"', *Spiked Online*, 1 September 2004. Online. Available HTTP: www.spiked-online.com/index.php/site/article/2236/ (accessed 11 April 2012).

76. Al-Qaq, *Managing World Order*, p. 7.

77. Ibid., p. 34.

78. Guéhenno, cited in Thierry Tardy, 'A Critique of Robust Peacekeeping in Contemporary Peace Operations', *International Peacekeeping* 18, no. 2, 2011, p. 159.

79. Michael Pugh, 'Peacekeeping and IR Theory: Phantom of the Opera?', *International Peacekeeping* 10, no. 4, 2003, p. 106. Paris, 'Broadening the Study of Peace Operations', p. 34

80. Paris, 'Broadening the Study of Peace Operations', p. 34.

81. Fabian, *Soldiers without Enemies*, p. vii.

2. PEACE OF THE VICTORS: PEACEKEEPING IN THE POST-COLD WAR ERA

1. Michael Barnett and Martha Finnemore, 'The Power, Politics and Pathologies of International Organizations', *International Organization* 53, no. 4, 1999, pp. 714–5. There is a vast literature on the 'liberal peace'; see further references below.

2. The political economy of peacekeeping and peacebuilding is comparatively under-researched and in any case carried out through a different set of institutions—international economic agencies and development bodies. This will be discussed further below. For one effort to grapple with the political economy of

post-conflict countries, see Michael Pugh, Neil Cooper and Mandy Turner (eds), *Whose Peace? Critical Perspectives on the Political Economy of Peacebuilding*, Basingstoke: Palgrave Macmillan, 2008.

3. Marc Lacey, 'After failures, UN peacekeepers get tough "Robust" new tactics to support aggressive operations against militants in Congo', *International Herald Tribune*, 24 May 2005.

4. Cited in Denis M. Tull, 'Peacekeeping in the Democratic Republic of Congo', *International Peacekeeping* 16, no. 2, 2009, p. 224. Henceforward all references to 'Congo' can be assumed to refer to the Democratic Republic of Congo (Congo-Kinshasa), rather than the Republic of Congo (Congo-Brazzaville).

5. Patrick Jackson, 'When the gloves of peace come off', 18 April 2007, BBC News. Online. HTTP: news.bbc.co.uk/1/hi/6542399.stm (accessed 6 January 2011).

6. Center on International Cooperation, *Annual Review of Global Peace Operations 2012*, Boulder, CO: Lynne Rienner, 2012.

7. Michael J. Jordan, 'UN Forces Toughen Up', *Christian Science Monitor*, 15 June 2005. For the discussion of 'pitched battles' see Michael Pugh, 'Peace Enforcement' in Thomas G. Weiss and Sam Daws (eds), *The Oxford Handbook on the United Nations*, Oxford: Oxford University Press, 2007, p. 377. On the use of heavy weapons and air support in Monuc operations, see Karsten Friis, 'Peacekeeping and Counter-insurgency—Two of a kind?', *International Peacekeeping* 17, no. 1, 2010, p. 61.

8. See David Bosco, 'When peacekeepers go to war', *Foreign Policy*, 1 April 2013. Online. Available HTTP: bosco.foreignpolicy.com/posts/2013/03/28/when_peacekeepers_go_to_war (accessed 12 April 2013).

9. On Sierra Leone, see Alan Bullion, 'India in Sierra Leone: A Case of Muscular Peacekeeping?', *International Peacekeeping* 8, no. 4, 2001, pp. 80–1; 85. On Untac, see Bruce Jones with Feryal Cherif, 'External Study: Evolving Models of Peacekeeping: Policy Implications and Responses', Peacekeeping Best Practices Unit (undated). Online. Available HTTP: pksoi.army.mil/doctrine_concepts/documents/UN%20Policy%20Documents/evolving%20models.pdf (accessed 13 April 2012), p. 21. On Côte d'Ivoire, see further below. Note that I have focused purely on the use of force by peacekeepers under the command of the United Nations, and not those forces deployed alongside UN peacekeepers but outside of UN command structures—for example, the British intervention in Sierra Leone (Operations Palliser and Barras, 2000). These hybrid missions that combine UN peacekeepers alongside non-UN military forces will be discussed in greater detail in chapter four.

10. See further Ryan C. Hendrickson, 'Crossing the Rubicon', *NATO Review*, August 2005. Online. Available HTTP: www.nato.int/docu/review/2005/issue3/offprint_autumn_eng.pdf (accessed 13 April 2012); and Robert C. Owen, 'Operation Deliberate Force: A Case Study on Humanitarian Constraints in Aerospace Warfare', Carr Center for Human Rights Policy Web Working Papers, Kennedy School of Government, University of Harvard, 2001. Online. Available HTTP: http://pksoi.army.mil/doctrine_concepts/docu-

ments/UN%20Policy%20Documents/evolving%20models.pdf (accessed 13 April 2012). NATO estimates direct civilian casualties from the bombing at thirty and an unknown number of Bosnian Serb soldiers (see Owen report).

11. Despite the growing military assertiveness of peacekeepers on the ground and the strategic success of the NATO air campaign, the clumsiness of the 'dual key' joint UN-NATO command system for unleashing NATO air power, as well as the failure of Unprofor to defend the 'safe havens' designated by the Security Council, prompted the disentanglement of NATO and UN peacekeeping efforts—the significance of which will be examined in greater detail in chapter four. On the tank battle, see Peter Viggo Jakobsen, 'The Danish Approach to UN Peace Operations After the Cold War', *International Peacekeeping* 5, no. 3, 1998. p. 106.

12. Norrie MacQueen, *United Nations Peacekeeping in Africa since 1960*, London: Pearson Education, 2002, p. 214.

13. Ibid.

14. Ibid., p. 213.

15. Under the aegis of the United Nations Stand-by Arrangements System established in 1994, member states earmarked military units and equipment for rapid deployment in peacekeeping, thereby enhancing the UN ability to plan operations and helping to ensure that missions were put together more quickly. See further Michael Pugh, 'Maintaining Peace and Security', in David Held and Anthony McGrew (eds) *Governing Globalisation: Power, Authority and Global Governance*, Cambridge: Polity Press, 2002, p. 222. Linked to this concept for rapid deployment was a Danish initiative established in 1996 known as the Stand-by High Readiness Brigade (Shirbrig), a multinational brigade of up to 5,000 troops designed to be ready for immediate deployment to the field between 15 and 30 days' notice and to subsist in the field for up to 6 months. Supported by a permanent planning centre in Denmark, this unit doubles up as the core of the headquarters staff for a Shirbrig deployment. Shirbrig troops are made up of soldiers from different nations trained to the same standard, using the same operating procedures and inter-operable equipment and that regularly take part in combined exercises. The UN has availed itself of Shirbrig in Ethiopia, Liberia and Sudan. Gary Anderson, 'Preparing for the Worst: Military Requirements for Hazardous Missions', in D.C.F. Daniel *et al.* (eds), *Peace Operations: Trends, Progress, and Prospects*, Washington, D.C.: 2008, p. 69.

16. Alex J. Bellamy and Paul D. Williams with Stuart Griffin, *Understanding Peacekeeping*, Cambridge: Polity Press, 2010, p. 52.

17. See Gregory P. Giletti, 'The UN's capacities for strategic lift', *International Peacekeeping* 5, no. 3, 1998, p. 42.

18. United Nations, 'Fifth Committee Takes up $68 million Budget for Logistics Base in Brindisi', 4 June 2009. Online. Available HTTP: www.un.org/News/Press/docs/2009/gaab3912.doc.htm (accessed 13 April 2012)

19. This is from the Report of the Panel on United Nations Peace Operations,

2000, §51, henceforward the 'Brahimi Report', discussed in greater detail below. See further Karsten Friis, 'Peacekeeping and Counter-insurgency—Two of a Kind?', p. 60.

20. Simon Chesterman, 'Does the UN Have Intelligence?' *Survival: Global Politics and Strategy* 48, no. 3, 2006.

21. Ibid., p. 157.

22. Friis, 'Peacekeeping and Counter-insurgency—Two of a Kind?', p. 60.

23. A. Walter Dorn, 'United Nations Peacekeeping Intelligence' in L.K. Johnson (ed.), *The Oxford Handbook of National Security Intelligence*, New York: Oxford University Press, p. 282; see also Simon Chesterman, 'Does the UN Have Intelligence?', p. 153. The disquiet of developing countries over the growth in UN infrastructure for intelligence gathering prompted the General Assembly in 1999 to close down the discreet intelligence bureau established by Boutros-Ghali in the peacekeeping department in 1993, which had hitherto been staffed by intelligence officers freely 'loaned' by the permanent members of the Security Council.

24. See Stathis Kalyvas, '"New" and "Old" Civil Wars: A Valid Distinction?', *World Politics* 54, no. 1, 2001, pp. 99–118.

25. Alex J. Bellamy, 'The "Next Stage" in Peace Operations Theory?', *International Peacekeeping* 11, no. 1, 2004, p. 28.

26. Boutros-Ghali, Boutros. *An Agenda for Peace,* 2nd ed., New York: United Nations, 1995, §44.

27. The 1989–90 Untag mission to Namibia is something of an exception, as we shall see below. Subsequent missions to Angola were less successful.

28. Bush, cited in Michael G. MacKinnon, *The Evolution of US Peacekeeping Under Clinton: A Fairweather Friend?*, London: Frank Cass, 2000, p. 15.

29. On questions of peacekeeping doctrine stemming from the operations of the 1990s, see J.G. Ruggie, 'The United Nations and the Collective Use of Force: Whither or Whether?', *International Peacekeeping* 3, no. 4, 1996, pp. 1–20.

30. Michael Barnett, 'The New United Nations Politics of Peace: From Juridical to Empirical Sovereignty', *Global Governance* 1, no. 1, 1995, 92–93.

31. Blanca Antonini, 'El Salvador' in D. Malone (ed.), *The UN Security Council: From the Cold War to the 21st Century*, Boulder: Lynne Rienner, 2004, p. 431.

32. Ugurhan G. Berkok and Binyam Solomon, 'Peacekeeping, private benefits and common agency' in D. L. Braddon and K. Hartley (eds), *Handbook on the Economics of Conflict*, Cheltenham: Edward Elgar, 2011, p. 266.

33. Andrea K. Talentino, *Military Intervention after the Cold War: The Evolution of Theory and Practice*, Athens: Ohio University Press, 2005, p. 3.

34. Perry Anderson, 'Made in USA', *The Nation*, 2 April 2007.

35. UN, Brahimi report, §51. See also United Nations, *United Nations Peacekeeping Operations: Principles and Guidelines*, 2008, p. 24 (henceforward the 'Capstone Doctrine'). Online. Available HTTP: http://www.peacekeepingbest-practices.unlb.org/pbps/library/capstone_doctrine_eng.pdf (accessed 12 December 2011).

36. UN, Brahimi report, §50.

37. Ibid., p. xi.

38. United Nations, Department of Peacekeeping Operations and Department of Field Support, *A New Partnership Agenda: Charting a New Horizon for UN Peacekeeping*, July 2009, p. 21. Online. Available HTTP: www.un.org/en/peacekeeping/documents/newhorizon.pdf (accessed 13 April 2012).

39. For example see Tull, 'Peacekeeping in the Democratic Republic of Congo'.

40. *Agenda*, §44.

41. Capstone Doctrine, p. 19.

42. Ibid.

43. Here I am focusing on the violent paradoxes resulting from peacekeepers' use of force. Other abuses committed by peacekeepers will be discussed in greater depth below.

44. Mats Berdal, *Building Peace After War*, Abingdon: Routledge, 2009, p. 112.

45. Cited in Richard Gowan, 'The Tragedy of 21ˢᵗ Century Peacekeeping', *World Politics Review*, 19 May 2010.

46. Daniel H. Levine, 'Civilian protection and the image of the "total spoiler": reflections on MONUC support to Kimia II', *African Security Review* 20, no. 1, 2011, p. 101.

47. Human Rights Watch, 'DR Congo: Civilian Cost of Military Operations is Unacceptable', 13 October 2009. Online. Available HTTP: www.hrw.org/news/2009/10/12/dr-congo-civilian-cost-military-operation-unacceptable (accessed 13 April 2012).

48. Berdal, *Building Peace After War*, p. 114.

49. In the words of Levine, 'The approach taken by MONUC and the FARDC was one that was likely to increase FDLR abuses against civilians', p. 102 and *passim*, and Berdal, *Building Peace*, p. 114.

50. For some interesting reflections on ideological aspects of peacekeeping, see W. M. Reisman, 'Stopping Wars and Making Peace: Reflections on the Ideology and Practice of Conflict Termination in Contemporary World Politics', *Tulane Journal of International and Comparative Law* 6, no. 1, 1998, 5–56.

51. Richard Gowan, 'Diplomatic Fallout: U.N.'s "Intervention Brigade" Raises Cost of Interference in DRC', *World Politics Review*, 8 April 2013.

52. MacQueen, *United Nations in Peacekeeping in Africa*, p. 116.

53. Thomas G. Weiss and Meryl A. Kessler, 'Resurrecting Peacekeeping: The super-powers and conflict management', *Third World Quarterly* 12, no. 3/4, 1990, p. 141. See further MacQueen, ibid., pp. 115–6. MacQueen puts Plan casualties at 300 (out of a force of over 1,500) resulting from a 'series of unequal engagements' between the guerrillas and apartheid forces.

54. Alex de Waal, 'US War Crimes in Somalia', *New Left Review* 23, Jul-Aug 1998, p. 137. See also Sherene H. Razack, *Dark Threats and White Knights: The Somalia Affair, Peacekeeping, and the New Imperialism*, Toronto, London: University of Toronto Press, 2004, ch. 2 and Ramesh Thakur, 'From Peace-Keeping to Peace-Enforcement: The UN Operation in Somalia', *The Journal of Modern African Studies* 32, no. 3, 1994, pp. 399–400.

55. de Waal, ibid.

56. According to de Waal 'the Canadians deserve credit for thoroughly investigat-

ing every case that came to light. According to Somalis, the Canadians were some of the best behaved of the peacekeeping forces.' The elite Canadian Airborne Regiment, whose troops were convicted of torture and murder, was subsequently disbanded. The same was not true of other countries' forces, while de Waal also records that 'The US was the *only* contingent in Mogadishu to have an office that entertained complaints from the Somali public and made compensation payments, chiefly to the victims of traffic accidents; only the Canadians and Australians (outside Mogadishu) had similar arrangements.' de Waal, ibid. On the results of the Italian investigation into Italian peacekeepers' behaviour, see Razack, *Dark Threats and White Knights*, pp. 150–1.

57. The phrase is that of Ian Johnstone in his piece 'Dilemmas of Robust Peace Operations', in Center on International Cooperation, *Annual Review of Global Peace Operations*, London, Boulder: Lynne Rienner Publishers, 2006, p. 5.

58. Patrick Jackson, 'When the gloves of peace come off'.

59. Arturo C. Sotomayor, 'Peacekeeping Effects in South America: CommonExperiences and Divergent Effects in Civil-Military Relations', *International Peacekeeping* 17, no. 5, 2010, pp. 629–43, p. 638.

60. See A. Walter Dorn, 'Intelligence-led Peacekeeping: The United Nations' Stabilization Mission in Haiti (MINUSTAH), 2006–07', *Intelligence and National Security* 24, no. 6, 2009, p. 812. See further the website of the Cite Soleil Massacre Declassification Project for discussion of redacted US diplomatic cables relating to civilian casualties in Minustah raids: www.cod.edu/people/faculty/yearman/cite_soleil.htm (accessed 6 September 2011). Varying numbers of casualties are given for the raids. See further Matt Halling, 'Peacekeeping in Name Alone: Accountability for the UN in Haiti', *Hastings Journal of International and Comparative Law*, 31, no. 1, 2007, pp. 461–486 and Naomi Klein, '6/7: the massacre of the poor that the world ignored', *The Guardian*, 18 July 2005. According to local residents cited in Klein's report, the number of dead was put at least twenty. According to China Miéville the 'gang leader' Emmanuel 'Dred' Wilme, who was the target of the 2005 raid, was a community organiser and activist supporter of Aristide's political movement Funmi Lavalas (China Miéville, 'Multilateralism as Terror: International Law, Haiti and Imperialism', *Finnish Yearbook of International Law*, 18, 2007, p. 35).

61. Alex Diceanu, 'Haiti Deserves Better from the United Nations', *Peace Magazine*, Apr-Jun 2006, p. 16.

62. See further Sandra Jordan, 'Haiti's children die in UN cross fire', *The Observer*, 1 April 2007 and Dorn, 'Intelligence-led Peacekeeping', pp. 812–13.

63. The figure of eighty injuries is given by Vetëvendosje! leader Albin Kurti. See Albin Kurti, 'JISB Interview: Kosova in Dependence: From Stability in Crisis to Crisis of Stability', *Journal of Intervention and Statebuilding* 5, no. 1, 2011, pp. 89–97. See further the Amnesty UK Report 'Kosovo (Serbia): Vetevendosje! Activists beaten during Kurti arrest', 21 June 2010, Amnesty UK. Online. HTTP: www.amnesty.org.uk/news_details.asp?NewsID=18835 (accessed 6 September 2011).

64. See Ian Johnstone 'Dilemmas of Robust Peace Ops' pp. 3–4. See also Tim John-

ston, 'Peacekeeping forces kill 4 rebels in East Timor', *International Herald Tribune*, 4 March 2007.

65. On this point, see Mahmood Mamdani, 'The Politics of Naming: Genocide, Civil War, Insurgency', *London Review of Books* 29, no. 5, 2007, 5–8.

66. Capstone Doctrine, p. 34.

67. For a partial critique of the 'spoiler' ideology and its potentially pernicious consequences in relation to peacekeeping, see Levine, 'Civilian protection and the image of the "total spoiler"'. On political questions of citizenship and identity pertaining to the conflict in eastern Congo, see also Mahmood Mamdani, 'The Invention of the Indigène', *London Review of Books* 33, no. 2, 2011, 31–33.

68. See, *inter alia*, David Keen, 'War and Peace: What's the difference?', *International Peacekeeping* 7, no. 4, 2000, p. 9; Berdal, *Building Peace After War*, pp. 49–50.

69. Séverine Autesserre, *The Trouble with Congo: Local Violence and the Failure of International Peacebuilding*, Cambridge: Cambridge University Press, 2010, p. 79.

70. Ibid., *passim*.

71. See B.S. Chimni, 'Refugees, Return and Reconstruction of "Post-Conflict" Societies: a Critical Perspective', *International Peacekeeping* 9, no. 2, 2002, p. 165. On *refoulement* in Congo specifically, see Jacob Stevens, 'Prisons of the Stateless: The Derelictions of UNHCR', *New Left Review* 42, Nov-Dec 2006.

72. See for example Jessica Hatcher and Alex Perry, 'Defining Peacekeeping Downward: The U.N. Debacle in Eastern Congo', *Time*, 26 November 2012. Online. Available HTTP: world.time.com/2012/11/26/defining-peacekeeping-downward-the-u-n-debacle-in-eastern-congo/ (accessed 12 April 2013).

73. My discussion here draws on Mark Duffield, *Global Governance and the New Wars: The Merging of Development and Security*, London: Zed Books, 2001; Jacob Stevens, 'Prisons of the Stateless', *New Left Review* 42, Nov-Dec 2006, and chapter 4 in Michael Barnett and Martha Finnemore, *Rules for the World: International Organization in Global Politics*, Ithaca, London: Cornell University Press, 2004).

74. Capstone Doctrine, p. 24.

75. Tara McCormack, 'Power and Agency in the Human Security Framework', *Cambridge Review of International Affairs* 21, no. 1, 2008, p. 124.

76. 'U.N., French attack Gbagbo heavy weapons in Ivory Coast', Reuters, 10 April 2011. Online. Available HTTP: www.reuters.com/article/2011/04/10/us-ivory-coast-idUSTRE73014Z20110410 (accessed 12 September 2011). A spokesman for President Laurent Gbagbo responded to the UN attacks, saying: 'The residence of the head of state is not a heavy weapon.' See Tarak Barkawi, 'The Shield of Innocence', Al Jazeera, 13 April 2011. Online. Available HTTP: english.aljazeera.net/indepth/opinion/2011/04/201141112379523528.html# (accessed 13 September 2011).

77. Alex J. Bellamy and Paul D. Williams, 'The new politics of protection? Côte d'Ivoire, Libya and the responsibility to protect', *International Affairs* 87, no. 4, 2011, p. 835.

78. Ibid, p. 845.
79. On war crimes attributed to Republican Forces, including a massacre of up to 1,000 civilians, see ibid., p. 834.
80. Voting irregularities were confirmed by African Union and civil society observer missions in the north, and the report of an Ecowas election observer mission has not been released. See Thabo Mbeki, 'What the World Got Wrong in Côte d'Ivoire', *Foreign Policy*, 29 April 2011. Online. Available HTTP: www.foreignpolicy.com/articles/2011/04/29/what_the_world_got_wrong_in_cote_d_ivoire?page=0,1 (accessed 13 April 2012).
81. Ibid.
82. Bellamy and Williams, 'Politics of protection', p. 833.
83. Giulia Piccolino, 'David Against Goliath in Cote d'Ivoire? Laurent Gbagbo's War against Global Governance' *African Affairs* 111, no. 442, 2012, p. 20. The definition of neotrusteeship is taken from James D. Fearon and David D. Laitin, 'Neotrusteeship and the Problem of Weak States' *International Security* 28, no. 4, 2004, p. 7 and *passim*.
84. Boutros Boutros-Ghali, *Unvanquished: A U.S.—U.N. Saga*, London: I.B. Tauris, 1999, p. 68.
85. Douglas Hurd cited in Marrack Goulding, 'The Evolution of United Nations Peacekeeping', *International Affairs* 69, no. 3, 1993, p. 453.
86. Agenda, §21 and §59 respectively.
87. Ibid., §59. The 'rule of law' is one trope that continues to appreciate in rhetorical significance in relation to peacekeeping. See Jean-Marie Guéhenno, 'Giving peace a chance', *The Economist: The World in 2005*, 17 November 2004, pp. 91–2.
88. Berdal, *Building Peace After War*, p. 13.
89. Here I am drawing on the discussion in chapter one of Oliver P. Richmond's *The Transformation of Peace*, Basingstoke: Palgrave, 2005. See also, *inter alia*, Kimberly Marten, *Enforcing the Peace: Learning from the Imperial Past*, New York: Columbia University Press, 2004, p. 23.
90. *Agenda*, §17.
91. Ibid., §20.
92. Unmik still operates in independent Kosova, though in a diminished role since the country declared independence in 2008. The reality and substance of that independence is questionable, as the country is effectively a protectorate of the European Union. See Philip Cunliffe, 'The legacy of Kosovo? International paternalism', *Spiked Online*, 24 March 2009. Online. Available HTTP: http://www.spiked-online.com/newsite/article/6388#.Ue5iueD3Dj0 (accessed 25 June 2013).
93. See for example Jarat Chopra, 'The UN's Kingdom of East Timor', *Survival: Global Politics and Strategy* 42, no. 3, 2000, pp. 27–40; Jarat Chopra, 'Building State Failure in East Timor', *Development and Change* 33, no. 5, 2002, pp. 979–1000; Alexandros Yannis, 'The UN as Government in Kosovo', *Global Governance: A Review of Multilateralism and International Organiza-*

tions 10, no. 1, 2004, pp. 67–91. See more widely Conor Foley, *The Thin Blue Line: How Humanitarianism Went to War*, London: Verso, 2008, passim. Cf. former UN peacekeeping boss Jean-Marie Guéhenno's robust defence of the East Timor mission: 'Few peoples in the post-Second World War era have ever been given such an opportunity to determine their destiny in relative freedom and security, and with the luxury of an unprecedented amount of international assistance and good will.' in Jean-Marie Guéhenno, 'On the Challenges and Achievements of Reforming UN Peace Operations', *International Peacekeeping* 9, no. 2, 2002, pp. 77–8.

94. Bosnia-Herzegovina is often spoken of in the same breath as East Timor and Kosovo as it too has been administered by international viceroys since the end of the war there in 1995. However, the internationally-led administration of Bosnia is not carried out by the United Nations but rather through a Peace Implementation Council led by Western states and established by the Dayton Peace Accords. Latterly the functions of international administration in Bosnia have been increasingly taken up by the European Union. This makes Bosnia, like newly independent Kosova, more a part of the 'European Raj' than a UN one, as suggested in the title of Gerald Knaus and Felix Martin's article 'Lessons from Bosnia-Herzegovina: Travails of the European Raj', *Journal of Democracy* 14, no. 3, 2003, pp. 60–74. As the post-Unprofor administration of Bosnia is not undertaken by the United Nations, I will not discuss it in this book in any depth. The classic critique of international rule in Bosnia is David Chandler's book *Bosnia: Faking Democracy after Dayton*, 2nd ed., London: Pluto Press, 2000.

95. Roland Paris, 'International peacebuilding and the "mission civilisatrice"', *Review of International Studies* 28, no. 4, 2002, p. 650.

96. Roland Paris, 'Broadening the Study of Peace Operations', *International Studies Review* 2, no. 3, 2000, p. 43. See further Barnett and Finnemore, 'The Power, Politics and Pathologies of International Organizations', pp. 712–13.

97. Eşref Aksu, *The United Nations, intra-state peacekeeping and normative change*, Manchester, New York: Manchester University Press, 2003, p. 92. See further Thierry Tardy 'UN Peace Operations in Light of the Events of 11 September 2001' in Thierry Tardy (ed.), *Peace Operations after 11 September 2001*, London: Frank Cass, 2004, p. 21.

98. Michael W. Doyle and Nicholas Sambanis, *Making War and Building Peace: United Nations Peace Operations*, Princeton: Princeton University Press, 2006, p. 325.

99. Roland Paris, 'Peacekeeping and the Constraints of Global Culture', *European Journal of International Relations* 9, no. 3, 2003, pp. 449–450.

100. Paris, '"mission civilisatrice"', pp. 644–5.

101. Michael Lipson, 'Peacekeeping: Organized Hypocrisy?', *European Journal of International Relations* 13, no. 1, 2007, p. 19.

102. Doyle and Sambanis, *UN Peace Operations*, p. 198; see further p. 312 and p. 320 on the intrusion into domestic sovereignty by UN peacekeeping.

103. Ibid, p. 327.

104. Fearon and Laitin, 'Neotrusteeship', p. 9.

105. *Economist*, 'Helping to calm a continent', 9 June 2012.

106. S. Neil MacFarlane, 'International Politics, Local Conflicts and Intervention' in T.M. Shaw and N. Mychajlyszyn (eds), *Twisting Arms and Flexing Muscles: Humanitarian Intervention and Peacebuilding in Perspective*, Aldershot: Ashgate, 2005, p. 12.

107. See further the discussion in chapter six.

108. See Paris, 'limits of liberal internationalism', p. 61 on the character of democracy in the peacebuilding of the new liberal internationalism.

109. Roland Paris, *At War's End: Building Peace After Civil Conflict*, Cambridge: Cambridge University Press, 2004, p. 65.

110. Ibid., p. 123.

111. Ibid., pp. 138–9.

112. Ibid., p. 145.

113. The narrative in this paragraph is based on the argument of William I. Robinson, *Promoting Polyarchy: Globalization, US Intervention, and Hegemony*, Cambridge: Cambridge University Press, 1996.

114. Barry Gills and Joel Rocamora, 'Low Intensity Democracy', *Third World Quarterly* 13, no. 3, 1992, pp. 501–23.

115. Doyle and Sambanis, *Making War and Building Peace*, p. 197.

116. For a general account of the shift in policy and vision, see Francis Fukuyama (ed.), *State-Building: Governance and World Order in the 21st Century*, Ithaca: Cornell University Press, 2004.

117. Paris provides a useful and succinct summary of this evolution in his article 'Saving liberal peacebuilding', *Review of International Studies* 36, no. 2, 2010, pp. 341–3.

118. See Simon Chesterman, 'Virtual Trusteeship', in D. Malone (ed.), *The UN Security Council*.

119. Autesserre, *The Trouble with Congo*, p. 3.

120. Kant attributed the latter to the Chinese empire of his day. See Kant, 'Speculative Beginning of Human History' in Immanuel Kant, *Perpetual Peace and Other Essays*, Trans. Ted Humphrey, Indianapolis, IL: Hackett Publishing, 1983, p. 58.

121. For the classic theoretical expression of the theory on which I base the following argument, see Michael W. Doyle, 'Kant, liberal legacies and foreign affairs', Parts I & II, *Philosophy and Public Affairs* 12, no. 4, 1983, pp. 323–53.

122. Michael Pugh, 'Peacekeeping and Critical Theory', *International Peacekeeping* 11, no. 1, 2004, p. 46.

123. Doyle and Sambanis, *United Nations Peace Operations*, p. 13. For another conceptualisation of peacekeeping as policing, see Martin Shaw, *The New Western Way of War: Risk-Transfer War and Its Crisis in Iraq*, Cambridge: Polity Press, 2005, p. 142.

124. Richard Kareem Al-Qaq, *Managing World Order: United Nations Peace Operations and the Security Agenda*, London: I. B. Tauris, 2009, p. 15.

125. Cited in Tom Woodhouse and Oliver Ramsbotham, 'Cosmopolitan Peace-keeping and the Globalisation of Security', *International Peacekeeping* 12, no. 2, 2005, p. 139. On the UN more generally, see Hidemi Suganami, *The Domestic Analogy and World Order Proposals*, Cambridge: Cambridge University Press, 1989. According to Suganami, 'The police analogy was at the centre of United Nations thinking.' (p. 201)

126. Details available on the UN policing website. Online. Available HTTP: http://www.un.org/en/peacekeeping/sites/police/policing.shtml (accessed 12 December 2011).

127. Cammaert cited in Jackson, 'When the gloves of peace come off'.

128. Ibid.

129. Brahimi report, §50.

130. Aksu, *intra-state peacekeeping and normative change*, p. 92.

131. Here I am drawing on Ramsbotham and Woodhouse 'Cosmopolitan Peace-keeping'; Mary Kaldor, *New and Old Wars: Organized Violence in a Global Era*, 2nd ed., Cambridge: Polity Press, 2007; Lorraine Elliott and Graeme Cheeseman (eds), *Forces for Good: Cosmopolitan militaries in the twenty-first century*, Manchester: Manchester University Press, 2004; Michael O'Connor, 'Policing the peace' in A. Schnabel and R. Thakur (eds), *United Nations Peacekeeping Operations: Ad Hoc Missions, Permanent Engagement*, Tokyo: United Nations University Press, 2001.

132. 'Post-Westphalian' in that the origin of the modern states system is conventionally dated to the Peace of Westphalia in 1648.

133. Kaldor, *New and Old Wars*, p. 133.

134. Ibid.

135. William Durch, 'Are We Learning Yet? The Long Road to Applying Best Practices' in W.J. Durch (ed.), *Twenty-First-Century Peace Operations*, Washington, D.C.: United States Institute of Peace and The Henry L. Stimson Centre, 2006, p. 592.

136. Fearon and Laitin, 'Neo-trusteeship', p. 23. The RUC was renamed the Police Service of Northern Ireland in 2001.

137. See Ramsbotham and Woodhouse, 'Cosmopolitan Peacekeeping', *passim* and Kaldor, *New and Old Wars*, chapter 6.

138. Kaldor, *New and Old Wars*, p. 139.

139. Alan Ryan, 'Cosmopolitan objectives and the strategic challenges of multinational military operations' in Elliott and Cheeseman (eds), *Forces for Good*, p. 77.

140. Ibid., p. 67.

141. Wight's term was in fact 'sphere of interest', which exists 'where an international police authority is assumed by the presiding power and exercised by means of intervention'. *Power Politics*, H. Bull and C. Holbraad (eds), London: Penguin Books, 1979, p. 194.

142. Barnett, 'empirical to juridical sovereignty', p. 94.

143. Matteo Tondini, 'From Neo-Colonialism to a "Light Footprint" Approach: Restoring Justice Systems', *International Peacekeeping* 15, no. 2, 2008, p. 237.

144. Shaw, *The New Western Way of War*, p. 142.

145. Lawrence Freedman, 'The Changing Forms of Military Conflict', *Survival: Global Politics and Strategy* 40, no. 4, 1998–99, p. 47.

146. BBC, 'Brazil army to take up "peacekeeping" in Rio slums', BBC News, 5 December 2010. Online. Available HTTP: www.bbc.co.uk/news/world-latin-america-11920645 (accessed 13 April 2012).

147. Freedman, 'The Changing Forms of Military Conflict', p. 47.

148. Paris, '"mission civilisatrice"', 670.

149. Pugh, 'Peacekeeping and Critical Theory', pp. 48–9.

150. As Alejandro Bendaña observes of peacebuilding practice, democracy cannot be sundered from self-determination: they are part of a single issue 'since there is no such thing as democratic colonies or partially sovereign democracies'. Alejandro Bendaña, 'From Peacebuilding to Statebuilding: One step forward, two steps back', *Development* 48, no. 3, 2005, p. 14.

151. On the decline of international equality between the developed and less developed countries and its ramifications, see *inter alia*, David Chandler, *From Kosovo to Kabul and Beyond: Human Rights and International Intervention* 2nd ed., London: Pluto Press, 2005, ch. 7; Benedict Kingsbury, 'Sovereignty and Inequality' in A. Hurrell and N. Woods (eds), *Inequality, Globalization and World Politics*, Oxford: Oxford University Press, 1999; Will Bain, 'The political theory of trusteeship and the twilight of international equality', *International Relations* 17, no. 1, 2003, pp. 59–77; Mohammed Ayoob, 'Humanitarian intervention and state sovereignty', *International Journal of Human Rights* 6, no. 1, 2002, pp. 81–102.

3. THE HIGHEST FORM OF LIBERAL IMPERIALISM

1. For example, Andrew Williams, 'Reconstruction: The Bringing of Peace and Plenty or Occult Imperialism?', *Global Society* 21, no. 4, 2007, p. 551; Kimberly Marten, *Enforcing the Peace: Learning from the Imperial Past*, New York: Columbia University Press, 2004, p. 13.

2. James Rubin, 'Base motives', *The Guardian*, 7 May 2004.

3. Perry Anderson, 'Made in USA', *The Nation*, 2 April 2007.

4. Michael Hardt and Antonio Negri, *Empire*, London, Cambridge: Harvard University Press, 2000, p. 189. Although Hardt and Negri are attentive to the way in which the authority to use force increasingly shades over from nation state to supra-state agencies, these insights are by no means unique to their work. Some time ago Hedley Bull observed that political leaders' rhetoric betrayed the diminishing political appeal of the sovereign state when military alliances had to be described as 'regional security systems' and 'war [as] police action'. Bull, 'Society and Anarchy in International Relations' in J. Der Derian (ed.), *International Theory: Critical Investigations*, Basingstoke, Macmillan, 1995, p. 76.

5. Roland Paris, 'International peacebuilding and the "mission civilisatrice"', *Review of International Studies* 28, no. 4, 2002, p. 638. See further Marten, *Enforcing the Peace*, pp. 3–5.

6. Paris, ibid.

7. Roland Paris, 'Saving liberal peacebuilding', *Review of International Studies* 36, no. 2, 2010, p. 350.

8. Marina Ottoway and Bethany Lacina, 'International Interventions and Imperialism', *SAIS Review* 23, no. 2, 2003, p. 74.

9. Foley, *The Thin Blue Line: How Humanitarianism Went to War*, London: Verso, 2008, p. 194. Foley is referring to Sierra Leone and Liberia.

10. Ibid, p. 222.

11. Michael Gilligan and Stephen J. Stedman, 'Where Do Peacekeepers Go?' *International Studies Review* 5, no. 4, 2003. Their findings are echoed by Marten, *Enforcing the Peace*, p. 7 and endorsed by Paul Diehl, *Peace Operations*, Cambridge: Polity Press, 2008, p. 60. The claim that peacekeepers are deployed in order to secure access to strategic sources of raw materials was suggested by David N. Gibbs, 'Is peacekeeping a new form of imperialism?', *International Peacekeeping* 4, no. 1, 1997, pp. 122–8; and Hirofumi Shimizu, 'An Economic Analysis of the UN Peacekeeping Assessment System', *Defence and Peace Economics* 16, no. 1, 2005, p. 2. Outside the academy, such claims have featured more prominently in popular journalism. John Pilger for example claimed that 'Britain is recolonising Sierra Leone in an attempt to get its hands on the country's diamonds', *New Statesman*, 18 September 2000.

12. Ottoway and Lacina, 'Imperialism and Intervention', pp. 74–5. For similar arguments distinguishing peacekeeping from colonialism, see further Jarat Chopra, 'Introducing Peace-Maintenance' in Jarat Chopra (ed.), *The Politics of Peace Maintenance*, Boulder, CO: Lynne Rienner, 1998: pp. 9–10.

13. Paris, 'Saving liberal peacebuilding', p. 348.

14. Michael W. Doyle and Nicholas Sambanis, *Making War and Building Peace: United Nations Peace Operations*, Princeton: Princeton University Press, 2006. p. 318. The authors contradict themselves on this point of effectiveness elsewhere, as we shall see below.

15. James D. Fearon and David D. Laitin, 'Neotrusteeship and the Problem of Weak States', *International Security* 28, no. 4, 2004, p. 7. Hardt and Negri put this more lyrically: 'The distinct national colours of the imperialist map of the world have merged and blended into the imperial global rainbow.' *Empire*, p. xiii.

16. Doyle and Sambanis, *Making War and Building Peace*, p. 318. In support of this point, see also Marrack Goulding, 'The Evolution of United Nations Peacekeeping', *International Affairs* 69, no. 3, 1993, p. 462 and Chopra, 'Introducing peace-maintenance', p. 9.

17. Ottoway and Lacina, 'Imperialism and Intervention', p. 75.

18. Ibid., p. 77; 83.

19. Ibid., p. 85.

20. On these points, see Richard Gowan, 'The Tragedy of 21st Century Peacekeeping', *World Politics Review*, 19 May 2010.

21. Doyle and Sambanis, *Making War and Building Peace*, p. 318.

22. Michael W. Doyle, 'The new interventionism', *Metaphilosophy* 32, nos. 1–2, 2001, p. 227.

23. James Mayall, 'Introduction', in Mats Berdal and Spyros Economides, *United Nations Interventionism 1991–2004*, Cambridge: Cambridge University Press, 2007, p. 31.

24. Roland Paris, 'Peacekeeping and the Constraints of Global Culture', *European Journal of International Relations* 9, no. 3, 2003, p. 457.

25. Marten, *Enforcing the Peace*, p. 17. The sub-title of Marten's book is 'Learning from the Imperial Past'. See further Ottoway and Lacina, 'Imperialism and Intervention', p. 82; 87.

26. Simon Chesterman, *You, the People: The United Nations, Transitional Administration and State-building*, Oxford: Oxford University Press, 2004, p. 253.

27. Lenin by contrast had a more flexible approach to modelling imperialism: he stressed the 'conditional and relative value of all definitions' in characterising the imperialism of his day, noting that fixed definitions could not encompass 'all the concatenations of a phenomenon in its complete development'. Vladimir I. Lenin, *Imperialism: The Highest Stage of Capitalism: A Popular Outline*, London: Pluto Press, 1996, p. 90.

28. Mats Berdal, 'The UN After Iraq', *Survival: Global Politics and Strategy* 46, no. 3, 2004, p. 88.

29. Cited in Alejandro Colás, *Empire*, Cambridge: Polity, p. 169.

30. David N. Gibbs's review essay is often taken as a stand-in to represent all arguments regarding the imperial character of contemporary peacekeeping. Yet the specific claims in Gibbs' essay are more modest and circumspect than the way in which his arguments have often been invoked in the literature. Gibbs does not claim a systematic correlation between peacekeeping deployments and the existence of strategic raw materials, but rather makes a more general point about *realpolitik* and the spheres of influence behind peacekeeping.

31. On this point, see Ray Kiely, *Rethinking Imperialism*, Basingstoke: Palgrave Macmillan, 2010, p. 83. See further David Horowitz, *Empire and Revolution: A Radical Interpretation of Contemporary History*, New York: Vintage Books, 1969.

32. Paris, 'Saving liberal peacebuilding', p. 349.

33. See Michael Pugh, Neil Cooper, Mandy Turner (eds), *Whose Peace? Critical Perspectives on the Political Economy of Peacebuilding*, Basingstoke: Palgrave Macmillan, 2008.

34. Eric Ouellet, 'Multinational counterinsurgency: the Western intervention in the Boxer Rebellion 1900–1901', *Small Wars and Insurgencies* 20, nos. 3–4, 2009, pp. 507–27.

35. There was intervention in the Greek War of Independence in 1827 and multinational interventions by Austrian, British and French forces in Lebanon in 1840 and 1860.

36. Interestingly, some of these nineteenth century expeditions against the Ottoman Empire are also cited as prototypes of humanitarian intervention. There are earlier examples from the nineteenth century too, such as military cooperation between the European powers against the Barbary pirates until 1830. See Erwin Schmidl, 'The Evolution of Peace Operations from the Nineteenth Cen-

tury', *Small Wars and Insurgencies* 10, no. 2, 1999, pp. 4–20. Schmidl also covers the counter-revolutionary interventions of the Congress and Holy Alliance powers within Europe itself.

37. Ibid. The expedition to Albania never materialised due to the outbreak of the First World War, though Albania survived as a nominally independent state until it was annexed to the Italian empire.

38. Fabian, *Soldiers without Enemies: Preparing the United Nations for Peacekeeping*, Washington, D.C.: The Brookings Institution, 1971, pp. 43–4. Fabian calls these colonial ventures early 'adumbrations' of peacekeeping.

39. Ibid.

40. Chesterman, *You, the People*, p. 45.

41. Paris, 'Broadening the Study of Peace Operations', *International Studies Review* 2, no. 3, 2000, p. 43.

42. Michael Ignatieff, *Empire Lite: Nation-Building in Bosnia, Kosovo and Afghanistan*, London: Vintage, 2003, p. 95.

43. Ibid., p. 94.

44. Chesterman, *You, the People*, p. 46.

45. Béatrice Pouligny, *Peace Operations Seen from Below: UN Missions and Local People*, London: C.H. Hurst & Co., 2006, p. 43. The quotes are from those interviewed by Pouligny. The irony in this discussion is that, in many respects, racism was a product of the imperial encounter, not its source. Indeed, racism coalesced as a way of ideologically systematising precisely the kinds of views relayed to Pouligny by UN peacekeepers. See Kenan Malik, *The Meaning of Race: Race, History and Culture in Western Society*, New York: New York University Press, 1996.

46. Victor G. Kiernan, *Colonial Empires and Armies 1850–1960*, Stroud: Sutton Publishing, 1999, p. 24.

47. See Chandler, *Faking Democracy After Dayton*.

48. See supra n. 47 in chapter one.

49. Ignatieff, *Empire-Lite*, p. 72.

50. Lord Paddy Ashdown, former viceroy of Bosnia-Herzegovina, is reported to have claimed that he would have been granted the 'droit de seigneur' if he had asked for it—the ancient apocryphal right of the feudal lord to sleep with any woman in his domain on the night of her wedding. Cited in Christopher Bickerton, 'State-building: exporting state failure' in Christopher Bickerton, Philip Cunliffe and Alexander Gourevitch (eds), *Politics without Sovereignty: A critique of contemporary international relations*, London: UCL Press, 2007, p. 99.

51. See for example, Michael Barnett and Christoph Zurcher, 'The peacebuilder's contract: how external statebuilding reinforces weak statehood' in R. Paris and T. Sisk (eds), *The Dilemmas of Statebuilding: confronting the contradictions of post-war peace operations*, Abingdon: Routledge, 2009.

52. Robert O. Keohane, 'Political authority after intervention: gradations in sovereignty' in J.L. Holzgrefre and R.O. Keohane (eds), *Humanitarian Intervention: Ethical, Legal and Political Dilemmas*, Cambridge: Cambridge University Press, 2003, p. 277.

53. See for example Stephen Krasner, 'Sharing sovereignty: New Institutions for Collapsed and Failing States', *International Security* 29, no. 2, 2004, pp. 85–120.

54. Guéhenno wrote these words in a previous role as French ambassador to the European Union. Jean-Marie Guéhenno, *The End of the Nation-State*, Trans. Victoria Elliott, Minneapolis: University of Minnesota Press, 1993, pp. 121–2.

55. See Sankar Muthu, *Enlightenment against Empire*, Princeton: Princeton University Press, 2003.

56. This section draws on the work of David Long, Mark Mazower and Bernard Porter (see bibliography for references).

57. Cited in David Long, 'Paternalism and the Internationalization of Imperialism' in D. Long and B.C. Schmidt (eds) *Imperialism and Internationalism in the Discipline of International Relations*, Albany, NY: State University of New York Press, 2005, p. 75.

58. See Paris, '"mission civilisatrice"', p. 651.

59. Hobson, cited in Bernard Porter, *Critics of Empire: British Radicals and the Imperial Challenge*, London: I.B. Tauris, 2008, p. 231.

60. Long, 'Paternalism', p. 78.

61. Ibid., p. 80.

62. Hobson proposed rules and regulations in this regard, which are incorporated into the definition of regimes used in regime theory today. See David Long, 'Liberalism, Imperialism and Empire', *Studies in Political Economy* 78, 2006, pp. 201–23.

63. Hobson, cited in Porter, *Critics of Empire*, p. 232.

64. Hobson, cited in Long, 'Paternalism', p. 77.

65. Ibid., p. 85.

66. Ibid., p. 91.

67. Ibid., p. 84.

68. Long, 'Liberalism, Imperialism and Empire', p. 208.

69. See Long, 'Paternalism'. p. 80, and Porter, *Critics of Empire*, p. 232. Both of these were founded on the idea that colonial peoples need internationally directed tutelage before they are ready for political independence. Hobson's ideas also interlocked with the development of the theory of indirect rule in Africa (which he welcomed as a progressive reform towards his own vision of 'responsible' imperialism) and the policies of Sir Fredrick (later Lord) Lugard, who would formulate the 'dual mandate' theory of imperial rule in the inter-war period. Hobson's ideas also intersected with those of Fabian imperial reformers, whom he admired, although Hobson insisted that if the 'interests of civilization as a whole' were to be the guide of imperial policy as the Fabians desired, the only guarantee of this was international institutions and rules that would ensure such an outcome beyond the claims of the interfering power (Porter, *Critics of Empire*, p. 231). The compliment was not returned: according to David Long, Hobson rankled the Fabians with his criticism of their justifications of imperial rule on the grounds that it would foster social reform

and benefit the working classes (Long, 'Liberalism, Imperialism and Empire', p. 204). As Hobson's friend and intellectual collaborator Ramsay MacDonald shifted from the milieu of late nineteenth century radical and social liberalism to the Labour party of the early twentieth century, he took with him many of Hobson's ideas to equip with an 'ethical' theory of imperialism a party already anticipating having to rule a global empire once in office (Porter, *Critics of Empire*, pp. 237–9).

70. Long, 'Paternalism', p. 82.

71. Long, 'Liberalism, Imperialism, Empire' p. 208.

72. Long, 'Paternalism', p. 87.

73. Hobson, cited in Paris, '"mission civilisatrice"', p. 651. It could also be argued that Paris dilutes his defence of peacebuilding by his ambivalence: on the one hand he claims that peacebuilding is not imperialistic, and on the other, he claims peacebuilding is the realisation of Hobson's 'sane imperialism'.

74. Paris, 'Saving liberal peacebuilding', pp. 349–50.

75. An argument inspired by Karuna Metana, *Alibis of Empire: Henry Maine and the Ends of Liberal Imperialism*, Princeton: Princeton University Press, 2010.

76. Oliver P. Richmond, *The Transformation of Peace*, Basingstoke: Palgrave, 2005, p. 70.

77. Alex J. Bellamy and Paul Williams, 'Introduction: Thinking anew about peace operations', *International Peacekeeping*, 11, no. 1, 2004, p. 6.

78. See Paris, 'Broadening', *passim*.

79. Canadian feminist scholars have the distinction of being among the few academic observers of peacekeeping to have systematically explored crimes by peacekeepers and sought to understand their roots, rather than leaving them to the realm of scandal for journalists and evasive national commissions of inquiry. Most academic studies of peacekeeping focus on the institutional and organisational failures of peacekeeping, sins of omission rather than sins of commission. See also Sharene Razack, *Dark Threats and White Knights: The Somalia Affair, Peacekeeping and the New Imperialism*, Toronto: University of Toronto Press, 2004.

80. Sandra Whitworth, *Men, Militarism, and UN Peacekeeping*, Boulder, CO: Lynne Rienner, 2004, *passim*.

81. Whitworth, *Men, Militarism, and UN Peacekeeping*, p. 186.

82. See for example, Roberto J. González, 'Human terrain: past, present and future applications', *Anthropology Today* 24, no. 1, 2008, pp. 21–6.

83. Séverine Autesserre, *The Trouble With Congo: Local Violence and the Failure of International Pacebuilding*, Cambridge: Cambridge University Press, 2010, pp. 249–50.

84. Alex J. Bellamy and Paul D. Williams, 'Conclusion: What Future for Peace Operations? Brahimi and Beyond', *International Peacekeeping* 11, no. 1, 2004, pp. 199–200. Beyond rhetorically invoking 'neo-imperialism', neither author makes clear what would constitute 'neo-imperialism' according to their view.

85. Alex J. Bellamy and Paul D. Williams, 'Introduction: Thinking anew about peace operations', *International Peacekeeping* 11, no. 1, 2004, p. 7.

86. Paul D. Williams, 'Peace Operations and the International Financial Institutions: Insights from Rwanda and Sierra Leone', *International Peacekeeping*, 11, no. 1, 2004, pp. 103–23.

87. Bellamy and Williams, 'Thinking anew', p. 8.

88. Bellamy and Williams, 'Conclusion', p. 190.

89. Ibid., p. 207.

90. Neil Cooper, Mandy Turner and Michael Pugh, 'The end of history and the last liberal peacebuilder: a reply to Roland Paris', *Review of International Studies* 37, no. 4, 2011, p. 2000.

91. This is the point made by David Chandler, 'The uncritical critique of "liberal peace"', *Review of International Studies* 36, SI, 2010, p. 16.

92. Roger Mac Ginty, 'Hybrid Peace: The Interaction between Top-Down and Bottom-Up Peacebuilding', *Security Dialogue* 41, no. 4, 2010, p. 397.

93. Roger Mac Ginty, 'Gilding the lily? International support for indigenous and traditional peacebuilding' in O.P. Richmond (ed.), *Palgrave Advances in Peacebuilding: Critical Developments and Approaches*, Basingstoke: Palgrave Macmillan, 2010, p. 355. Note that East Timor is known as Timor-Leste since independence from UN rule in 2002.

94. Ibid., pp. 357–8.

95. Roberto J. González, 'Going "tribal": Notes on pacification in the 21st century', *Anthropology Today* 25, no. 2, 2009, pp. 15–19.

96. Chandler, 'uncritical critique', p. 17.

97. Mahmood Mamdani, 'Historicizing power and responses to power: indirect rule and its reform', *Social Research* 66, no. 3, 1999, p. 870. On the timing of the adoption of indirect rule by the various European empires, see p. 869.

98. The iconic example is Ian Martin, 'All Peace Operations are Political: a Case for Designer Missions and the Next UN Reform'. Online. Available HTTP: http://cic.nyu.edu/sites/default/files/political_missions_2010_martin_all-peace2.pdf (accessed 10 April 2013).

99. Mamdani, 'Historicizing Power', p. 869. Mamdani traces this crisis to the First Indian War of Independence in 1857, with indirect rule subsequently being systematised by the British in early twentieth century Africa.

100. Chandler, 'uncritical critique', p. 10.

101. Ibid., p. 3.

102. Ibid., p. 18.

103. It is worth noting that this latter claim, that the retreat from liberal peace occurred much earlier in the twentieth century, contradicts Chandler's other line of argument, observing the rise of a more self-consciously illiberal form of peacebuilding in response to the early failures of peacebuilding in the post-Cold War period. Chandler, 'uncritical critique', p. 9.

104. Chesterman, *You, the People*, p. 1.

105. John A. Hobson, *Imperialism: A Study*, Nottingham: Spokesman, 2011 [1902], p. 145.

4. CONSTRUCTING IMPERIAL SECURITY: FROM COLONIAL ARMIES TO CAPACITY-BUILDING

1. Paul F. Diehl, 'Forks in the Road: Theoretical and Policy Concerns for 21st Century Peacekeeping', *Global Society* 14, no. 3, 2000, p. 337.
2. United Nations, *United Nations Peacekeeping Operations: Principles and Guidelines*, p. 36; henceforward 'Capstone Doctrine'.
3. According to Finnemore: '[multilateral principles] require that intervening forces be composed not just of troops of more than one state but of troops from disinterested states other than Great Powers.' Martha Finnemore, *The Purpose of Intervention: Changing Beliefs about the Use of Force*, Ithaca: Cornell University Press, 2003, p. 81.
4. Ibid., p. 82.
5. Cynthia Enloe, *The Morning After: Sexual Politics at the end of the Cold War*, University of California Press, 1993, p. 30.
6. Andrea K. Talentino, *Military Intervention after the Cold War: The Evolution of Theory and Practice*, Athens: Ohio University Press, 2005, p. 89.
7. Pearson, cited in Larry F. Fabian, *Soldiers without Enemies: Preparing the United Nations for Peacekeeping*, Washington, D.C.: The Brookings Institution, 1971, p. 94.
8. O'Neill and Rees identify the major Cold War peacekeeping contributors as Australia, Austria, Canada, Denmark, Fiji, Finland, Ghana, India, Ireland, Italy, Nepal, New Zealand, Norway, Pakistan, Senegal, Sweden and Holland. The scale of the operations was very different to today's routinely massive operations, with only five missions exceeding 3,000 troops in the Cold War—namely, Unef I and Unef II, Onuc, Unficyp and Unifil. John T. O'Neill and Nicholas Rees, *United Nations Peacekeeping in the Post Cold War Era*, London: Routledge, 2005, p. 23.
9. Danilo Zolo, *Cosmopolis: Prospects for World Government*, Trans. David McKie, Cambridge: Polity Press, 1997, p. xiii.
10. Jerzy Ciechanski, 'Enforcement Measures under Chapter VII of the UN Charter: UN Practice after the Cold War' in Michael Pugh (ed.), *The UN, Peace and Force*, London: Frank Cass, 1997, p. 88. Further examples of UN authority being extended to cover 'spheres of influence' peacekeeping was the Italian-led Operation Alba in Albania (1997), the Nigerian-led intervention in Liberia (1990–99) and later, the Australian-led operation in East Timor (1999–2000). See further Peter Viggo Jakobsen 'The Transformation of United Nations Peace Operations in 1990s: Adding Globalization to the Conventional "End of the Cold War" Explanation', *Conflict and Cooperation: Journal of the Nordic Studies Association* 37, no. 2, 2002, p. 273.
11. Trevor Findlay, 'The new peacekeepers and the new peacekeeping' in T. Findlay (ed.), *Challenges for the New Peacekeepers*, New York: Oxford University Press, 1996, p. 2. Another twenty-one states became first-time peacekeepers in regional operations in the same period (p. 6).
12. Alex J. Bellamy and Paul D. Williams with Stuart Griffin, *Understanding Peacekeeping*, 2nd ed., Cambridge: Polity Press, 2010, p. 109.

13. The NATO operations (Ifor/Sfor) in Bosnia after 1995, later metamorphosed into an EU operation; the Italian-led Operation Alba in Albania, Misab in Central African Republic; the Ecowas Monitoring Group (Ecomog) in Sierra Leone (1998–2000); the Australian-led Interfret in East Timor (1999–2000); the Peace-Truce Monitoring Group in Bougainville (Belisi) (1998–2003); the EU Operation Concordia in Macedonia (2003); the EU Operation Artemis in DRC (2003); the African Mission in Burundi (Amib, 2003), and the Ecowas operation in Liberia (2003). At the same time as the three Western permanent members retrenched their peacekeeping commitments, so too did their European 'middle power' allies, who had dominated peacekeeping in the Cold War period (Sweden, Denmark, Norway, Finland and Ireland; see Alex J. Bellamy and Paul D. Williams, 'The West and Contemporary Peace Operations', *Journal of Peace Research* 46, no. 1, 2009, p. 43).

14. Davis B. Bobrow and Mark A. Boyer, 'Maintaining System Stability: Contributions to Peacekeeping Operations', *Journal of Conflict Resolution* 41, no. 6, 1997, p. 731. See further James H. Lebovic, 'Uniting for Peace? Democracies and United Nations Peace Operations After the Cold War', *Journal of Peace Research* 48, no. 6, 2004, p. 917.

15. On the behaviour of the Western former neutral powers, see further Bellamy and Williams, 'The West and Contemporary Peace Operations', pp. 43–4.

16. Ibid., p. 44.

17. See United Nations Security Council, 'Report of the Secretary-General on the situation in Mali', 26 March 2013, S/2013/189.

18. Bellamy and Williams define these operations in the following ways: in spearhead operations Western troops prepare the security environment for UN forces; in stabilisation operations Western forces work alongside UN forces to provide stability, 'fire-fighting' operations provide military support to beleaguered UN operations in theatre and 'over-the-horizon' operations involve Western forces in a deterrent posture where they are deployed within striking distance of the theatre in question. Ibid, p. 47.

19. Donald C.F. Daniel, 'Contemporary Patterns in Peace Operations, 2000–2010', in Bellamy and Williams, *Providing Peacekeepers*, p. 43.

20. Bellamy and Williams, 'The West and Contemporary Peace Operations', p. 50.

21. See SIPRI, 'Background paper on SIPRI military expenditure data', 11 April 2011. Online. Available HTTP: www.sipri.org/research/armaments/milex/factsheet2010SIPRI overview (accessed 13 April 2012).

22. Bastian Giegerich, 'Europe: Looking Near and Far' in D.C.F. Daniel, P. Taft and S. Wiharta (eds), *Peace Operations: Trends, Progress, and Prospects*, Washington, D.C.: Georgetown University Press, 2008, p. 130.

23. Richard Norton-Taylor, 'Asia's military spending likely to overtake Europe this year', *Guardian*, 7 March 2012.

24. Giegerich, 'Europe', p. 130.

25. This group of states is taken from Michael O'Hanlon and Peter W. Singer, 'The Humanitarian Transformation: Expanding Global Intervention Capacity', *Survival: Global Politics and Strategy* 46, no. 1, 2004, p. 84.

26. See D.C.F. Daniel *et al.*, *Peace Operations*, and O'Hanlon and Singer, 'The Humanitarian Transformation', pp. 77–99.

27. Richard Gowan, 'UN Peace Operations: The Case for Strategic Investment', Centre for International Peace Operations Policy Briefing, August 2010, p. 2. Online. Available HTTP: www.zif-berlin.org/fileadmin/uploads/analyse/dokumente/veroeffentlichungen/Policy_Briefing_Richard_Gowan_Aug_2010_ENG.pdf (accessed 16 April 2012).

28. James Dobbins *et al.*, *The UN's Role in Nation-Building: From the Congo to Iraq*, Santa Monica, CA: RAND Corporation, 2005, p. xxii.

29. Ibid., p. xxviii.

30. Finnemore, *Purpose*, p. 74.

31. Ibid., p. 81.

32. Neil MacFarquhar, 'Gentle Questioning for U.N. Nominee', *The New York Times* 15 January 2009.

33. See for example, Richard Gowan, 'UN peace operations: the case for strategic investment'; Tom Freke, 'If it didn't exist, we'd have to invent it', *New Statesman*, 13 September 2004; William J. Durch with Tobias C. Berkman, 'Restoring and Maintaining Peace: What We Know So Far' in W.J. Durch (ed.), *Twenty-First-Century Peace Operations*, United States Institute of Peace, 2006, p. 44; Vincenzo Bove and Ron Smith, 'The economics of peacekeeping' in D.L. Braddon and K. Hartley (eds), *Handbook on the Economics of Conflict*, Cheltenham: Edward Elgar, 2011, p. 237.

34. Hervé Ladsous, Fourth Committee, 24 October 2011. Online. Available HTTP: www.un.org/en/peacekeeping/articles/4thc_dpkousg_24102011.pdf (accessed 13 April 2012).

35. RAND, *UN's Role in Nation-Building*, p. xxxvi.

36. Nina M. Serafino, 'The Global Peace Operations Initiative: Background and Issues for Congress', Congressional Research Service, 11 June 2009, p. 2. Online. Available HTTP: www.effectivepeacekeeping.org/reports/issue/usg-issues (accessed 13 April 2012).

37. Bellamy and Williams, *Understanding Peacekeeping*, p. 62.

38. In Claude's original formulation, he warned against missing the substance of the UN's activity: 'If we can learn to judge the United Nations less in terms of its failure to attain the ideals that we postulate … we shall be in a better position to analyse its development. Approaching the Organisation in this spirit, we find that its debating society aspect is not to be deplored and dismissed as evidence of a "slump" but that it deserves to be examined for evidence of the functional adaptation and innovation that it may represent.' Inis L. Claude, Jr, 'Collective Legitimisation as a Political Function of the United Nations', *International Organization* 20, no. 3, 1996, p. 379.

39. O'Brien, cited in Mats Berdal, 'The UN Security Council: Ineffective but Indispensable', *Survival: Global Politics and Strategy* 46, no. 3, 2004, p. 9. O'Brien, who was instrumental in bringing the Onuc operation to a close with the final assault of UN troops on Katangan secessionists, may have taken this observation from U Thant, who used precisely this justification in relation to the Onuc

operation: 'One of the most important roles of the United Nations ... is that of the old English institution, Aunt Sally—the large and conspicuous figure at which things can be thrown with impunity and with almost complete certainty of hitting the target ...' U Thant, cited in Andrew Boyd, *United Nations: Piety, Myth and Truth*, London: Penguin, 1964, p. 180. On the 'Aunt Sally' analogy see further, Fabian, *Soldiers without Enemies*, pp. 35–6.

40. Conor Cruise O'Brien, 'Faithful scapegoat to the world', *The Independent*, 1 October 1993.

41. O'Brien, 'Faithful scapegoat'.

42. Cited in James Lunt, *Imperial Sunset: Frontier Soldiering in the 20ᵗʰ Century*, London: Macdonald Futura, 1981, p. xii.

43. Lunt, *Imperial Sunset*, ibid.

44. Paul Kennedy, *The Parliament of Man: The United Nations and the Quest for World Government*, London, Allen Lane, 2006. Kennedy omits both Jordan and South Africa from his list.

45. Ashley Jackson, *Distant Drums: The Role of Colonies in British Imperial Warfare*, Brighton: Sussex Academic Press, 2010, p. 13.

46. Kennedy, *The Parliament of Man*, p. 83.

47. Dan Plesch, 'How the United Nations Beat Hitler and Prepared the Peace', *Global Society* 22, no. 1, 2008, pp. 137–58.

48. See ibid., *passim*.

49. BBC, 'Germans crush Jewish uprising'. Online. Available HTTP: news.bbc.co.uk/onthisday/hi/dates/stories/may/16/newsid_3501000/3501730.stm (accessed 13 April 2012). On German use of East European askari during the Second World War, see Gerard Reitlinger, *The S.S.: Alibi of a Nation*, New York: Viking Press, 1957, p. 126. For the so-called 'Stroop report' concerning the use of askari in the crushing of the ghetto uprising, see HTTP: www.holocaust-history.org/works/stroop-report/htm/intro000.htm (accessed 24 April 2012).

50. Jackson, *Distant Drums*, p. 1.

51. Ibid., p. 14. See also Victor G. Kiernan, *Colonial Empires and Armies 1815–1960*, Stroud: Sutton Publishing, 1998, p. 207.

52. Jackson, ibid.

53. Tarak Barkawi, *Globalization and War*, Lanham: Rowman and Littlefield Publishers, 2006, p. 85.

54. Ashley Jackson, *The British Empire and the Second World War*, London: Hambledon Continuum, 2006.

55. Barkawi, *Globalization and War*, pp. 86–8; Kiernan, *Colonial Empires and Armies*, p. 207; Jackson, *British Empire*, p. 243.

56. Ashley Jackson, *British Empire*, p. 532.

57. On the Military Staff Committee, see John G. Ruggie, 'The United Nations and the Collective Use of Force: Whither or Whether?' in Pugh (ed.), *UN, Peace and Force*, p. 3. The Committee met 152 times in the first fifteen months of its existence before sinking under the rising tide of Cold War rivalries. On the international institutional innovation spurred by the global war effort, see Inis

L. Claude, Jr., *Swords into Plowshares: The Problems and Progress of International Organization*, 4th ed., New York: Random House, p. 47. On the history and politics of proposals for a standing UN army, see Stephen Kinloch-Pichat, *A UN 'Legion': Between Utopia and Reality*, Abingdon: Frank Cass, 2004, p. 14.

58. Darryl Li, 'UN Peacekeepers and the Countries that Send Them', 20 September 2003 (unpublished), p. 6.

59. David Smith, 'Etiquette, deference, tradition and tea amid an unsung tour of duty', *The Guardian*, 3 February 2010.

60. Adam Bernstein, 'I.J. Rikhye; Indian Major General Oversaw U.N. Peacekeeping Efforts', *The Washintgon Post*, 25 May 2007.

61. *The Economist*, 'Indar Jit Rikhye', 7 June 2007.

62. Josy Joseph, 'Warriors of Peace: Should the Indian soldier shed his blood for the UN?' (undated). Online. Available HTTP: www.rediff.com/news/2000/jun/30un.htm (accessed 13 April 2012).

63. Michael W. Doyle and Nicholas Sambanis, *Making War and Building Peace: United Nations Peace Operations*, Princeton: Princeton University Press, p. 273.

64. *The Telegraph*, 'Lieutenant General Dewan Prem Chand', 20 December 2003.

65. Lunt, *Imperial Sunset*, p. 172.

66. Barkawi, *Globalization and War*, p. 62. See also Dipankar Banerjee, 'South Asia: Contributors of Global Significance' in D.C.F. Daniel *et al.*, *Peace Operations*, p. 189.

67. Lunt, *Imperial Sunset*, p. 234.

68. Ibid., p. 302.

69. Ibid., p. 235.

70. Anthony Clayton, *France, Soldiers and Africa*, London: Brassey's Defence Publishers, 1988, p. 244.

71. Ibid., p. 3.

72. Bruce Vandervort, 'Review Essay: The Thin Black Line of Heroes', *The Journal of Military History*, 65, no. 4, 2004, p. 1071. Although called *Sénégalais*, the *tirailleurs* came from all over French West Africa.

73. Barkawi, *Globalization and War*, p. 49.

74. Kiernan, *Colonial Empires and Armies*, p. 217.

75. Tarak Barkawi and Mark Laffey, 'The Imperial Peace: Democracy, Force and Globalization', *European Journal of International Relations* 5, no. 4, 1999, p. 413.

76. Patricia Taft, 'Preparing Nations for Peace: Specialized Requirements for Complex Missions', in D.C.F. Daniel *et al.*, *Peace Operations*, p. 73.

77. The exception is perhaps Bangladesh, although this state seceded from West Pakistan rather than from the old imperial metropole. 'Algeria apart, no former colonial territory [in Africa] gained statehood with indigenous, nationalist-oriented military institutions.' Chester Crocker, 'Military Dependence: The Colonial Legacy in Africa', *The Journal of Modern African Studies* 12, no. 2, 1974, p. 267.

78. See further Kevin Blackburn, 'Colonial forces as postcolonial memories: the commemoration and memory of the Malay Regiment in modern Malaysia and Singapore', in K. Hack and T. Rettig (eds), *Colonial Armies in Southeast Asia*, London: Routledge, 2006.

79. See Jaap de Moor, 'The recruitment of Indonesian soldiers for the Dutch Colonial Army, c. 1700–1950' in D. Killingray and D. Omissi (eds), *Guardians of Empire: The Armed Forces of the Colonial Empires c. 1700–1964*, Manchester: Manchester University Press, 2000.

80. Crocker, 'Military Dependence', p. 276; Li, 'UN Peacekeepers and the Countries That Send Them', pp. 8–9.

81. Clayton, *France, Soldiers, Africa*, p. 6.

82. Li, ibid.

83. On the history of Ceylonese colonial militarization, see Jackson, *Distant Drums*, pp. 57–9.

84. China is a partial exception, as there was a British Chinese colonial unit, but it was small. See Lunt, *Imperial Sunset*, ch. 15.

85. David Killingray, 'Guardians of Empire' in Killingray and Ornissi (eds), *Guardians of Empire*, p. 10.

86. Ibid., p. 7.

87. Ibid. p. 4.

88. Kiernan, *Colonial Empires and Armies*, pp. 202–3.

89. Lunt, *Imperial Sunset*, p. x.

90. Killingray, 'Guardians of Empire', p. 10.

91. Crocker, 'Military Dependence', p. 273.

92. Jackson, *Distant Drums*, p. 19.

93. Barkawi, *Globalization and War*, p. 75.

94. Killingray, 'Guardians of Empire', p. 6.

95. Ibid., p. 8.

96. Ibid., p. 10.

97. Ibid., p. 2.

98. Cited in Callinicos, *Imperialism and Global Political Economy*, p. 194.

99. Killingray, 'Guardians of Empire', p. 6.

100. Norrie MacQueen, *United Nations Peacekeeping in Africa since 1960*, London: Pearson Education, 2002, p. 208.

101. Killingray, 'Guardians of Empire', p. 2.

102. Kiernan, *Colonial Empires and Armies*, p. 228.

103. Killingray, 'Guardians of Empire', p. 18.

104. See Bruno Charbonneau, 'Dreams of Empire: France, Europe, and the New Interventionism in Africa', *Modern and Contemporary France* 16, no. 3, 2008, p. 282; Clayton, *France, Soldiers and Africa*, p. 382.

105. Alexander Wendt, 'Dependent state formation and Third World militarization', *Review of International Studies* 19, no. 4, 1993, pp. 321–47.

106. Robert E. Harkavy, *Bases Abroad: The Global Foreign Military Presence*, Oxford: Oxford University Press, 1989, pp. 119–20.

107. On the importance of the Cuban role in militarily exhausting the apartheid

system in the war in Angola, see Piero Gleijeses, *Conflicting Missions: Havana, Washington, and Africa 1959–1976*, Chapel Hill and London: The University of North Carolina Press, 2002.

108. Harkavy, *Bases Abroad*, pp. 119–120.

109. Karl Hack with Tobias Rettig, 'Imperial systems of power, colonial forces and the making of modern Southeast Asia' in Hack and Rettig, *Colonial Armies in Southeast Asia*, p. 30.

110. Bruno Charbonneau, *France and the New Imperialism: Security Policy in Sub-Saharan Africa*, Aldershot: Ashgate, 2008, p. 114.

111. G8, 'G8 Action Plan: Expanding Global Capacity for Peace Support Operations', 10 June 2004. Online. Available HTTP: www.g8.utoronto.ca/summit/2004seaisland/peace.html (accessed 17 April 2012).

112. Serafino, 'The Global Peace Operations Initiative', p. 3.

113. Ibid., *passim*.

114. John T. Fishel, 'Latin America: Haiti and Beyond', in D.C.F. Daniel *et al.* (eds), *Peace Operations*, p. 158. See also James D. Fearon and David D. Laitin, 'Neotrusteeship and the Problem of Weak States', *International Security* 28, no. 4, 2004, p. 33.

115. Banerjee, 'South Asia', p. 198.

116. Serafino, 'Global Peace Operations Initiative', p. 13; see also p. 2.

117. Ibid., p. 13.

118. Ibid.

119. Mark Malan, 'Africa: Building Institutions on the Run' in D.C.F. Daniel *et al.* (eds), *Peace Operations*, p. 103.

120. See for example, ibid., p. 104.

121. Gorm Rye Olsen, 'The EU and Military Conflict Management in Africa: For the Good of Europe or Africa?', *International Peacekeeping* 16, no. 2, 2009, p. 252.

122. Charbonneau, *France and the New Imperialism*, p. 115.

123. Olsen, 'The EU and Military Conflict Management in Africa', p. 252.

124. Charbonneau, *France and the New Imperialism*, p. 117.

125. Ibid., pp. 115–6; Malan, 'Africa: Building Institutions on the Run', p. 103.

126. Interview with author, TCC3, 5 March 2005.

127. On US-Francophone competition over training programmes, see Fearon and Laitin, 'Neo-trusteeship', p. 32.

128. Olsen, 'The EU and Military Conflict Management in Africa', p. 257.

129. Malan, 'Africa: Building Institutions on the Run', p. 103.

130. A. Sarjoh Bah, and Kwesi Aning, 'US Peace Operations Policy in Africa: From ACRI to AFRICOM', *International Peacekeeping* 15, no. 1, 2008, p. 128.

131. Malan, 'Africa: Building Institutions on the Run', p. 89.

132. On African scepticism, see ibid. and Bah and Aning, 'US Peace Operations Policy in Africa', p. 120; 128.

133. Charbonneau, *France and the New Imperialism*, p. 113.

134. Malan, 'Africa: Building Institutions on the Run', p. 104.

135. Center on International Cooperation, *Annual Review of Global Peace Operations 2011*, Boulder, CO: Lynne Rienner, 2011, pp. 120–1.

136. David N. Gibbs, 'The United Nations, international peacekeeping and the question of "impartiality": revisiting the Congo operation of 1960', *The Journal of Modern African Studies* 38, no. 3, 2000, p. 375 and *passim*; Ludo de Witte, *The Assassination of Lumumba*, London: Verso, 2002, p. 130 and *passim*.

137. Cited in de Witte, *Assassination of Lumumba*, flyleaf.

138. Ibid., p. 66.

139. Gibbs, 'The United Nations, international peacekeeping and the question of "impartiality"', p. 374.

140. Lakhdar Brahimi, 'The Debate on the Report on UN Peace Operations: Fighting battles on the wrong grounds?', Alastair Buchan Memorial Lecture, 22 March 2001, London, p. 6. Online. Available HTTP: www.iiss.org/conferences/alastair-buchan/alastair-buchan-lecture-transcripts/ (accessed 16 April 2012).

141. Both cited in Killingray, 'Guardians of Empire', p. 10.

5. ASKARIS AND SEPOYS OF THE NEW WORLD ORDER

1. Laura Neack, 'UN Peace-keeping: In the Interest of Community or Self?', *Journal of Peace Research* 32, no. 2, 1995, p. 181.

2. On the specifics see discussion below.

3. Alan Ryan, 'Cosmopolitan objectives and the strategic challenges of multinational military operations' in L. Elliott and N. Cheeseman (eds), *Forces for Good: Cosmopolitan militaries in the twenty-first century*, Manchester: Manchester University Press, 2004, p. 67. This was confirmed to me in interviews with UN officials (UN2, 8 December 2005). See also Ioan Lewis and James Mayall: 'Supplying troops was … a profitable business, especially for Third World countries short of hard currency'; 'Somalia' in M. Berdal and S. Economides (eds), *United Nations Interventionism: 1991–2004*, Cambridge: Cambridge University Press, p. 136. See also Kgomotso Monnakgotla, 'The Naked Face of UN Peacekeeping: Noble Crusade or National Self-interest?', *African Security Review* 5, no. 5, 1996, pp. 53–61; William J. Durch 'Paying the Tab: Financial Crises' in W.J. Durch (ed.), *The Evolution of UN Peacekeeping: Case Studies and Comparative Analysis*, New York: St. Martin's Press, 1993, p. 50.

4. *Economist*, 'Helping to calm a continent', 9 June 2012. The same article claims that India has only recently started to subsidise its peacekeeping deployments from its own funds. On this, see the discussion further below.

5. Stephen Kinloch-Pichat, *A UN 'Legion': Between Utopia and Reality*, Abingdon: Frank Cass, 2004, p. 178.

6. Ibid.

7. Cited in Patrick Jackson, 'The UN's South Asian workhorse', BBC News, 19 April 2007. Online. Available HTTP: news.bbc.co.uk/1/hi/6542405.stm (accessed 17 April 2012)

8. *The Economist*, 'Supply-side peacekeeping', 21 February 2007. Cf. Zaman and Biswas, who suggest that national economic growth is changing the incentive

structures confronting Bangladeshi officers, Rashed Uz Zaman and Niloy R. Biswas, 'Bangladesh' in Alex J. Bellamy and Paul D. Williams (eds), *Providing Peacekeepers: The Politics, Challenges, and Future of United Nations Peacekeeping Contribution*, Oxford: Oxford University Press, 2013, pp. 194–5. Estimates of earnings from peacekeeping vary widely. Cf. the *Economist* figures with the discussion below.

9. Dipankar Banerjee, 'South Asia: Contributors of Global Significance' in D.C.F. Daniel, P. Taft and S. Wiharta (eds), *Peace Operations: Trends, Progress, and Prospects*, Washington, D.C.: Georgetown University Press, 2008, p. 196.

10. Mark Tran, 'Q&A: the Bangladesh border guards mutiny', *The Guardian*, 26 February 2009. Online. Available HTTP: www.guardian.co.uk/world/2009/feb/26/bangladesh-mutiny1 (accessed 17 April 2012).

11. Kai Michael Kenkel, 'Stepping out of the Shadow: South America and Peace Operations', *International Peacekeeping* 17, no. 5, 2010, p. 589.

12. Arturo C. Sotomayor, 'Peacekeeping Effects in South America: Common Experiences and Divergent Effects in Civil-Military Relations', *International Peacekeeping* 17, no. 5, 2010, pp. 632–4.

13. Satish Nambiar, 'South Asian contributions to United Nations peacekeeping operations, with particular reference to India's participation' in R. Thakur and O. Wiggan (eds), *South Asia in the World: Problem Solving Perspectives on Security, Sustainable Government and Good Governance*, Tokyo: United Nations University Press, 2004, p. 114. More research is needed to explore the dynamics and market structures of UN procurement in relation to 'post-conflict capitalism'.

14. Nina M. Serafino, 'The Global Peace Operations Initiative: Background and Issues for Congress', Congressional Research Service, 11 June 2009, p. 2. Online. Available HTTP: www.effectivepeacekeeping.org/reports/issue/usg-issues (accessed 13 April 2012).

15. Ugurhan G. Berkok and Binyam Solomon, 'Peacekeeping, private benefits and common agency' in D.L. Braddon and K. Hartley (eds), *Handbook on the Economics of Conflict*, Cheltenham: Edward Elgar, 2011, p. 282.

16. The data excludes earnings that countries gain from contributing specialists (who are reimbursed at higher rates by the United Nations), as well as reimbursement for countries supplying their own (so-called 'contingent-owned') equipment, recreational leave allowance for peacekeepers, and payments made to individually deployed police officers, who are paid a retainer by the United Nations itself while retaining their nationally paid salary (according to William Durch and Madeline England, a slight majority of police peacekeepers deploy as individuals—see William J. Durch with Madeline L. England (eds), *Enhancing United Nations Capacity to Support Post-Conflict Policing and the Rule of Law: Revised and Updated*, Henry Stimson Center, August 2010. Online. Available HTTP: www.stimson.org/images/uploads/research-pdfs/Enhancing_United_Nations_Capacity_2010_revision.pdf [accessed 12 May 2012]). By contrast, for the deployment of formed police units—officers deployed together as a self-sufficient unit—countries are reimbursed at the standard flat rate of

reimbursement for military peacekeepers, which includes the following per month per contingent member: $1,028 plus $68 for personal clothing, gear and equipment allowances, plus $5 per month per contingent member for personal weaponry, ammunition and training, and a daily allowance of $1.28. The figures were calculated by multiplying the monthly peacekeeping deployment figures from table 1.2 by twelve ([1028 + 68 + 5 + 1.27] x 12), which was then divided by that country's annual military expenditure. The figures given are from 2002 as this was the last date that peacekeeping reimbursement rates were fixed. Data on UN reimbursement taken from United Nations, 'Force Generation Process', p. 10. Online. Available HTTP: www.cc.unlb.org/UNSAS%20Training%20Documents/Force%20Generation%20Documents/1.%20Force%20GenerationProcess.doc (accessed 11 April 2013).

17. Cf. Vincenzo Bove and Leandro Elia, 'Supplying peace: Participation in and troop contribution to peacekeeping missions', *Journal of Peace Research* 48, no. 6, 2011, *passim.*

18. Zaman and Biswas, 'Bangladesh', p. 189.

19. On the opportunity costs of peacekeeping participation, see further Ross Fetterly, 'A Review of Peacekeeping Financing Methods', *Defence and Peace Economics* 17, no. 5, 2006, p. 397.

20. Donald C.F. Daniel, 'Why So Few Troops from Among So Many?', in D.C.F. Daniel *et al.*, *Peace Operations*, pp. 57–8.

21. Sotomayor, 'Peacekeeping Effects in South America: Common Experiences and Divergent Effects in Civil-Military Relations', p. 639.

22. Inam-ur-Rahman Malik, 'Pakistan' in Bellamy and Williams (eds), *Providing Peacekeepers*, p. 219.

23. Paul LaRose-Edwards, cited in Anthony McDermott, *The New Politics of Financing the UN*, Basingstoke: Macmillan, 2000, p. 97. Even McDermott himself is suspicious of developing countries' commitment and irresponsibility as regards financial motivations in peacekeeping contribution, for example ibid., p. 89.

24. Cited in Davis B. Bobrow and Mark A. Boyer, 'Maintaining System Stability: Contributions to Peacekeeping Operations', *Journal of Conflict Resolution* 41, no. 6, 1997, p. 736.

25. See 'Tables and Charts on UN Peacekeeping Operations Budget', Global Policy Forum. Online. Available HTTP: www.globalpolicy.org/images/pdfs/Z/pk_tables/expendarrears.pdf (accessed 23 April 2012). On UN arrears to Bangladesh, one of the largest peacekeeping contributors, see Kabilan Krishnasamy, 'Bangladesh and UN Peacekeeping: The Participation of a "Small" State', *Commonwealth and Comparative Politics* 41, no. 2, 2003, p. 37. On UN arrears to India, see Dipankar Banerjee, 'India', in Bellay and Williams, *Providing Peacekeepers*, p. 241. On UN underfunding and arrears in general during the mid-1990s, see Victoria K. Holt, 'Reforming UN Peacekeeping: The U.S. Role and the UN Financial Crisis', *Brown Journal of World Affairs* 3, no. 1, 1996, pp. 126–7 and *passim*. Findlay argues that 'the UN is usually so slow in paying and the amount so relatively niggardly that this cannot be a sole

motivating factor' and 'Even Fiji threatened to quit peacekeeping unless it is "reimbursed" more promptly.' Trevor Findlay, 'The new peacekeepers and the new peacekeeping' in T. Findlay (ed.), *Challenges for the New Peacekeepers*, Oxford: Oxford University Press, 1996, p. 9. Angela Kane estimates that at one point in the early 1990s Egypt was owed $4.6 million for troop costs and had claimed another $103 million for equipment costs; Angela Kane, 'Other new and emerging peacekeepers', in T. Findlay (ed.), *Challenges for the New Peacekeepers*, p. 118. Deborah Norden notes, 'Peacekeeping costs money, and so far the United Nations has not been able to pay. Without that external aid, consolidating the [Argentinean] military's internationalist role will be difficult.' Deborah Norden, 'Keeping the Peace, Outside and In: Argentina's UN missions', *International Peacekeeping* 2, no. 3, 1995, p. 344. See further 'UN owes $70m. to India', *The Hindu*, 15 March 2007. Simon Tisdall of *The Guardian* writes: 'developing countries, that provide the majority of peacekeeping troops, were footing the bill for richer countries. Bangladesh holds a $77m unpaid invoice because donor nations, the US in particular, are not paying their bills in full', in 'Darfur mission faces US funding hurdle', *The Guardian*, 18 June 2007. More recently at the Open Debate on Peacekeeping held by the UN Security Council in August 2011, both Fiji and Pakistan claimed that they were subsidising peacekeeping themselves given the range of arrears that they were owed. Security Council, 'Security Council commits to strengthening partnership with Troop, Police Contributors in Debate on United Nations Peacekeeping Operations', 26 August 2011. Online. Available HTTP: www.un.org/News/Press/docs/2011/sc10368.doc.htm (accessed 17 April 2012).

26. A view originally suggested to me by an official from the Department of Peacekeeping Operations in an interview with the author, UN7, 9 March 2005.

27. Norden, 'Keeping the Peace, Outside and In', pp. 340–1. A representative with the permanent mission to the United Nations of another significant Latin American contributor to peacekeeping told me that having a large immigrant population from the Old World endowed his country with an external orientation that facilitated an internationalist perspective and foreign policy supportive of peacekeeping. TCC3, 8 March, 2005.

28. Sotomayor, 'Peacekeeping Effects in South America: Common Experiences and Divergent Effects in Civil-Military Relations', p. 631.

29. David Smith, 'Etiquette, deference, tradition and tea amid an unsung tour of duty', *The Guardian*, 3 February 2010.

30. Cited in Adam Bernstein, 'Obituary: I.J. Rikhye; Indian Major General Oversaw U.N. Peacekeeping Efforts', *The Washington Post*, 25 May 2007.

31. See further Katharina P. Coleman, 'Token Troop Contributions to United Nations Peacekeeping Operations', in Bellamy and Williams (eds), *Providing Peacekeepers*, p. 58.

32. *The Economist*, 'Supply-side peacekeeping', 21 February 2007.

33. Zaman and Biswas, 'Bangladesh', p. 195.

34. Cited in Andrew Scobell, 'Politics, Professionalism and Peacekeeping', *Comparative Politics* 26, no. 2, 1994, p. 190.

35. Kenkel, 'Stepping out of the Shadow: South America and Peace Operations', p. 588.

36. See Kabilan Krishnasamy, '"Recognition" for Third World Peacekeepers: India and Pakistan', *International Peacekeeping* 8, no. 4, 2001, pp. 56–76; see further Kabilan Krishnasamy, 'Pakistan's peacekeeping experience', *International Peacekeeping* 9, no. 4, 2001, pp. 112–13.

37. John T. Fishel, 'Latin America: Haiti and Beyond', p. 164.

38. Banerjee, 'South Asia', p. 194; Malik, 'Pakistan', in Bellamy and Williams (eds), *Providing Peacekeepers*, p. 210–12.

39. TCC4, 9 March 2005.

40. See *supra* n. 23.

41. Findlay, 'The new peacekeepers and the new peacekeeping', in Findlay (ed.), *Challenges for the New Peacekeepers*, pp. 8–9. On Nepal, see Arturo Sotomayor, 'Nepal', in Bellamy and Williams (eds), *Providing Peacekeepers*, p. 296.

42. Malik, 'Pakistan', in Bellamy and Williams, *Providing Peacekeepers*, p, 212.

43. *Supra* n. 23.

44. A point stressed to me in an interview with an UN peacekeeping official. UN7, 9 March 2005.

45. James D. Fearon and David D. Laitin, 'Neotrusteeship and the Problem of Weak States', *International Security* 28, no. 4, 2004, p. 25.

46. TCC5, 9 March 2005.

47. TCC1, 7 March 2005.

48. TCC9, 11 March 2005.

49. *Supra* n. 23.

50. The phrase is taken from Arturo C. Sotomayor, 'Diversionary Peace in the Southern Cone: From Praetorianism to Peacekeeping?', American Political Science Association Annual Meeting, Boston, 30 August 2002.

51. Fishel, 'Latin America: Haiti and Beyond', p. 164. See further Norden, 'Keeping the Peace, Outside and In' and Cynthia A. Watson, 'Argentina' in D. Sorenson and P. C. Wood (eds), *The Politics of Peacekeeping in the Post-Cold War Era*, London: Frank Cass, 2005.

52. Kane, 'New and Emerging Peacekeepers', p. 119. The role of peacekeeping in restoring the moral authority and purpose of national armed forces is not confined to the South: peacekeeping has helped to bolster the reputation of military forces in countries such as South Korea, Spain and of course Germany and Japan. See also Zaman and Biswas, 'Bangladesh', p. 198; Krishnasamy, 'Bangladesh and UN Peacekeeping', p. 39, Banerjee, 'South Asia: Contributors of Global Significance', in Daniel *et al.* (eds), *Peace Operations*, p. 195.

53. Cited in Roland Buerk, 'The cream of UN peacekeepers', BBC News, 18 January 2006. Online. Available HTTP: news.bbc.co.uk/1/hi/world/south_asia/3763640.stm (accessed 17 April 2012).

54. Kai Michael Kenkel, 'South America's Emerging Power: Brazil as Peacekeeper', *International Peacekeeping* 17, no. 5, 2010, p. 653.

55. Victor G. Kiernan, *Colonial Empires and Armies 1815–1960*, Stroud: Sutton Publishing, 1998, p. 227.

56. 'If stability is the security goal of the status quo, then change is the banner of revisionism.' Barry Buzan, *People, Stages and Fear: An Agenda for International Security Studies in the Post-Cold War Era*, 2nd ed., New York: Harvester Wheatsheaf, 1991, p. 303.

57. Gideon Rachman, *Zero-Sum World: Politics, Power and Prosperity After the Crash*, London: Atlantic Books, 2011, p. 76.

58. For an argument along these lines, see Walter Ladwig, 'An Artificial Bloc Built on a Catchphrase', *The New York Times*, 26 March 2012.

59. Ibid.

60. S. Neil MacFarlane, 'International Politics, Local Conflicts and Intervention', in T.M. Shaw and N. Mychajlyszyn (eds), *Twisting Arms and Flexing Muscles: Humanitarian Intervention and Peacebuilding in Perspective*, Aldershot: Ashgate, 2005, p. 30.

61. *The Economist*, 'Brazil's foreign policy: A giant stirs', 12 June 2004. *The Economist* correspondent omits Brazil's participation in Operation Condor, the systematic campaign of anti-leftist political repression coordinated across the continent by the military dictatorships of the time.

62. On the PT under Lula, see Perry Anderson, 'Lula's Brazil', *London Review of Books* 33, no. 7, 2011.

63. Emir Sader, 'Taking Lula's Measure', *New Left Review* 33, May-June 2005, p. 72.

64. Cited in Mark Goldberg, 'The Coming Peacekeeping Crunch', *The American Prospect*, 21 May 2007.

65. *The Economist*, 'Brazil and peacekeeping: policy, not altruism', 23 September 2010. Initially there were two peacekeeping training centres, one for the Army and one for the Marine Corps (Navy); these were fused so as to focus more resources onto peacekeeping training (I owe this point to Kai Michael Kenkel).

66. Sotomayor, 'Peacekeeping Effects in South America', p. 636.

67. I owe this point to Kai Michael Kenkel.

68. See Frank D. McCann, 'Brazil and World War II: The Forgotten Ally: What did you do in the war, Zé Carioca?', *Estudios Interdisciplinarios de America Latina y El Carib* 6, no. 2, 1995 (unpaginated).

69. See 'Permanent Mission of Brazil to the United Nations'. Online. Available HTTP: www.un.int/brazil/book/conselhoSecuranca_index.html (accessed 17 April 2012).

70. Fishel, 'Latin America: Haiti and Beyond', p. 155.

71. Sotomayor, 'Peacekeeping Effects in South America', p. 632; Bastian Giegerich, 'Europe: Looking Near and Far', in Daniel *et al.* (ed.), *Peace Operations*, p. 127.

72. *The Economist*, 'Policy, not altruism'.

73. These points are based on exchanges with Kai Michael Kenkel and Danilo Marcondes.

74. MercoPress, 'Lula's Party Fearful of "Brazilian sub-imperialism" and arrogance', 8 February 2010. Online. Available HTTP: en.mercopress.com/2010

/02/08/lula-da-silva-s-party-fearful-of-brazilian-sub-imperialism-and-arrogance (accessed 17 April 2012).

75. See for example, Eduard Jordaan, 'The concept of a middle power in international relations: distinguishing between emerging and traditional middle powers', *Politikon: South African Journal of Political Studies* 30, no. 1, 2003, pp. 165–81.

76. Matthew Flynn, 'Between Sub-imperialism and Globalization: A Case Study in the Internationalization of Brazilian capital', *Latin American Perspectives* 34, no. 6, 2007, p. 12.

77. See Sader, 'Taking Lula's Measure'.

78. Flynn, 'Between Sub-imperialism and Globalization', p. 23.

79. Ibid., p. 24.

80. Sotomayor, 'Peacekeeping Effects in South America', p. 637.

81. According to Clovis Brigagão of Candido Mendes University. Cited in *The Economist*, 'Policy, not altruism'.

82. Sotomayor, 'Peacekeeping Effects in South America', pp. 637–8.

83. For example, Andres Smith Serrano claims that the Russian-led peacekeeping operation in Tajikistan was characterised 'by an aggressive and asymmetrical approach to the conflicting parties', and therefore belonged to a 'different category' than 'the internationally accepted definition of traditional peacekeeping'—presumably not a category that includes Somalia and the Congo. 'CIS peacekeeping in Tajikistan' in J. Mackinlay and P. Cross (eds), *Regional Peacekeepers: The Paradox of Russian Peacekeeping*, Tokyo: United Nations University Press, 2003, p. 156. See further S. Neil MacFarlane and Albrecht Schnabel, 'Russia's approach to peacekeeping', *International Journal* 50, no. 2, 1995, pp. 294–324.

84. Isabelle Facon, 'Integration of Retrenchment? Russian Approaches to Peacekeeping' in R.E. Utley (ed.), *Major Powers and Peacekeeping: Perspectives, Priorities and the Challenge of Military Intervention*, Aldershot: Ashgate, 2006, p. 36. See also Alexander I. Nikitin and Mark A. Loucas, 'Peace Support in the New Independent States: Different from the Rest' in Daniel *et al.* (ed.), *Peace Operations*, p. 146.

85. Michael O'Hanlon and P.W. Singer estimate that of twenty million people under arms across the world, discounting the US only a few hundred thousand military personnel are capable of being deployed at great distances. Ukraine too enjoys some vestigial capacities for strategic lift inherited from the USSR. Michael O'Hanlon and P.W. Singer, 'The Humanitarian Transformation: Expanding Global Intervention Capacity', *Survival: Global Politics and Strategy* 46, no. 1, 2004, p. 80.

86. Nikitin and Loucas, 'Peace Support in the New Independent States: Different from the Rest', p. 146.

87. Notably the GUAM grouping of Georgia, Ukraine, Azerbaijan and Moldova.

88. See further Alexander Nikitin, 'The Russian Federation' in Bellamy and Williams, *Providing Peacekeepers*.

89. On Indian contribution and casualty figures, see Colum Lynch, 'The blue hel-

met caste system', *Foreign Policy*, 11 April 2013. Online. Available HTTP: turtlebay.foreignpolicy.com/posts/2013/04/11/the_blue_helmet_caste_system (accessed 12 April 2013).

90. Even before its involvement in UN peacekeeping proper beginning in 1956, India contributed a medical unit to Commonwealth forces fighting in the Korean War and Indian soldiers acted in de facto peacekeeping roles in the Korean (1950–53) and Indochinese wars (1956–70). Indian soldiers were variously involved in supervising the repatriation of prisoners of war, patrolling buffer zones, monitoring the stability of ceasefires and the movements of armaments across borders (the latter tasks in particular were conducted in Indochina). Army Training Command, *The Indian Army: United Nations Peacekeeping Operations*, New Delhi: Lancer Publishers, 1997, pp. 9–16.

91. Banerjee, 'South Asia', p. 191. This has changed recently; see Banerjee, 'India', in Bellamy and Williams (eds), *Providing Peacekeepers*, p. 242.

92. Alan Bullion, 'India', in D. Sorenson and P. C. Wood (eds), *The Politics of Peacekeeping in the Post-Cold War Era*, London: Frank Cass, 2005, p. 108.

93. *Supra* n. 23.

94. Bullion, 'India', p. 202.

95. Cited in ibid., p. 206.

96. Banerjee, 'South Asia', p. 200.

97. Josy Joseph, 'Warriors of Peace: Should the Indian soldier shed his blood for the UN?' (undated). Online. Available HTTP: www.rediff.com/news/2000/jun/30un.htm (accessed 13 April 2012).

98. Guha, quoted in Perry Anderson, 'Gandhi and After', Letters, *London Review of Books* 34, no. 17, 13 Sept 2012.

99. See for example C. Rajah Mohan, *Washington Quarterly*.

100. This is an argument made by Kimberly Marten Zisk, 'Canada, India and UN Peacekeeping', Paper delivered at annual convention of the International Studies Association, 2000, pp. 7–10. See further Dipankar Banerjee, 'India', in Bellamy and Williams (eds), *Providing Peacekeepers*, p. 239. This might be beginning to change however since the signing of the US-India Civilian Nuclear Agreement in 2005, when one of the constituents of the ruling Congress-led coalition almost toppled the government in protest at its foreign policy on nuclear energy (I owe this point to Rahul Rao).

101. Nirupam Sen, 'Statement by Mr Nirupam Sen on the Report of the IGH Level Panel on Threats, Challenges and Change at the Informal Meeting of the Plenary of the 59 Session of the General Assembly', 27 January 2005.

102. Alan Bullion, 'India and UN Peacekeeping', *International Peacekeeping* 4, no. 1, 2004, p. 99. In the event of course, UN intervention in Yugoslavia accelerated and solidified that partition.

103. C. Raja Mohan, 'Balancing Interests and Values: India's Struggle with Democracy Promotion', *Washington Quarterly* 30, no. 3, 2007, p. 106.

104. Ibid., p. 99 and *passim*.

105. The term is Walter Russell Mead's, cited in Thomas J. Knock, 'Playing for a Hundred Years Hence', in G. John Ikenberry *et al.*, *The Crisis of American*

Foreign Policy: Wilsonianism in the Twenty-first Century, Princeton: Princeton University Press, 2009, p. 31.

106. C. Raja Mohan, 'The Return of the Raj', *The American Interest*, May/June 2010. Online. Available HTTP: www.the-american-interest.com/article. cfm?piece=803 (accessed 19 April 2012).

107. Raja Mohan, 'Balancing Interests and Values', p. 106.

108. Colum Lynch, 'India's withdrawal of helicopters points to wider trend', *The Washington Post*, 14 June 2011.

109. Ramesh Thakur, 'India and the United Nations', *Strategic Analysis* 35, no. 6, 2011, p. 900.

110. See International Institute for Strategic Studies, *The Military Balance 2011*, London: International Institute for Strategic Studies.

111. For a sober assessment of the failures of the Indian time on the Security Council, see Richard Gowan, 'India's big bet at the UN', *Pragati: The Indian National Interest Review*, 8 Feb 2013. Online. Available HTTP: pragati. nationalinterest.in/2013/02/indias-big-bet-at-the-un/ (accessed 12 April 2013).

112. Banerjee, 'South Asia', p. 191.

113. *The Economist*, 'Calming a continent', 9 June 2012.

114. Specifically, the posts of military adviser and civilian police adviser. See *supra* no. 111.

115. See Keerthi Sampath Kumar and Saurabh Mishra, 'India's Presidency in the UN Security Council—An Evaluation', 19 September 2011. Online. HTTP: www.idsa.in/idsacomments/IndiasPresidencyintheUNSecurityCouncil_kskumar_190911 (accessed 12 May 2012).

116. Raja Mohan, 'Balancing Interests and Values', p. 101; 106.

117. See C. Raja Mohan, *Crossing the Rubicon: The Shaping of India's New Foreign Policy*, Basingstoke: Palgrave, 2005, *passim*. Curzon also presided over the formation of an elite Indian officer corps that paved the way for the Indianisation of the British Indian army and, less propitiously, the famine of 1899–1900—Mike Davis estimates between six and nine million died during the famine. Mike Davis, *Late Victorian Holocausts: El Nino Famines and the Making of the Third World*, London: Verso, 2002, p. 158.

118. Raja Mohan, 'Return of the Raj'.

119. See Siddharth Varadarajan, 'Trading one hyphen for another', *The Hindu*, 11 November 2010. Online. Available HTTP: www.thehindu.com/opinion/columns/siddharth-varadarajan/trading-one-hyphen-for-another/article880277. ece (accessed 12 April 2013).

120. See for example, Army Training Command, *The Indian Army*, pp. 27–31.

121. On US influence in Cold War-era Congo/Zaïre, see David N. Gibbs, *The Political Economy of Third World Intervention: Mines, Money and U.S. Policy in the Congo Crisis*, Chicago: University of Chicago Press, 1993.

122. See data on peacekeeping contribution for March 2003. Available from the UN Department of Peacekeeping Operations.

123. Nambiar, 'South Asian contributions to United Nations peacekeeping', p. 113.

124. Nirmala George, 'India upgrades its military with China in mind', *The Guardian*, 8 February 2012.

125. See Stuenkel, 'India's National Interests and Diplomatic Activism' and Iskender Rehman, 'The Military Dimensions of India's Rise' in Nicholas Kitchen (ed.), *India: The Next Superpower?*, London: LSE Ideas, 2012.

126. See Anderson, 'Gandhi and After'.

127. See further Bullion, 'India', p. 199.

128. Perry Anderson, 'After Nehru', *London Review of Books* 34, no. 15, 2 August 2012.

129. Smith, 'Etiquette, deference, tradition and tea amid an unsung tour of duty'.

130. Bruce Cumings, *The Korean War: A History*, New York: The Modern Library, 2010, p. 35. UN casualty figures exclude South Korean casualties (415,004 war dead) and North Korean casualties (two million, including one million civilians).

131. Cited in Liu Tiewa, 'Marching for a More Open, Confident and Responsible Great Power; Explaining China's Involvement in UN Peacekeeping Operations', *Journal of International Peacekeeping* 13, nos. 1–2, 2009, p. 105. Although the US contributed the overwhelming majority of forces to UN Command, the United Nations was instrumental to the legitimacy of the multinational anti-communist war effort. Coming only five years after the atomic bombing of Japan and in the midst of European nations' efforts to restore their colonial empires in the Asia-Pacific region, Western leaders were concerned with allaying the suspicions of 'Asiatic peoples' that the intervention in the Korean civil war was yet another imperialist bout of racial subjugation. See Kinloch-Pichat, *A UN 'Legion'*, p. 53.

132. Cited in Yongjin Zhang, 'China and UN peacekeeping: from condemnation to participation', *International Peacekeeping* 3, no. 3, 1996, p. 3.

133. BBC, 'UN peacekeepers prepare to leave Macedonia', BBC News, 1 March 1999. Online. Available HTTP: news.bbc.co.uk/1/hi/world/europe/288402.stm (accessed 17 April 2012).

134. Mark Doyle, 'China peacekeepers in Liberia', BBC News, 20 January 2004. Online. Available HTTP: news.bbc.co.uk/1/hi/world/africa/3412317.stm (accessed 17 April 2012).

135. Bates Gill and Chin-Hao Huang, 'China's Expanding Role in Peacekeeping', *SIPRI Policy Paper*, November 2009, p. 13. Online. Available HTTP: books.sipri.org/files/PP/SIPRIPP25.pdf (accessed 17 April 2012).

136. Zhang, 'China and UN Peacekeeping', p. 4.

137. Tiewa, 'Marching for a More Open, Confident and Responsible Great Power', p. 108.

138. Ibid., p. 105.

139. Gary D. Rawnsley, 'China, Japan and Peacekeeping' in R.E. Utley (ed.), *Major Powers and Peacekeeping*, p. 86.

140. Cited in Colum Lynch, 'China Filling Void Left by West in U.N. Peacekeeping', *The Washington Post*, 24 November 2006.

141. Courtney J. Richardson, 'A Responsible Power? China and the UN Peacekeeping Regime', *International Peacekeeping* 18, no. 3, 2011, p. 289.

142. Cited in Mark Armstrong, 'U.N. Peacekeeping as Public Diplomacy', *World Politics Review*, 19 May 2010.

143. Zhao Lei, 'Two Pillars of China's Global Peace Engagement Strategy: UN Peacekeeping and International Peacebuilding', *International Peacekeeping* 18, no. 3, p. 356.

144. Ibid., p. 348.

145. Armstrong, 'U.N. Peacekeeping as Public Diplomacy'.

146. Chin-Hao Huang, 'Principles and Praxis of China's Peacekeeping', *International Peacekeeping* 18, no. 3, 2011, p. 262.

147. See Richardson, 'A Responsible Power?', p. 288.

148. See for example, Tiewa, 'Marching for a More Open, Confident and Responsible Great Power', pp. 110–12.

149. Shogo Suzuki, 'Why Does China Participate in Intrusive Peacekeeping? Understanding Paternalistic Chinese Discourses on Development and Intervention', *International Peacekeeping* 18, no. 3, 2011, p. 279.

150. See further Bates Gill and Chin-Hao Huang 'The People's Republic of China' in Bellamy and Williams (eds), *Providing Peacekeepers*, p 143.

151. Barry Buzan, 'China in International Society: Is "Peaceful Rise" Possible?', *The Chinese Journal of International Politics* 3, no. 1, 2010, p. 18.

152. The Shanghai Cooperation Council, for example, is a fledging organisation at best. See Nikitin and Loucas, 'Peace Support in the New Independent States', p. 148.

153. Kai Michael Kenkel, 'Brazil', in Bellamy and Williams (eds), *Providing Peacekeepers*, p. 345.

154. On Brazil's vision of peacebuilding, see ibid., p 351.

155. See for example Global Center on the Responsibility to Protect, 'The Georgia-Russia Crisis and the Responsibility to Protect: Background Note', 19 August 2008. Online. Available HTTP: www.globalr2p.org/pdf/related/GeorgiaRussia.pdf (accessed 20 April 2012); and Gareth Evans, 'Russia and the "responsibility to protect"', *Los Angeles Times*, 31 August 2008. Online. Available HTTP: http://www.latimes.com/news/opinion/commentary/la-oe-evans31–2008aug31,0,3632207.story (accessed 20 August 2012).

156. Andreas Andersson, 'Democracies and UN Peacekeeping Operations, 1990–1996', *International Peacekeeping* 7, no. 2, 2000, p. 2.

157. Richard Perkins and Eric Neumayer, 'Extra-territorial interventions in conflict spaces: Explaining the geographies of post-Cold War peacekeeping', *Political Geography* 27, no. 8, 2008, p. 910.

158. James H. Lebovic, 'Uniting for Peace? Democracies and United Nations Peace Operations after the Cold War', *Journal of Conflict Resolution* 48, no. 6, 2004, p. 920. Original emphasis. Some of the states that Lebovic places outside the West—Australia, New Zealand, Japan—are just as often classified as belonging to the 'West' or 'greater West' by virtue of their economic development, history and political and security links.

159. Andersson, 'Democracies and UN Peacekeeping Operations', p. 129. Andersson only argues this point in relation to Latin America; but on this point

more generally see Norrie MacQueen, *Peacekeeping in the International System*, London: Routledge, 2006, p. 129.

160. Andersson, 'Democracies and UN Peacekeeping Operations', p. 5.

161. Andersson's study covers the 1990–96 period. Jonah Victor's study covers 1989 to 2001 and Lebovic 1993–2001. Only Picker and Neumayer go up to 2005.

162. Andrew Scobell, 'Politics, Professionalism, and Peacekeeping'. On the growth in the size of the Fijian military as a result of peacekeeping, see *The Economist*, 'Utility of peacekeeping', 29 September 2007.

163. Scobell, 'Politics, Professionalism and Peacekeeping', p. 192; 197.

164. *The Economist*, 'Utility of peacekeeping', 29 September 2007.

165. Jean-Marie Guéhenno, Letters to the editor, *The Economist*, 25 October 2007.

166. Eboe Hutchful, 'Military policy and reform in Ghana', *The Journal of Modern African Studies* 35, no. 2, 1997, p. 253.

167. Ibid., p. 258. Abdoulaye S.M. Saine credits peacekeeping participation with a similar role in the overthrow of one of Africa's oldest multiparty democracies in The Gambia in 1994 (albeit this was participation in regional peacekeeping rather than UN peacekeeping). Putsch leader Captain Yahya Jammeh modeled his rule on Rawlings's own populist praetorianism, inviting Rawlings to preside as guest of honour over the celebrations marking the Armed Forces' Provisional Ruling Council's first year in office. Abdoulaye S.M. Saine, 'The Coup D'Etat in The Gambia, 1994: The End of the First Republic', *Armed Forces and Society* 23, no. 1, 1996, p. 103. One of the supposed mechanisms of democratic peacekeeping is the suggestion that transitional governments have used peacekeeping to consolidate civilian rule by entangling meddlesome militaries in adventures abroad. But there is no reason in principle why authoritarian regimes cannot also avail themselves of this technique. Herbert M. Howe argues that military dictatorship was a precondition of Nigeria's costly regional peacekeeping efforts in the early post-Cold War period, the military regime channelling the energies of its large army into a bid for regional hegemony that was unpopular with a Nigerian public chafing under military rule, but that gave Nigerian officers plenty of opportunity for personal enrichment. Herbert M. Howe, 'Nigeria', in Sorenson and Wood (eds), *The Politics of Peacekeeping*, *passim*.

168. Matthew Russell Lee, 'Niger Coup Leader Reportedly Served on UN Missions, France, UN and Council Shrug, on Guinea', 19 February 2012. Online. Available HTTP: www.innercitypress.com/uncoup1niger021910.html (accessed 17 April 2012).

169. Pervez Musharraf, *In the Line of Fire: A Memoir*, Simon and Schuster, London, 2006, p. 77.

170. On the links between peacekeeping and the 2006 coup, see *The Economist*, 'Supply-side peacekeeping'.

171. Jalal Alamgir, 'Lessons in Democracy from Bangladesh', *The Nation*, 16 March 2009. See also Jalal Alamgir, 'Bangladesh's Fresh Start', *Journal of Democracy* 20, no. 3, 2009, pp. 41–55.

172. Alamgir, 'Lessons in Democracy from Bangladesh'.

173. Alamgir, 'Bangladesh's Fresh Start', p. 48.

174. Nurul Islam, 'The Army, UN Peacekeeping Mission and Democracy in Bangladesh', *Economic and Political WEEKLY* XLV, no. 29, 2010, p. 79.

175. *The Economist*, 'Supply-side peacekeeping'.

176. Alamgir, 'Lessons in Democracy from Bangladesh'.

177. Islam, 'The Army, UN Peacekeeping Mission and Democracy in Bangladesh', p. 79.

178. Ibid.

179. For example, Devin T. Hagerty, 'Bangladesh in 2006: Living in "Interesting Times"', *Asian Survey* 47, no. 1, 2007, p. 112. See further, C.S.R. Murthy, 'Unintended Consequences of Peace Operations for Troop-Contributing Countries from South Asia' in Chiyuki Aoi, Cedric de Coning and Ramesh Thakur (eds), *Unintended Consequences of Peacekeeping Operations*, Tokyo: United Nations University Press, 2007.

180. J.A. Hobson, *Imperialism: A Study*, Intro. Nathaniel Mehr. Nottingham: Spokesman, 2011, p. 145.

181. For examples of these apologetics see *The Economist*, 'Supply-side peacekeeping'; and Smruti S. Pattanaik, 'Re-emergence of the Military and the Future of Democracy in Bangladesh', *Strategic Analysis* 32, no. 6, 2008, esp. pp. 982–6.

182. Michael Mann, 'The Roots and Contradictions of Modern Militarism', *New Left Review* I/162, Mar-Apr 1987, p. 35.

183. Perkins and Neumayer, 'Extra-territorial interventions in conflict spaces', p. 910.

184. Sotomayor, 'Peacekeeping Effects in South America: Common Experiences and Divergent Effects in Civil-Military Relations', p. 639.

185. Ibid.

186. Ibid., p. 640.

187. Robin Luckham, 'Democracy and the military: An epitaph for Frankenstein's monster?', *Democratization* 3, no. 2, 1996, p. 14.

188. Ibid., p. 13.

189. O'Hanlon and Singer, 'The Humanitarian Transformation', p. 82.

190. Alex J. Bellamy and Paul D. Williams with Stuart Griffin, *Understanding Peacekeeping*, 2nd ed., Cambridge: Polity Press, 2010, p. 58.

191. Jean-Marie Guéhenno, Letters to the editor, *The Economist*.

6. THE UNITED NATIONS: LAST REFUGE OF EMPIRE

1. Kimberly Marten, *Enforcing the Peace: Learning from the Imperial Past*, New York: Columbia University Press, 2004, p. 19.

2. Much of the argument developed in this chapter draws its inspiration from Mark Mazower, *No Enchanted Palace: The End of Empire and the Ideological Origins of the United Nations*, Princeton: Princeton University Press, 2009 and Perry Anderson, 'Internationalism: a breviary', *New Left Review* 143, Mar-Apr 2002.

3. Ironically, a prominence that was in part a result of the Assembly being rallied by the US during the Korean War in order to outflank Soviet vetoes on the Council.

4. Inis L. Claude, Jr, *Swords into Plowshares: The Problems and Progress of International Organization*, 4th ed., New York: Random House, 1971, p. 215.

5. Nigel D. White, 'The UN Charter and Peacekeeping Forces—Constitutional Issues' in M. Pugh (ed.), *The UN, Peace and Force*, London: Frank Cass, 1997, p. 53.

6. Peter Wallensteen and Patrik Johansson, 'Security Council Decisions in Perspective', in D.M. Malone (ed.), *The UN Security Council: From the Cold War to the 21st Century*, Boulder, CO: Lynne Rienner, 2004, p. 21. This came to the fore in the diplomatic crisis over Iraq according to Berdal: 'In the negotiations over Resolution 1441, the non-permanent or elected members of the Council were, in effect, entirely excluded from detailed consultations over various drafts, to the point where some draft resolutions appeared in the *New York Times* before they were seen by non-permanent members.' Berdal, 'The UN Security Council: Ineffective but Indispensable', *Survival: Global Politics and Strategy* 46, no. 3, 2004, p. 20.

7. David M. Malone, 'Introduction' in D.M. Malone (ed.), *The UN Security Council*, p. 5. See further Hisako Shimura, 'The role of the UN Secretariat in organizing peacekeeping' in R. Thakur and A. Schnabel (eds), *United Nations Peacekeeping Operations: Ad hoc Missions, Permanent Engagement*, Tokyo: United Nations University Press, 2001, p. 51. On the role of Soviet 'new thinking' in relation to the United Nations and the end of the Cold War, see also Adam Roberts and Benedict Kingsbury, 'Introduction' in A. Roberts and B. Kingsbury (eds), *United Nations, Divided World: The UN's Roles in International Relations*, 2nd ed., New York: Oxford University Press, 1993, p. 46. For more on the post-Cold War Security Council, see Michael J. Matheson, *Council Unbound: The Growth of UN Decision Making on Conflict and Postconflict Issues after the Cold War*, Washington, D.C.: United States Institute of Peace, 2006.

8. Jerzy Ciechanski, 'Enforcement Measures under Chapter VII of the UN Charter: UN Practice after the Cold War' in M. Pugh (ed.), *The UN, Peace and Force*, London: Frank Cass, 1997, pp. 90–1.

9. Thomas G. Weiss and Meryl A. Kessler, 'Resurrecting Peacekeeping: The superpowers and conflict management', *Third World Quarterly* 12, no. 3/4, 1990, p. 12. With the notable exception of Untag in Namibia, these operations were small-scale affairs consisting of scores of military observers rather than the brigades of infantry and massed police forces that would become routine in later missions.

10. Malone, 'Introduction', pp. 6–8. 'It has been clear for some years, perhaps most strikingly since the Dayton Accords of late 1995, that the United States has emerged not only as the sole remaining superpower but also as the principal driver of the Council's agenda and decisions, passively and actively.' Ibid., p. 8. The Council also did not bother to require states acting under its authori-

sation to report on those measures to the Council, or member states at large. Martti Koskenniemi, 'The Police in the Temple: Order, Justice and the UN: A Dialectical View', *European Journal of International Law* 6, no. 3, 1995, p. 346.

11. Wallensteen and Johansson, 'Security Council Decisions in Perspective', p. 21. 'Increasingly, it has been seen as irresponsible to force other members of the Council to veto a proposed resolution.' Ibid., p. 20. See also Anthony Parsons, 'The UN and the National Interests of States', in Roberts and Kingsbury (eds), *United Nations, Divided World*, p. 117.

12. Susan C. Hulton, 'Council Working Methods and Procedure', in Malone (ed.), *The UN Security Council*, p. 247. Paradoxically, however, the greater cooperation among a few select countries means that the five permanent powers have to some extent boxed themselves into a corner, whereby they rely on the Council more on the one hand, while on the other hand, the greater authority of the Council is constantly seen to be undermined by double standards arising from the parochial concerns of these powerful states. See Wallensteen and Johansson, 'Security Council Decisions in Perspective', p. 30.

13. Wallensteen and Johansson, 'Security Council Decisions', p. 20.

14. See further Norrie MacQueen, *Peacekeeping in the International System*, London: Routledge, p. 112.

15. Danilo Zolo, *Cosmopolis: Prospects for World Government*, Trans. David McKie, Cambridge: Polity Press, 1997, p. 20.

16. Thomas Weiss, 'The Illusion of Security Council Reform', *The Washington Quarterly* 26, no. 4, 2003, p. 150. Cf. Ian Hurd, 'Legitimacy, Power, and the Symbolic Life of the UN Security Council', *Global Governance* 8, no. 1, 2002, *passim.*

17. Anthony Parsons, 'The UN and the National Interests of States', p. 117. According to Malone, 'the ability and disposition of the five permanent members … to cooperate with each other seriously diminished the margin for manoeuvre of other Council members …'. Malone, 'Introduction', p. 7.

18. Malone, 'Introduction', p. 7.

19. See Security Council Resolution 1353 (2001). See Hurd, 'Legitimacy, Power, and the Symbolic Life of the UN Security Council', p. 42.

20. Susan C. Hulton, 'Council Working Methods and Procedures', pp. 240–1.

21. Wallensteen and Johansson, 'Security Council Decisions in Perspective', p. 21.

22. 'Almost every formal Council meeting now is a pro forma affair, scripted in … advance informal consultations [among the Permanent Five]'. Hurd, 'The Symbolic Life of the UN Security Council', p. 43.

23. Ibid., p. 42. Hurd notes that these benefits of non-permanent membership have diminished in recent years. Despite the lack of real power, the fact that non-permanent membership is 'a source of authority by association' reflects the enhanced power of the Council itself. Ibid., p. 43.

24. In 1963 the United Nations decided that ten non-permanent members should be elected to the Council, with five states from among African and Asian states; one from Eastern Europe, two from Latin American and Caribbean states; and

two from Western European and 'Other' states. The first such expanded Council was elected in 1965.

25. Hurd, 'The Symbolic Life of the UN Security Council', p. 42.

26. Lise Morjé Howard, 'Sources of Change in United States-United Nations Relations', *Global Governance* 16, no. 4, 2010, p. 22.

27. MacQueen, *Peacekeeping in the International System*, p. 158; Peter Viggo Jakobsen, 'The Transformation of United Nations Peace Operations in the 1990s: Adding Globalization to the Conventional "End of the Cold War Explanation"', *Cooperation and Conflict: Journal of the Nordic Studies Association* 37, no. 3, 2002, p. 273.

28. UN, 'Remarks of Mr. Hervé Ladsous Under-Secretary-General of Peacekeeping Operations to the Special Committee on Peacekeeping Operations', 19 February 2013. Online. Available HTTP: www.un.org/en/peacekeeping/articles/hl_speech_C34_19_February%20_with_french.pdf (accessed 15 April 2013).

29. Berdal, 'Ineffective but Indispensable', p. 8.

30. Cf. Hobsbawm on the early nineteenth century: 'The statesmen of 1815 were wise enough to know that no settlement, however carefully carpentered, would in the long run withstand the strain of state rivalries and changing circumstance.' Hobsbawm, *The Age of Revolution: Europe 1789–1848*, London: Abacus, 1962, p. 131.

31. Berdal, 'The UN After Iraq', *Survival: Global Politics and Strategy* 46, no. 3, 2004, p. 88. Examples include UN peacekeeping operations launched in Haiti and eastern Congo.

32. Howard, 'Sources of Change in United States-United Nations Relations', p. 497.

33. Ibid., p. 495.

34. Ibid.

35. Eric P. Schwartz, 'US Policy Towards Peace Operations', in T. Tardy (ed.), *Peace Operations After 11 September 2001*, London: Frank Cass, 2004, pp. 44–6.

36. Michael G. MacKinnon, *The Evolution of US Peacekeeping Under Clinton: A Fairweather Friend?*, Frank Cass: London, 2000, pp. 17–8.

37. Michael W. Bhatia, *War and Intervention: Issues for Contemporary Peace Operations*, Sterling, VA: Kumarian Press, 2003, p. 20.

38. Andrea K. Talentino, *Military Intervention after the Cold War: The Evolution of Theory and Practice*, Athens: Ohio University Press, 2005, p. 3.

39. William E. Rappard, 'The United Nations as Viewed From Geneva', *The American Political Science Review* 40, no. 3, 1946, p. 545.

40. J. David Singer, cited in Anthony McDermott, *The New Politics of Financing the UN*, Basingstoke: Macmillan, 2000, p. 1.

41. According to Kabilan Krishnasamy: 'The difference in the way the UN values the contributions of its major financiers vis-à-vis other contributors to UN peacekeeping operations needs to be addressed, for without this the UN's fundamental premise of universality and equality is a myth…'; '"Recognition" for Third World Peacekeepers: India and Pakistan', *International Peacekeeping* 8, no. 4, 2001, p. 73.

42. See Articles 17 and 18 in Chapter V of the UN Charter.

43. The Fifth Committee (Administrative and Budgetary) of the General Assembly apportions peacekeeping costs based on a special scale of assessments specifically for peacekeeping (that is, calculated differently from the regular UN budget). This peacekeeping financing system is still based on the relative economic wealth of member states (average per capita gross national product). The committee reviews and adjusts the budget for operations throughout the year and, like the operations themselves, the budget will tend to vary widely from year to year. The evolution of financial contributions to peacekeeping is itself complex: in its history, peacekeeping finance has veered from exceeding the entire budget of the world organisation as a whole to peacekeeping surpluses being raided in order to informally supplant the deficit in the regular UN budget. The early peacekeeping observation operations—Unscob, UNTSO—were financed out of the UN's regular budget (Untso still is). Thus the Unef force was pioneering not only in terms of the diplomacy and conduct of peacekeeping, but also in its financing, for the mechanism of separate assessment for peacekeeping was developed as a way of breaking the diplomatic gridlock posed by the question of how to maintain this force in the field. McDermott, *The New Politics of Financing the UN*, pp. 80–3. The USSR at first insisted that the aggressors, Britain, France and Israel be made to pay for the force. The compromise solution led to the US shouldering the burden. Separate financing arrangements for peacekeeping were formalised by a two-thirds majority vote of the General Assembly in November 1956. By making financial responsibility for peacekeeping collective, the General Assembly formalised peacekeeping as a de facto collective obligation of the United Nations, with costs to be borne collectively on the basis of compulsory, universal payments. See ch. 5 in ibid. Other anomalous operations include Unyom (financed by Egypt and Saudi Arabia), Unikom (financed two-thirds by Kuwait), UNSF (equally financed by the Netherlands and Indonesia) and Unficyp (initially financed on a voluntary basis by personnel contributors rather than from general assessments, and latterly by a combination of assessments, troop-contributors' donations, Cyprus and Greece, ibid., pp. 85–6). The notorious dispute over contributions to the Onuc operation, while historically important, is not relevant to the argument here. For one account of this dispute, see Andrew Boyd, *United Nations: Myth, Piety and Truth*, Harmondsworth: Penguin, 1964, ch. 6.

44. According to McDermott, 'The UN's figures for expenditures on peace-keeping operations on an annual basis are notional for the reason that mandates, which include financial appropriations, are renewed usually for six months and with different starting dates. This rarely coincides with a calendar or fiscal year. In addition, the inflow of funds may not be regular …' McDermott, *The New Politics of Financing the UN*, p. 81.

45. Noted by the Department of Peacekeeping Operations itself. Online. Available HTTP: www.un.org/Depts/dpko/dpko/contributors/financing.html (accessed 30 June 2008).

46. Note however, that this does not mean that everyone in each band pays an

equivalent amount; the actual amount paid is related to regular budget contributions. So for example, although China is in the top band of peacekeeping assessments it pays less than the US, because its regular budget contribution is less than the US. See 'Implementation of General Assembly resolutions 55/235 and 55/236: Report of the Secretary-General' A/61/129, 13 July 2006, p. 3.

47. See further Ross Fetterly, 'A Review of Peacekeeping Financing Methods', *Defence and Peace Economics* 17, no. 5, 2006, p. 399.

48. Alex J. Bellamy and Paul D. Williams, 'The West and Contemporary Peace Operations', *Journal of Peace Research* 46, no. 1, 2009, p. 46.

49. Durch, cited in ibid.

50. William J. Durch with Tobias C. Berkman, 'Restoring and Maintaining Peace: What We Know So Far' in W.J. Durch (ed.), *Twenty-First-Century Peace Operations*, Washington, D.C.: United States Institute of Peace, 2006, p. 39.

51. See the data in Center on International Cooperation, *Annual Review of Global Peace Operations* 2011, Boulder, CO: Lynne Rienner, 2011. One exception to this is Mexico, which contributed 2.3 per cent of assessed costs in 2007.

52. Colum Lynch, 'U.S. and Europe fight over cuts in peacekeeping', *Foreign Policy*, 10 October 2011. Online. Available HTTP: turtlebay.foreignpolicy.com/posts/2011/10/10/us_and_europe_fight_over_cuts_in_peacekeeping (accessed 20 April 2012).

53. Cited in ibid.

54. Ibid.

55. Durch with Berkman, 'Restoring and Maintaining Peace', p. 38.

56. Fetterly, 'A Review of Peacekeeping Financing Methods', p. 400.

57. Victoria K. Holt, 'Reforming UN Peacekeeping: The U.S. Role and the UN Financial Crisis', *Brown Journal of International Affairs* 3, no. 1, 1996, pp. 125–134.

58. Khrusrav Gaibulloev, Todd Sandler and Hirofumi Shimizu, 'Demands for UN and Non-UN Peacekeeping: Nonvoluntary versus Voluntary Contributions to a Public Good', *Journal of Conflict Resolution* 53, no. 6, 2009, p. 829.

59. Germany and Japan, for example, consciously pay heavily to the UN in order to build their credibility and reputation within the organisation, both to reverse their lingering status as the 'defeated powers' mentioned in the Charter, and in the hope of securing permanent seats on the Security Council.

60. Michael W. Doyle and Nicolas Sambanis, *Making War and Building Peace: United Nations Peace Operations*, Princeton: Princeton University Press, 2006, p. 188. For this type of argument, see further Michael Lipson, 'Peacekeeping: Organized Hypocrisy?', *European Journal of International Relations* 13, no. 1, 2007, pp. 5–34.

61. Jean-Marie Guéhenno, 'On the Challenges and Achievements of Reforming UN Peace Operations', *International Peacekeeping* 9, no. 2, 2002, p. 76.

62. Ibid., *passim*.

63. Cited in Perry Anderson, 'Made in USA', *The Nation*, 2 April 2007.

64. Michael Pugh, 'Maintaining Peace and Security', in David Held and Anthony McGrew (eds), *Governing Globalisation: Power, Authority and Global Governance*, Cambridge: Polity Press, 2003, p. 222.

65. Jocelyn Coulon, *Soldiers of Diplomacy: The United Nations, Peacekeeping and the New World Order*, Trans. Phyllis Aronoff and Howard Scott, Toronto: University of Toronto Press, 1998, p. 152.

66. Ibid., p. 165.

67. James Bone and Richard Beeston, 'America fights to take charge of UN peacekeepers around world: Move could help exit strategy in Iraq', *The Times*, 3 November 2006.

68. Laura Trevelyan, 'All change at the UN', BBC News, 9 December 2006. Online. Available HTTP: news.bbc.co.uk/1/hi/programmes/from_our_own_correspondent/6162695.stm (accessed 18 April 2012).

69. In 2000, the Fourth Committee found that developed countries occupied two thirds of professional positions in the Department of Peacekeeping Operations. Krishnasamy, '"Recognition" for Third World Peacekeepers', p. 69. The post of military advisor since the end of the Cold War has mainly been appointed from Europe.

70. Krishnasamy, '"Recognition" for Third World Peacekeepers', p. 62. See further the data available in the *Annual Review of Global Peace Operations*, Boulder, CO: Lynne Rienner.

71. Ibid., p. 71.

72. Figures taken from *Annual Review of Global Peace Operations*; the claims here are approximate, as the precise proportions fluctuate from year to year. Here, Northern states have been counted as high-income members of the OECD; the figures given by the *Annual Review* sometimes include the personnel at the logistics depot in Brindisi, sometimes not. See the *Review* for more details.

73. Trevelyan, 'All change at the UN'.

74. Richard Kareem Al-Qaq, *Managing World Order: United Nations Peace Operations and the Security Agenda*, London: I.B. Tauris, 2009, pp. 65–6.

75. Ibid., p. 68.

76. Ibid., p. 56.

77. Ibid., p. 244.

78. The other two being 'freedom from want' and 'freedom to live in dignity for all'.

79. I focus on the work of Bobrow and Boyer in this section because they best elaborate the conceptual logic of the theory; see further the bibliography for discussion of other explanations of this type.

80. Davis B. Bobrow and Mark A. Boyer, 'Maintaining System Stability: Contributions to Peacekeeping Operations', *Journal of Conflict Resolution* 41, no. 6, 1997, p. 726. Bobrow and Boyer's data are out of date, but of course this does not invalidate the theory by default.

81. 'Models of public good provision predict that poor nations will be able to free ride off the contributions of wealthier nations and that the public good will be underprovided because contributors do not take into account the spillover benefits that their support confers to others.' Erik Voeten, 'The Political Origins of the UN Security Council's Ability to Legitimize the Use of Force', *International Organization*, 59, no. 3, 2005, p. 539.

82. Of course, the spread of democratic peace can also be treated in public goods terms as effecting 'transnational benefit spillovers by extending political freedoms and fostering peace'. Hirofumi Shimizu and Todd Sandler, 'Peacekeeping and Burden-Sharing', *Journal of Peace Research* 39, no. 6, 2002, p. 655. For our purposes here and given that we have already dealt with democratic peacekeeping theories in the previous chapter, it makes sense to focus on self-interest as the demiurge of public goods peacekeeping theories.

83. Vincenzo Bove and Leandro Elia, 'Supplying peace: Participation in and troop contribution to peacekeeping mission', *Journal of Peace Research* 48, no. 6, 2011, p. 701. The examples of the different types of goods are the author's own; the quote on privately consumable benefits is taken from Bobrow and Boyer, 'Maintaining System Stability', p. 726.

84. Bobrow and Boyer, 'Maintaining System Stability', p. 725.

85. Gaibulloev *et al.*, 'Demands for UN and Non-UN Peacekeeping', p. 847; Shimizu and Sandler, 'Peacekeeping and Burden-Sharing', pp. 666–7.

86. Elia and Bove, 'Supplying peace', p. 712.

87. Andrew Blum, 'Blue Helmets from the South: Accounting for the Participation of Weaker States in Peacekeeping Operations', *Journal of Conflict Studies* 20, no. 1, 2000, p. 8. This problem could be overcome if one made certain assumptions about institutionally embedded multilateralism, for instance. In these theories though, multilateralism simply exists as the convergence of interests through a constant process of calculation on the part of states. For criticism of this approach, see Martha Finnemore, *The Purpose of Intervention: Changing Beliefs about the Use of Force*, Ithaca: Cornell University Press, 2003, p. 81.

88. Bobrow and Boyer, 'Maintaining System Stability', p. 727.

89. Gaibulloev *et al.*, 'Demands for UN and Non-UN Peacekeeping', p. 830.

90. Laura Neack, 'UN Peace-keeping: In the Interest of Community or Self?', *Journal of Peace Research* 32, no. 2, 1995, p. 198.

91. Paul D. Williams, 'Peace Operations and the International Financial Institutions: Insights from Rwanda and Sierra Leone', *International Peacekeeping* 11, no. 1, 2004, pp. 103–23.

92. On this thorny question, see Roland Paris, 'Post-Conflict Peacebuilding', in T.G. Weiss and S. Daws, *The Oxford Handbook on the United Nations*, Oxford: Oxford University Press, 2007, p. 412.

93. Bobrow and Boyer, 'Maintaining System Stability', pp. 727–8.

94. Shimizu and Sandler, 'Peacekeeping and Burden-Sharing', p. 654 and *passim*; Gaibulloev *et al.*, 'Demands for UN and Non-UN Peacekeeping', p. 829.

95. UN Security Council, 'Security Council commits to strengthening partnership with troop, police contributors in debate on United Nations Peacekeeping Operations' 26 August 2011. SC/10368. Online. Available HTTP: http://www.un.org/News/Press/docs/2011/sc10368.doc.htm (accessed 26 March 2012).

96. Doyle and Sambanis, *Making and Building Peace*, p. 345.

97. Bobrow and Boyer, 'Maintaining System Stability', p. 741.

98. James D. Fearon and David D. Laitin, 'Neotrusteeship and the Problem of Weak States', *International Security* 28, no. 4, 2004, p. 25.

99. TCC8, 11 March 2005. See also Jean-Marie Guéhenno, 'The Way We Operate is Dangerous and Problematic: *Spiegel* interview with UN Peacekeeping Boss', interview by Georg Mascolo, *Spiegel Online*, 7 January 2007. Online. Available HTTP: www.spiegel.de/international/spiegel/0,1518,458801,00. html (accessed 30 June 2008).

100. Duane Bratt, 'Critiquing Peace-Maintenance', in Jarat Chopra (ed.), *Politics of Peace-Maintenance*, Boulder, CO: Lynne Rienner, 1998, p. 127.

101. Bobrow and Boyer, 'Maintaining System Stability', p. 736.

102. Marten, *Enforcing the Peace*, p. 122.

103. Berdal, 'UN After Iraq', p. 88.

104. Peter Hallward, 'Option Zero in Haiti', *New Left Review* 27, May-June 2004. See also S. Neil MacFarlane 'International Politics, Local Conflicts and Intervention', p. 29.

105. MacQueen, *Peacekeeping in the International System*, p. 158.

106. Perry Anderson, 'Internationalism: a breviary', *New Left Review* 143, Mar-Apr 2002.

107. See Marc Peceny, 'A Constructivist Interpretation of the Liberal Peace: The Ambiguous Case of the Spanish-American War', *Journal of Peace Research* 34, no. 4, 1997, 415–30.

108. See for example Ellen Meiksins Wood, *The Empire of Capital*, London: Verso, 2005.

109. Or, as MacQueen puts it in relation to the decolonisation of Cyprus, Unficyp provided cover for the colonial power, Britain 'anxious to extricate itself from an uncomfortable unilateral peacekeeping role'. *Peacekeeping in the International System*, p. 95.

110. Cf. MacQueen, who describes these operations as 'at the most fundamental level … attempts to reduce the pressures put on the international system by the end of empire and the construction of new states that came as a consequence of this'. Ibid., p. 79.

111. East Timor became known as Timor-Leste upon independence in 2002.

112. 'Class B' mandates were territories that the administering powers were forbidden from militarising and in which they were under nominal obligations to protect freedom of conscience and religion. Class Bs were seen to be further from self-determination than class A mandates. In practice, class B mandates were the territories of Germany's African empire, divided up among the victors of the First World War, Belgium in this case being responsible for 'Ruanda-Burundi'. Italian Somaliland, which had endured both British and Italian colonialism at different stages of the twentieth century, united with the British protectorate of Somaliland to form Somalia upon independence in 1960. See Anthony Anghie, 'Colonialism and the Birth of International Institutions: Sovereignty, Economy, and the Mandate System of the League of Nations', *New York University Journal of International Law and Politics* 34, no. 3, 2002, p. 513.

113. Al-Qaq, *Managing World Order*, p. 76.

114. Ibid., p. 106.

115. I owe this point to Emily Paddon.
116. According to Stephen Kinloch-Pichat, the first truly international military force of the twentieth century was deployed by the League of Nations when 1,500 British, 1,300 Italian and 250 Swedish troops were deployed to the Saar Basin in December 1934 to oversee a plebiscite as to whether the territory would be restored to German sovereignty. *A UN 'Legion': Between Utopia and Reality*, Abingdon: Frank Cass, 2004, p. 15. Interestingly, Larry Fabian observes that the British drew on their doctrines of imperial warfare when deploying to the Saarland in the League mission there in 1935; Fabian, *Soldiers Without Enemies: Preparing the United Nations for Peacekeeping*, Washington, D.C.: The Brookings Institution, 1971, p. 52. The Leticia operation in South America (1933–34) was the first time specifically international emblems were used. As the peacekeeping force was Colombian, League of Nations armbands and flags were needed, as the border dispute the peacekeepers were trying to resolve was between Peru and Colombia. MacQueen, *Peacekeeping in the International System*, p. 41.
117. Unscob 1947–51 (Balkans/Greek Civil War); UNTSO (Middle East; 1948-present), Unmogip (Kashmir; 1949–present).
118. For pointed criticisms of this nostalgia for Cold War peacekeeping, see Terence O'Neill and Nicholas Rees, *United Nations Peacekeeping in the Post-Cold War Era*, London: Routledge, 2005, pp. 24–5; 185.
119. MacQueen, *Peacekeeping in the International System*, p. 73.
120. Al-Qaq, *Managing World Order*, p. 20. Original emphasis.
121. Neack, 'UN Peace-keeping: In Interest of Community or Self?, p. 189.
122. Al-Qaq, *Managing World Order*, p. 23. According to Al-Qaq, Canada's diplomatic entrepreneurship in this regard reflected Canadian alarm at being squeezed between the US on the one hand and the British on the other.
123. Ibid., p. 181.
124. Sandra Whitworth makes this argument in *Men, Militarism and UN Peacekeeping: A Gendered Analysis*, Boulder, CO: Lynne Rienner, 2004, pp. 30–1.
125. Al-Qaq, *Managing World Order*, p. 24.
126. Ibid., pp. 20–1.
127. Michael Oren, 'The Revelations of 1967: New Research on the Six Day War and Its Lessons for the Contemporary Middle East', *Israel Studies* 10, no. 2, 2005, p. 312.
128. On the trusteeship character of peacekeeping, see Kenneth W. Abbot and Duncan Snidal, 'Why states act through formal organizations', *Journal of Conflict Resolution* 42, no. 1, 1998, p. 20.
129. Adam Roberts lists the crises from which the United Nations was absent as the 1948 Berlin Blockade, the Soviet invasions of Hungary (1956) and Czechoslovakia (1968), US intervention in South East Asia (1948–91), the Indonesian invasion of East Timor (1975–99), the Iran-Iraq War (1980–88), superpower disarmament works, and the Helsinki Accords. 'Towards a World Community? The United Nations and International Law', in M. Howard and W.R. Louis (eds), *The Oxford History of the Twentieth Century*, New York: Oxford University Press, 1998, p. 311.

130. Roberts, 'Towards a World Community?', pp. 310–1. See further Claude, *Swords into Plowshares*, pp. 375–6.
131. See for instance Mohammed Ayoob, *The Third World Security Predicament: State Making, Regional Conflict and the International System*, Boulder, CO: Lynne Rienner, 2004, p. 72; see further pp. 103–5 on the Non-Aligned Movement.
132. As described by an analyst at the time, '… one of the UN's most striking characteristics is the extent to which it has frustrated the Communist powers' hopes of directing the Afro-Asian anti-colonial movement … the development of the UN … has helped the Africans and Asians to "choose their own way".' Boyd, *United Nations: Piety, Myth and Truth*, p. 186.
133. Martin Wight, *Four Seminal Thinkers in International Theory: Machiavelli, Grotius, Kant and Mazzini*, Oxford: Oxford University Press, 2004, p. 146. Koskenniemi points out that the Council is like a Hobbesian sovereign in that there is only ever one extraction of political legitimacy upon entry into the social contract, after which rights over the sovereign no longer exist. Koskenniemi, 'Police in the Temple', p. 326.
134. Martin Wight, *Power Politics*, H. Bull and C. Holbraad (eds), Harmondsworth: Penguin Books, 1979, p. 216.
135. Ibid., p. 217.
136. This section draws on Hinsley's comparison, *Power and the Pursuit of the Peace: Theory and Practice in the Relations Between States*, Cambridge: Cambridge University Press, 1967, pp. 337–8.
137. Ibid., p. 339.
138. Zolo, *Cosmopolis*, p. 76. See also Morgenthau: 'It is significant that the Charter is most explicit in elaborating and implementing the first two purposes [international peace and collective security] … and that it is virtually silent with regard to prohibition of the use of force, maintenance of justice, national self-determination'. Hans J. Morgenthau, *Politics Among Nations: The Struggle for Power and Peace*, 7th ed., rev. by Kenneth W. Thompson and W. David Clinton, Boston: McGraw Hill, 2006, p. 487.
139. Claude, *Swords into Plowshares*, p. 215.
140. See further Claude, *Swords into Plowshares*, pp. 359–60.
141. Andrew Williams traces trusteeship back through Jan Smuts, the former Boer commando turned imperial statesman. The 1902 Peace of Vereeniging, which ended the Boer Wars between the breakaway republics and the British empire, led to self-rule for the Boers under British guidance and within a larger international framework of imperial relations coordinated by London, as well as reconstruction aid pledged by the British Empire. Williams takes this as the progenitor of later models of internationally led reconstruction. 'Reconstruction: The Bringing of Peace and Plenty or Occult Imperialism?', *Global Society* 21, no. 4, 2007, p. 545.
142. Claude suggested that trusteeship be seen as serving a 'post-natal' function just as important as the pre-natal function it served prior to independence. *Swords into Plowshares*, p. 376.

EPILOGUE: CONCLUDING THOUGHTS ON UN PEACEKEEPING,
        CONTRIBUTION TO UN PEACEKEEPING, AND
        INTERNATIONAL ORDER

1. See Danilo Zolo, *Cosmopolis: Prospects for World Government*, Trans. David McKie, Cambridge: Polity Press, 1997, p. 181.
2. Conor Cruise O'Brien and Feliks Topolski, *The United Nations: Sacred Drama*, New York: Simon Schuster, 1968. Original emphasis. Cf. Leon Gordenker, 'Conor Cruise O'Brien and the Truth about the United Nations', *International Organization* 23, no. 4, 1969, pp. 897–913.
3. Ibid.
4. Ibid.
5. A point made by David N. Gibbs, 'Is peacekeeping a new form of imperialism?', *International Peacekeeping* 4, no. 1, 1997, p. 122.

BIBLIOGRAPHY

United Nations

Boutros-Ghali, Boutros. *An Agenda for Peace*, 2ⁿᵈ ed., New York: United Nations, 1995.

Ladsous, Hervé, Fourth Committee, 24 October 2011. Online. Available HTTP: www.un.org/en/peacekeeping/articles/4thc_dpkousg_24102011.pdf (accessed 13 April 2012).

UN, *Report of the Panel on United Nations Peace Operations*, 2000.

UN, *A More Secure World: Our Shared Responsibility*, Report of the High-Level Panel on Threats, Challenges and Change, 2004.

UN, *United Nations Peacekeeping Operations: Principles and Guidelines*, 2008.

UN, Department of Peacekeeping Operations and Department of Field Support, *A New Partnership Agenda: Charting a New Horizon for UN Peacekeeping*, 2009.

Security Council Resolutions

Security Council Resolution 1353 on strengthening cooperation with troop contributing countries. S/RES/1353, 2001.

Security Council Resolution 1325 on women, peace and security. S/RES/1325, 2000.

Security Council Resolution 1612 on Children in Armed Conflict. S/RES/1612, 2005.

Security Council Resolution 1674 on Protection of Civilians in Armed Conflict. S/RES/1674, 2006.

Security Council, 'Report of the Secretary-General on the situation in Mali'. S/2013/189, 26 March 2013.

Data

Center on International Cooperation, *Annual Review of Global Peace Operations*.

International Institute for Strategic Studies, *The Military Balance*.
Stockholm Institute for Peace Research, *Yearbook*.

Books & Book Chapters

Aksu, Eşref, *The United Nations, intra-state peacekeeping and normative change*, Manchester: Manchester University Press, 2003.

Al-Qaq, Richard Kareem, *Managing World Order: United Nations Peace Operations and the Security Agenda*, London: I.B. Tauris, 2009.

Army Training Command, *The Indian Army: United Nations Peacekeeping Operations*, New Delhi: Lancer Publishers, 1997.

Anderson, Gary, 'Preparing for the Worst: Military Requirements for Hazardous Missions' in D.C.F. Daniel *et al.* (eds), *Peace Operations: Trends, Progress, and Prospects*, Washington, D.C.: 2008.

Antonini, Blanca, 'El Salvador' in David M. Malone (ed.), *The UN Security Council: From the Cold War to the 21st Century*, Boulder, CO: Lynne Rienner, 2004.

Autesserre, Séverine, *The Trouble with Congo: Local Violence and the Failure of International Peacebuilding*, Cambridge: Cambridge University Press, 2010.

Ayoob, Mohammed, *The Third World Security Predicament: State Making, Regional Conflict and the International System*, Boulder, CO: Lynne Rienner, 1995.

Bacevich, Andrew, *Washington Rules: America's Path to Permanent War*, New York: Metropolitan Books, 2010.

Barkawi, Tarak, *Globalization and War*, Lanham: Rowman and Littlefield Publishers, 2006.

Barnett, Michael N. and Martha Finnemore, 'The power of liberal international organizations' in Michael N. Barnett and Raymond Duvall (eds), *Power in Global Governance*, Cambridge: Cambridge University Press, 2005.

——— *Rules for the World: International Organization in Global Politics*, Ithaca, London: Cornell University Press, 2004.

Barnett, Michael N. and Christoph Zurcher, 'The peacebuilder's contract: how external statebuilding reinforces weak statehood' in R. Paris and T. Sisk (eds), *The Dilemmas of Statebuilding: confronting the contradictions of post-war peace operations*, Abingdon: Routledge, 2009.

Banerjee, Dipankar, 'South Asia: Contributors of Global Significance' in D.C.F. Daniel, P. Taft and S. Wiharta (eds), *Peace Operations: Trends, Progress, and Prospects*, Washington, D.C.: Georgetown University Press, 2008.

Bellamy, Alex J., Paul D. Williams with Stuart Griffin, *Understanding Peacekeeping*, Cambridge: Polity Press, 2010.

Bellamy, Alex J. and Paul D. Williams (eds), *Providing Peacekeepers: The Politics, Challenges, and Future of United Nations Peacekeeping Contributions*, Oxford: Oxford University Press, 2013.

Berdal, Mats, *Whither UN Peacekeeping?*, Adelphi Paper 281, London: Brassey's for the International Institute for Strategic Studies, 1993.

——— *Building Peace After War*, Abingdon: Routledge, 2009.

Berkok, Ugurhan G. and Binyam Solomon, 'Peacekeeping, private benefits and common agency' in D. L. Braddon and K. Hartley (eds), *Handbook on the Economics of Conflict*, Cheltenham: Edward Elgar, 2011.

Bhatia, Michael, *War and Intervention: Issues for Contemporary Peace Operations*, Bloomfield, CT: Kumerian Press, 2003.

Bickerton, Christopher J., 'State-building: exporting state failure' in Christopher J. Bickerton, Philip Cunliffe and Alexander Gourevitch (eds), *Politics without Sovereignty: A critique of contemporary international relations*, London: UCL Press, 2007.

Blackburn, Kevin, 'Colonial forces as postcolonial memories: the commemoration and memory of the Malay Regiment in modern Malaysia and Singapore' in K. Hack and T. Rettig (eds), *Colonial Armies in Southeast Asia*, London: Routledge, 2006.

Boutros-Ghali, Boutros, *Unvanquished: A U.S.—U.N. Saga*, London: I.B. Tauris, 1999.

Bove, Vincenzo and Ron Smith, 'The economics of peacekeeping' in D.L. Braddon and K. Hartley (eds), *Handbook on the Economics of Conflict*, Cheltenham and Northampton, MA: Edward Elgar, 2011.

Boyd, Andrew, *United Nations: Piety, Myth, and Truth*, Harmondsworth: Penguin, 1964.

Bratt, Duane, 'Critiquing Peace-Maintenance' in Jarat Chopra (ed.), *The Politics of Peace-Maintenance*, Boulder, CO: Lynne Rienner, 1998.

Brown, Chris, *Understanding International Relations*, London: Macmillan Press, 1997.

Brown, Chris, 'International Political Theory and the Idea of World Community' in Ken Booth and Steve Smith (eds), *International Relations Theory Today*, Cambridge: Polity Press, 1995.

Brown, Michael E., Sean M. Lynn-Jones and Steven E. Miller (eds), *Debating the Democratic Peace*, Cambridge, MA: MIT Press, 1996.

Bull, Hedley, 'Society and Anarchy in International Relations' in J. Der Derian (ed.), *International Theory: Critical Investigations*, Basingstoke, Macmillan, 1995.

——— *The Anarchical Society: A Study of Order in World Politics*, 3rd ed., Basingstoke: Palgrave, 2002.

Bullion, Alan J., 'India' in D.C.F. Daniel, P. Taft and S. Wiharta (eds), *Peace Operations: Trends, Progress and Prospects*, Washington, D.C.: Georgetown University Press, 2008.

Buzan, Barry, *People, States and Fear: An Agenda for International Security Studies in the Post-Cold War Era*, 2nd ed., New York: Harvester Wheatsheaf, 1991.

Callinicos, Alex, *Imperialism and Global Political Economy*, London: Polity Press, 2009.

Carr, E. H., *The Twenty Years' Crisis 1919–1939: An Introduction to the Study of International Relations*, Basingstoke: Palgrave, 2001.

Chandler, David, *From Kosovo to Kabul and Beyond: Human Rights and International Intervention*, 2nd ed., London: Pluto Press, 2005.

Charbonneau, Bruno, *France and the New Imperialism: Security Policy in Sub-Saharan Africa*, Aldershot: Ashgate, 2008.

Chesterman, *Just War of Just Peace? Humanitarian Intervention and International Law*, Oxford: Oxford University Press, 2001.

———— *You, the People: The United Nations, Transitional Administration, and State-Building*, Oxford: Oxford University Press, 2004.

———— 'Virtual Trusteeship' in David M. Malone (ed.), *The UN Security Council: From the Cold War to the 21st Century*, Boulder, CO: Lynne Rienner, 2004.

Ciechanski, Jerzy, 'Enforcement Measures under Chapter VII of the UN Charter: UN Practice after the Cold War' in M. Pugh (ed.), *The UN, Peace and Force*, London: Frank Cass, 1997.

Chopra, Jarat *et al.*, 'The Political Tasks of Peace Maintenance' in Erwin A. Schmidl (ed.), *Peace Operations Between War and Peace*, London: Frank Cass, 2000.

Chopra, Jarat, 'Introducing Peace-Maintenance' in Jarat Chopra (ed.), *The Politics of Peace-Maintenance*, Boulder, CO: Lynne Rienner, 1998.

Claude, Jr, Inis L., *Swords into Plowshares: The Problems and Progress of International Organization*, 4th ed., New York: Random House, 1971.

Clayton, Anthony, *France, Soldiers and Africa*, London: Brassey's Defence Publishers, 1988.

Coicaud, Jean-Marc, *Beyond the National Interest: The Future of UN Peacekeeping and Multilateralism in an Era of US Primacy*, Washington, D.C.: United States Institute of Peace, 2007.

Colás, Alejandro, *Empire*, Cambridge: Polity Press, 2007.

Coleman, Katharina P., *International Organisations and Peace Enforcement: The Politics of International Legitimacy*, Cambridge: Cambridge University Press, 2007.

———— 'Token Troop Contributions to United Nations Peacekeeping Operations' in Alex J. Bellamy and Paul D. Williams (eds), *Providing Peacekeepers: The Politics, Challenges, and Future of United Nations Peacekeeping Contribution*, Oxford: Oxford University Press, 2013.

Cooper, Andrew F., 'Niche Diplomacy' in Andrew F. Cooper (ed.), *Niche Diplomacy: Middle Powers after the Cold War*, Basingstoke: Macmillan Press, 1997.

Cumings, Bruce, *The Korean War: A History*, New York: The Modern Library, 2010.

Dallaire, Romeo with Brent Beardsley, *Shake Hands with the Devil: The Failure of Humanity in Rwanda*, London: Arrow Books, 2004.

Dallmeyer, Dorinda G., 'National Perspectives on International Intervention: From the Outside Looking In' in Donald C.F. Daniel and Bradd C. Hayes (eds), *Beyond Traditional Peacekeeping*, Basingstoke: Macmillan Press, 1995.

Daniel, Donald C.F., 'Why So Few Troops from Among So Many?' in Donald C.F. Daniel, P. Taft and S. Wiharta (eds), *Peace Operations: Trends, Progress, and Prospects*, Washington, D.C.: Georgetown University Press, 2008.

———— 'Contemporary Patterns in Peace Operations, 2000–2010' in Alex J. Bellamy and Paul D. Williams (eds), *Providing Peacekeepers: The Politics, Challenges, and Future of United Nations Peacekeeping Operations*, Oxford: Oxford University Press, 2013.

Daniel, Donald C.F., Katrin Heuel and Benjamin Margo, 'Distinguishing Among Military Contributors' in D.C.F. Daniel, P. Taft and S. Wiharta (eds), *Peace Operations: Trends, Progress, and Prospects*, Washington, D.C.: Georgetown University Press, 2008.

Daniel, Donald C.F. and Michael Pugh. 'Conclusion: Change, Continuity and Conceptions of World Order' in Thierry Tardy (ed.), *Peace Operations After 11 September 2001*, London: Routledge, 2004.

Davis, Mike, *Late Victorian Holocausts: El Nino Famines and the Making of the Third World*, London: Verso, 2002.

De Witte, Ludo, *The Assassination of Lumumba*, London: Verso, 2002.

Debrix, François, *Re-Envisioning Peacekeeping: The United Nations and the Mobilisation of Ideology*, London: University of Minnesota Press, 1999.

Deng, Francis M. *et al.*, *Sovereignty as Responsibility: Conflict Management in Africa*, Washington, D.C.: The Brookings Institution, 1996.

Diehl, Paul F., *Peace Operations*, Cambridge: Polity Press, 2008.

Diehl, Paul F., *International Peacekeeping*, Baltimore: Johns Hopkins University Press, 1994.

Dobbins, James, *et al.*, *The UN's Role in Nation-Building: From the Congo to Iraq*, Santa Monica, CA: RAND Corporation, 2005.

Dorn, A. Walter., 'United Nations Peacekeeping Intelligence' in L. K. Johnson (ed.), *The Oxford Handbook of National Security Intelligence*, New York: Oxford University Press.

Doyle, Michael W. and Nicholas Sambanis, *Making War and Building Peace: United Nations Peace Operations*, Princeton: Princeton University Press, 2006.

Duffield, Mark, *Global Governance and the New Wars: The Merging of Development and Security*, London: Zed Books, 2001.

Durch, William J., 'Introduction' in William J. Durch (ed.), *The Evolution of UN Peacekeeping: Case Studies and Comparative Analysis*, New York: St. Martin's Press, 1993.

———— 'Paying the Tab: Financial Crises' in William J. Durch (ed.), *The Evolution of UN Peacekeeping: Case Studies and Comparative Analysis*, New York: St. Martin's Press, 1993.

———— 'Are We Learning Yet? The Long Road to Applying Best Practices' in W.J. Durch (ed.), *Twenty-First-Century Peace Operations*, Washington, D.C.: United States Institute of Peace/Henry L. Stimson Centre, 2006.

Durch, William J. with Tobias C. Berkman 'Restoring and Maintaining Peace: What We Know So Far' in William J. Durch (ed.), *Twenty-First-Century Peace Operations*, Washington, D.C.: United States Institute of Peace/Henry L. Stimson Centre, 2006.

Elliott, Lorraine and Graeme Cheeseman (eds), *Forces for Good: Cosmopolitan militaries in the twenty-first century*, Manchester: Manchester University Press, 2004.

Enloe, Cynthia, *The Morning After: Sexual Politics at the end of the Cold War*, University of California Press, 1993.

Fabian, Larry L., *Soldiers Without Enemies: Preparing the United Nations for Peacekeeping*, Washington, D.C.: The Brookings Institution, 1971.

Facon, Isabelle, 'Integration or Retrenchment? Russian Approaches to Peacekeeping' in Rachel E. Utley (ed.), *Major Powers and Peacekeeping: Perspectives, Priorities and the Challenges of Military Intervention*, Aldershot: Ashgate, 2006.

Findlay, Trevor, 'The new peacekeepers and the new peacekeeping' in Trevor Findlay (ed.), *Challenges for the New Peacekeepers*, New York: Oxford University Press, 1996.

———— *The Use of Force in Peace Operations*, Oxford: Oxford University Press for the Stockholm International Peace Research Institute, 2002.

Finnemore, Martha, *The Purpose of Intervention: Changing Beliefs about the Use of Force*, Ithaca: Cornell University Press, 2004.

Fishel, John T., 'Latin America: Haiti and Beyond' in D.C.F. Daniel, P. Taft and S. Wiharta (eds), *Peace Operations: Trends, Progress, and Prospects*, Washington, D.C.: Georgetown University Press, 2008.

Foley, Conor, *The Thin Blue Line: How Humanitarianism Went to War*, London: Verso, 2008.

Fortna, Virginia Page, *Does Peacekeeping Work? Shaping Belligerents' Choices After Civil War*, Princeton: Princeton University Press, 2008.

Francis, David J., 'Peacekeeping in Africa' in Rachel E. Utley (ed.), *Major Powers and Peacekeeping: Perspectives, Priorities and the Challenges of Military Intervention*, Aldershot: Ashgate, 2006.

Franck, Thomas, *The Power of Legitimacy Among Nations*, Oxford: Oxford University Press, 1990.

Frantzen, Henning-A., *NATO and Peace Support Operations 1991–1999: Policies and Doctrines*, London: Frank Cass, 2005.

Gibbs, David N., *The Political Economy of Third World Intervention: Mines, Money and U.S. Policy in the Congo Crisis*, Chicago: University of Chicago Press, 1993.

Giegerich, Bastian, 'Europe: Looking Near and Far' in D.C.F. Daniel, P. Taft and S. Wiharta (eds), *Peace Operations: Trends, Progress, and Prospects*, Washington, D.C.: Georgetown University Press, 2008.

Gill, Bates and Huang, Chin-Hao, 'The People's Republic of China', in Alex J. Bellamy and Paul D. Williams (eds), *Providing Peacekeepers: The Politics, Challenges, and Future of United Nations Peacekeeping Operations*, Oxford: Oxford University Press, 2013.

Gleijeses, Piero, *Conflicting Missions: Havana, Washington, and Africa 1959–1976*, Chapel Hill and London: The University of North Carolina Press, 2002.

Gray, Colin S., *Modern Strategy*, Oxford: Oxford University Press, 1999.

Guéhenno, Jean-Marie, *The End of the Nation-State*, Trans. Victoria Elliott, Minneapolis: University of Minnesota Press, 1993.

Hack, Karl with Tobias Rettig, 'Imperial systems of power, colonial forces and the making of modern Southeast Asia' in Karl Hack and Tobias Rettig (eds), *Colonial Armies in Southeast Asia*, London: Routledge, 2006.

Halliday, Fred, *Rethinking International Relations*, Basingstoke: Palgrave, 1994.

Handel, Michael, *Weak States in the International System*, London: Frank Cass, 1981.

Hardt, Michael and Antonio Negri, *Empire*, London, Cambridge: Harvard University Press, 2000.

Harkavy, Robert E., *Bases Abroad: The Global Foreign Military Presence*, Oxford: Oxford University Press, 1989.

Heldt, Birger, 'Trends from 1948 to 2005: How to View the Relation between the United Nations and non-UN Entities' in D.C.F. Daniel, P. Taft and S. Wiharta (eds), *Peace Operations: Trends, Progress, and Prospects*, Washington D.C.: Georgetown University Press, 2008.

Hey, Jeanne A.K. (ed.), *Small States in World Politics: Explaining Foreign Policy Behavior*, Boulder, CO: Lynne Rienner, 2003.

Hey, Jeanne A.K., 'Refining Our Understanding of Small State Foreign Policy' in Jeanne A.K. Hey (ed.), *Small States in World Politics: Explaining Foreign Policy Behavior*, Boulder, CO: Lynne Rienner, 2003.

Higgott, Richard, 'Issues, Institutions and Middle-Power Diplomacy: Action and Agendas in the Post-Cold War Era' in Andrew F. Cooper (ed.), *Niche Diplomacy: Middle Powers after the Cold War*, Basingstoke: Macmillan Press, 1997.

Hill, Christopher, *The Changing Politics of Foreign Policy*, Basingstoke: Palgrave Macmillan, 2003.

Hinsley, F.H., *Power and the Pursuit of Peace: Theory and Practice in the Relations Between States*, Cambridge: Cambridge University Press.

Hobsbawm, Eric, *The Age of Revolution: Europe 1789–1848*, London: Abacus, 1962.

⸻ *The Age of Empire: 1875–1914*, London: Abacus, 1987.

Hobson, John A., *Imperialism: A Study*, Nottingham: Spokesman, 2011 [1902].

Hoffman, Peter J. and Thomas G. Weiss, *Sword and Salve: confronting new wars and humanitarian crisis*, Oxford: Rowman and Littlefield, 2006.

Holbraad, Carsten, *Middle Powers in International Politics*, Basingstoke: Macmillan, 1984.

Hollis, Martin and Steve Smith, *Explaining and Understanding International Relations*, Oxford: Clarendon Press, 1990.

Holsti, Kalevi J., *The State, War and the State of War*, Cambridge: Cambridge University Press, 1996.

Horowitz, David, *Empire and Revolution: A Radical Interpretation of Contemporary History*, New York: Vintage Books, 1969.

Howard, Michael, *The Causes of War*, London: Unwin Paperbacks, 1984.

Howe, Herbert M., 'Nigeria' in David S. Sorenson and Pia C. Wood (eds), *The Politics of Peacekeeping in the Post-Cold War Era*, London: Frank Cass, 2005.

Huldt, Bo, 'Working Multilaterally: The Old Peacekeepers' Viewpoint' in Donald C.F. Daniel and Bradd C. Hayes (eds), *Beyond Traditional Peacekeeping*, Basingstoke: Macmillan Press, 1995.

Hulton, Susan C., 'Council Working Method and Procedure' in David M. Malone (ed.), *The UN Security Council: From the Cold War to the 21st Century*, Boulder, CO: Lynne Rienner, 2004.

Hurd, Ian, *After Anarchy: Legitimacy and Power in the United Nations Security Council*, Princeton: Princeton University Press, 2007.

Hurd, Ian, and Bruce Cronin (eds), *The UN Security Council and the Politics of International Authority*, London: Routledge, 2008.

Huntington, Samuel P., *The Third Wave: Democratization in the Late Twentieth Century*, Norman, OK: University of Oklahoma Press, 1993.

Ignatieff, Michael, *Empire Lite: Nation-Building in Bosnia, Kosovo and Afghanistan*, London: Vintage, 2003.

Ikenberry, John G. *et al.*, *The Crisis of American Foreign Policy: Wilsonianism in the Twenty-first Century*, Princeton: Princeton University Press, 2009.

Ishisuka, Katsumi, *Ireland and International Peacekeeping 1960–2000*, London: Frank Cass, 2004.

Jackson, Ashley, *The British Empire and the Second World War*, London: Hambledon Continuum, 2006.

——— *Distant Drums: The Role of Colonies in British Imperial Warfare*, Brighton: Sussex Academic Press, 2010.

James, Alan, *Peacekeeping in International Politics*, New York: St. Martin's Press, 1990.

Kagan, Robert, *The Return of History and the End of Dreams*, London: Atlantic Books, 2008.

Kaldor, Mary, *New and Old Wars: Organized Violence in a Global Era*, 2nd ed., Cambridge: Polity Press, 2007.

Kane, Angela, 'Other Selected States: Motivations and Factors in National Choices' in Donald C.F. Daniel and Bradd C. Hayes (eds), *Beyond Traditional Peacekeeping*, Basingstoke: Macmillan Press, 1995.

——— 'Other new and emerging peacekeepers' in Trevor Findlay (ed.), *Challenges for the New Peacekeepers*, New York: Oxford University Press, 1996.

Kant, Immanuel, *Perpetual Peace and Other Essays*, Trans. Ted Humphrey, Indianapolis, IL: Hackett Publishing, 1983.

Katzenstein, Peter J. (ed.), *The Culture of National Security: Norms and Identity in World Politics*, New York: Columbia University Press, 1996.

Kenkel, Kai Michael, 'Brazil' in Alex J. Bellamy and Paul D. Wiliams (eds), *Providing Peacekeepers: The Politics, Challenges, and Future of United Nations Peacekeeping Contributions*, Oxford: Oxford University Press, 2013.

Kennedy, Paul, *The Parliament of Man: The United Nations and the Quest for World Government*, London: Allen Lane, 2006.

Keohane, Robert O., 'Political authority after intervention: gradations in sovereignty' in J.L. Holzgrefre and R.O. Keohane (eds), *Humanitarian Intervention: Ethical, Legal and Political Dilemmas*, Cambridge: Cambridge University Press, 2003.

Kiely, Ray, *Rethinking Imperialism*, Basingstoke: Palgrave Macmillan, 2010.

Kiernan, Victor G., *Colonial Empires and Armies 1815–1960*, Stroud: Sutton Publishing, 1998.

Killingray, David, 'Guardians of Empire' in David Killingray and David Ornissi (eds), *Guardians of Empire: The Armed Forces of the Colonial Empires c. 1700–1964*, Manchester: Manchester University Press, 2000.

Kingsbury, Benedict, 'Sovereignty and Inequality' in A. Hurrell and N. Woods (eds), *Inequality, Globalization and World Politics*, Oxford: Oxford University Press, 1999.

Kinloch-Pichat, Stephen, *A UN 'Legion': Between Utopia and Reality*, Abingdon: Frank Cass, 2004.

Klein, Naomi, *The Shock Doctrine*, London: Penguin, 2008.

Koskenniemi, Martti, 'The Place of Law in Collective Security: Reflections on the Recent Activity of the Security Council' in Albert J. Paolini, Anthony P. Jarvis and Christian Reus-Smit (eds), *Between Sovereignty and Global Governance: The United Nations, the State and Civil Society*, London: Macmillan, 1998.

Leonard, Mark, *What does China Think?*, London: Fourth Estate, 2008.

Lenin, Vladimir, 'The Question of Peace' in Lenin, *On National Liberation and Social Emancipation*, Moscow: Progress Publishers, 1986.

—— *Imperialism: The Highest Stage of Capitalism: A Popular Outline*, London: Pluto Press, 1996.

Lewis, Ioan and James Mayall, 'Somalia' in Mats Berdal and Spyros Economides (eds), *United Nations Interventionism 1991–2004*, Cambridge: Cambridge University Press, 2007.

Long, David, 'Paternalism and the Internationalization of Imperialism' in D. Long and B.C. Schmidt (eds), *Imperialism and Internationalism in the Discipline of International Relations*, Albany, NY: State University of New York Press, 2005.

Lunt, James, *Imperial Sunset: Frontier Soldiering in the 20th Century*, London: Macdonald Futura, 1981.

Lyons, Gene M. and Michael Mastanduno (eds), *Beyond Westphalia? National Sovereignty and Interventional Intervention*, Baltimore: John Hopkins University Press, 1995.

Mac Ginty, Roger, 'Gilding the lily? International support for indigenous and traditional peacebuilding' in O. P. Richmond (ed.), *Palgrave Advances in Peacebuilding: Critical Developments and Approaches*, Basingstoke: Palgrave Macmillan, 2010.

MacFarlane, S. Neil, 'International Politics, Local Conflicts and Intervention' in Timothy M. Shaw and Nathalie Mychajlyszyn (eds), *Twisting Arms and Flexing Muscles: Humanitarian Intervention and Peacebuilding in Perspective*, Aldershot: Ashgate, 2005.

Mackinlay, John, 'Conclusion: The paradox of Russian peacekeeping' in John Mackinlay and Peter Cross (eds), *Regional Peacekeepers: The Paradox of Russian Peacekeeping*, Tokyo: United Nations University Press, 2003.

MacKinnon, Michael G., *The Evolution of US Peacekeeping Under Clinton: A Fairweather Friend?*, London: Frank Cass, 2000.

MacQueen, Norrie, *United Nations Peacekeeping in African since 1960*, Edinburgh: Pearson Education, 2002.

—— *Peacekeeping in the International System*, London: Routledge, 2006.

Malan, Mark, 'Africa: Building Institutions on the Run' in D.C.F. Daniel, P. Taft and S. Wiharta (eds), *Peace Operations: Trends, Progress, and Prospects*, Washington, D.C.: Georgetown University Press, 2008.

Malik, Kenan, *The Meaning of Race: Race, History and Culture in Western Society*, New York: New York University Press, 1996.

Malone, David M., 'Introduction' in David M. Malone (ed.), *The UN Security Council: From the Cold War to the 21st Century*, Boulder, CO: Lynne Rienner, 2004.

Marten, Kimberly, *Enforcing the Peace: Learning from the Imperial Past*, New York: Columbia University Press, 2004.

Matheson, Michael J., *Council Unbound: The Growth of UN Decision Making on Conflict and Postconflict Issues after the Cold War*, Washington, D.C.: United States Institute of Peace, 2006.

Mayall, James, 'Humanitarian Intervention and International Society: Lessons from Africa' in Jennifer Welsh (ed.), *Humanitarian Intervention and International Relations*, Oxford: Oxford University Press, 2004.

—— 'Introduction' in Mats Berdal and Spyros Economides, *United Nations Interventionism 1991–2004*, Cambridge: Cambridge University Press, 2007.

Mazower, Mark, *No Enchanted Palace: The End of Empire and the Ideological Origins of the United Nations*, Princeton: Princeton University Press, 2009.

—— *Governing the World: The History of an Idea*, London: Allen Lane, 2012.

McDermott, Anthony, *The New Politics of Financing the UN*, Basingstoke: Macmillan, 2000.

Metana, Karuna, *Alibis of Empire: Henry Maine and the Ends of Liberal Imperialism*, Princeton: Princeton University Press, 2010.

C. Wright Mills, *The Sociological Imagination*, New York: Oxford University Press, 1999.

Mohan, C. Raja, *Crossing the Rubicon: The Shaping of India's New Foreign Policy*, Basingstoke: Palgrave, 2005.

de Moor, Jaap, 'The recruitment of Indonesian soldiers for the Dutch Colonial Army, c. 1700–1950' in D. Killingray and D. Omissi (eds), *Guardians of Empire: The Armed Forces of the Colonial Empires c.* 1700–1964, Manchester: Manchester University Press, 2000.

Morgenthau, Hans J., *Politics Among Nations: The Struggle for Power and Peace,* 7th ed., rev. by Kenneth W. Thompson and W. David Clinton, Boston: McGraw Hill, 2006.

Murray, Leonie G., *Clinton, Peacekeeping and Humanitarian Intervention: Rise and Fall of a Policy,* London: Routledge, 2008.

Murthy, C.S.R., 'Unintended Consequences of Peace Operations for Troop-Contributing Countries from South Asia' in Chiyuki Aoi, Cedric de Coning and Ramesh Thakur (eds), *Unintended Consequences of Peacekeeping Operations,* Tokyo: United Nations University Press, 2007.

Musharraf, Pervez, *In the Line of Fire: A Memoir,* Simon and Schuster: London, 2006.

Muthu, Sankar, *Enlightenment Against Empire,* Princeton: Princeton University Press, 2003.

Nambiar, Satish, 'South Asian contributions to United Nations peacekeeping operations, with particular reference to India's participation' in Ramesh Thakur and Oddriy Wiggan (eds), *South Asia in the World: Problem Solving Perspectives on Security, Sustainable Government and Good Governance,* Tokyo: United Nations University Press, 2004.

Nikitin, Alexander I. and Mark A. Loucas, 'Peace Support in the New Independent States: Different from the Rest' in D.C.F. Daniel, P. Taft and S. Wiharta (eds), *Peace Operations: Trends, Progress, and Prospects,* Washington, D.C.: Georgetown University Press, 2008.

Nikitin, Alexander, 'The Russian Federation' in Alex J. Bellamy and Paul D. Williams (eds), *Providing Peacekeepers: The Politics, Challenges, and Future of United Nations Peacekeeping Operations,* Oxford: Oxford University Press, 2013.

O'Neill, John T. and Nicholas Rees, *United Nations Peacekeeping in the Post Cold War Era,* London: Routledge, 2005.

O'Brien, Conor Cruise and Feliks Topolski, *The United Nations: Sacred Drama,* New York: Simon Schuster, 1968.

Paris, Roland, *At War's End: Building Peace After Civil Conflict,* Cambridge: Cambridge University Press, 2004.

—— 'Post-Conflict Peacebuilding' in T.G. Weiss and S. Daws, *The Oxford Handbook on the United Nations,* Oxford: Oxford University Press, 2007.

Parsons, Anthony, 'The UN and the National Interests of States' in Adam Roberts and Benedict Kingsbury (eds), *United Nations, Divided World: The UN's Roles in International Relations,* 2nd ed., Oxford: Clarendon Press, 1995.

Pillar, Paul R., 'The Greater Middle East: Problems of Priorities and Agendas' in D.C.F. Daniel, P. Taft and S. Wiharta (eds), *Peace Operations: Trends, Progress and Prospects,* Washington, D.C.: Georgetown University Press, 2008.

Porter, Bernard, *Critics of Empire: British Radicals and the Imperial Challenge*, London: I.B. Tauris, 2008.

Pouligny, Béatrice, *Peace Operations Seen from Below: UN Missions and Local People*, London: C. Hurst & Co., 2006.

Prashad, Vijay, *The Darker Nations: A People's History of the Third World*, New York: The New Press, 2006.

Pugh, Michael, 'Maintaining Peace and Security' in David Held and Anthony McGrew (eds), *Governing Globalisation: Power, Authority and Global Governance*, Cambridge: Polity Press, 2002.

———— 'Peace Enforcement' in Thomas G. Weiss and Sam Daws (eds), *The Oxford Handbook on the United Nations*, Oxford: Oxford University Press, 2007.

Pugh, Michael (ed.), *The UN, Peace and Force*, London: Frank Cass, 1997.

Pugh, Michael, Neil Cooper and Mandy Turner (eds), *Whose Peace? Critical Perspectives on the Political Economy of Peacebuilding*, Basingstoke: Palgrave Macmillan, 2008.

Rachman, Gideon, *Zero-Sum World: Politics, Power and Prosperity After the Crash*, London: Atlantic Books, 2011.

Ragin, Charles, *Constructing Social Research: The Unity and Diversity of Method*, Thousand Oaks, CA: Pine Forge Press, 1994.

Razack, Sherene H., *Dark Threats and White Knights: The Somalia Affair, Peacekeeping, and the New Imperialism*, Toronto, London: University of Toronto Press, 2004.

Reitlinger, Gerard, *The S.S.: Alibi of a Nation*, New York: Viking Press, 1957.

Richmond, Oliver P., *The Transformation of Peace: Rethinking Peace and Conflict Studies*, Basingstoke: Palgrave, 2005.

Risse-Kappen, Thomas, 'Between a New World Order and None: Explaining the Re-emergence of the United Nations in World Politics', in Keith Krause and Michael C. Williams (eds), *Critical Security Studies: Cases and Concepts*, London: UCL Press, 1997.

Roberts, Adam and Benedict Kingsbury (eds), *United Nations, Divided World: The UN's Roles in International Relations*, 2nd ed., New York: Oxford University Press, 1993.

Roberts, Adam, 'Intervention: Beyond "dictatorial interference"' in William Bain (ed.), *The Empire of Security and the Safety of the People*, London: Routledge, 2006.

Roberts, Adam, 'Towards a World Community? The United Nations and International Law' in Michael Howard and William Roger Louis (eds), *The Oxford History of the Twentieth Century*, New York: Oxford University Press, 1998.

Robinson, William I., *Promoting Polyarchy: Globalization, US Intervention, and Hegemony*, Cambridge: Cambridge University Press, 1996.

Roomy, Fatemy Ahmed, 'The United Nations and South Asia: Bangladesh's contribution to UN peacekeeping' in Ramesh Thakur and Oddriy Wiggan (eds), *South Asia in the World: Problem Solving Perspectives on Security,*

Sustainable Government and Good Governance, Tokyo: United Nations University Press, 2004.

Ruggie, John G., *Constructing the World Polity: Essays on International Institutionalization*, London: Routledge, 1998.

Ryan, Alan, 'Cosmopolitan objectives and the strategic challenges of multinational military operations' in Lorraine Elliott and Graeme Cheeseman (eds), *Forces for Good: Cosmopolitan militaries in the twenty-first century*, Manchester: Manchester University Press, 2004.

Schwartz, Eric P., 'US Policy Towards Peace Operations' in Thierry Tardy (ed.), *Peace Operations After 11 September 2001*, London: Frank Cass, 2004.

Shaw, Martin, *The New Western Way of War: Risk-Transfer War and Its Crisis in Iraq*, Cambridge: Polity Press, 2005.

Shimura, Hisako, 'The role of the UN Secretariat in organizing peacekeeping' in Ramesh Thakur and Albrecht Schnabel (eds), *United Nations Peacekeeping Operations: Ad hoc Missions, Permanent Engagement*, Tokyo: United Nations University Press, 2001.

Sorenson, David S. and Pia C. Wood (eds), *The Politics of Peacekeeping in the Post-Cold War Era*, London: Frank Cass, 2005.

Sotomayor, Arturo, 'Nepal' in Alex J. Bellamy and Paul D. Williams (eds), *Providing Peacekeepers: The Politics, Challenges, and Future of United Nations Peacekeeping Operations*, Oxford: Oxford University Press, 2013.

Stuenkel, Oliver, 'India's National Interests and Diplomatic Activism' in Nicholas Kitchen (ed.), *India: The Next Superpower?*, London: LSE Ideas, 2012.

Suganami, Hidemi, *The Domestic Analogy and World Order Proposals*, Cambridge: Cambridge University Press, 1989.

Taft, Patricia, 'Preparing Nations for Peace: Specialized Requirements for Complex Missions' in D.C.F. Daniel, P. Taft and S. Wiharta (eds), *Peace Operations: Trends, Progress and Prospects*, Washington, D.C.: Georgetown University Press, 2008.

Talentino, Andrea K., *Military Intervention After the Cold War: The Evolution of Theory and Practice*, Athens: Ohio University Press, 2005.

Tardy, Thierry, 'Introduction' in Thierry Tardy (ed.), *Peace Operations After 11 September 2001*, London: Frank Cass, 2004.

———— 'UN Peace Operations in Light of the Events of 11 September 2001' in Thierry Tardy (ed.), *Peace Operations After 11 September 2001*, London: Frank Cass, 2004.

Thakur, Ramesh, *The United Nations, Peace and Security: From Collective Security to the Responsibility to Protect*, Cambridge: Cambridge University Press, 2006.

Thakur, Ramesh and Albrecht Schanebel (eds), *United Nations Peacekeeping Operations: Ad hoc Missions, Permanent Engagement*, Tokyo: United Nations University Press, 2001.

Utley, Rachel E., 'A Means to Wider Ends? France, Germany and Peacekeeping' in Rachel E. Utley (ed.), *Major Powers and Peacekeeping: Perspectives, Priorities and the Challenges of Military Intervention*, Aldershot: Ashgate, 2006.

Utley, Rachel E. (ed.), *Major Powers and Peacekeeping: Perspectives, Priorities and the Challenges of Military Intervention*, Aldershot: Ashgate, 2006.

Vincent, R. J., *Nonintervention and International Order*, Princeton: Princeton University Press, 1974.

Wallensteen, Peter and Patrik Johansson, 'Security Council Decisions in Perspective' in David M. Malone (ed.), *The UN Security Council: From the Cold War to the 21st Century*, Boulder, CO: Lynne Rienner, 2004.

Watson, Cynthia A., 'Argentina' in David S. Sorenson and Pia C. Wood (eds), *The Politics of Peacekeeping in the Post-Cold War Era*, London: Frank Cass, 2005.

Weiss, Thomas G., 'The Humanitarian Impulse' in David M. Malone (ed.), *The UN Security Council: From the Cold War to the 21st Century*, Boulder, CO: Lynne Rienner, 2004.

———— 'On the Brink of a New Era? Humanitarian Intervention, 1991–94' in Donald C.F. Daniel and Bradd C. Hayes (eds), *Beyond Traditional Peacekeeping*, Basingstoke: Macmillan Press, 1995.

Welsh, Jennifer, 'Taking Consequences seriously' in Jennifer Welsh (ed.), *Humanitarian Intervention and International Relations*, Oxford: Oxford University Press, 2006.

Westad, Odd Arne, *The Global Cold War: Third World Interventions and the Making of Our Times*, Cambridge: Cambridge University Press, 2004.

Wheeler, Nicholas J., *Saving Strangers: Humanitarian Intervention in International Society*, Oxford: Oxford University Press, 2000.

———— 'The Humanitarian Responsibilities of Sovereignty: Explaining the Development of a New Norm of Military Intervention for Humanitarian Purposes in International Society' in Jennifer Welsh (ed.), *Humanitarian Intervention and International Relations*, Oxford: Oxford University Press, 2006.

White, Nigel D., 'The UN Charter and Peacekeeping Forces—Constitutional Issues' in M. Pugh (ed.), *The UN, Peace and Force*, London: Frank Cass, 1997.

Whitworth, Sandra, *Men, Militarism and UN Peacekeeping: A Gendered Analysis*, Boulder, CO: Lynne Rienner, 2004.

Wight, Martin, *Power Politics*, Hedley Bull and Carsten Holbraad (eds), Harmondsworth: Penguin Books, 1979.

———— *International Theory: The Three Traditions*, Gabriele Wight and Brian Porter (eds), London: Leicester University Press for The Royal Institute of International Affairs, 1991.

Winslow, Donna, 'The UN: multinational cooperation in peace operations' in Joseph Soeters and Philippe Manigart (eds), *Military Cooperation in Multinational Peace Operations*, Routledge: London, 2008.

Zaman, Rashed Uz and Niloy R. Biswas, 'Bangladesh' in Alex J. Bellamy and Paul D. Williams (eds), *Providing Peacekeepers: The Politics, Challenges, and Future of United Nations Peacekeeping Contribution*, Oxford: Oxford University Press, 2013.

Zolo, Danilo, *Cosmopolis: Prospects for World Government*, Trans. David McKie, Cambridge: Polity Press, 1997.

Zwanenburg, Marten, *Accountability of Peace Support Operations*, Leiden: Martinus Nijhoff, 2005.

Journal Articles

Abbot, Kenneth W. and Duncan Snidal, 'Why states act through formal organisations', *Journal of Conflict Resolution* 42, no. 1, 1998, pp. 3–32.

Alamgir, Jalal, 'Bangladesh's Fresh Start', *Journal of Democracy* 20, no. 3, 2009, pp. 41–55.

Anderson, Perry, 'Internationalism: a breviary', *New Left Review* 143, Mar-Apr 2002, pp. 5–25.

Andersson, Andreas, 'Democracies and UN Peacekeeping Operations, 1990–1996', *International Peacekeeping* 7, no. 2, 2000, pp. 1–22.

—— 'Democracy and Susceptibility to UN Intervention', *International Peacekeeping* 13, no. 2, 2006, pp. 184–99.

Anghie, Anthony, 'Colonialism and the Birth of International Institutions: Sovereignty, Economy, and the Mandate System of the League of Nations', *New York University Journal of International Law and Politics* 34, no. 3, 2002, pp. 513–634.

Askandar, Kamarulzaman, 'A Regional Perspective on UN Peace Operations in Southeast Asia', *International Peacekeeping* 12, no. 1, 2005, pp. 34–48.

Ayoob, Mohammed, 'Inequality and Theorizing in International Relations: The Case for Subaltern Realism', *International Studies Review* 4, no. 3, 2002, pp. 27–48.

—— 'Humanitarian intervention and state sovereignty', *International Journal of Human Rights* 6, no. 1, 2002, pp. 81–102.

Bah, A. Sarjoh and Kwesi Aning, 'US Peace Operations Policy in Africa: From ACRI to AFRICOM', *International Peacekeeping* 15, no. 1, 2008, pp. 118–32.

Bain, Will, 'The political theory of trusteeship and the twilight of international equality', *International Relations* 17, no. 1, 2003, pp. 59–77.

Barkawi, Tarak and Mark Laffey, 'The Imperial Peace: Democracy, Force and Globalization', *European Journal of International Relations* 5, no. 4, 1999, pp. 403–34.

Barnett, Michael N. and Martha Finnemore, 'The Power, Politics and Pathologies of International Organizations', *International Organization* 53, no. 4, 1999, pp. 699–732.

Barnett, Michael N. 'The New United Nations Politics of Peace: From Juridical to Empirical Sovereignty', *Global Governance* 1, no. 1, 1995, pp. 79–97.

Barnett, Michael, Hunjoon Kim, Madelene O'Donnell, Laura Sitea, 'Peacebuilding: what is in a name?', *Global Governance* 13, no. 1, 2007, pp. 35–58.

Banerjee, Dipankar, 'Current Trends in UN Peacekeeping: A Perspective from Asia', *International Peacekeeping* 12, no. 1, 2005, pp. 18–33.

Berdal, Mats, 'The UN Security Council: Ineffective but Indispensable', *Survival: Global Politics and Strategy* 45, no. 2, 2003, pp. 7–30.

―――― 'The UN After Iraq', *Survival: Global Politics and Strategy* 46, no. 3, 2004, pp. 83–101.

―――― 'The UN's Unnecessary Crisis', *Survival: Global Politics and Strategy* 47, no. 3, 2005, pp. 7–32.

Bellamy, Alex J. and Paul D. Williams, 'Introduction: Thinking anew about peace operations', *International Peacekeeping* 11, no. 1, 2004, pp. 1–15.

―――― 'The "Next Stage" in Peacekeeping Operations Theory?', *International Peacekeeping* 11, no. 1, 2004, pp. 17–38.

―――― 'Conclusion: What Future for Peace Operations? Brahimi and Beyond', *International Peacekeeping* 11, no. 1, 2004, pp. 183–212.

―――― 'Who's keeping the peace?', *International Security* 29, no. 4, 2005, pp. 157–95.

―――― 'The West and Contemporary Peace Operations', *Journal of Peace Research* 46, no. 1, 2009, pp. 39–57.

―――― 'The new politics of protection? Côte d'Ivoire, Libya and the responsibility to protect', *International Affairs* 87, no. 4, 2011, pp. 825–50.

Bendaña, Alejandro, 'From Peacebuilding to Statebuilding: One step forward, two steps back', *Development* 48, no. 3, 2005, pp. 5–15.

Andrew Blum, 'Blue Helmets from the South: Accounting for the Participation of Weaker States in Peacekeeping Operations', *Journal of Conflict Studies* 20, no. 1, 2000.

Bickerton, Christopher J., 'The Perils of Performance: EU Foreign Policy and the Problem of Legitimization', *Perspectives: The Central European Review of International Affairs* 28, 2007, pp. 24–42.

Bobrow, Davis B. and Mark A. Boyer. 'Maintaining System Stability: Contributions to Peacekeeping Operations', *Journal of Conflict Resolution* 41, no. 6, 1997, pp. 723–48.

Bove, Vincenzo and Leandro Elia, 'Supplying Peace: Participation in and troop contribution to peacekeeping', *Journal of Peace Research* 48, no. 6, 2011, pp. 699–714.

Boulden, Jane, 'Double Standards, Distance and Disengagement: Collective Legitimization in the Post-Cold War Security Council', *Security Dialogue* 37, no. 3, 2006, pp. 409–23.

Breau, Susan C., 'The Impact of the Responsibility to Protect on Peacekeeping', *Journal of Conflict and Security Law* 11, no. 3, 2006, pp. 429–64.

Bull, Hedley, 'International Theory: The Case for a Classical Approach', *World Politics* 18, no. 3, 1966, pp. 361–77.

Bullion, Alan, 'India in Sierra Leone: A Case of Muscular Peacekeeping?', *International Peacekeeping* 8, no. 4, 2001, pp. 77–91.

Bures, Oldrich, 'Wanted: A Mid-Range Theory of International Peacekeeping', *International Studies Review* 9, no. 3, 2007, pp. 407–36.

Buzan, Barry, 'China in International Society: Is "Peaceful Rise" Possible?', *The Chinese Journal of International Politics* 3, no. 1, 2010, pp. 5–36.

Chandler, David, 'Rhetoric without responsibility: the attraction of "ethical" foreign policy', *The British Journal of Politics and International Relations* 5, no. 3, 2003, pp. 295–322.

—— 'Introduction: Peace without Politics?' *International Peacekeeping* 12, no. 3, 2005, pp. 1–15.

—— 'The uncritical critique of "liberal peace"', *Review of International Studies* 36, SI, 2010, pp. 137–55.

Charbonneau, Bruno, 'Dreams of Empire: France, Europe, and the New Interventionism in Africa', *Modern and Contemporary France* 16, no. 3, 2008, pp. 279–95.

Chesterman, Simon, 'Does the UN Have Intelligence?', *Survival: Global Politics and Strategy* 48, no. 3, 2006, pp. 149–64.

Chimni, B.S., 'Refugees, Return and Reconstruction of "Post-Conflict" Societies: A Critical Perspective', *International Peacekeeping* 9, no. 2, 2002, pp. 163–80.

Chopra, Jarat, 'The UN's Kingdom of East Timor', *Survival: Global Politics and Strategy* 42, no. 3, 2000, pp. 27–40.

—— 'Building State Failure in East Timor', *Development and Change* 33, no. 5, 2002, pp. 979–1000.

Claude, Jr, Inis L., 'Collective Legitimization as a Political Function of the United Nations', *International Organization* 20, no. 3, 1996, pp. 367–79.

—— 'Peace and 'Peace and Security: Prospective Roles for the Two United Nations', *Global Governance* 2, no. 3, 1996, pp. 289–98.

Cooper, Neil, Mandy Turner and Michael Pugh, 'The end of history and the last liberal peacebuilder: a reply to Roland Paris', *Review of International Studies* 37, no. 4, 2011, pp. 1995–2007.

Crocker, Chester, 'Military Dependence: The Colonial Legacy in Africa', *The Journal of Modern African Studies* 12, no. 2, 1974, pp. 265–86.

Daniel, D.C.F. and Leigh C. Caraher, 'Characteristics of troop contributors to peace operations and implications for global capacity', *International Peacekeeping* 13, no. 3, 2006, pp. 297–315.

Diehl, Paul F., 'Forks in the Road: Theoretical and Policy Concerns for 21st Century Peacekeeping', *Global Society* 14, no. 3, 2000, pp. 337–60.

Diehl, Paul F., 'Peacekeeping Operations and the Quest for Peace', *Political Science Quarterly* 103, no. 3, 1988, pp. 485–507.

Dorn, A. Walter, 'Intelligence-led Peacekeeping: The United Nations' Stabilization Mission in Haiti (MINUSTAH), 2006–07', *Intelligence and National Security* 24, no. 6, 2009, pp. 805–35.

Doyle, Michael W., 'Kant, liberal legacies and foreign affairs', Parts I & II, *Philosophy and Public Affairs* 12, no. 4, 1983, pp. 323–53.

—— 'The new interventionism', *Metaphilosophy* 32, nos. 1–2, 2001, pp. 212–35.

Duffield, Mark, 'NGO Relief in War Zones: towards an analysis of the new aid paradigm', *Third World Quarterly* 108, no. 3, 1997, pp. 527–42.

Fearon, James D. and David D. Laitin, 'Neotrusteeship and the Problem of Weak States', *International Security* 28, no. 4, 2004, pp. 5–43.

Fetterly, Ross, 'A Review of Peacekeeping Financing Methods', *Defence and Peace Economics* 17, no. 5, 2006, pp. 395–411.

——— 'The Demand and Supply of Peacekeeping Troops', *Defence and Peace Economics* 17, no. 5, 2006, pp. 457–71.

Finnemore, Martha and Kathryn Sikkink, 'International Norms and Political Change', *International Organization* 53, no. 4, 1998, pp. 887–917.

Freedman, Lawrence, 'The Changing Forms of Military Conflict', *Survival: Global Politics and Strategy* 40, no. 4, 1998–99, pp. 39–56.

Friis, Karsten, 'Peacekeeping and Counter-insurgency—Two of a Kind?', *International Peacekeeping* 17, no. 1, 2010, pp. 49–66.

Flynn, Matthew, 'Between Sub-imperialism and Globalization: A Case Study in the Internationalization of Brazilian Capital', *Latin American Perspectives* 34, no. 6, 2007, pp. 9–27.

Gaibulloev, Khrusrav Todd Sandler and Hirofumi Shimizu, 'Demands for UN and Non-UN Peacekeeping: Nonvoluntary versus Voluntary Contributions to a Public Good', *Journal of Conflict Resolution* 53, no. 6, 2009, pp. 827–52.

Giletti, Gregory P., 'The UN's capacities for strategic lift', *International Peacekeeping* 5, no. 3, 1998, pp. 42–57.

Gibbs, David N., 'The United Nations, international peacekeeping and the question of "impartiality": revisiting the Congo operation of 1960', *The Journal of Modern African Studies* 38, no. 3, 2000, pp. 359–83.

——— 'Is peacekeeping a new form of imperialism?', *International Peacekeeping* 4, no. 1, 1997, pp. 122–8.

Gilligan, Michael and Stephen J. Steadman, 'Where Do the Peacekeepers Go?', *International Studies Review* 5, no. 4, 2003, pp. 37–54.

Gills, Barry and Joel Racamora, 'Low Intensity Democracy', *Third World Quarterly* 13, no. 3, 1992, pp. 501–23.

Glennon, Michael J., 'The New Interventionism: The Search for Just International Law', *Foreign Affairs* 78, no. 3, 1999, pp. 2–7.

Gordenker, Leon, 'Conor Cruise O'Brien and the Truth about the United Nations', *International Organization* 23, no. 4, 1969, pp. 897–913.

González, Roberto J. 'Human terrain: past, present and future applications', *Anthropology Today* 24, no. 1, 2008, pp. 21–6.

Goulding, Marrack, 'The Evolution of United Nations Peacekeeping', *International Affairs* 69, no. 3, 1993, pp. 451–64.

Gowan, Peter, 'US:UN', *New Left Review* no. 24, 2003, pp. 5–28.

Guéhenno, Jean-Marie, 'On the Challenges and Achievements of Reforming UN Peace Operations', *International Peacekeeping* 9, no. 2, 2002, pp. 69–80.

Hagerty, Devin T., 'Bangladesh in 2006: Living in "Interesting Times"', *Asian Survey* 47, no. 1, 2007, pp. 105–12.

Halling, Matt, 'Peacekeeping in Name Alone: Accountability for the UN in Haiti', *Hastings Journal of International and Comparative Law* 31, no. 1, 2007, pp. 461–86.

Hallward, Peter, 'Option Zero in Haiti', *New Left Review* 27, May-June 2004.

Holt, Victoria K., 'Reforming UN Peacekeeping: The U.S. Role and the UN Financial Crisis', *Brown Journal of World Affairs* 3, no. 1, 1996, pp. 125–34.

Howard, Lise-Morjé, 'Sources of Change in United States-United Nations Relations', *Global Governance* 16, no. 4, 2010, pp. 485–503.

Hurd, Ian, 'Legitimacy and Authority in International Politics', *International Organization* 53, no. 2, 1999, pp. 125–34.

——— 'Legitimacy, Power, and the Symbolic Life of the UN Security Council', *Global Governance* 8, no. 1, 2002, pp. 35–51.

Hutchful, Eboe, 'Military policy and reform in Ghana', *The Journal of Modern African Studies* 35, no. 2, 1997, pp. 535–60.

Islam, Nurul, 'The Army, UN Peacekeeping Mission and Democracy in Bangladesh', *Economic and Political WEEKLY* XLV, no. 29, 2010, pp. 77–85.

Jakobsen, Peter Viggo, 'National Interest, Humanitarianism or CNN: What Triggers Peace Enforcement After the Cold War', *Journal of Peace Research* 33, no. 2, 1996, pp. 205–15.

——— 'The Danish Approach to UN Peace Operations after the Cold War', *International Peacekeeping* 5, no. 3, 1998, pp. 106–23.

——— 'The Transformation of United Nations Peace Operations in the 1990s: Adding Globalization to the Conventional "End of the Cold War Explanation"', *Cooperation and Conflict: Journal of the Nordic International Studies Association* 37, no. 3, 2002, pp. 267–82.

Jordaan, Eduard, 'The concept of a middle power in international relations: distinguishing between emerging and traditional middle powers', *Politikon: South African Journal of Political Studies* 30, no. 1, 2003, pp. 165–81.

Kalyvas, Stathis, '"New" and "Old" Civil Wars: A Valid Distinction?', *World Politics* 54, no. 1, 2001, pp. 99–118.

Keen, David, 'War and Peace: What's the difference?', *International Peacekeeping* 7, no. 4, 2000, pp. 1–22.

Keohane, Robert O., 'Lilliputians' Dilemmas: Small States in International Politics', Review of George Liska, *Alliances and the Third World*, Robert E. Osgood, *Alliances and American Foreign Policy*, Robert L. Rothstein, *Alliances and Small Powers* and David Vital *The Inequality of States*, *International Organization* 23, no. 2, 1969, pp. 291–310.

Kenkel, Kai Michael, 'Stepping out of the Shadow: South America and Peace Operations', *International Peacekeeping* 17, no. 5, 2010, pp. 584–97.

——— 'South America's Emerging Power: Brazil as Peacekeeper', *International Peacekeeping* 17, no. 5, 2010, pp. 644–61.

Knaus, Gerald and Felix Martin, 'Lessons from Bosnia-Herzegovina: Travails of the European Raj', *Journal of Democracy* 14, no. 3, 2003, pp. 60–74.

Koskenniemi, Martti, 'The Police in the Temple: Order, Justice and the UN: A Dialectical View', *European Journal of International Law* 6, no. 3, 1995, pp. 325–48.

Krasner, Stephen, 'Sharing Sovereignty: New Institutions for Collapsed and Failing States', *International Security* 29, no. 2, 2004, pp. 85–120.

Kratochwil, Friedrich and John G. Ruggie, 'International Organization: A State of the Art on an Art of the State', *International Organization* 40, no. 4, 1986, pp. 753–75.

Krishnasamy, Kabilan, 'Pakistan's Peacekeeping Experiences', *International Peacekeeping* 9, no. 3, 2002, pp. 103–20.

———— '"Recognition" for Third World Peacekeepers: India and Pakistan', *International Peacekeeping* 8, no. 4, 2001, pp. 56–76.

———— 'Bangladesh and UN Peacekeeping: The Participation of a "Small" State', *Commonwealth and Comparative Politics* 41, no. 1, 2003, pp. 24–47.

Kurti, Albin, 'JISB Interview: Kosova in Dependence: From Stability in Crisis to Crisis of Stability', *Journal of Intervention and Statebuilding* 5, no. 1, 2011, pp. 89–97.

Lebovic, James H., 'Uniting for Peace? Democracies and United Nations Peace Operations after the Cold War', *Journal of Conflict Resolution* 48, no. 6, 2004, pp. 910–36.

Levine, Daniel H., 'Civilian protection and the image of the "total spoiler": reflections on MONUC support to Kimia II', *African Security Review* 20, no. 1, 2011, pp. 95–113.

Lipson, Michael, 'Peacekeeping: Organized Hypocrisy?', *European Journal of International Relations* 13, no. 1, 2007, pp. 5–34.

———— 'A Garbage Can Model of UN Peacekeeping', *Global Governance* 13, no. 1, 2007, pp. 79–97.

Long, David, 'Liberalism, Imperialism and Empire', *Studies in Political Economy* 78, 2006, pp. 201–23.

Luckham, Robin, 'Democracy and the military: An epitaph for Frankenstein's monster?', *Democratization* 3, no. 2, 1996, pp. 1–16.

Luttwak, Edward, 'Give war a chance', *Foreign Affairs* 78, no. 4, 1999, pp. 36–44.

MacFarlane, Neil S., and Albrecht Schnabel, 'Russia's approach to peacekeeping', *International Journal* 50, no. 2, 1995, pp. 294–324.

Mac Ginty, Roger, 'Hybrid Peace: The Interaction between Top-Down and Bottom-Up Peacebuilding', *Security Dialogue* 41, no. 4, 2010, pp. 391–412.

Mamdani, Mahmood, 'Historicizing power and responses to power: indirect rule and its reform', *Social Research* 66, no. 3, 1999, pp. 859–86.

Mann, Michael, 'The Roots and Contradictions of Modern Militarism', *New Left Review* I/162, Mar-Apr 1987.

March, James G. and Johan P. Olsen, 'The Institutional Dynamics of International Political Orders', *International Organization* 52, no. 4, 1998, pp. 943–69.

McCann, Frank D., 'Brazil and World War II: The Forgotten Ally: What did you do in the war, Zé Carioca?', *Estudios Interdisciplanarios de America Latina y El Carib* 6, no. 2, 1995 (unpaginated).

McCormack, Tara, 'Power and Agency in the Human Security Framework', *Cambridge Review of International Affairs* 21, no. 1, 2008, pp. 113–28.

Mersiades, Michael, 'Peacekeeping and Legitimacy: Lessons from Cambodia and Somalia', *International Peacekeeping* 12, no. 2, 2005, pp. 205–21.

Miéville, China, 'Multilateralism as Terror: International Law, Haiti and Imperialism', *Finnish Yearbook of International Law*, 18, 2007, pp. 63–92.

Mohan, C. Raja, 'Balancing Interests and Values: India's Struggle with Democracy Promotion', *Washington Quarterly* 30, no. 3, 2007, pp. 99–116.

Monnakgotla, Kgomotso, 'The Naked Face of UN Peacekeeping: Noble Crusade or National Self-Interest?', *African Security Review* 5, no. 5, 1996, pp. 53–61.

Moore, John N., 'Grenada and the International Double Standard', *American Journal of International Law* 78, no. 1, 1984, pp. 145–68.

Mullenbach, Mark J., 'Deciding to Keep Peace: An Analysis of International Influences on the Establishment of Third-Party Peacekeeping Missions', *International Studies Quarterly* 49, no. 3, 2005, pp. 529–56.

Neack, Laura, 'UN Peace-keeping: In the Interest of Community or Self?', *Journal of Peace Research* 32, no. 2, 1995, pp. 181–96.

Norden, Deborah, 'Keeping the Peace, Outside and In: Argentina's UN Missions', *International Peacekeeping* 2, no. 3, 1995, pp. 330–49.

O'Hanlon, Michael and P.W. Singer, 'The Humanitarian Transformation: Expanding Global Intervention and Capacity', *Survival: Global Politics and Strategy* 46, no. 1, 2004, pp. 77–100.

Olsen, Gorm Rye, 'The EU and Military Conflict Management in Africa: For the Good of Europe or Africa?', *International Peacekeeping* 16, no. 2, 2009, pp. 245–60.

Oren, Michael, 'The Revelations of 1967: New Research on the Six Day War and its Lessons for the Contemporary Middle East', *Israel Studies* 10, no. 2, 2005, pp. 1–14.

Ottoway, Marina and Bethany Lacina, 'International Interventions and Imperialism: Lessons from the 1990s', *SAIS Review* 23, no. 2, 2003, pp. 71–92.

Ouellet, Eric, 'Multinational counterinsurgency: the Western intervention in the Boxer Rebellion 1900–1901', *Small Wars and Insurgencies* 20, nos. 3–4, 2009, pp. 507–27.

Paris, Roland, 'Broadening the Study of Peace Operations', *International Studies Review* 2, no. 3, 2000, pp. 27–44.

———— 'International Peacebuilding and the "Mission Civilisatrice"', *Review of International Studies* 28, no. 4, 2002, pp. 637–56.

———— 'Peacekeeping and the Constraints of Global Culture', *European Journal of International Relations* 9, no. 3, 2003, pp. 441–73.

———— 'Saving liberal peacebuilding', *Review of International Studies* 36, no. 2, 2010, pp. 337–65.

Pattanaik, Smruti S., 'Re-emergence of the Military and the Future of Democracy in Bangladesh', *Strategic Analysis* 32, no. 6, 2008, pp. 975–95.

Peceny, Marc, 'A Constructivist Interpretation of the Liberal Peace: The Ambiguous Case of the Spanish-American War', *Journal of Peace Research* 34, no. 4, 1997, pp. 415–30.

Peou, Sorpong, 'The UN, Peacekeeping, and Collective Human Security: From An Agenda for Peace to the Brahimi Report', *International Peacekeeping* 9, no. 2, pp. 51–68.

Perkins, Richard and Eric Neumayer, 'Extra-territorial interventions in conflict spaces: Explaining the geographies of post-Cold War peacekeeping', *Political Geography* 27, no. 8, 2008, pp. 895–914.

Piccolino, Giulia, 'David Against Goliath in Côte d'Ivoire? Laurent Gbagbo's War against Global Governance', *African Affairs* 111, no. 442, 2012, pp. 1–23.

Plesch, Dan, 'How the United Nations Beat Hitler and Prepared the Peace', *Global Society* 22, no. 1, 2008, pp. 137–58.

Pugh, Michael, 'Peacekeeping and IR Theory: Phantom of the Opera?', *International Peacekeeping* 10, no. 4, 2003, pp. 104–12.

——— 'Peacekeeping and Critical Theory', *International Peacekeeping* 11, no. 1, 2004, pp. 39–58.

Ramsbotham, Oliver and Tom Woodhouse, 'Cosmopolitan Peacekeeping and the Globalization of Security', *International Peacekeeping* 12, no. 2, 2005, pp. 139–56.

Rappard, William E., 'The United Nations as Viewed From Geneva', *The American Political Science Review* 40, no. 3, 1946, pp. 545–51.

Reisman, W. M., 'Stopping Wars and Making Peace: Reflections on the Ideology and Practice of Conflict Termination in Contemporary World Politics', *Tulane Journal of International and Comparative Law* 6, no. 1, 1998, pp. 5–56.

Reus-Smit, Chris, 'Human Rights and the Social Construction of Sovereignty', *Review of International Studies* 27, no. 4, 2001, pp. 1–20.

Roberts, Adam, 'The United Nations and international security', *Survival: Global Politics and Strategy* 35, no. 2, 1993, pp. 3–30.

Ruggie, John G., 'Multilateralism: The Anatomy of an Institution', *International Organization* 46, no. 3, 1993, pp. 561–98.

——— 'The UN and the Collective Use of Force: Whither or Whether?', *International Peacekeeping* 3, no. 4, 1996, pp. 1–20.

Sader, Emir, 'Taking Lula's Measure', *New Left Review* 33, May-June 2005.

Saine, Abdoulaye S.M., 'The Coup D'Etat in The Gambia, 1994: The End of the First Republic', *Armed Forces and Society* 23, no. 1, 1996, pp. 97–111.

Schmidl, Erwin, 'The Evolution of Peace Operations from the Nineteenth Century', *Small Wars and Insurgencies* 10, no. 2, 1999, pp. 4–20.

Scobell, Andrew, 'Politics, Professionalism, and Peacekeeping: An Analysis of the 1987 Military Coup in Fiji', *Comparative Politics* 26, no. 2, 1994, pp. 187–201.

Shimizu, Hirofumi, 'An Economic Analysis of the UN Peacekeeping Assessment System', *Defence and Peace Economics* 16, no. 1, 2005, pp. 1–18.

Shimizu, Hirofumi and Todd Sandler, 'Peacekeeping and Burden-Sharing', *Journal of Peace Research* 39, no. 6, 2002, pp. 651–68.

Stamnes, Eli, 'Critical Security Studies and the United Nations Preventive

Deployment in Macedonia', *International Peacekeeping* 11, no. 1, 2004, pp. 161–81.

Stevens, Jacob, 'Prisons of the Stateless: The Derelictions of UNHCR', *New Left Review* 42, 2006.

Sotomayor, Arturo C., 'Peacekeeping Effects in South America: Common Experiences and Divergent Effects in Civil-Military Relations', *International Peacekeeping* 17, no. 5, 2010, pp. 629–43.

Suzuki, Shogo, 'Why Does China Participate in Intrusive Peacekeeping? Understanding Paternalistic Chinese Discourses on Development and Intervention', *International Peacekeeping* 18, no. 3, 2011, pp. 275–81.

Tardy, Thierry, 'A Critique of Robust Peacekeeping in Contemporary Peace Operations', *International Peacekeeping* 18, no. 2, 2011, pp. 152–67.

Thakur, Ramesh, 'From Peace-Keeping to Peace-Enforcement: The UN Operation in Somalia', *The Journal of Modern African Studies* 32, no. 3, 1994, pp. 387–410.

Thakur, Ramesh, 'India and the United Nations', *Strategic Analysis* 35, no. 6, 2011, pp. 898–905.

Tiewa, Liu, 'Marching for a More Open, Confident and Responsible Great Power: Explaining China's Involvement in UN Peacekeeping Operations', *Journal of International Peacekeeping* 13, nos. 1–2, 2009, pp. 101–30.

Tondini, Matteo, 'From Neo-Colonialism to a "Light Footprint" Approach: Restoring Justice Systems', *International Peacekeeping* 15, no. 2, 2008, pp. 237–51.

Tull, Denis M., 'Peacekeeping in the Democratic Republic of Congo', *International Peacekeeping* 16, no. 2, 2009, pp. 215–30.

Vandervort, Bruce, 'Review Essay: The Thin Black Line of Heroes', *The Journal of Military History*, 65, no. 4, 2004, pp. 1067–73.

Väyrynen, Tarja, 'Gender and UN Peace Operations: The Confines of Modernity', *International Peacekeeping* 11, no. 1, 2004, pp. 125–42.

Victor, Jonah, 'African peacekeeping in Africa: Warlord politics, defence economics, and state legitimacy', *Journal of Peace Research* 47, no. 2, 2010, pp. 217–29.

Voeten, Erik, 'The Political Origins of the UN Security Council's Ability to Legitimize the Use of Force', *International Organization* 59, no. 3, 2005, pp. 527–57.

de Waal, Alex, 'US War Crimes in Somalia', *New Left Review* 23, Jul-Aug 1998.

Weiss, Thomas G., 'The Illusion of UN Security Council Reform', *The Washington Quarterly* 26, no. 4, 2003, pp. 147–61.

Weiss, Thomas G. and Meryl A. Kessler, 'Resurrecting Peacekeeping: The superpowers and conflict management', *Third World Quarterly* 12, no. 3/4, 1990, pp. 124–44.

Wendt, Alexander, 'On Constitution and Causation in International Relations', *Review of International Studies* 24, no. 5, 1998, pp. 101–17.

——— 'Dependent state formation and Third World militarization', *Review of International Studies* 19, no. 4, 1993, pp. 321–47.

Wheeler, Nicholas J. and Tim Dunne, 'Good International Citizenship: A Third Way for British Foreign Policy', *International Affairs* 74, no. 4, 1998, pp. 847–70.

———— 'Humanitarian vigilantes or legal entrepreneurs: Enforcing human rights in international society', *Critical Review of International Social and Political Philosophy* 3, no. 1, 2000, pp. 139–62.

Whitworth, Sandra. 'Where is the politics in peacekeeping?', Review of *International Peacekeeping* by Paul H. Diehl, *Peacekeeping in Transition: The United Nations in Cambodia* by Janet E. Heininger, *Canada and International Peacekeeping* by Joseph T. Jockel, *Peacekeeping: The Road to Sarajevo* by Lewis Mackenzie, *Keeping the Peace in the Post-Cold War Era: Strengthening Multilateral Peacekeeping* by John Roper, Masashi Nishihara, Olar A. Otunnu and Enid C.B. Schoettle and *The Wave of the Future: The Untied Nations and Naval Peacekeeping* by Robert Stephens, *International Journal* 50, 1995, pp. 427–35.

Williams, Andrew, 'Reconstruction: The Bringing of Peace and Plenty or Occult Imperialism?', *Global Society* 21, no. 4, 2007, pp. 539–51.

Williams, Paul D., 'Peace Operations and the International Financial Institutions: Insights from Rwanda and Sierra Leone', *International Peacekeeping*, 11, no. 1, 2004, pp. 103–23.

Wohlforth, William C., 'Realism and the End of the Cold War', *International Security* 19, no. 3, 1994/95, pp. 91–129.

Yannis, Alexandros, 'The UN as Government in Kosovo', *Global Governance: A Review of Multilateralism and International Organizations* 10, no. 1, 2004, pp. 67–91.

Yongjin, Zhang, 'China and UN Peacekeeping: From Condemnation to Participation', *International Peacekeeping* 3, no. 3, 1996, pp. 1–15.

Zanotti, Laura, 'Taming Chaos: A Foucauldian View of UN Peacekeeping, Democracy and Normalization', *International Peacekeeping* 13, no. 2, 2006, pp. 150–67.

News Sources, Newspapers, Periodicals

Alamgir, Jalal, 'Lessons in Democracy from Bangladesh', *The Nation*, 16 March 2009.

Anderson, Perry, 'Made in USA', *The Nation*, 2 April 2007.

———— 'Lula's Brazil', *London Review of Books* 33, no. 7, 2011.

———— 'Gandhi and After', Letters, *London Review of Books* 34, no. 17, 13 September 2012.

Barkawi, Tarak, 'The Shield of Innocence', Al Jazeera, 13 April 2011. Online. Available HTTP: english.aljazeera.net/indepth/opinion/2011/04/201141 112379523528.html# (accessed 13 September 2011).

BBC, 'Brazil army to take up "peacekeeping" in Rio slums', BBC News, 5 December 2010. Online. Available HTTP: www.bbc.co.uk/news/world-latin-america-11920645 (accessed 13 April 2012).

—— 'Germans crush Jewish uprising', BBC News. Online. Available HTTP: news.bbc.co.uk/onthisday/hi/dates/stories/may/16/newsid_3501000/350 1730.stm (accessed 13 April 2012).

Bernstein, Adam, 'I.J. Rikhye; Indian Major General Oversaw U.N. Peacekeeping Efforts', *The Washington Post*, 25 May 2007.

Bone, James and Richard Beeston, 'America fights to take charge of UN peacekeepers around world: Move could help exit strategy in Iraq', *The Times*, 3 November 2006.

Bosco, David, 'When peacekeepers go to war', *Foreign Policy*, 1 April 2013. Online. Available HTTP: bosco.foreignpolicy.com/posts/2013/03/28/when_peacekeepers_go_to_war (accessed 12 April 2013).

Buerk, Roland, 'The cream of UN peacekeepers', BBC News, 18 January 2006. Online. Available HTTP: news.bbc.co.uk/1/hi/world/south_asia/3763640.stm (accessed 17 April 2012).

Philip Cunliffe, 'The legacy of Kosovo? International paternalism', *Spiked Online*, 24 March 2009. Online. Available HTTP: http://www.spiked-online.com/newsite/article/6388#.Ue5iueD3Dj0 (accessed 25 June 2013).

Diceanu, Alex, 'Haiti Deserves Better from the United Nations', *Peace Magazine*, April–June 2006.

The Economist, 'Indar Jit Rikhye', 7 June 2007.

—— 'Helping to calm a continent', 9 June 2012.

—— 'Call the blue helmets', 12 January 2007.

—— 'Supply-side Peacekeeping', 21 February 2007.

—— 'Utility of peacekeeping', 29 September 2007.

—— 'Brazil's foreign policy: A giant stirs', 12 June 2004.

—— 'Charlemagne: Berlin Minus', 10–16 February 2007.

—— 'Policy, not altruism', 23 Sept 2010.

Evans, Gareth, 'Russia and the "responsibility to protect"', *Los Angeles Times*, 31 August 2008.

Freke, Tom, 'If it didn't exist, we'd have to invent it', *New Statesman*, 13 September 2004.

George, Nirmala, 'India upgrades its military with China in mind', *The Guardian*, 8 February 2012.

Goldberg, Mark, 'The Coming Peacekeeping Crunch', *The American Prospect*, 21 May 2007.

Gowan, Richard, 'The Tragedy of 21st Century Peacekeeping', *World Politics Review*, 19 May 2010.

—— 'Diplomatic Fallout: U.N.'s "Intervention Brigade" Raises Cost of Interference in DRC', *World Politics Review*, 8 Apr 2013.

—— 'India's big bet at the UN', *Pragati: The Indian National Interest Review*, 8 February 2013. Online. Available HTTP: pragati.nationalinterest.in/2013/02/indias-big-bet-at-the-un/ (accessed 12 April 2013).

Guéhenno, Jean-Marie, 'Giving peace a chance', *The Economist: The World in 2005*, 17 November 2004.

—— 'The Way We Operate is Dangerous and Problematic: *Spiegel* interview with UN Peacekeeping Boss', interview by Georg Mascolo, *Spiegel Online*,

7 January 2007. Online. Available HTTP: www.spiegel.de/international/spiegel/0,1518,458801,00.html (accessed 30 June 2008).

—— Letters to the editor, *The Economist*, 25 October 2007.

Hatcher, Jessica and Alex Perry, 'Defining Peacekeeping Downward: The U.N. Debacle in Eastern Congo', *Time*, 26 November 2012. Online. Available HTTP: world.time.com/2012/11/26/defining-peacekeeping-downward-the-u-n-debacle-in-eastern-congo/ (accessed 12 Apr 2013).

Heartfield, James, 'Zombie anti-imperialists vs. the "Empire"', *Spiked Online*, 1 September 2004. Online. Available HTTP: www.spiked-online.com/index.php/site/article/2236/ (accessed 11 April 2012).

Hendrickson, Ryan C., 'Crossing the Rubicon', *NATO Review*, August 2005. Online. Available HTTP: www.nato.int/docu/review/2005/issue3/offprint_autumn_eng.pdf (accessed 13 April 2012).

Jackson, Patrick, 'When the gloves of peace come off', BBC News, 18 April 2007. Online. Available HTTP: news.bbc.co.uk/1/hi/6542399.stm (accessed 6 January 2011).

—— 'The UN's South Asian workhorse', BBC News, 19 April 2007. Online. Available HTTP: news.bbc.co.uk/1/hi/6542405.stm (accessed 17 April 2012)

Johnston, Tim, 'Peacekeeping forces kill 4 rebels in East Timor', *International Herald Tribune*, 4 March 2007.

Jordan, Michael J., 'UN Forces Toughen Up', *Christian Science Monitor*, 15 June 2005.

Jordan, Sandra, 'Haiti's children die in UN cross fire', *The Observer*, 1 April 2007.

Joseph, Josy, 'Warriors of Peace: Should the Indian soldier shed his blood for the UN?' (undated). Online. Available HTTP: www.rediff.com/news/2000/jun/30un.htm (accessed 13 April 2012).

Judt, Tony, 'Is the UN Doomed?', review of *The UN Exposed* by Eric Shawn, *The Parliament of Man* by Paul Kennedy, *The Best Intentions* by James Traub, *New York Review of Books* 54, no. 2, 15 February 2007.

Klein, Naomi, '6/7: the massacre of the poor that the world ignored', *The Guardian*, 18 July 2005.

Lacey, Marc, 'After failures, UN peacekeepers get tough "Robust" new tactics to support aggressive operations against militants in Congo', *International Herald Tribune*, 24 May 2005.

Ladwig, Walter, 'An Artificial Bloc Built on a Catchphrase', *The New York Times*, 26 March 2012.

Lee, Matthew Russell, 'Niger Coup Leader Reportedly Served on UN Missions, France, UN and Council Shrug, on Guinea', *Inner City Press*, 19 February 2012. Online. Available HTTP: www.innercitypress.com/uncoup1niger021910.html (accessed 17 April 2012).

Lynch, Colum, 'The blue helmet caste system', *Foreign Policy*, 11 Apr 2013. Online. Available HTTP: turtlebay.foreignpolicy.com/blog/16159 (accessed 12 Apr 2013).

—— 'India's withdrawal of helicopters points to wider trend', *The Washington Post*, 14 June 2011.

—— 'U.S. and Europe fight over cuts in peacekeeping' *Foreign Policy*, 10 October 2011. Online. Available HTTP: turtlebay.foreignpolicy.com/posts/2011/10/10/us_and_europe_fight_over_cuts_in_peacekeeping (accessed 11 April 2012).

MacFarquhar, Neil, 'Gentle Questioning for U.N. Nominee', *The New York Times*, 15 January 2009.

Mamdani, Mahmood, 'The Politics of Naming: Genocide, Civil War, Insurgency', *London Review of Books* 29, no. 5, 2007.

—— 'The Invention of the Indigène', *London Review of Books* 33, no. 2, 2011.

Mbeki, Thabo, 'What the World Got Wrong in Côte d'Ivoire', *Foreign Policy*, 29 April 2011. Online. Available HTTP: www.foreignpolicy.com/articles/2011/04/29/what_the_world_got_wrong_in_cote_d_ivoire?page=0,1 (accessed 13 April 2012).

MercoPress, 'Lula's Party Fearful of "Brazilian sub-imperialism" and arrogance', 8 February 2010. Online. Available HTTP: en.mercopress.com/2010/02/08/lula-da-silva-s-party-fearful-of-brazilian-sub-imperialism-and-arrogance (accessed 17 April 2012).

Mohan, C. Raja, 'The Return of the Raj', *The American Interest*, May/June 2010. Online. Available HTTP: www.the-american-interest.com/article.cfm?piece=803 (accessed 19 April 2012).

Norton-Taylor, Richard, 'Asia's military spending likely to overtake Europe this year', *The Guardian*, 7 March 2012.

Pilger, John, 'Britain is recolonising Sierra Leone in an attempt to get its hand's on the country's diamonds', *New Statesman*, 18 September 2000.

Reuters, 'U.N., French attack Gbagbo heavy weapons in Ivory Coast', Reuters, 10 April 2011. Online. Available HTTP: www.reuters.com/article/2011/04/10/us-ivorycoast-idUSTRE73014Z20110410 (accessed 12 September 2011).

Rubin, James, 'Base motives', *The Guardian*, 7 May 2004.

Smith, David, 'Etiquette, deference, tradition and tea amid an unsung tour of duty', *The Guardian*, 3 February 2010.

The Telegraph, 'Lieutenant General Dewan Prem Chand', 20 December 2003.

Tisdall, Simon, 'Darfur mission faces US funding hurdle', *The Guardian*, 18 June 2007.

Tran, Mark, 'Q&A: the Bangladesh border guards mutiny', *The Guardian*, 26 February 2009.

Trevelyan, Laura, 'All change at the UN', BBC News, 9 December 2006. Online. Available HTTP: news.bbc.co.uk/1/hi/programmes/from_our_own_correspondent/6162695.stm (accessed 18 April 2012).

Urquhart, Brian, 'Looking for the Sheriff', Review of *FDR and the Creation of the UN* by Townsend Hoopes and Douglas Brinkley, *United Nations* by Stanley Meisler, *The Reluctant Sheriff* by Richard N. Haass, and *Preventing Deadly Conflict*, New York Review of Books, 16 July 1998.

Varadarajan, Siddharth, 'Trading one hyphen for another', *The Hindu*, 11 November 2010.

Wole, Soyinka, 'A fate worse than imperialism', *New Perspectives Quarterly*, 2000. Online. Available HTTP: www.digitalnpq.org/archive/2000_summer/fate_worse.html. (accessed 30 June 2008).

Other Sources

Brahimi, Lakhdar, 'The Debate on the Report on UN Peace Operations: Fighting battles on the wrong grounds?', Alastair Buchan Memorial Lecture, 22 March 2001, London, Online. Available HTTP: www.iiss.org/conferences/alastair-buchan/alastair-buchan-lecture-transcripts/ (accessed 16 April 2012).

Chesterman, Simon, 'The Use of Force in UN Peace Operations', Peacekeeping Best Practices Unit (undated), p. 11. Online. Available HTTP: smallwarsjournal.com/documents/useofforceunpko.pdf (accessed 6 April 2012).

Durch, William J. with Madeline L. England (eds), *Enhancing United Nations Capacity to Support Post-Conflict Policing and the Rule of Law: Revised and Updated*, Henry Stimson Center, August 2010. Online. Available HTTP: www.stimson.org/images/uploads/research-pdfs/Enhancing_United_Nations_Capacity_2010_revision.pdf (accessed 12 May 2012).

Global Center on the Responsibility to Protect, 'The Georgia-Russia Crisis and the Responsibility to Protect: Background Note', 19 August 2008. Online. Available HTTP: www.globalr2p.org/pdf/related/GeorgiaRussia.pdf (accessed 20 April 2012).

Gowan, Richard, 'UN Peace Operations: The Case for Strategic Investment', Centre for International Peace Operations Policy Briefing, August 2010, p. 2. Online. Available HTTP: www.zif-berlin.org/fileadmin/uploads/analyse/dokumente/veroeffentlichungen/Policy_Briefing_Richard_Gowan_Aug_2010_ENG.pdf (accessed 16 April 2012).

G8, 'G8 Action Plan: Expanding Global Capacity for Peace Support Operations', 10 June 2004. Online. Available HTTP: www.g8.utoronto.ca/summit/2004seaisland/peace.html (accessed 17 April 2012).

Johnstone, Ian, 'Peace Operations Literature Review', Center on International Cooperation, 2005. Online. Available HTTP: www.cic.nyu.edu/internationalsecurity/docs/Peace%20operations%20final%20literature%20review4.pdf (accessed 30 June 2008).

Johnstone, Ian, 'Recent Thinking on Peacekeeping: Literature Review No. 1', Center on International Cooperation, 2004.

Johnstone, Ian, 'Recent Thinking on Peacekeeping: Literature Review No. 3', Center on International Cooperation, 2005.

Kumar, Keerthi Sampath and Saurabh Mishra, 'India's Presidency in the UN Security Council—An Evaluation', 19 September 2011. Online. Available HTTP: www.idsa.in/idsacomments/IndiasPresidencyintheUNSecurityCouncil_kskumar_190911 (accessed 12 May 2012).

Li, Darryl, 'Peacekeepers and the Countries that Send Them', unpublished, 2003.

Owen, Robert C., 'Operation Deliberate Force: A Case Study on Humanitarian Constraints in Aerospace Warfare', Carr Center for Human Rights Policy Web Working Papers, Kennedy School of Government, University of Harvard, 2001. Online. Available HTTP: http://pksoi.army.mil/doctrine_concepts/documents/UN%20Policy%20Documents/evolving%20models.pdf (accessed 13 April 2012).

Sen, Nirupam, 'Statement by Mr Nirupam Sen on the Report of IGH Level Panel on Threats, Challenges and Change at the Informal Meeting of the Plenary of the 59 Session of the General Assembly', 27 January 2005. Online. Available HTTP: www.un.int/india/2005/ind1059.pdf (accessed 30 June 2008).

Serafino, Nina M., 'The Global Peace Operations Initiative: Background and Issues for Congress', Congressional Research Service, 11 June 2009. Online. Available HTTP: www.effectivepeacekeeping.org/reports/issue/usg-issues (accessed 13 April 2012).

SIPRI, 'Background paper on SIPRI military expenditure data', 11 April 2011. Online. Available HTTP: www.sipri.org/research/armaments/milex/factsheet2010SIPRI overview (accessed 13 April 2012).

Williams, Paul D., 'Agency, Authority and Effect in Contemporary Peace Operations', paper presented to the British International Studies Association conference, 19–21 December 2005.

Zisk, Kimberly Marten, 'Lending Troops: Canada, India and UN Peacekeeping', paper delivered at the annual meeting of the International Studies Association, Los Angeles, March 2000.

INDEX

for Rwanda (Unamir) (1993–6), 45, 62, 127; Centre on Transnational Corporations (UNCTC), 237; Charter, xv, 48–9, 53, 84, 96, 196, 223–4, 230, 233, 255–8; 'Civpols', 74–5; criticisms of, 135, 137; Declaration of (1942), 140, 184; Department of Economic and Social Development, 237; Department of Field Support, 43, 234, 236–7; Department of Humanitarian Affairs, 236–7; Department of Peacekeeping Operations, 43, 47, 192, 218, 234, 236–7; Department of Political Affairs, 5, 235–6; Development Programme (UNDP), 110; Disengagement Observer Force Zone (Undof) (1974–), 222; Economic and Social Council (Ecosoc), 223; Emergency Force (Unef I/II) (1956)(1973–9), 141, 220, 222, 249–53; excessive force used by personnel, 51–2; financial reimbursement for peacekeeping operations provided by, 171, 173–4; funding shortcomings of, 230–1; General Assembly, 2, 44, 158–9, 191–2, 197, 218, 220, 223, 225, 234, 256; Good Offices Mediation in Afghanistan and Pakistan (Ungomap) (1988–91), 221; Interim Administration Mission in Kosovo (Unmik) (1999), 21, 61, 66, 98, 126, 250; Interim Force in Lebanon (Unifil I/II) (1978–), 129, 177, 182, 206, 222, 226; Iran-Iraq Military Observer Group (Uniimog) (1988–91), 221; member states of, 16, 85, 123–4, 223, 225–6, 231, 255; Military Staff Committee, 140, 228, 257; Mission in Bosnia and Herzegovina (UNMIBH) (1995–2002), 61, 90, 126; Mission in Democratic

Republic of Congo (Monuc)/ Stabilization Mission in the Democratic Republic of Congo (Mousco)(1999–), 1, 40–1, 46, 49, 51, 67, 90, 193, 239; Mission in East Timor (1999), 21; Mission in Liberia (UNMIL) (2003–), 21, 41, 44, 46, 49, 57, 62, 129, 162, 198; Mission in Sierra Leone (UNAMSIL) (1999–2005), 21, 41, 44, 48, 153, 178, 189, 234; Mission in South Sudan (2011–), 21–2, 49; N10 group, 14–15, 146, 225; Observer group in Central America (Onuca) (1989–92), 62; Observer Mission in El Salvador (Onusal), 46, 62; Operation in Burundi (2004–7), 21, 44, 49, 163; Operation in Côte d'Ivoire (Unoci) (2003–), 21, 49, 59, 154; Operation in Mozambique (1992–4), 62; Operation in Somalia (Unosom I/II) (1992–5), 42, 62, 107, 126, 177, 190, 229; Organization in the Congo (Onuc), 1, 21, 141, 146, 249–50; Peacebuilding Commission, 225; Peacekeepers, 2–4, 6, 9, 22–3, 37, 39, 41, 47, 50, 56–9, 63–4, 69–71, 117, 121, 127, 132, 134–5, 141, 217, 227–8, 235, 253, 261; Peacekeeping Force in Cyprus (Unficyp) (1964–), 249–50; personnel of, xiv–xv, 21–2, 40, 43, 50, 57–9, 66, 81, 91, 93, 96–9, 128, 132–3, 135, 163–4, 183, 206, 208–9, 223, 225, 230, 234–5, 237, 251, 260; Preventive Deployment Force (Unpredep) (1995–9), 196; Protection Force (Unprofor), 42, 61, 127, 135, 169, 171, 189–90, 194; role in Suez Crisis (1956), 69; Security Council, xiii, 1–2, 21–2, 24, 41–6, 53, 55, 58, 66, 70, 126, 128, 177–8, 182–3, 185–6, 189,